For: My Family

I give to you all I know.

We have established a Facebook group for our descendants. Those of you who would like an easy way to contact members of our family are encouraged to join our Facebook group: Caribbean Genealogy Struggles. This group includes members of the Sheppard, Begg, Kirk, Anderson, Martin, Richards, and Gruny families and is private for these family members. Please visit https://www.facebook.com/groups/529811485161441 and request to join.

I love you all, and love the connections we can make.

Table of Contents

Sheppard

11	Arleen Lorraine Olive Sheppard
37	David Allan Sheppard
292	**Spouse:** Teresa "Pamela" Audra Martin
75	Walter Cyril Sheppard
109	**Spouse:** Olive Lyle Begg
103	Arthur Sheppard
128	**Spouse:** Adeline Alston Richards

Sheppard Siblings

29	Arleen Sheppard Siblings
55	David Sheppard Siblings
91	Walter Sheppard Siblings
107	Arthur Sheppard Siblings

Begg

109	Olive Lyle Begg
75	**Spouse:** Walter Sheppard
161	James Bowhill Begg
171	**Spouse:** Kathleen Cunningham Paterson
166	James Begg Siblings
167	Alexander Begg (No Siblings known)
168	**Spouse:** Emily Grace Gordon Bowhill
169	Emily Grace Gordon Bowhill Siblings

Richards/Hazel

128	Adeline Alston Richards
103	**Spouse:** Arthur Sheppard
131	Adeline Alston Richards Sibling
132	William Richards
137	Hercules Hazel
139	**Story:** Marooned by Pirates
155	**Story:** Emancipation School

Paterson

171	Kathleen Cunningham Paterson
161	**Spouse:** James Bowhill Begg
177	Kathleen Paterson Siblings
181	James Paterson
191	**Spouse:** Minnie Kirk
188	James Paterson Siblings
185	John Paterson
187	**Spouse:** Margaret Thorburn
191	Alexander Paterson
191	**Spouse:** Mary Stewart

Table of Contents

Kirk - Children

191	Minnie Kirk
181	**Spouse:** James Paterson
193	**Spouse:** Dr. Richard Anderson
207	Minnie Kirk Siblings
209	Jane Kirk and Spouse
210	Elizabeth Kirk and Spouse
211	Catherine Kirk and Spouses
212	James Kirk, JR - No Spouse

Kirk - Chapters

223	Kirk to Tobago
226	Appointments and Accolades
228	Kirk and Jardine
234	Kirk and Jardine - Letter Summaries
239	Kirk and Birds
243	Kirk, Sugar and the Enslaved
263	Kirk Jr and Sr - Estates
286	Kirk, Jr and the Rest of the Story

Anderson

193	Richard Benjamin Anderson
191	**Spouse:** Minnie Kirk
120	Mary Olive Elizabeth Anderson

Martin

292	Pamela Martin
37	**Spouse:** David Allan Sheppard
304	Pamela Martin Siblings
324	Joseph Martin
335	**Spouse:** Theresa Bertha Stoute
338	**Spouse:** Gwendolyn Stewart
338	**Spouse:** Ethel B. Rosenthal
339	Luis Martin
343	**Spouse:** Bernardine "Eleonore" Angelique Gruny

Gruny

343	Bernardine "Eleonore" Gruny
339	**Spouse:** Luis Martin
349	Bernadine Gruny Siblings
358	Leonisse Gruny
362	Leonisse Gruny Sibling
362	Leonisse Gruny Half Siblings
375	Armand Gruny
379	**Spouse:** Etinnette Cointree
378	**Spouse:** Marie Dite Anne Babut

Ancestor Fan Chart

GEN 1: Arleen Lorraine Sheppard, 1959–Living

GEN 2:
- David Allan Sheppard, 1931–2022
- Teresa Pamela Audra Martin, 1934–2021

GEN 3:
- Walter Cyril Sheppard, 1898–1974
- Olive Lyle Begg, 1904–1949
- Joseph Gabriel Martin, 1913–1986
- Theresa Bertha Stoute, 1912–1956

GEN 4:
- Arthur Sheppard, 1859–1925
- Adeline Alston Richards, 1878–1957
- James Bowhill Begg, 1878–Deceased
- Kathleen Cunnin... Patterson, 1879–1905
- Luis Martin, 1873–1924
- Bernardine Eleo... Gruny, 1884–1944
- Stoute, Deceased
- Margaret

GEN 4++:
- Sheppard, 1841–Deceased
- William H Richards, 1842–1933
- Alexander Begg, 1850–Deceased
- Emily Grace Gordon Bowhill, 1850–Deceased
- James Bowhill, 1811–Deceased
- Ann Gray, 1820–Deceased
- John Paterson, 1808–1884
- Margaret Thorburn, 1809–1894
- James Kirk, 1800–1874
- Minnie Cunningham, 1825–Deceased
- Thomas Thorburn
- Mary Stewart
- Alexander Paterson
- Margaret McCall
- William Richards, 1814–Deceased
- Mary, Deceased
- Ann Elizabeth Hazel
- John Richards
- Leonisse Sitheph... Gruny, 1854–Deceased
- Armand Gruny, 1820–1898
- Etiennette Cointree, –1864
- Eleonis Gruny
- Nicolas Cointre
- Celeste Bede

This chart has quite a few blank spaces. This is a representation of my ThruLines; that means they are my direct ancestors. It does not account for cousins, aunts and uncles who are represented in this work.

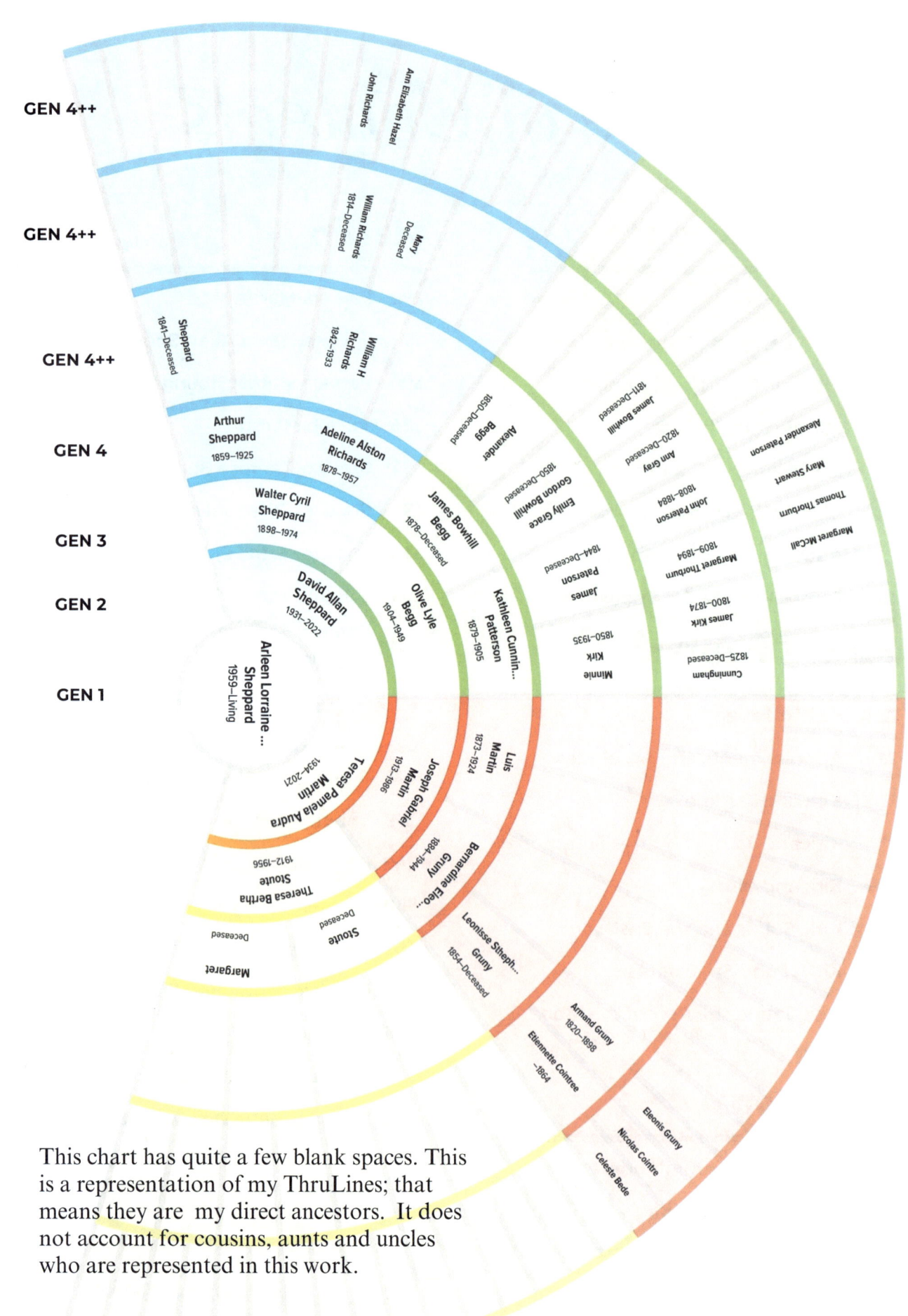

4

FOREWARD

It is imperative that I give thanks to the members of our family who worked tirelessly to uncover copious amounts of genealogical information. These family members diligently captured and recorded the details of our family's history. That effort took years to compile, and I stand on their shoulders.

My first cousin, once removed, Kelvin Pierre, is the most substantial contributor. His work was based on the memories of surviving family members, oral family histories, Bibles, scrapbooks, and, as in every family, urban legends. Additionally, his research was supported by interviews he conducted, as well as by others who sought to support his efforts.

I remember my father working diligently to contact family members in order to gather information about their relatives—such as aunts, uncles, siblings, cousins, nieces, and nephews—on the Sheppard side. He loved doing the work and sharing his findings with Kelvin. They truly bonded over creating our large family tree. Moreover, Kelvin did all of his documentation work by hand, providing page after page of handwritten details. Then my niece, Renee Mangum (née Sheppard), took those pages and painstakingly entered the information into online databases: familysearch.org (free) and ancestry.com (subscription required). Even if you had enough information to perform a search, trying to find the right results on Ancestry wasn't always easy. With thousands of returns, it was hard to determine which, if any, applied to our family. I could move forward with some details, but I couldn't be certain that the work was meeting the minimum requirements of the Genealogy Proof Standards.

I was at a standstill until I was given a copy of some scrapbook-like pages created and maintained by my Aunt Pat Torry (née Sheppard) and her ancestors. On these pages, I noticed that my great-grandmother's sister was named Wilhemia Arnold Richards. That was a very unusual and specific name. I decided to do an internet search for her in Google.com. I used her name using the spelling of her name as listed, Wilhemia, and also as the common spelling of her name, Wilhelmina. The latter returned hits. The first return was for a website owned by Kingsley McCartney, A descendant of Wilhelmina.

The site was ***http://www.kingsleymccartney.com/www/trinity/index.php?ctype=gedcom***. This turned out to be a fantastic source for the Richards line/Hazel line. It was also the place that the genealogy bug bit BAD. Through this website, I was able to track back to Hercules Hazel line, and it was amazing. I wanted to do more.

The Clue

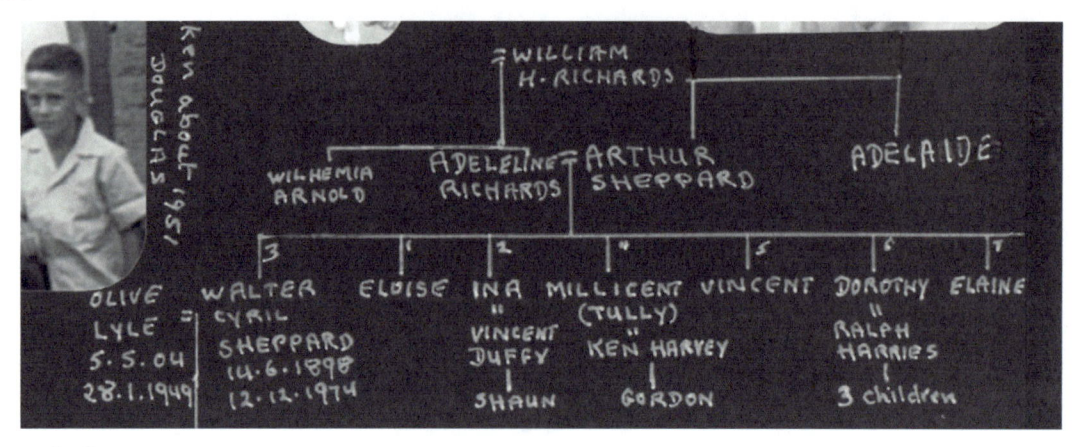

The Search Query

Wilhelmina Arnold Richards

The Google Search Results - For Wilhelmina Arnold Richards

kingsleymccartney.com
http://www.kingsleymccartney.com › www › wilhelmina

Families, Richards, Bayne and McArtney

Wilhelmina Arnold Richards (left) married Reginald Augustus McArtney. Her father was William H Richards, her mother's name is unknown. Wilhelmina had a ...

The results for Wilhelmina Arnold Richards

2	I55	Richards, Ann Elizabeth	15 December 1844	179		8	Yes			
3	I147	Richards, Leonora Augusta	1839	185	St Vincent	3	Yes			22 July 2021 - 10:25:58am
4	I52	Richards, Wilhelmina Arnold / McArtney, Wilhelmina Arnold	1875	149	Georgetown	4	1948	76	73	Port of Spain

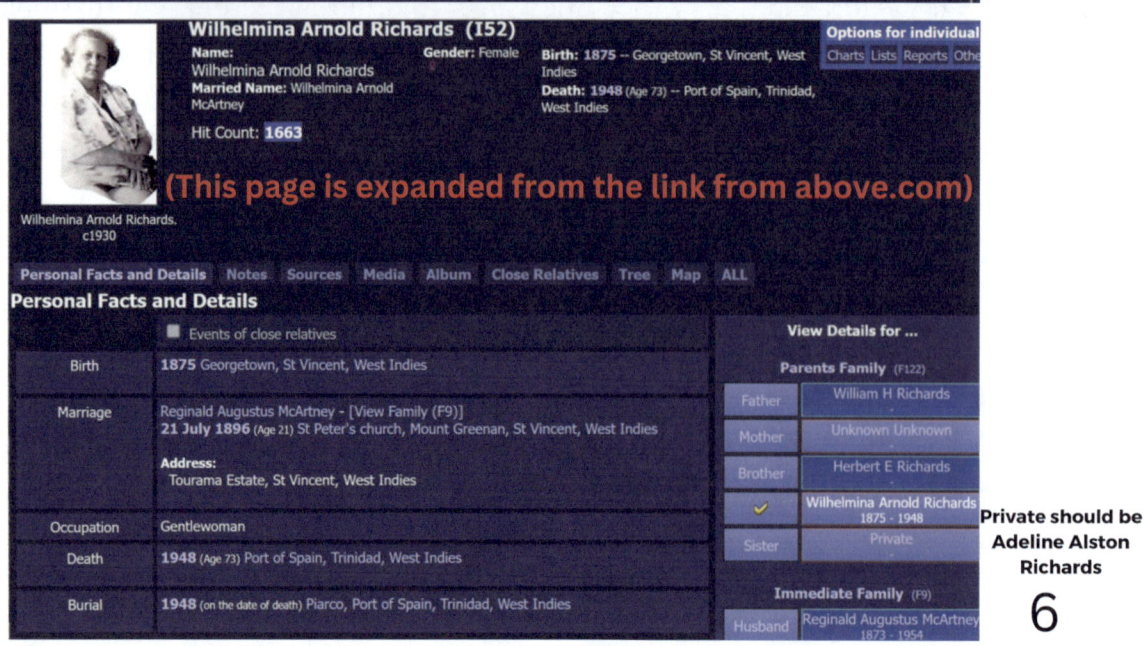

Wilhelmina Arnold Richards (I52)

Name: Wilhelmina Arnold Richards
Married Name: Wilhelmina Arnold McArtney
Gender: Female
Birth: 1875 -- Georgetown, St Vincent, West Indies
Death: 1948 (Age 73) -- Port of Spain, Trinidad, West Indies
Hit Count: 1663

(This page is expanded from the link from above.com)

Wilhelmina Arnold Richards. c1930

Personal Facts and Details | Notes | Sources | Media | Album | Close Relatives | Tree | Map | ALL

Personal Facts and Details

☐ Events of close relatives

Birth	1875 Georgetown, St Vincent, West Indies
Marriage	Reginald Augustus McArtney - [View Family (F9)] 21 July 1896 (Age 21) St Peter's church, Mount Greenan, St Vincent, West Indies
	Address: Tourama Estate, St Vincent, West Indies
Occupation	Gentlewoman
Death	1948 (Age 73) Port of Spain, Trinidad, West Indies
Burial	1948 (on the date of death) Piarco, Port of Spain, Trinidad, West Indies

View Details for ...

Parents Family (F122)
Father: William H Richards
Mother: Unknown Unknown
Brother: Herbert E Richards
✓ Wilhelmina Arnold Richards 1875 - 1948
Sister: Private

Private should be Adeline Alston Richards

Immediate Family (F9)
Husband: Reginald Augustus McArtney 1873 - 1954

6

The plethora of information housed on the kingsleymccartney.com website was wonderful (and free). Based on what was available, I was able to trace the family history of my great-grandmother's Richards/Hazel line back to the 1500s. What grieved me, however, was that Adeline, Wilhelmina's sister, was listed as private. I contacted the website owner several times and provided proof of their relationship, but he did not wish to address it at the time. In fact, he responded once to tell me that Wilhelmina's private sister was named "Joan." I know Joan to be Adeline's granddaughter. Nevertheless, it felt like the sun had just come out after a long season of cloudy weather. It was absolutely joyous to have identified one of my family history lines.

The next big breakthrough

The next big breakthrough came from a search conducted on MyHeritage.com (subscription required). I noticed that many Caribbean accounts are housed there. I came across a tree belonging to Carmen Martin Gruny. She was definitely related to me, though I could not figure out how at first. I found that one of her relatives was St. Ange Gruny. I was able to obtain a copy of his birth record that she had uploaded, and I had it translated from French to English. The man who translated it also provided information about his mother, Leonnise Sthéphanie Gruny. This was the "Mama Niese" that our family had learned about through the work of Renee Mangum.

Using www.filae.com (subscription required), I was able to find birth records for Leonnise, her entire family, and her father's and mother's families.

This discovery had been buried in family lore. The craziest family tale was that Leonnise was the daughter of a French general who was appointed governor of an island in the Caribbean. According to the story, Leonnise was disowned by the family because she fell in love with a local soldier. As it turns out, this is very close to what happened, though many details were lost over time. This was probably my most exciting find because we were able to clear up information that people had taken to their graves rather than divulge. I will forever be thankful to the man who translated St. Ange's record and provided me with more information.

Next, I joined a Facebook group called "Trinidad and Tobago Genealogy" (subscription required for searches) at https://www.facebook.com/groups/1400414593557228. On my first day on the website, I found a son of Arthur Sheppard, my great-grandfather. His name was Denis, and he passed away when he was 15. That was the beginning of copious amounts of research using that website, along with many documents providing proof of life.
Through their files, I found Arthur Sheppard's obituary, where I learned about his life. I discovered that he had traveled throughout the Caribbean before marrying in St. Vincent, then settled in Trinidad. From there, I was able to take off and learn so much more about my family. This document presents all the information I have uncovered. I hope you enjoy everything I will present to you. Hopefully, this will spur conversations in our Facebook group.

INTRODUCTION

I wish I had asked my father more questions about his ancestors while he was alive. We did a 3-hour DVD-recorded interview of his life, but for some reason, his tales did not include much information about his extended family. I wonder why our ancestors didn't tell us much about their past or the countries they came from. Walter Sheppard's father, Arthur, came from England, yet his grandchild—my father—never heard anything mentioned about him. Arthur passed away before his first grandchild was born, but why didn't his family know or share anything about him?

Now, in my senior years, I have a laundry list of questions that I would have asked if I had known that so much would be lost. That saddens me. I wish I had gotten to it sooner. I "get it" now. If there is blame to be placed, it likely rests on my shoulders. I have been under prophetic counsel to learn about my forebears since I joined The Church of Jesus Christ of Latter-day Saints in 1980.

At the time, my parents were my only source of content, and the road to getting family history from them was like trying to break into the Cheyenne Mountain Complex in Colorado. There were apparently stories my family felt embarrassed about. So many conversations were simply shut down. I felt like I was never going to find anything about my family from my parents.

It wasn't until my father passed away that I genuinely began attempting to learn about my heritage, and spending money was the key to finding long-lost data. I subscribed to genealogy websites, requested BMD (Birth, Marriage, Death) certificates, and subscribed to newspapers—all of which were absolutely critical to uncovering the information. My husband said I had spent enough. At that point, I had to get donations from family. I am so thankful to those who sent those precious dollars.

Shortly before my dad's death, I started a Facebook group called "Caribbean Genealogy Struggles" (https://www.facebook.com/groups/529811485161441). This group comprises my maternal (Martin) and paternal (Sheppard) relatives. Two cousins on the Sheppard side stood out: Maria Isabel Reilly (Mariabella) and Kathy Plimmer. On the Martin side, cousin Donna Carla. They have been a great resource to the family.
Another resource is Alan De Montbrun, an expert on the Minnie Kirk and Dr. Richard Benjamin Anderson side. Minnie is my 2x great-grandmother, and Dr. Anderson was her second husband. Their children were my great-uncles and great-aunts.

I truly believe I have captured a substantial amount of content. Have you ever watched "Who Do You Think You Are?" They start by searching on Ancestry.com, and once that is exhausted, they hop on a plane and meet with experts in the field. That's usually when they pull out a giant family chart and tell them everything they want to know. We may not be able to afford research like that, but we can still gather basic information using online resources. Lastly, perhaps a cousin in one of those locations might be open to taking a trip to a clerk's office.

I would love to go to Tobago, Scotland, or the UK. One day, I would also love to visit St. Vincent, St. Kitts, and Saba to search cemeteries, parish records, libraries, county courthouses, etc. That could be a boon

WHO IS THIS WORK FOR?

My primary focus for this entire project has been for my direct descendants—my children and grandchildren—to provide them with a knowledge I grew up without. I am writing and gathering this information for them: Glen, Cady, Kirsten, Harrison, Stella, Rictor, Jordan, Addi, Averly, and Jonah. I do this as a love letter to them.

My secondary focus is what comes in the next sections and the remainder of the content. This is for my direct descendants as well as my extended family, which includes aunts, uncles, cousins, and grandparents.

The way to organize and display this work has given me fits. Genealogy lines do not follow a simple, linear path. There are twists and turns in many different directions. I have decided to begin with myself as the access point, moving first to my descendants and then tracing the trail upwards to the ancestors who came before me.

Some important points to note:

- **Who**: I invited every family member I am in contact with to contribute to this book. All those who provided additional information will be included.
- **Sensitive Topics:** These will not be excluded from the book but will be presented without any moral commentary on my part. There are illegitimate births, slavery, and disowned family members. I will report these as facts, making an effort to respect those who have experienced these things by using politically correct terminology. But make no mistake, I will not add any judgments; readers can draw their own conclusions and decide what to do with the information.
- **Personal Information**: The most an extended family member can find about themselves is their name within a family unit. I will include: name, parents, and siblings. There will be no birthdates for living cousins, aunts, or uncles. I am writing this for them, sharing the work I did on their behalf.
- **Copyrights**: I have included website locations and book titles whenever I referenced sources. I did not compile notes at the end of each chapter. Again, this is not a work prepared for a mass or formal audience. It's for family.
- **Pictures:** I have decades of pictures currently stored away. I would have loved to include many pictures, but I cannot, as they are stored and I cannot access them at the moment.

Believe it or not, the organization for this book occurs in the Table of Contents. This is important to link all the data, so the table of content is the vehicle for it. You will also see chapters or pages listed multiple times. That is done in order to show the different relationships.

Generation One

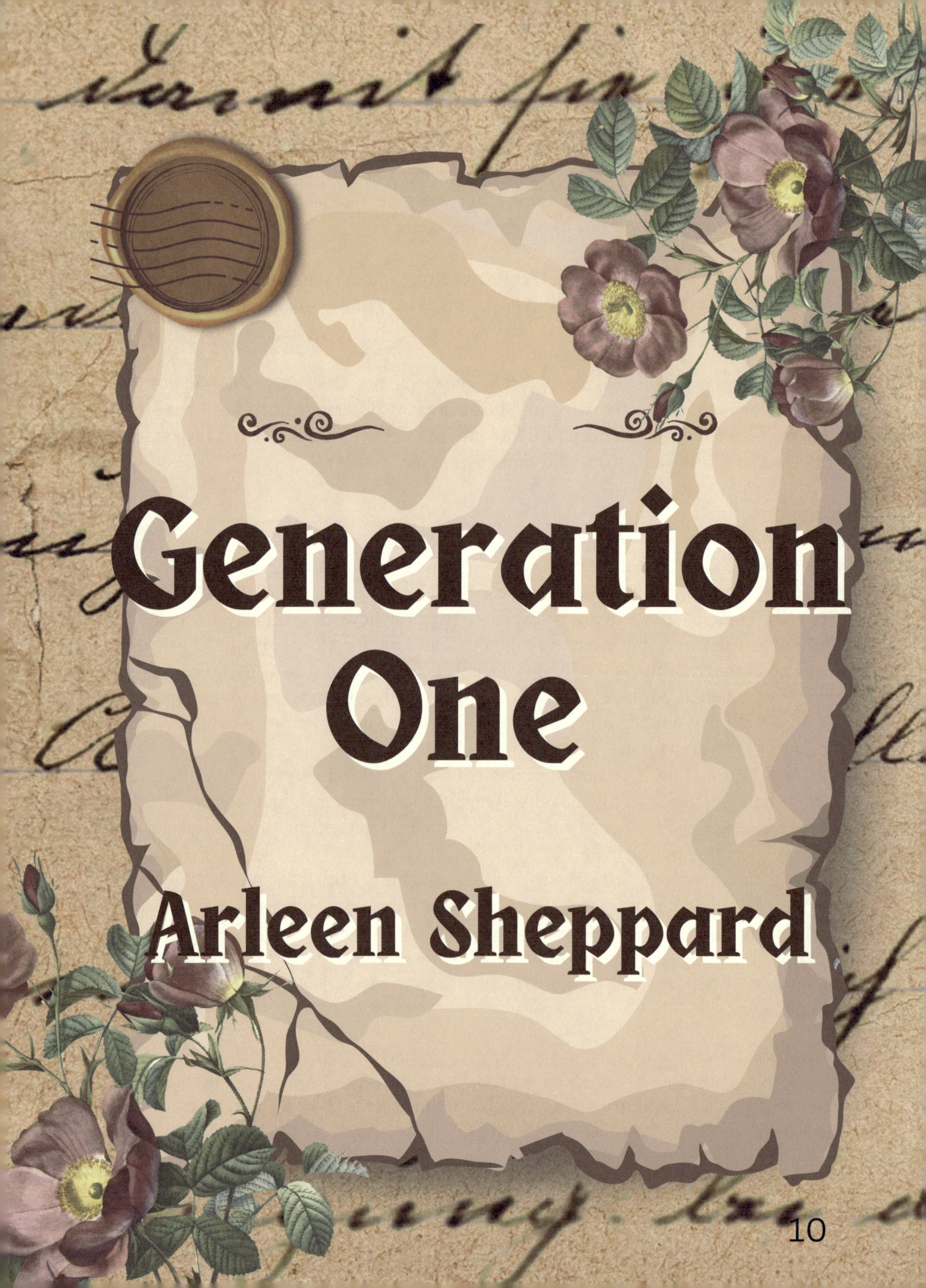

Arleen Sheppard

HISTORY OF
ARLEEN LORRAINE OLIVE MARIE SHEPPARD

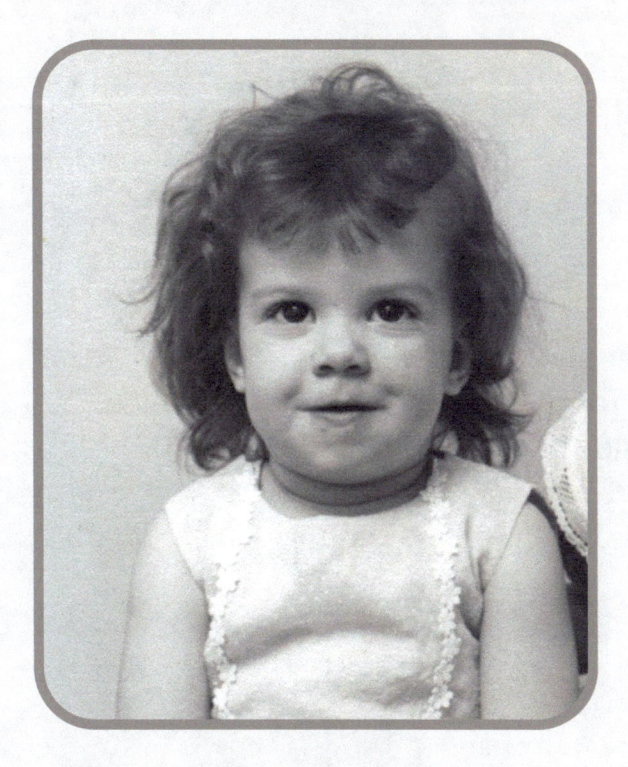

QUICK FACTS:

BORN
PORT OF SPAIN, TRINIDAD

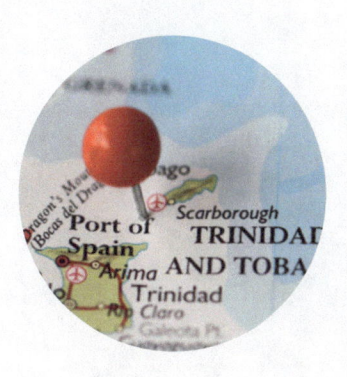

PARENTS
DAVID AND PAMELA SHEPPARD

CHILDREN
GLEN HOWELL
CADY HOWELL
LUMI FROEMMING
ADAM FROEMMING +

Family Tree

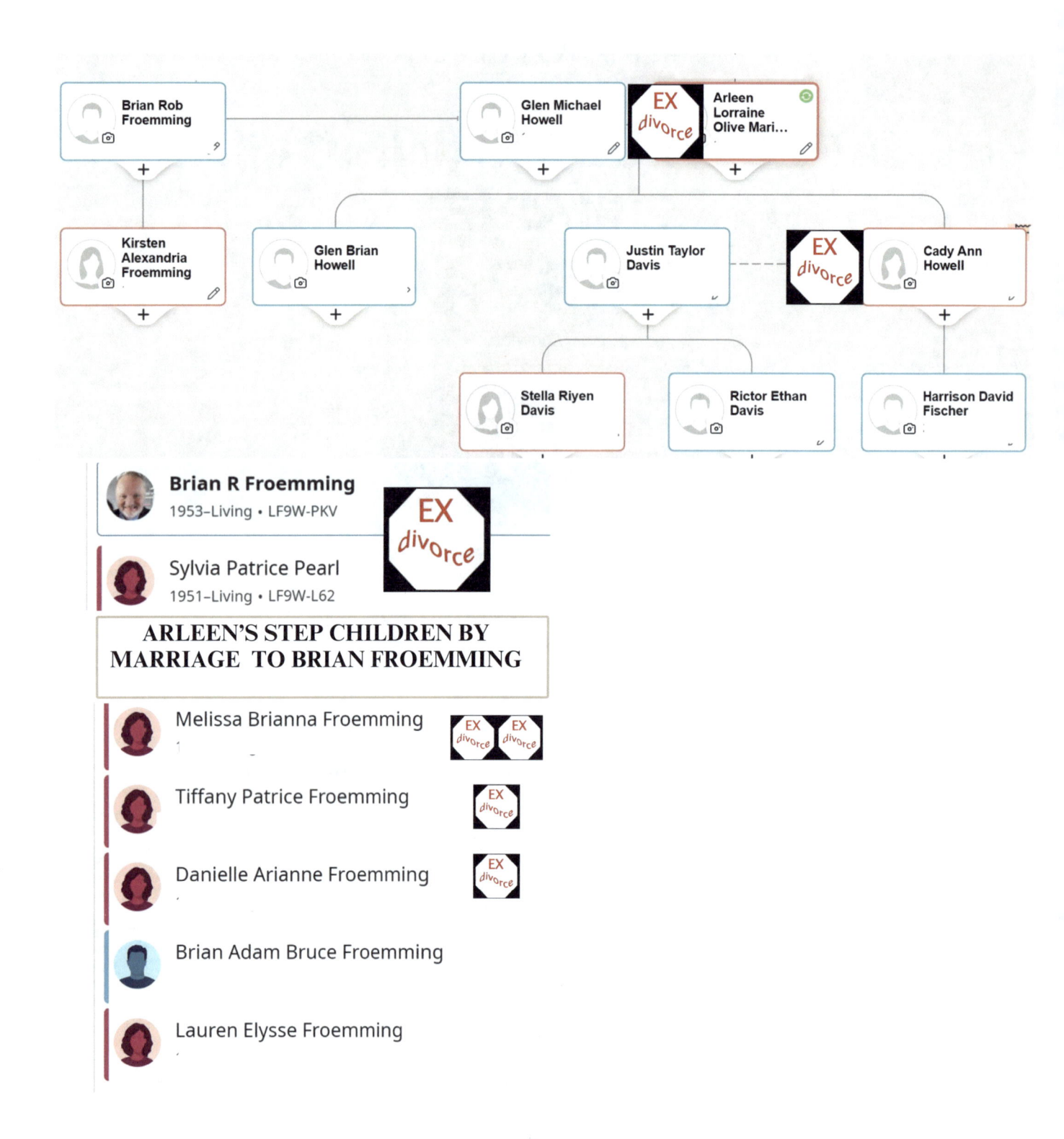

- **Brian Rob Froemming** + **Kirsten Alexandria Froemming**
- **Glen Michael Howell** [EX divorce] **Arleen Lorraine Olive Mari...**
  - **Glen Brian Howell**
  - **Justin Taylor Davis** [EX divorce] **Cady Ann Howell**
    - **Stella Riyen Davis**
    - **Rictor Ethan Davis**
    - **Harrison David Fischer**

Brian R Froemming
1953–Living • LF9W-PKV

[EX divorce]

Sylvia Patrice Pearl
1951–Living • LF9W-L62

ARLEEN'S STEP CHILDREN BY MARRIAGE TO BRIAN FROEMMING

- Melissa Brianna Froemming [EX divorce] [EX divorce]
- Tiffany Patrice Froemming [EX divorce]
- Danielle Arianne Froemming [EX divorce]
- Brian Adam Bruce Froemming
- Lauren Elysse Froemming

12

I was born in Port of Spain, Trinidad and Tobago, while my parents, David and Pamela, were permanently residing in Montreal, Canada. My mother didn't want to have her second baby so far away from family, so she returned to Trinidad to be in the company and comfort of her extended family.

When we returned to Montreal, I was just 8 months old. My parents often recounted the trouble they had crossing the border with me. They showed up at the border with a bundle they hadn't left Canada with, which understandably raised questions. My father said they went back and forth with the authorities about my paternity and permission to bring me into the country. Frustrated, he eventually held me out to them and declared, "Take her if you won't let her into the country!" Apparently, that dramatic gesture worked, and the officials found a solution. I was added as an immigrant without proper documentation. I suppose, technically, that made me an illegal immigrant in Canada's eyes—but thank goodness for having my parents as sponsors!

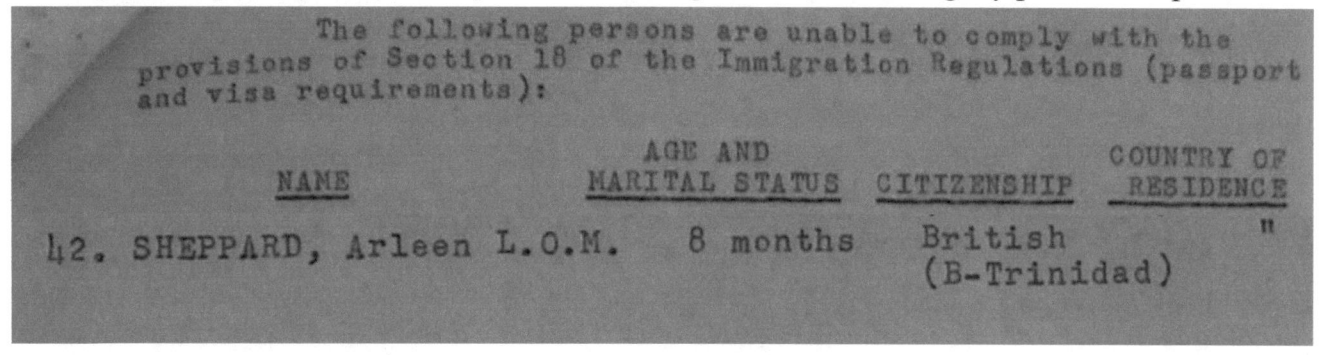

```
The following persons are unable to comply with the
provisions of Section 18 of the Immigration Regulations (passport
and visa requirements):

                         AGE AND                      COUNTRY OF
     NAME                MARITAL STATUS  CITIZENSHIP  RESIDENCE

42.  SHEPPARD, Arleen L.O.M.  8 months   British         "
                                         (B-Trinidad)
```

My father was a prolific storyteller, and he often entertained us with his wild tales. However, this particular story came with corroborating documentation from Canadian immigration, so I know it wasn't just another one of his "whoppers."

Growing up in Canada was wonderful. We were definitely outdoor kids, no matter the season. Having my dad around was like having a giant kid to play with. We had a simple swing set in the backyard, but he wasn't satisfied with "just plain." He rigged up two ladders—one to climb up and one to climb down—and turned the swing set into an obstacle course that could entertain a crowd of kids. In the winter, he'd tie a sled to the back of his car and drive around our icy cul-de-sac, slinging us across the road in fits of laughter.

We stayed in Canada until I was 8 years old. Eventually, my father decided he'd had enough of the cold. He complained that the frigid weather was affecting his left shoulder, the one closest to the car door. As a salesman, he was constantly in and out of his car, and the cold would seep into his muscles. He wanted to move somewhere with a milder climate.

He secured a transfer to Los Angeles, California, and we embarked on an epic road trip from Montreal to L.A.—a 41-hour journey. Along the way, he made sure we stopped to see some amazing sights: Niagara Falls in New York, herds of buffalo in the Midwest, and so much more. It was the perfect introduction to our new life in California.

My siblings and I had a lot of fun in Los Angeles, especially in our new neighborhood. There were so many kids to play with, and we even got to take swimming lessons at a neighborhood pool. I believe my love for water must be genetic because I adored swimming back then—and I still do to this day.

We were happy in Los Angeles. As usual, my father was up to his old tricks, finding ways to make life more fun for all the neighborhood children. One time, he made a harness for our Labrador, Nero, and hitched him to a wagon. The plan didn't go quite as expected. He told Nero to stay, then backed up some distance before calling him. The moment Nero bolted forward, the wagon tipped over immediately, leaving the riders crying in its wake. It was a short-lived but memorable experiment!

Despite our enjoyment, my father never truly took to life in Los Angeles. I vividly remember how he would come home from work visibly frazzled, almost vibrating from the hours spent driving in heavy traffic. He'd collapse into his chair in front of the TV, drink in hand, trying to unwind. It wasn't a sustainable routine, and he grew increasingly unhappy.
The final straw came during a massive rainstorm. After the storm passed, my father went outside and then called to us. In the distance, he pointed out something extraordinary—a mountain that none of us had ever noticed before. Hidden by smog, it had only become visible after the rain cleared the air. That moment seemed to spark something in him. Not long after, he took us up the mountain to the Griffith Observatory. Shortly after that visit, we were on a plane to Trinidad and Tobago, ready to start the next chapter of our lives.

Griffith Observatory
Los Angeles, California

I'll never forget our arrival at Piarco Airport for our return to Trinidad. As we got off the plane, I noticed a huge group of people waving at us. Confused, I turned to my father and asked who all those people were. His answer was simple: "Family."

I had never been surrounded by so much family before. Up until then, it had always been small groups—Auntie Joan and Uncle Brian in Montreal, Auntie Barbara in Virginia, Auntie Marie in San Diego. But this was different. It felt like there were a hundred people there to greet us, and the warmth of their welcome was unforgettable.

That first night in Trinidad, I experienced something entirely new. The TV was on, and I was captivated by what I saw—a beautiful East Indian woman singing while a man played the sitar. I had never heard music like that before; it was mesmerizing.
I also quickly learned something surprising: there was only three hours of TV a day, and just one channel! It was a far cry from what I was used to, but it marked the beginning of a fascinating new chapter in my life.

I believe we stayed with Auntie Kathleen for a while before we got our own home in Diego Martin and later moved to St. Ann's or Cascades. There were always lots of children around, and those days were incredible. We could leave the house in the morning and not return until evening, spending our time exploring and playing freely. We could eat fruit straight from the trees, with so many varieties to choose from. It was a magical time filled with family and joy—probably the closest to bliss I have ever experienced.

While we lived in Trinidad, my dad bought a boat. It was about 40 to 50 feet long, with a center inboard motor and seats all around. The boat had a canopy that stretched from the front to the back, providing shade for everyone onboard. I can't recall the exact type of boat, but it was big enough to fit quite a few family members. We'd often take it to Scotland's Bay for the day or enjoy a week together at a rental home Down d' Islands. Those outings were some of the best times we had as a family.

We might have stayed in Trinidad indefinitely if not for the Black Power Revolution in the Caribbean during the 1970s. My father felt it was no longer safe for us to remain there. At the time, he owned a flooring company called the Caribbean Carpet Company. He was a businessman through and through. He explained that his employees, who had been friendly and cordial when they left work on Friday, returned on Monday with hostility, talking about killing "Whitey." He said the change in attitude happened almost overnight. Concerned for our safety, he made the difficult decision to organize our return to the United States.

While we were still living on the island, I remember there was a curfew. One evening, as we were coming home, my father had us wait outside while he searched the house to ensure there hadn't been a break-in. To my young mind, it was terrifying. Another memory that stands out is of a Black man walking down the main road one day. Phone calls started spreading through the neighborhood, with families reporting his movements to one another, worried he might cause trouble. You could hear the phones ringing up and down the street as he passed. It gave me a sense that our neighborhood was watching out for each other, though the underlying tension of those times was palpable.

We moved to Florida just in time for the desegregation of public schools in the United States, a major milestone of the Civil Rights Movement. My parents enrolled Brent and me in a Catholic school, but Carol wanted to attend a public school, and they allowed her. I remember her telling me stories about fights breaking out at school. She also taught me an unusual lesson: that pulling someone's hair up hurts more than pulling it down. I've never had the chance to test that theory, though I can confirm from her demonstration that it really does hurt. I remember thinking that Carol was the last person I'd want to get into a conflict with.

Although I didn't move to Florida until I was 11, I consider it where I grew up. During our trip there, I recall a conversation about Americans. My father was commenting on their table manners, particularly how they used their thumbs to push food onto their forks or spoons. I'm sure the conversation was much longer and involved more critiques, but that's the part that stuck with me.

Looking back, I realize I was an odd child, and by "odd," I mean I struggled with mental health issues. I didn't feel everything a "normal" person would feel and often preferred to be alone. I also dealt with suicidal thoughts, though I never acted on them—I was too afraid to follow through. Instead, I just drifted through life for a time. Somehow, I managed to make it through, earning a college degree and finding a religion that gave me purpose and direction.
I left the Catholic Church in my mid-teens and set out on a spiritual journey. After briefly exploring another religion and realizing it wasn't the right fit, I eventually found The Church of Jesus Christ of Latter-Day Saints or should I say, it found me. For the first time, I felt at home. The church provided structure and religious guidelines that brought order to my life. It taught me the path to happiness and how to become a testifying disciple of Jesus Christ. It also required change—true repentance.

One of my favorite scriptures is *Doctrine and Covenants 58:43:*
"By this ye may know if a man repenteth of his sins—behold, he will confess them and forsake them."

Over the course of my life, I've continued to make mistakes, but my testimony of Jesus Christ has always kept me grounded. It has eliminated suicide as an option, giving me hope and purpose. I look forward to the day I can return to my Heavenly Father and Jesus Christ, who will act as my mediator before the Father. I love them both dearly. And I am deeply grateful for the Gift of the Holy Ghost, who guides me through life's challenges.

A SHORT STORY FROM ARLEEN

In 1978 while in the Air Force, I joined a Skydiving group on Fort Knox Army Post.

On my 6th jump, my chute was opened and I, as usual, was enjoying the peace and beauty I experienced on a regular basis.

All of a sudden, I noticed a tree in a wide opened field. I started having trouble getting away from the tree. I toggled left and the tree remained in my line of sight. The same thing happen when I toggled right. I could not get away from the tree no matter what I did. It stayed in my line of sight until it started getting closer and closer until there was no avoiding it.

I recalled my training and prepared for a tree landing. In order to prevent getting impaled by a tree limb or branch you have to place your palms in the opposite arm pit to protect arteries as well as burying your neck into your shoulder.

I made the tree landing unscathed. My jumpmaster came in a jeep zooming toward me while I was stuck in the tree. Once he found out that I was okay, he started yelling at me. "What were you doing?" I told him I could not get away from the hazard no matter how hard I tired. He yelled back that I focused on the tree, and maybe next time I should focus on the drop zone.

My very next jump, I focused on the drop zone, and landed within a few feet of it. It was a life lesson for me on focus, and to avoid the hazard, by focusing on the goal. Jesus Christ is my greatest goal.

A SHORT STORY FROM BRIAN

In 1973, Brian worked at a gas station that was next to a motorcycle shop. He was friends with a kid who worked there.

Being friendly, the kid kept inviting Brian to come over and test ride a new model, the 1973 CZ 250 bike they just got in stock.
Persistent, Brian agreed to come over and test drive the bike.

After getting set up on the bike, Brian rode in the field next to the shop. He spent several minutes riding around enjoying the new machine. After riding around the field for a bit, Brian headed back to the store. As he was pulling up he managed to ride over a sand pile that he could not see because of the tall grass. As he went over the it, the bike went airborne and he was thrown forward. His grip had tightened. As his hands came back and he shifted back into the seat, his hand came back revving the engine causing the bike to race forward.

It was only 20' to the side of the store wall, and he didn't have enough time to recover. He hit the side of the building as he was flying forward over the handle bars. Since it was a test drive in the grassy field, he was not given a helmet. He went head first over the handle bar and into the store wall.

Everyone at the store was so freaked out, they got the bike and offered Brian assistance. He declined and they were so happy to see him go back to the gas station.

Fast forward to September 2022, when he went to Minnesota for a class reunion, he stopped by the motorcycle shop which has long been closed, and the building was empty. To his surprise, the dents were still in the wall.

18

Brian Froemming

My husband Brian is a Viking. He is Nordic as Nordic can be with a minor helping of Aryan (German). He is 4th generation American. His great grandfather came to the United States and moved to Minnesota, which is a heavily populated Norse state along with family from Iowa and Wisconsin.

We have some pictures of him as a Viking Warrior. It is absolutely awesome.

I absolutely love being married to my Viking hero. He can do everything manly. Love it.

Arleen & Brian

January 5, 1993
St Petersburg, Florida

Cady Howell 3 years old

Glen Howell 5 years old

Cady Howell, Girl Froemming, Kirsten Froemming, Glen Howell

A Day at the Beach

KIRSTEN

RICTOR AND GRANDPA

STELLA AND GRANDMA

KIRSTEN, STELLA AND GRANDMA

22

Family Pics

My Stella Bella Cinderella

Rictor

23

More Fun Family Pictures

STELLA SAID SHE CAN JUMP TOO!!

Kirsten

Cady

Halloween

Kirsten and Stella

Great Grandma Sheppard

Cady with her babies

25

Random Family Pictures

26

Fun outings with Adam and Jessi Froemming

Bald Mountain, NC

The Virginia Creeper

Here's a fun story: While on the Virginia Creeper Trail, we spotted a baby black bear dart across our path. Those of us not from North Carolina—particularly the Floridians—stopped in our tracks and marveled at the little cub. "Look how cute!" we exclaimed, completely enchanted.

Moments later, we heard Jessi, a local, urgently whispering to Adam, "We need to get out of here. Now."

That snapped us out of our daze. We quickly realized the potential danger of sticking around, especially since where there's a cub, there's likely a protective mama bear nearby. We didn't need more convincing and made our way down the trail, ears perked for any signs of trouble.

The next day, Jessi came home from work laughing. "Guess what these crazy Floridians did on the trail?" she told her co-workers. "They stopped to look at a black bear cub! Isn't it cute!" Needless to say, we were the joke of the day—and a great source of amusement for her colleagues.

27

MY THREE BIO CHILDREN - TODAY

GLEN - 41

CADY - 39

Kirsten would prefer to be called Lumi

I want to apologize to my children. Most of the pictures of you from when you were younger have been packed away. They've been stored like this since 2012 and haven't been accessible. I'm truly sorry for this.

28

Generation One
Siblings Of Arleen Sheppard

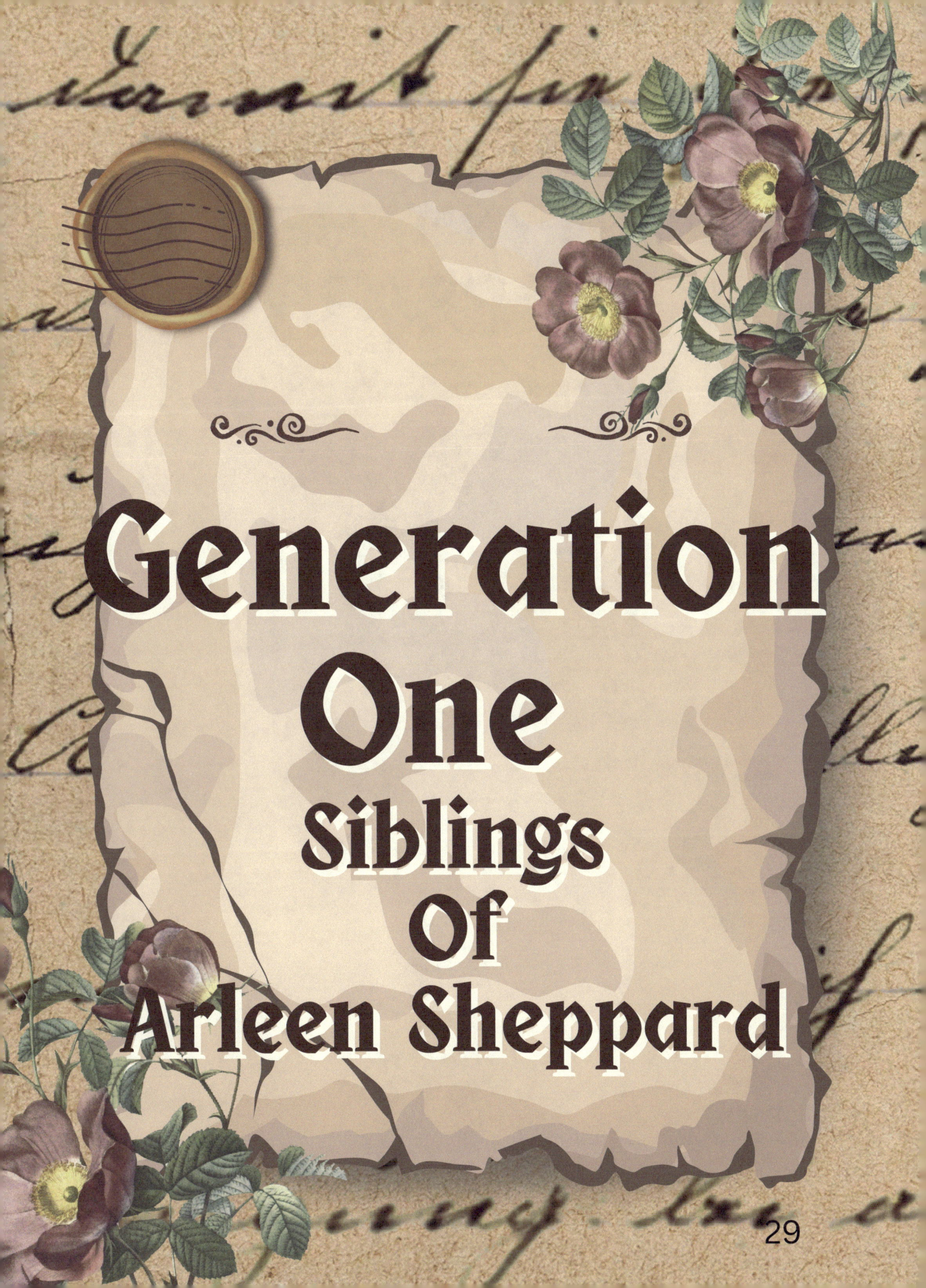

HISTORY OF CAROL-LYNN THERESA SHEPPARD

QUICK FACTS:

BORN
MONTREAL, QUEBEC
CANADA

PARENTS
DAVID AND PAMELA
SHEPPARD

CHILDREN
RENEE SHEPPARD
JAMES SHEPPARD
KRISTA VAN DE BOGART

Sheppard, Kirk, Begg, Gruny, Martin

Carol-Lynn Theresa Sheppard

Descendancy

1. Carol-Lynn Theresa Sheppard b: in Montreal Canada.
+ James Lee Vandebogart b: in Amsterdam, New York USA. m: 30 Dec 1982 in Adams, Colorado, United States of America. div: 20 Mar 2000 in St. Petersburg, Florida, U.S.A..
   2. Krista Van De Bogart b: in Denver, Colorado USA.
+ Rudy b: 21 AUG 1955. d: 1988; age: 32.
   2. Renee Sheppard b: in St. Petersburg, Florida, U.S.A..
   + Andrew Paul Cecere m: 12 Dec 1993 in Pinellas, Florida, USA.
     3. Brett Cerce b: in St. Petersburg, Florida, U.S.A..
     3. Haley Cerce b: in St. Petersburg, Florida, U.S.A
   + Ricky Toshina McSwain
   + Unknown
     3. Kiara Cerce
+ Unknown
   2. James Sheppard b: in Denver, Colorado USA.
   + Unknown
     3. Andrew Basehore

Carol-Lynn Theresa Sheppard

BIRTH Montreal Canada
DEATH Living

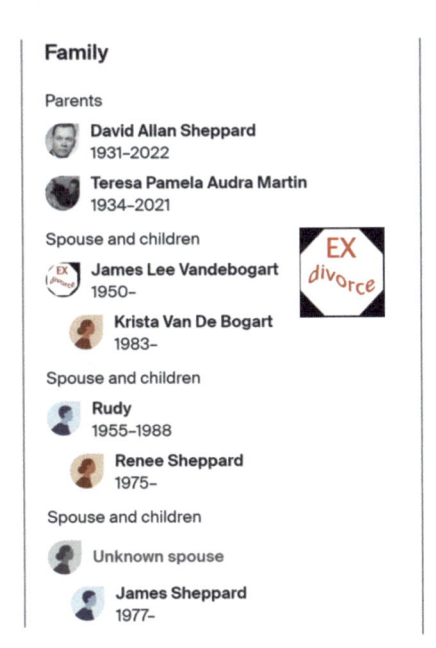

Family

Parents

David Allan Sheppard
1931–2022

Teresa Pamela Audra Martin
1934–2021

Spouse and children

James Lee Vandebogart *EX divorce*
1950–

  Krista Van De Bogart
  1983–

Spouse and children

Rudy
1955–1988

  Renee Sheppard
  1975–

Spouse and children

Unknown spouse

  James Sheppard
  1977–

Carol-Lyn Theresa Sheppard

I was born on a cold winter day in Montreal, Canada. Mom and Dad immigrated to Canada for Dad's job. That's the story I was told.

I was a difficult child, according to my mother. I was born with club foot, as the islanders say. I wore a brace which my father said he 'threw into the ocean,' because I cried all the time. I had some sort of imbalance or something because my energy was not the good kind. I was needy, insecure, and anxious with energy like a chihuahua. Mom said they used to call me Our Lady of Perpetual Motion. Speaking of perpetual motion, Dad seemed to like to travel, or something.

We left Canada when I was nine or ten, moved to California for two years; left school, family, friends, a dog and moved to Trinidad, lived there for two years, left school, family, friends, a dog, then moved to the US, I lived there for two years, then left school, family, friends, a dog…

I traveled around the US. I guess wandering rubbed off on me. I went to Boston and back, then back to Florida where I traveled (couch-surfed) around for a while. One day, I decided to leave Florida. That started some wild adventures, some of which were scary and dangerous, and some were hilariously funny in retrospect, but none of them should have been experienced by a 17-year-old.

When I was eighteen, I came back home pregnant with Renee. Not ready to be a mother, I left her at a farm, called The Farm, in Summertown Tennessee when she was one and a half years old. I read about it in Mother Earth News. I went back for her when she was three, after I made it to Colorado, met my future ex-husband who took a pregnant me in and I had my second child, Jimmy…James. Jimmy was one year-old when I went to get Renee.

I married my future ex-husband in 1982, and Krista was born in 1983. Renee is eight years older than Krista. Jimmy is six years older. We left Colorado, my husband, their father, in 1989 and moved in with my parents. I left my home, my family, friends, and the dog. I wasn't done traveling because I moved to Alabama.

The kids did not go with me. I moved back to Florida in September 1993. By that time, Renee was married to her first husband. I had reconnected with Renee and Jimmy. Krista was living with my ex-husband.

I got sober in March 1994 and have been in Florida ever since. I have reconnected with Krista. She lived with me in Florida for a little while. She is now a loving mother of a 23-year-old and an 8-year-old. She grows some of her own food in her large backyard in Colorado which apparently feed the squirrels more than they do her family. She is hilarious, one of the naturally funniest women I've ever known.

Jimmy was informally emancipated at 16 years old. He lives with his wife in a house they own in the mountains of Colorado with his stepson, and son. He and his wife are successful and both work at a hospital. He loves to go bike riding in the mountains with his wife and sons.

He has dogs, which surprises me because I never saw him expressing any interest in pets, or animals. He is tenderhearted soul who would drop everything and help someone in real need.

Renee met the love of her life and moved to North Carolina. She's a real estate agent now and a pretty successful one. She and her husband had three children each when they met and are putting the two who wanted to go through college. I am very proud of her. I tried to be a good mother and grandmother. Not sure how successful I was, but my grandkids talk to me tell me they love me, so maybe I did something right at some point.

And me, I stumbled into a career in the legal field the year I got sober. I started as a receptionist and worked my way up to a paralegal. Lucky for me, you don't need a degree to be a paralegal in Florida. I've worked for the same law firm for almost 12 years. I've gone as far as I can go in this field financially and by position. I expect to retire in three years, when I am seventy. After that, I want to sell my mobile home and move out of Florida.
So, that's it…67.9 years in two page and a half.

HISTORY OF BRENT ALLAN DAVID SHEPPARD

QUICK FACTS:

BORN
MONTREAL, QUEBEC
CANADA

PARENTS
DAVID AND PAMELA SHEPPARD

CHILDREN
NO ISSUE

My brother, Brent *by Arleen Froemming*

Brent was an amazing young man, the strongest person I've ever known. He was also an incredible athlete. In my mind, I had grand plans for his future—and mine. I imagined him becoming an MLB player, and through his career, I would get to know his teammates. My dream was to ride his coattails all the way to the altar with one of his teammates. Unfortunately, that dream never came to pass. Brent wasn't able to overcome the demons that ultimately took his life far too soon.

His strength always amazed me. Brent was powerful, even as a toddler. I remember my parents wanting him to join his sisters and their friends outside to play games. But he was too young to go out alone, so my parents came up with a creative solution: they harnessed him to an anchor

Brent used to pick on me if I got too close to him. One day, I saw a commercial on TV for Cheerios. The ad showed a character eating Cheerios and getting stronger. I remember thinking, If I eat Cheerios for breakfast, I'll be stronger than Brent.

So, I had my Cheerios and headed out to the front yard, feeling confident. My very next memory is running back into the house in tears, because I had been completely routed by my much stronger baby brother.

Brent's athletic ability was incredible. My dad wanted to make sure Brent saved his arm for the future. He thought Brent could pitch in high school, so they played him in center field. I remember one game where Richey Peterson was on third base, and the batter hit a ball deep to center field. Richey had to stay on base to see if Brent could catch it. He did. As soon as Brent made the catch, Richey bolted toward home. Brent threw the ball to home plate. It bounced once in the infield before the catcher caught it and tagged Richey out. That moment solidified it for me—Brent was an exceptional athlete. I don't think any of the other boy could have done that.

Brent's freshman year of high school was his best. He played both football and baseball, and his future seemed set. I was sure I was going to marry a baseball player. But then, my parents separated, and my mom moved us to Canada. I think that event really impacted Brent. He stepped away from sports and turned to drinking. Alcohol was always in the house, so it wasn't hard for him to get his hands on it. Unfortunately, his weaknesses took over, and his strengths were forgotten.

Brent and I grew distant after high school. He used to torment me. One time, he pinned me to the ground and threatened to spit on me. He would also needle me right behind Mom's back, and I would retaliate because I'm a bit of a hothead. But whenever there was a fight, Mom only saw me hitting Brent and assumed I was the instigator. She'd tell me I was "malicious and vicious." Brent would just giggle behind her back.

One night, he was driving me absolutely crazy. After an incident where he pushed me too far, I grabbed a knife and chased him out of the house. Of course, when the police arrived, I had to explain that I wasn't trying to harm him, I just wanted him to leave me alone.

Unfortunately, I never got to know the gregarious, humorous Brent that others did. I only knew the mean Brent.

Brent Sheppard Obituary

SHEPPARD, Brent 58, formerly of Shore Acres, Florida, passed away on Sunday, May 3, 2020. Brent is survived by his parents, David and Pamela Sheppard; sisters, Carol Sheppard and Arleen Froemming, and many relatives. He is beloved by family and friends for his extraordinary wit, humor and gregarious personality.

Brent in Trinidad 1965

Brent in Canada 1967

Brent in California 1969

Brent in Trinidad 1970
Brent is holding a bottle of alcohol

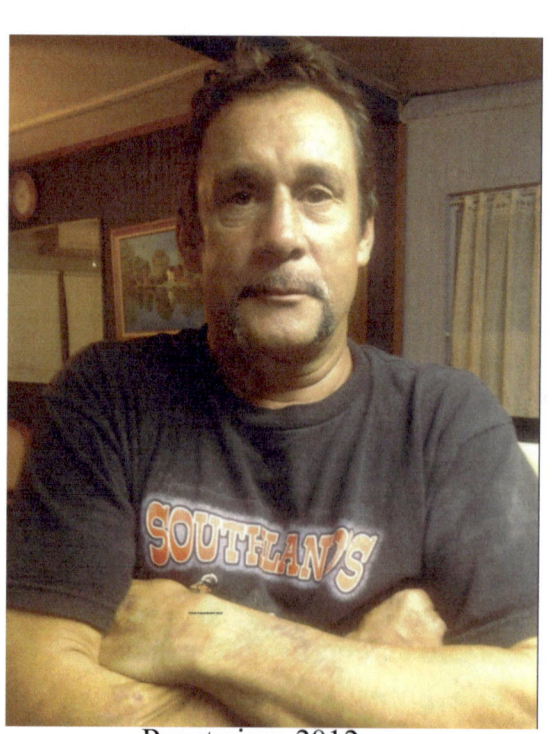

Brent circa 2012

36

Generation Two Paternal

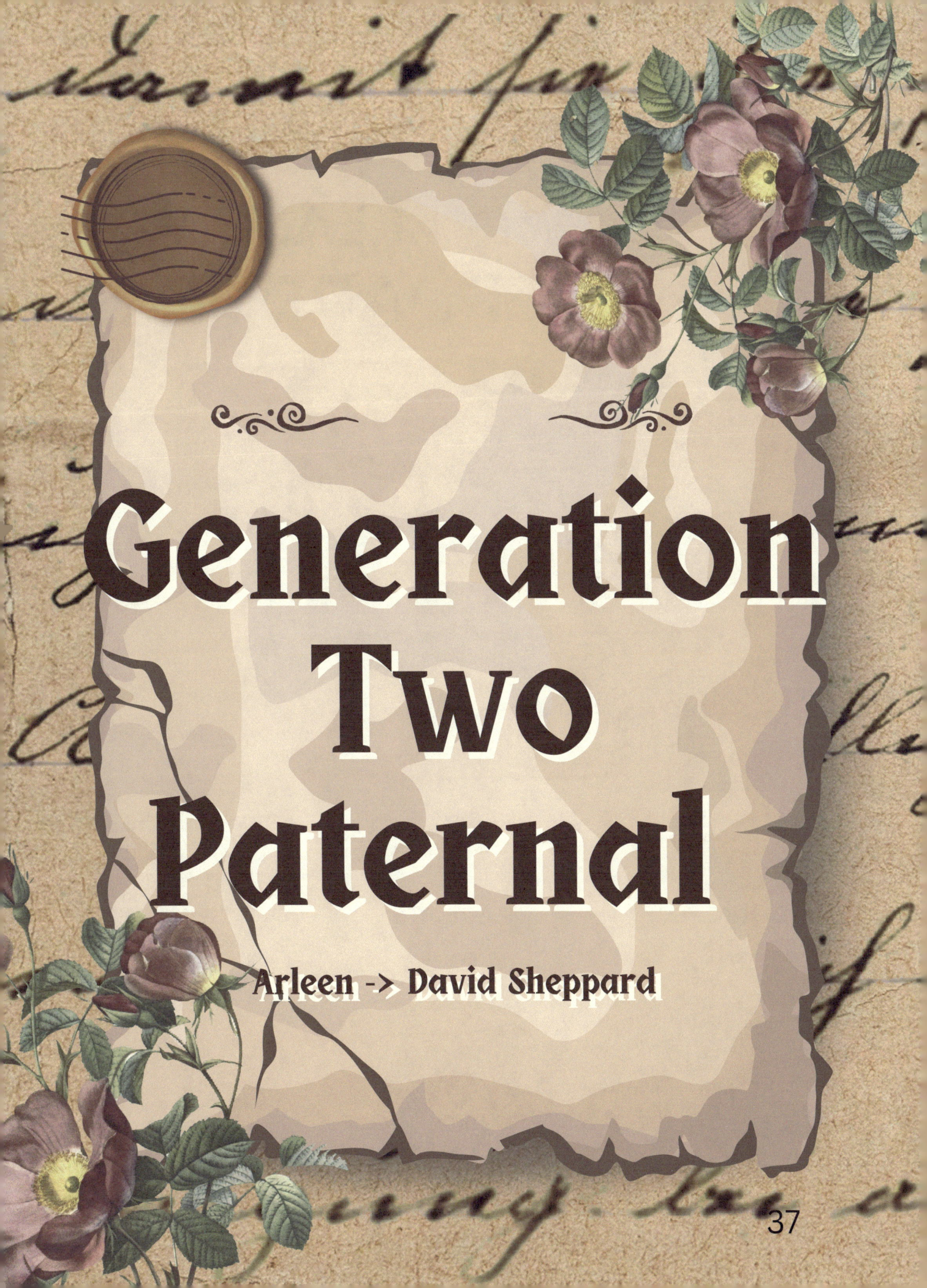

Arleen -> David Sheppard

HISTORY OF DAVID ALLAN SHEPPARD

QUICK FACTS:

BORN
PORT OF SPAIN, TRINIDAD

PARENTS
WALTER AND OLIVE SHEPPARD

CHILDREN
CAROL-LYNN THERESA
ARLEEN LORRAINE OLIVE
BRENT ALLAN DAVID

Descendancy

1. David Allan Sheppard b: 20 NOV 1931 in Port of Spain, Trinidad and Tobago, British West Indies. d: 02 Aug 2022 in Lecanto, Citrus, Florida, United States; age: 90.
+ Teresa Pamela Audra Martin b: 10 DEC 1934 in Port of Spain, Trinidad. m: 16 Apr 1955 in Montreal, Canada. d: 30 SEP 2021 in Lecanto, Citrus, Florida, USA; age: 86.
    2. Carol-Lynn Theresa Sheppard b: in Montreal Canada.
    + James Lee Vandebogart b: in Amsterdam, New York USA. m: 30 Dec 1982 in Adams, Colorado, United States of America. div: 20 Mar 2000 in St. Petersburg, Florida, U.S.A..
        3. Krista Van De Bogart b: 13 JUN 1983 in Denver, Colorado USA.
    + Rudy b: 21 AUG 1955. d: 1988; age: 32.
        3. Renee Sheppard b: in St. Petersburg, Florida.
        + Andrew Paul Cecere in Pinellas, Florida, USA
        + Ricky Toshina McSwain
    + Unknown
        3. James Sheppard b: in Denver, Colorado USA.
    2. Arleen Lorraine Olive Marie Sheppard b: in Port of Spain, Trinidad and Tobago, British West Indies.
    + Glen Michael Howell b: in Dover, Morris, New Jersey, USA. m: 20 May 1983 in Morristown, NJ. div: 14 Aug 1986 in St. Petersburg, Pinellas, Florida, USA.
        3. Glen Brian Howell b: in Dover, NJ.
        3. Cady Ann Howell b: in Dover, NJ.
        + Justin Taylor Davis b: in Orlando, Florida. m: 5 JUL 2005 in Goldsboro, North Carolina, USA. div: 2010 in Jacksonville, Duval, Florida, United States.
    + Brian Rob Froemming b: in Duluth, St. Louis, Minnesota, USA. m: 5 JAN 1993 in Saint Petersburg, Pinellas, Florida, United States.
        3. Kirsten Alexandria Froemming b: in Dunedin, Pinellas, Florida, USA.
    2. Brent Allan David Sheppard b: 10 JUN 1961 in Montreal, Canada. d: 3 MAY 2020 in Saint Petersburg, Pinellas, Florida, United States; age: 58.
    + Maureen H Hanley
    + Teresa K Monroe b: in Indianapolis, Indiana USA. m: 31 Dec 1988 in St. Petersburg, Florida, U.S.A.. div: 1 NOV 2001 in Pinellas, Florida, USA.

David Allan Sheppard

David grew up in Port of Spain, Trinidad and Tobago. He left Trinidad in the early 1950s. He was a young man with big dreams and jumped on an opportunity to work in Canada. He told stories of working on the Dew Line in the Artic, and then working as a salesman in Montreal. He also worked for a Cash Register repairman and that melded well with his youthful desire to figure out how things work.

In 1967 he left Canada to transfer to the American branch of Nelson Stud Welding in Los Angeles, California. He would come home from work shook because of the traffic he had to deal with in his daily grind, and to/fro home.

While living in California there was a hard rain. Unusual for the California climate. The next morning, we stepped outside to a beautiful smog free sky and saw a mountain we had never seen before. It was the Griffith Park Observatory 21 short miles away and 700' above our home in the foothills.

In what seemed to be a whirlwind, we loaded up our belongings and left for Trinidad. I'll never forget the amount of people who met us at the airport.

Date	Milestone Event
Early 1950s	Moved to Canada
04/16/1955	Married "Pamela" Martin
1967	Moved to California
1968	Moved to Trinidad
1970	Moved to Florida

In Trinidad it was a glorious time for our family. Life was certainly unlike anything, we had experienced before. There were family activities with the extended family and boat trips Down D' Island with the entire family in David's boat. Yes it sat quite a few people.

Unfortunately we had to leave Trinidad because of the Black Power Movement. We were no longer safe in Trinidad and had to move back to the US, where my father lived until his death. His eulogy appears next.

David Sheppard Eulogy by Carol Sheppard

It's hard to believe Dad's gone. He was such a big presence in our lives. He had a personality as big as he was. My father, David Sheppard, was born in Port of Spain, Trinidad, West Indies. He had 12 brothers and sisters. He said that not a year went by when a child wasn't born.

According to Dad's own words, he was a terror, always getting in trouble. He was very adventurous as a child who could never sit still. He always needed to know what was around the corner, what was on the next street.

I remember when, Brent, Arleen and I were young, our family went on long drives. I remember Dad saying he wanted to see "where this road went." Dad's adventuresome spirit took our family him from Trinidad to Canada, Canada to California, back to
Trinidad, and from Trinidad to Florida. A hurricane took Mom and Dad to Raleigh, NC, and Mom brought Dad back to Florida.

A Successful Man
A Poem By Bessie Anderson Stanley

That man is a success –
who has lived well, laughed often and loved much;

who has gained the respect of intelligent men and the love of children;
who has filled his niche and accomplished his task;
who leaves the world better than he found it;
who has never lacked appreciation of earth's beauty or failed to express it;
who looked for the best in others and gave the best he had.

Weep Not For Me
By Timothy Coote

Weep not for me though I have gone
Into that gentle night
Grieve if you will, but not for long
Upon my soul's sweet flight
I am at peace, my soul's at rest
There is no need for tears
For with your love I was so blessed
For all those many years
There is no pain, I suffer not
The fear is now all gone
Put now these things out of your thoughts
In your memory I live on
Remember not my fight for breath
Remember not the strife
Please do not dwell upon my death
But celebrate my life

DAVID SHEPPARD BIRTH CERTIFICATE

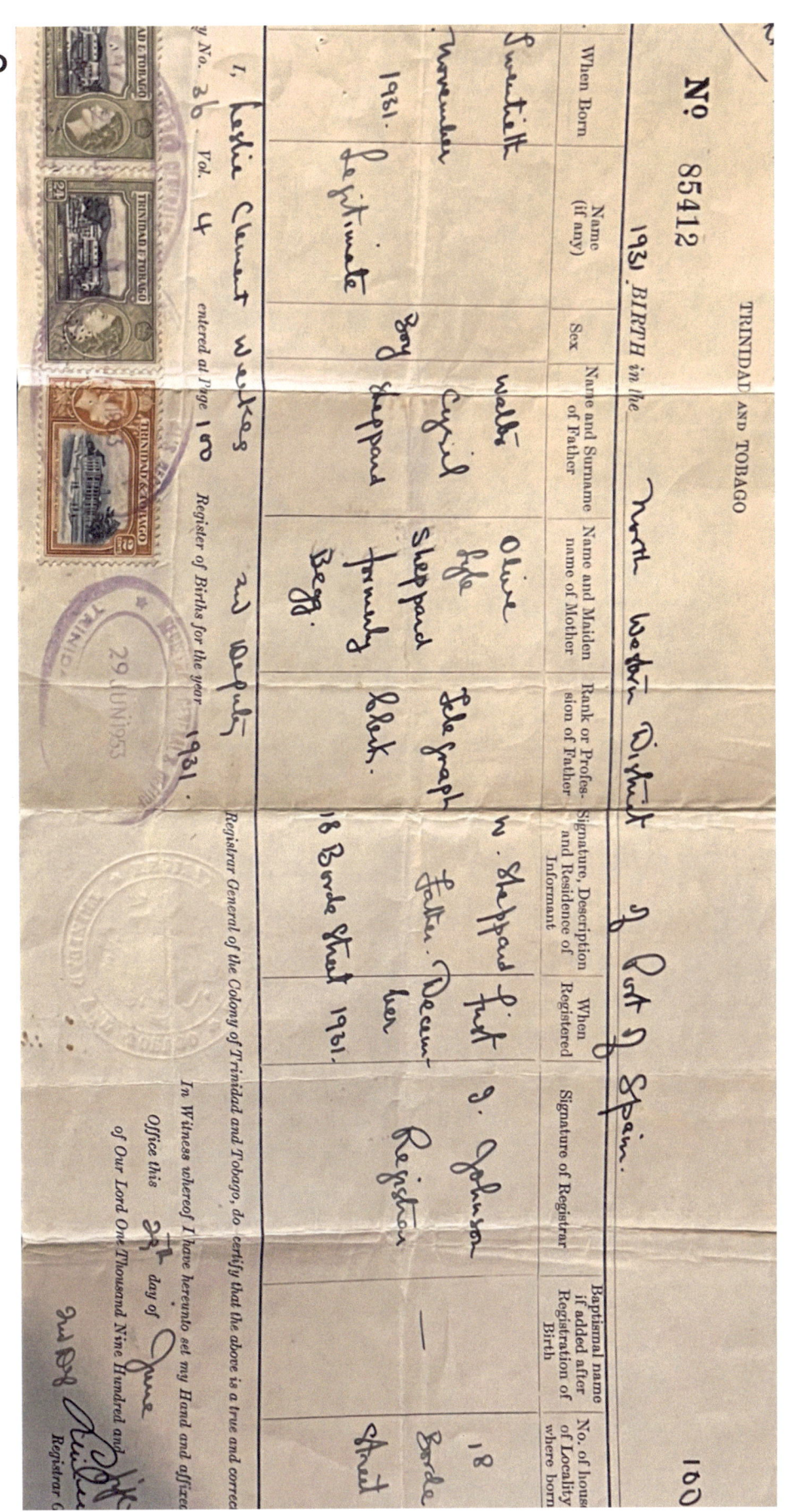

TRINIDAD AND TOBAGO

No. 85412

1931. BIRTH in the North Western District of Port of Spain.

When Born	Name (if any)	Sex	Name and Surname of Father	Name and Maiden name of Mother	Rank or Profession of Father	Signature, Description and Residence of Informant	When Registered	Signature of Registrar	Baptismal name if added after Registration of Birth	No. of house of Locality where born
Twentieth November 1931. Legitimate	Wallis Cyril Sheppard Begg.	Boy		Olive Lyle Sheppard formerly Begg.	Telegraph Clerk.	W. Sheppard Father. 18 Borde Street	First December 1931.	J. Johnson Registrar	—	18 Borde Street

I, Leslie Clement Walker, entered at Page 100 Register of Births for the year 1931. Entry No. 36 Vol. 4

29 JUN 1953

Registrar General of the Colony of Trinidad and Tobago, do certify that the above is a true and correct...

In Witness whereof I have hereunto set my Hand and affixed... Office this 29th day of June of Our Lord One Thousand Nine Hundred and...

Registrar

St. Monica's Parish
MONTREAL 28, QUE.

Certificate of Marriage

This is to certify that

David Allan Sheppard

and

Teresa Pamela Martin

were lawfully united in the Holy Bonds of Matrimony in this Church on the sixteenth day of April nineteen hundred and fifty five

in the presence of,

Louis Pitcher

and

Mrs Joan Marshall

The Priest officiating was: Rev. Frank McMahon

I certify that the foregoing has been correctly copied from the Register of Marriages of the above parish

this 16th day of April 19 55

_____
Priest

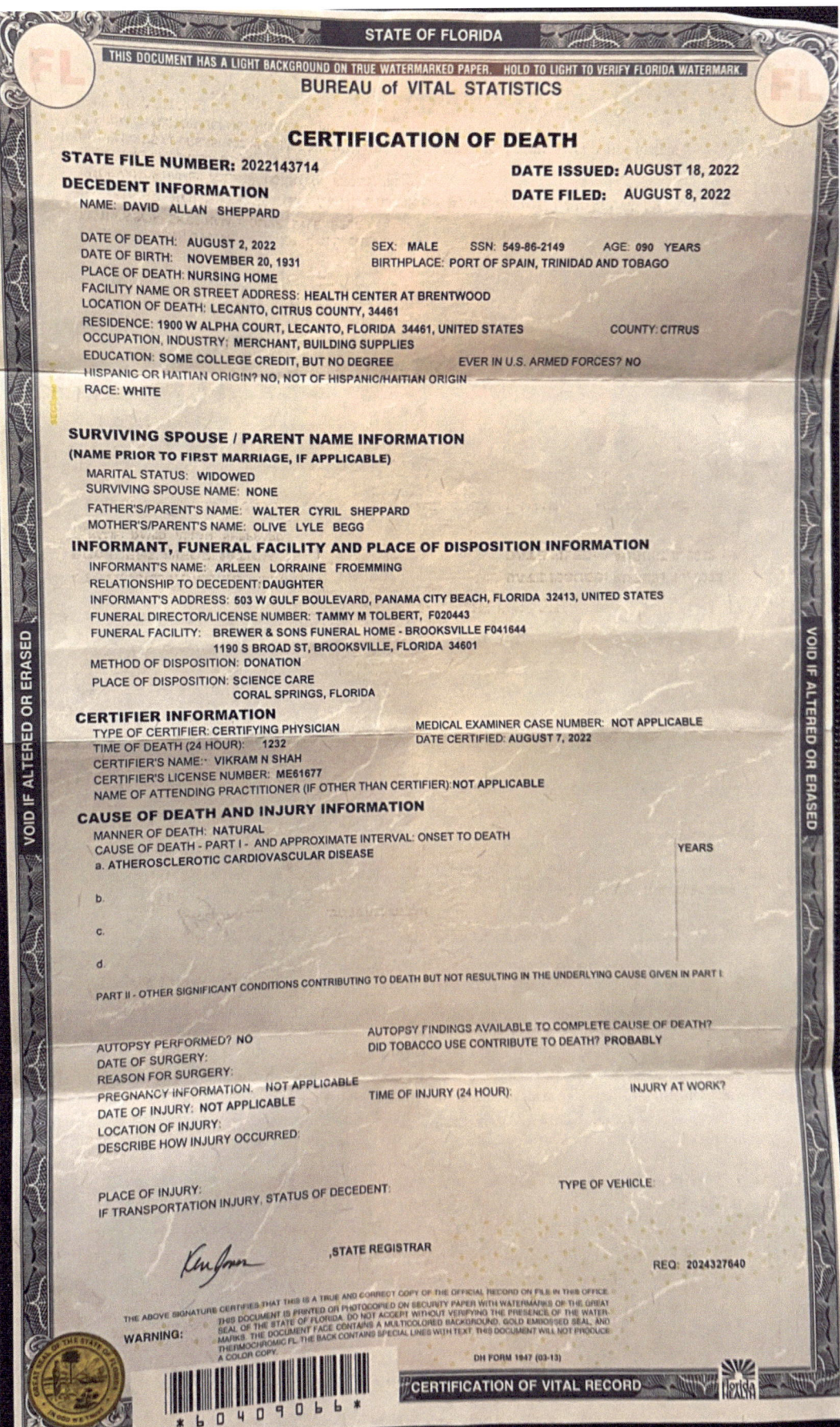

DAVID SHEPPARD DEATH CERTIFICATE

STATE OF FLORIDA
BUREAU of VITAL STATISTICS
CERTIFICATION OF DEATH

STATE FILE NUMBER: 2022143714
DATE ISSUED: AUGUST 18, 2022
DATE FILED: AUGUST 8, 2022

DECENT INFORMATION
NAME: DAVID ALLAN SHEPPARD
DATE OF DEATH: AUGUST 2, 2022
SEX: MALE
SSN: 549-86-2149
AGE: 090 YEARS
DATE OF BIRTH: NOVEMBER 20, 1931
BIRTHPLACE: PORT OF SPAIN, TRINIDAD AND TOBAGO
PLACE OF DEATH: NURSING HOME
FACILITY NAME OR STREET ADDRESS: HEALTH CENTER AT BRENTWOOD
LOCATION OF DEATH: LECANTO, CITRUS COUNTY, 34461
RESIDENCE: 1900 W ALPHA COURT, LECANTO, FLORIDA 34461, UNITED STATES
COUNTY: CITRUS
OCCUPATION, INDUSTRY: MERCHANT, BUILDING SUPPLIES
EDUCATION: SOME COLLEGE CREDIT, BUT NO DEGREE
EVER IN U.S. ARMED FORCES? NO
HISPANIC OR HAITIAN ORIGIN? NO, NOT OF HISPANIC/HAITIAN ORIGIN
RACE: WHITE

SURVIVING SPOUSE / PARENT NAME INFORMATION
(NAME PRIOR TO FIRST MARRIAGE, IF APPLICABLE)
MARITAL STATUS: WIDOWED
SURVIVING SPOUSE NAME: NONE
FATHER'S/PARENT'S NAME: WALTER CYRIL SHEPPARD
MOTHER'S/PARENT'S NAME: OLIVE LYLE BEGG

INFORMANT, FUNERAL FACILITY AND PLACE OF DISPOSITION INFORMATION
INFORMANT'S NAME: ARLEEN LORRAINE FROEMMING
RELATIONSHIP TO DECEDENT: DAUGHTER
INFORMANT'S ADDRESS: 503 W GULF BOULEVARD, PANAMA CITY BEACH, FLORIDA 32413, UNITED STATES
FUNERAL DIRECTOR/LICENSE NUMBER: TAMMY M TOLBERT, F020443
FUNERAL FACILITY: BREWER & SONS FUNERAL HOME - BROOKSVILLE F041644
1190 S BROAD ST, BROOKSVILLE, FLORIDA 34601
METHOD OF DISPOSITION: DONATION
PLACE OF DISPOSITION: SCIENCE CARE
CORAL SPRINGS, FLORIDA

CERTIFIER INFORMATION
TYPE OF CERTIFIER: CERTIFYING PHYSICIAN
MEDICAL EXAMINER CASE NUMBER: NOT APPLICABLE
TIME OF DEATH (24 HOUR): 1232
DATE CERTIFIED: AUGUST 7, 2022
CERTIFIER'S NAME: VIKRAM N SHAH
CERTIFIER'S LICENSE NUMBER: ME61677
NAME OF ATTENDING PRACTITIONER (IF OTHER THAN CERTIFIER): NOT APPLICABLE

CAUSE OF DEATH AND INJURY INFORMATION
MANNER OF DEATH: NATURAL
CAUSE OF DEATH - PART I - AND APPROXIMATE INTERVAL: ONSET TO DEATH
a. ATHEROSCLEROTIC CARDIOVASCULAR DISEASE — YEARS
b.
c.
d.

PART II - OTHER SIGNIFICANT CONDITIONS CONTRIBUTING TO DEATH BUT NOT RESULTING IN THE UNDERLYING CAUSE GIVEN IN PART I:

AUTOPSY PERFORMED? NO
AUTOPSY FINDINGS AVAILABLE TO COMPLETE CAUSE OF DEATH?
DID TOBACCO USE CONTRIBUTE TO DEATH? PROBABLY
DATE OF SURGERY:
REASON FOR SURGERY:
PREGNANCY INFORMATION: NOT APPLICABLE
TIME OF INJURY (24 HOUR):
INJURY AT WORK?
DATE OF INJURY: NOT APPLICABLE
LOCATION OF INJURY:
DESCRIBE HOW INJURY OCCURRED:
PLACE OF INJURY:
IF TRANSPORTATION INJURY, STATUS OF DECEDENT:
TYPE OF VEHICLE:

STATE REGISTRAR
REQ: 2024327640

DH FORM 1947 (03-13)
CERTIFICATION OF VITAL RECORD

60409066

DAVID SHEPPARD OBITUARY

NEWSPAPER:

SHEPPARD, David Allan 90, passed Aug. 2, 2022. Preceded in death by wife, Pamela and son, Brent, he is survived by daughters, Carol and Arleen and their families.

View Guest Book www.tampabay.com/obits

ONLINE:

David Allan Sheppard Obituary

David Sheppard, 90 passed peacefully away August 2, 2022.

David was born on 20 November 1931 in Port of Spain, Trinidad to Walter Sheppard and Olive Lyle Begg. He was the sixth of twelve children born into the family. He is preceded in death by his wife Pamela, son Brent Sheppard, parents Walter and Olive, siblings Richard, Kathleen, George, Joan, Patricia, Douglas and Brian.

He was survived by his daughters Carol Lynn Sheppard and Arleen Froemming (Brian). Siblings Barbara Williams (Harvey), Dorothy Martin, Michael (Heather) and Ken Sheppard (Maureen). Grandchildren Renee Mangum (Kelvin), Jim Sheppard (Michelle), Glen Howell, Krista VanDeBogart, Cady Howell and Kirsten Froemming. He leaves behind many loving nieces and nephews, and lots great grandchildren and great great grandchildren.

He will be remembered for his kindness, giving nature, and forgiving heart. He is beloved and missed. He always had a joke at the ready and wanted to make everyone around him laugh. In his final days, he spoke with his family daily almost to the end. God blessed him with his mental capacity and joyful attitude. Wonderful and lovely we're his most common responses to almost all good news.

Consensus amongst his family is that he is a great man. He loves the Lord, and the scriptures. He was eagerly awaiting his assignment from the Savior in the coming Kingdom and to be reunited with his wife and family.

Till we meet again.

David & Pamela

Young Love

Uncle Sam Marshall

Auntie Joan

Louis Pitcher

David and Pamela - Wedding Party

49

David & Pamela

David and Pamela - A Day at the Beach

Brent, Carol
and Arleen
Los Angeles 1968

Mom, Dad
and Kids
Circa - 1966 Montreal

Mom, Dad
and Kids
Circa - 1964 Montreal

51

Mom, Dad
and Kids
Circa - 1968 California

Dad
and Kids
Circa - 1962 Montreal

52

Arleen and Carol
Circa - 1961 Montreal

Brent, Arleen, Carol
Trinidad - Circa 1964

Carol, Arleen, Brent
Circa - 2010 St. Petersburg

Arleen, Pam, Cady
3 Generations

Generation Two

Siblings Of David Sheppard

Walter Cyril Sheppard
1898–1974 • LKYG-98Q

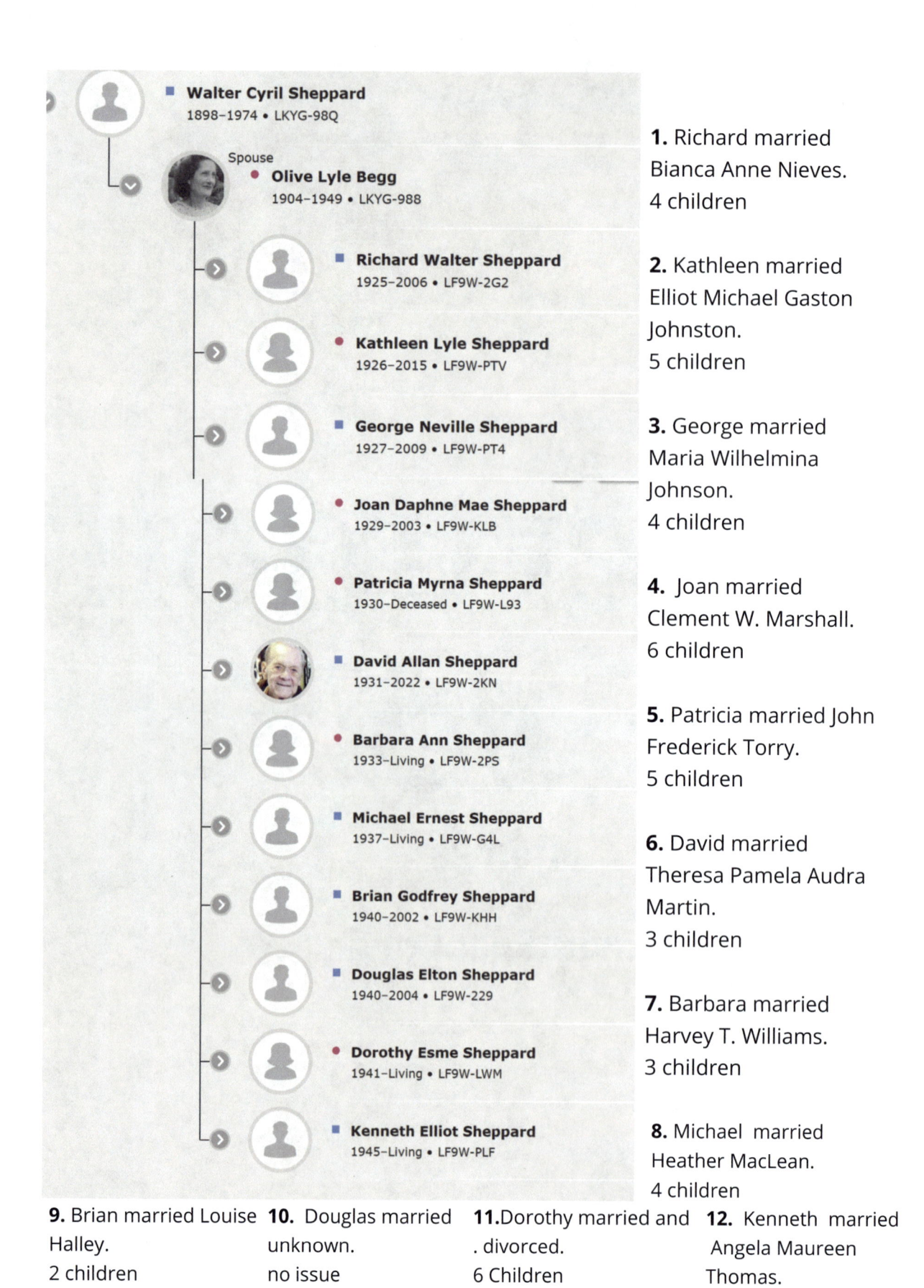

Spouse
Olive Lyle Begg
1904–1949 • LKYG-988

- **Richard Walter Sheppard**
  1925–2006 • LF9W-2G2
- **Kathleen Lyle Sheppard**
  1926–2015 • LF9W-PTV
- **George Neville Sheppard**
  1927–2009 • LF9W-PT4
- **Joan Daphne Mae Sheppard**
  1929–2003 • LF9W-KLB
- **Patricia Myrna Sheppard**
  1930–Deceased • LF9W-L93
- **David Allan Sheppard**
  1931–2022 • LF9W-2KN
- **Barbara Ann Sheppard**
  1933–Living • LF9W-2PS
- **Michael Ernest Sheppard**
  1937–Living • LF9W-G4L
- **Brian Godfrey Sheppard**
  1940–2002 • LF9W-KHH
- **Douglas Elton Sheppard**
  1940–2004 • LF9W-229
- **Dorothy Esme Sheppard**
  1941–Living • LF9W-LWM
- **Kenneth Elliot Sheppard**
  1945–Living • LF9W-PLF

1. Richard married Bianca Anne Nieves.
4 children

2. Kathleen married Elliot Michael Gaston Johnston.
5 children

3. George married Maria Wilhelmina Johnson.
4 children

4. Joan married Clement W. Marshall.
6 children

5. Patricia married John Frederick Torry.
5 children

6. David married Theresa Pamela Audra Martin.
3 children

7. Barbara married Harvey T. Williams.
3 children

8. Michael married Heather MacLean.
4 children

9. Brian married Louise Halley.
2 children

10. Douglas married unknown.
no issue

11. Dorothy married and . divorced.
6 Children

12. Kenneth married Angela Maureen Thomas.
4 Children

- **Richard Walter Sheppard**
  1925–2006

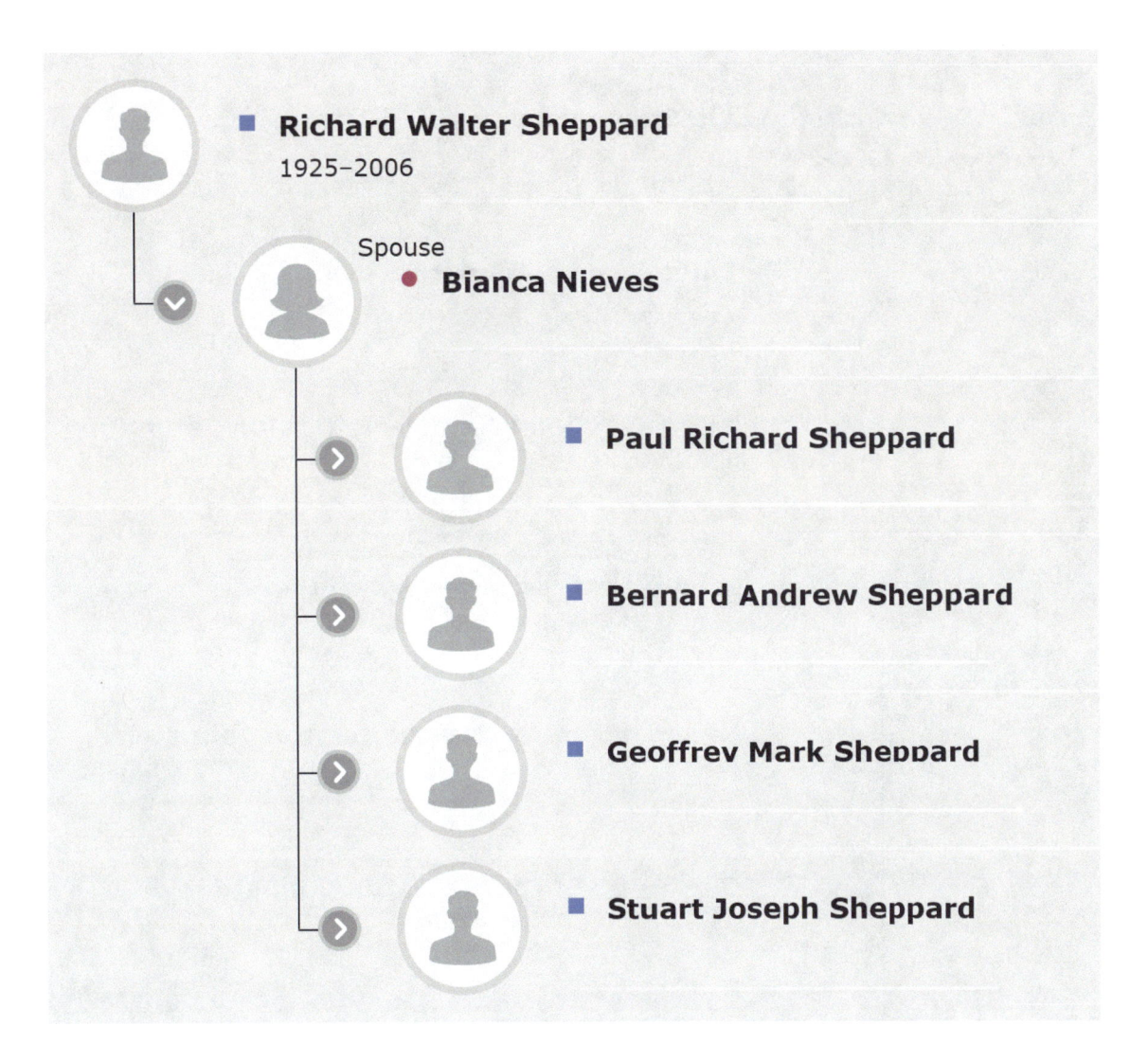

  Spouse
  - **Bianca Nieves**
    - **Paul Richard Sheppard**
    - **Bernard Andrew Sheppard**
    - **Geoffrey Mark Sheppard**
    - **Stuart Joseph Sheppard**

During the Black Power Revolution, Richard left Trinidad and moved his family to Scotland.

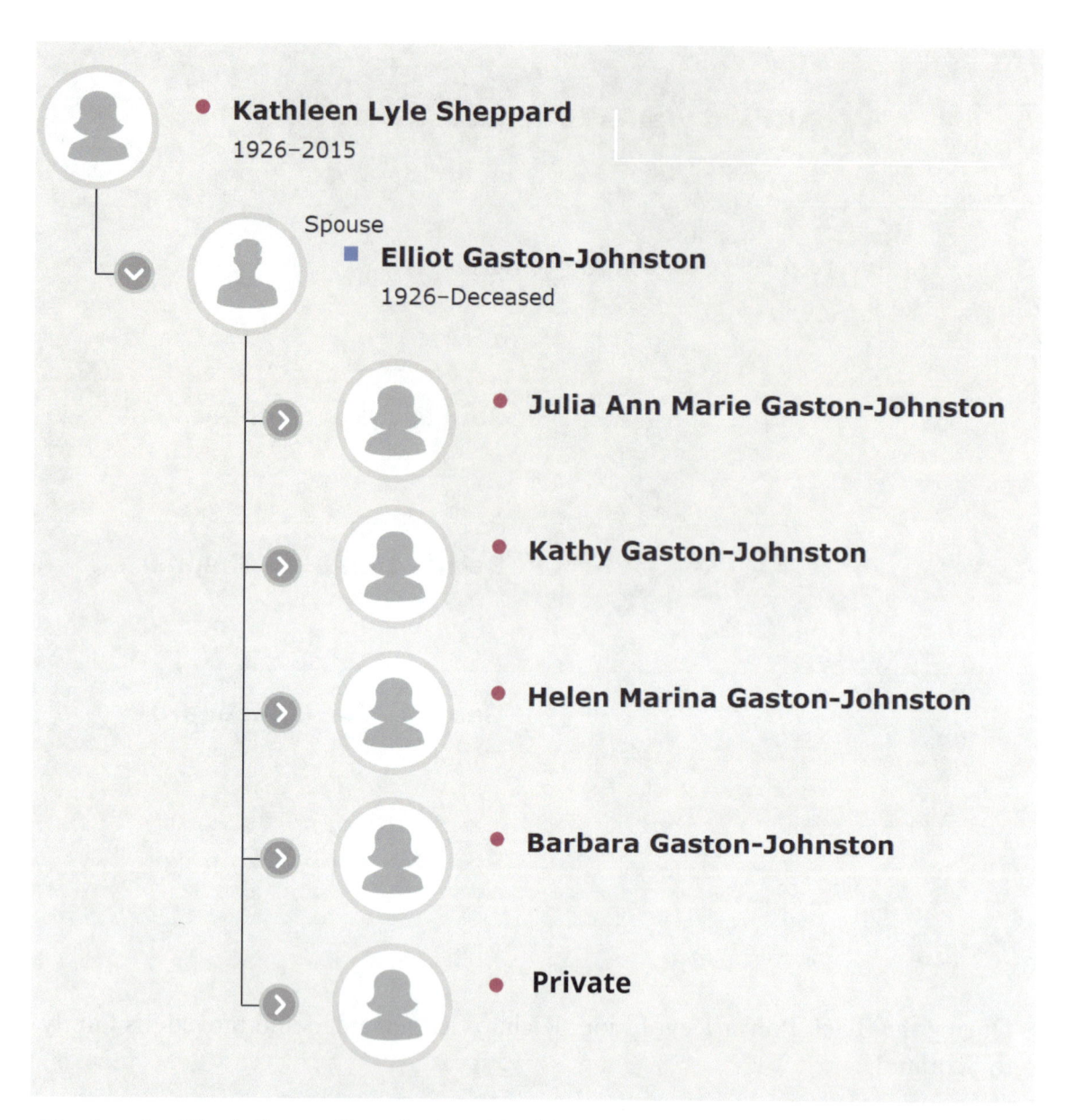

- **Kathleen Lyle Sheppard**
  1926–2015

  Spouse
  ■ **Elliot Gaston-Johnston**
  1926–Deceased

  - **Julia Ann Marie Gaston-Johnston**

  - **Kathy Gaston-Johnston**

  - **Helen Marina Gaston-Johnston**

  - **Barbara Gaston-Johnston**

  - **Private**

During the Black Power Revolution, Kathleen left Trinidad and moved her family to Toronto Canada.

Helen, Kathy, Julia and Barbara. Missing <private> sister.

58

Kathleen and Helen

George Neville Sheppard
1927–2009

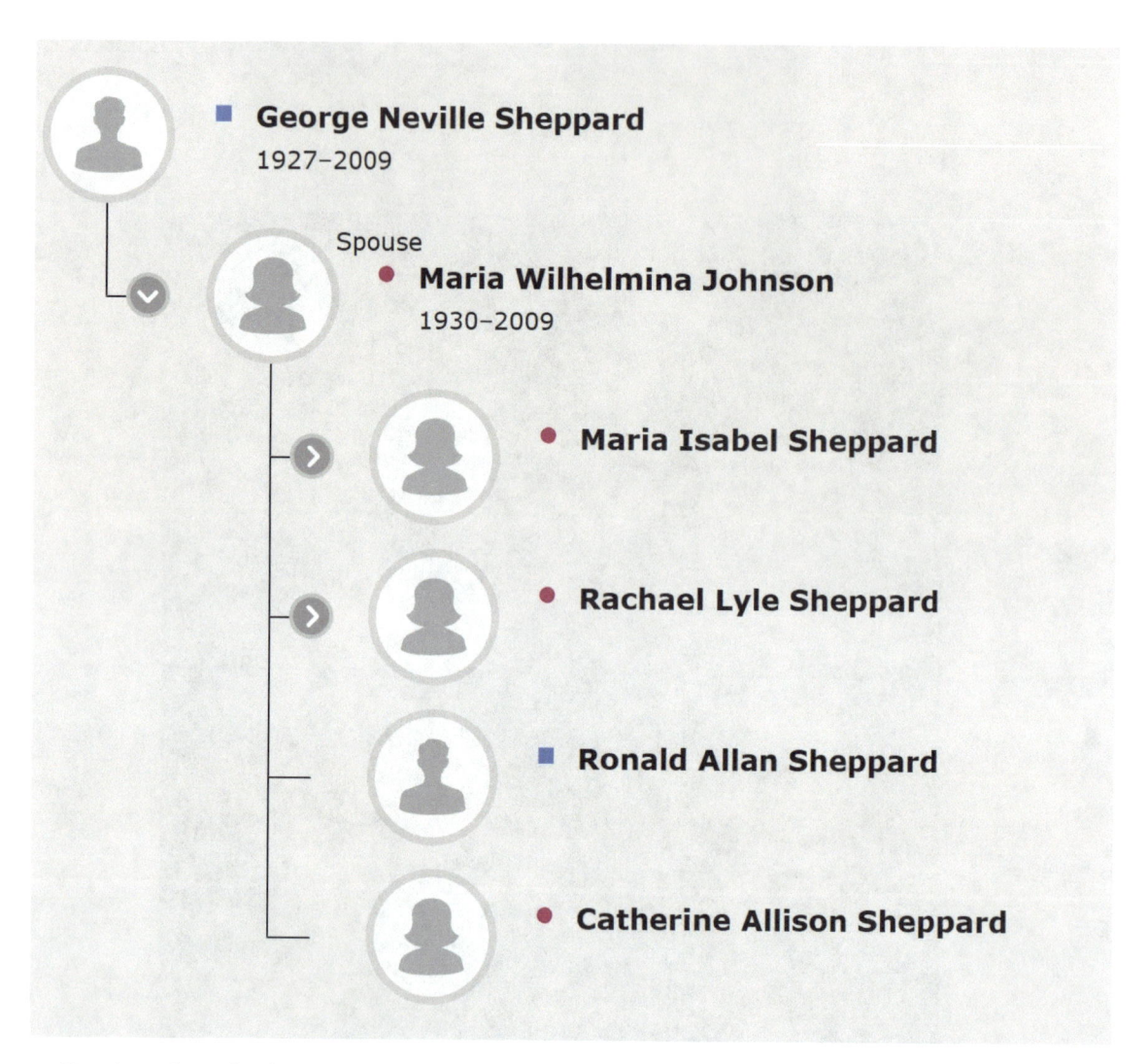

Spouse
Maria Wilhelmina Johnson
1930–2009

Maria Isabel Sheppard

Rachael Lyle Sheppard

Ronald Allan Sheppard

Catherine Allison Sheppard

During the Black Power Revolution, George left Trinidad and moved his family to Australia and later to Florida.

AUNTIE MARIA AND UNCLE GEORGE
ON THEIR WEDDING DATE
08/08/1952

Joan Daphne Mae Sheppard
1929–2003

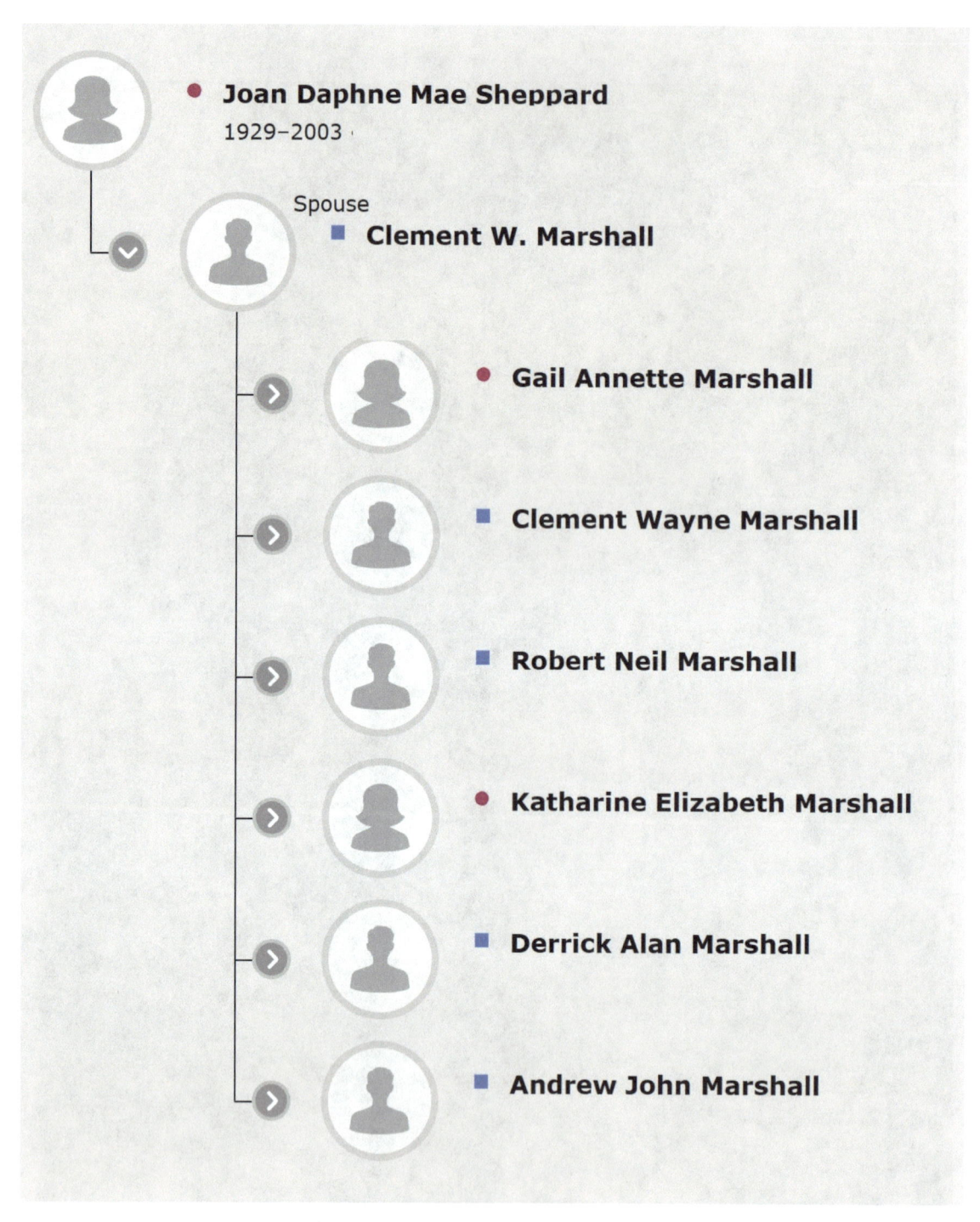

Spouse
- **Clement W. Marshall**

- **Gail Annette Marshall**

- **Clement Wayne Marshall**

- **Robert Neil Marshall**

- **Katharine Elizabeth Marshall**

- **Derrick Alan Marshall**

- **Andrew John Marshall**

Joan left Trinidad before I was born. She was already settled in Montreal, Canada.

- **Patricia Myrna Sheppard**
  1930–Deceased

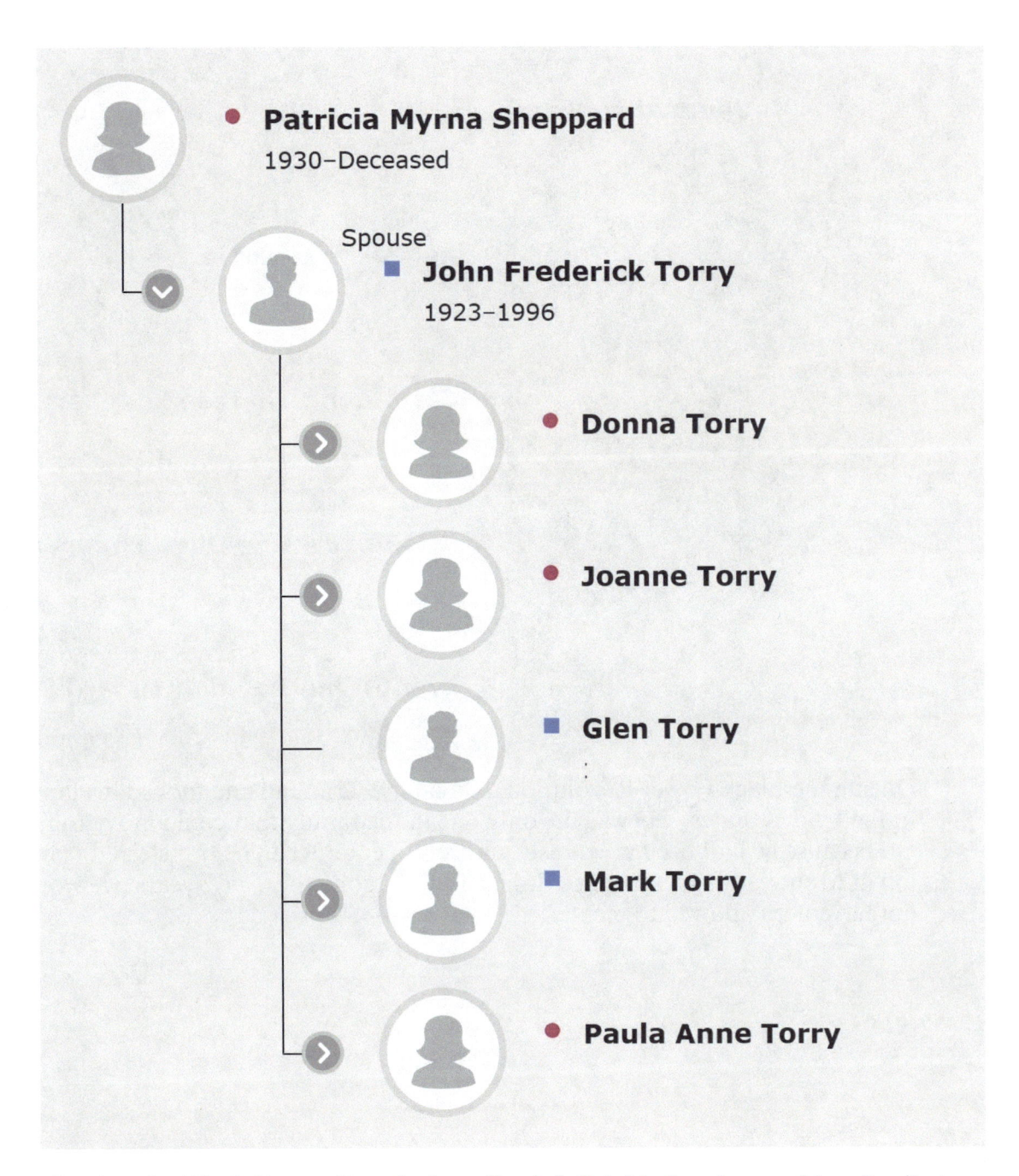

  Spouse
  ■ **John Frederick Torry**
  1923–1996

  - **Donna Torry**
  - **Joanne Torry**
  ■ **Glen Torry**
  ■ **Mark Torry**
  - **Paula Anne Torry**

During the Black Power Revolution, Pat left Trinidad and moved her family to Australia.

- **David Allan Sheppard**
  1931–2022

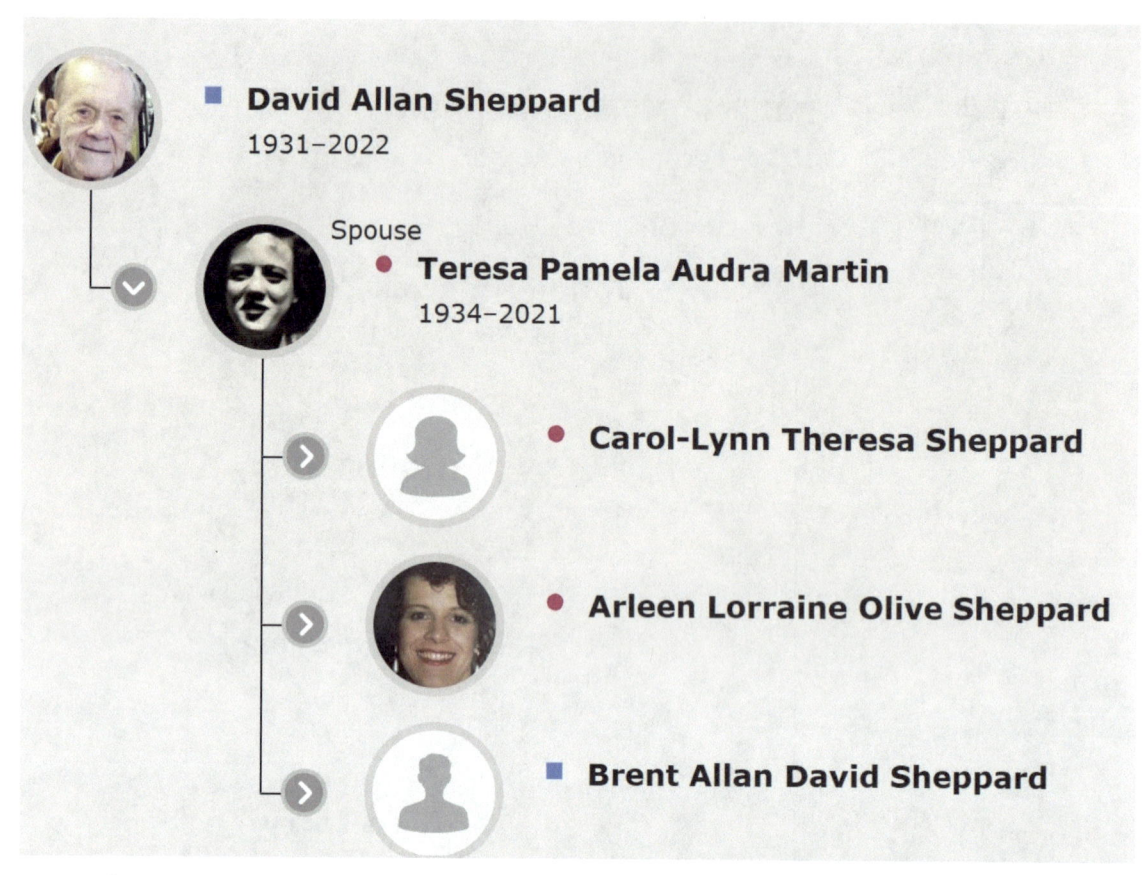

  Spouse
  - **Teresa Pamela Audra Martin**
    1934–2021
    - **Carol-Lynn Theresa Sheppard**
    - **Arleen Lorraine Olive Sheppard**
    - **Brent Allan David Sheppard**

During the Black Power Revolution, David left Trinidad and moved his family to the United States. He was the only one in the family that could move to the US because he had been previously allowed to enter when he transferred from a job in Montreal to Los Angeles. If he had been gone for over 2 years, we would not have been allowed to reenter.

- **Michael Ernest Sheppard**
  1937-

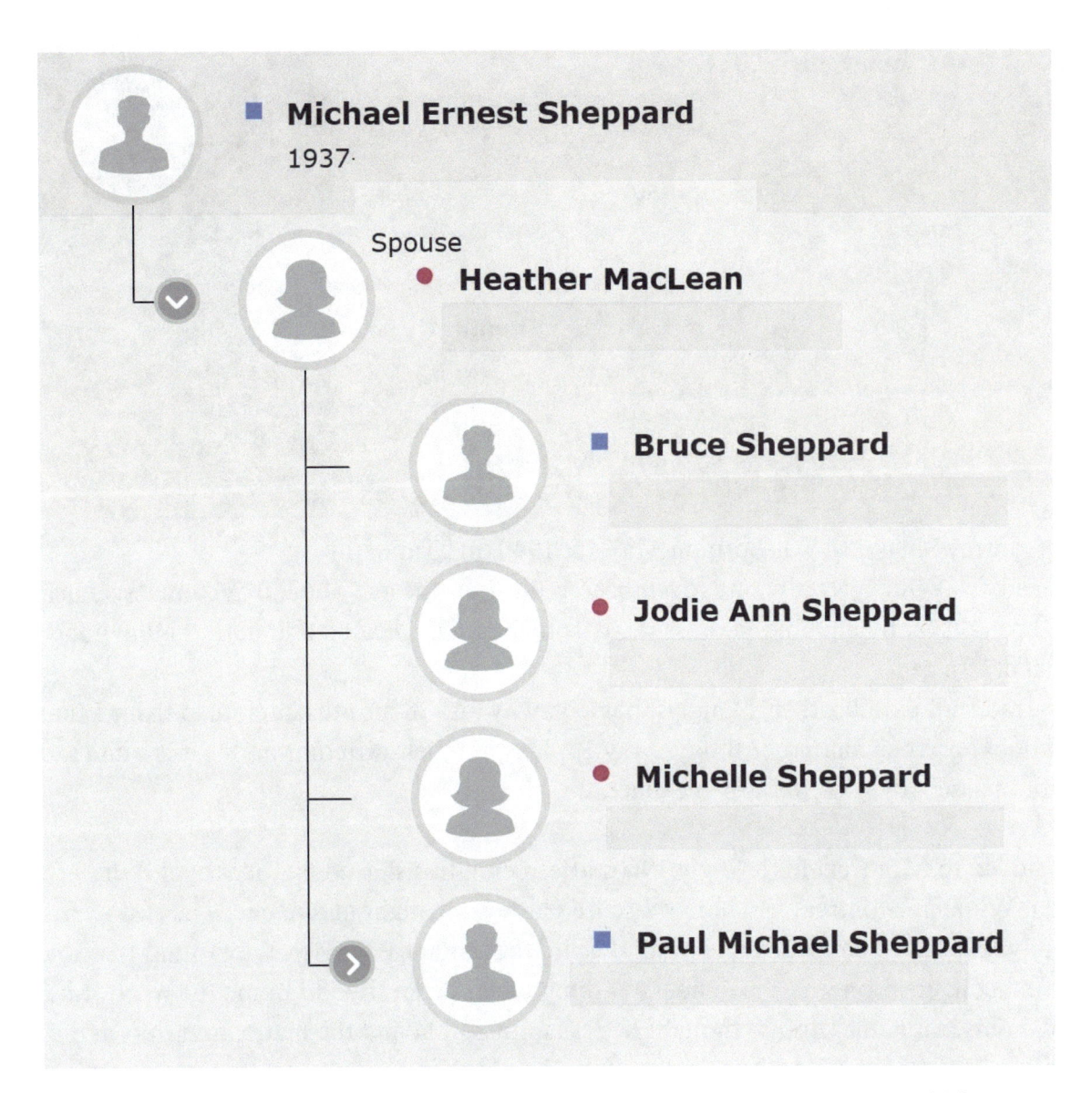

  Spouse
  - **Heather MacLean**

    - **Bruce Sheppard**

    - **Jodie Ann Sheppard**

    - **Michelle Sheppard**

    - **Paul Michael Sheppard**

During the Black Power Revolution, Michael left Trinidad and moved his family to Canada.

- **Brian Godfrey Sheppard**
  1940–2002

  Spouse
  - **Louise Halley**

  - **Christine Sheppard**

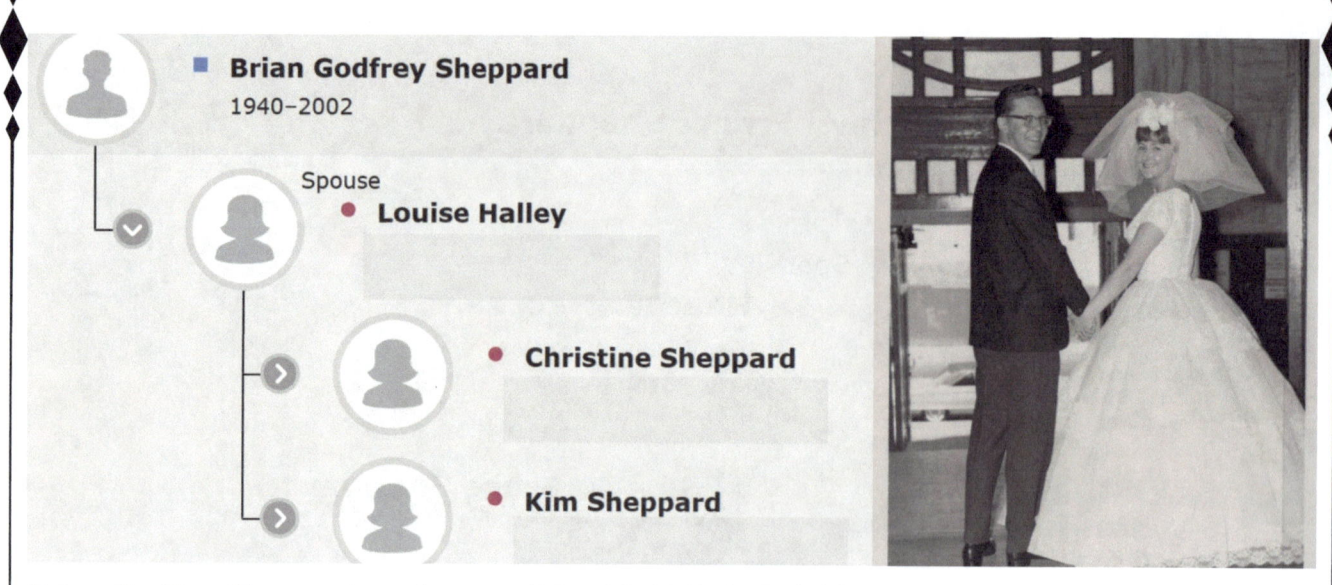

  - **Kim Sheppard**

Brian Godfrey Sheppard was born on May 15, 1940, in Trinidad.
He passed away unexpectedly on November 21, 2002, at the age of 62, from a massive heart attack brought on by high blood pressure, despite being medicated and maintaining good physical health.
Brian's fraternal twin brother, Douglas, passed away just 18 months later, also from a massive heart attack, on their shared birthday, May 15. Despite their different paths, it is quite sad that they both passed away from the same illness.

Brian moved to Montreal in the early 1960s after being transferred by the Royal Bank of Canada. While in Montreal, Brian met Louise Halley one night at a dance. The two were randomly selected to dance together and, despite the language barrier, they found true love. Their first conversation was a misunderstanding: when Brian tried to mime the word "Shepherd" to explain his last name, Louise thought he was miming playing the piano, and thus assumed his surname was "Chopin." Despite this, they found enough in common to continue their relationship.

Their early romance faced challenges, including a temporary breakup that led Brian to move to British Columbia. However, fate had other plans, and after Brian was transferred back to Montreal, he and Louise had a unforeseen reunion when they bumped into each other one day while Louise was window shopping. As she posed, sticking her butt out to make sure Brian saw her, it was clear that their connection was still strong. Three months later, they married. Brian's job transferred them shortly after to Trinidad.

Christine Sheppard was born on December 15, 1966, in Port of Spain, Trinidad. She was baptized there, with Brian's twin brother, Douglas, serving as her godfather. Despite the tropical setting, Louise found the heat, bugs, lizards, and snakes of Trinidad challenging, and the distance from her family in Montreal added to her discomfort. Still, she cherished the time spent with her extended family.

At one point, Louise's sister, Francine, visited them in Trinidad. The family's time in Trinidad was short-lived, as in 1970, they moved back to Montreal, partially due to political climate changes in the region, notably the rise of the Black Power movement.

They settled in Montreal North, and soon after, their second daughter, Kim, was born on October 17, 1971. In 1972, they moved to the West Island in Pierrefonds, where Christine and Kim grew up in a lively household full of light, laughter, music, and dance. Brian was a man of joy, and his love for dancing and singing was contagious. He also had a deep love for sports, particularly golf, lobball, volleyball and bowling, which he enjoyed with friends and family. He also enjoyed card games, which he spent evening on end playing with Kim.

Despite the warmth of their home life, Brian rarely spoke about his childhood in Trinidad, and when he did, it was often vague or contradictory. One claim he made, that he had not owned shoes until he was 12, was disputed by his sister Dorothy. Brian fondly remembered Caroline, the maid who worked in their house, and he often recounted how she saved him a plate of food when he was late for dinner, as there were so many people in their large family that food would often run out.

He also shared a memory of running into a burning building to save a child, showcasing his bravery and compassion. Brian also spoke about climbing trees to grab and eat mangos. Brian´s culinary traditions continued on with him to Canada, where he ate a banana with every dinner (instead of plantain, which was hard to find).

One sad memory that Brian remembered vividly and shared was going out in a boat in the murky waters when he was about 12 years old and being pushed over the edge "as a joke", as the boat rode off and Brian had to swim with all might back to land to avoid the sharks. (*Arleen Froemming believes that her father, David Sheppard may have been involved or the master planner of this.*) Despite these glimpses into his early life, we wish that we would have asked more questions.

Brian, Louise and Kim's at her baptism | Brian, Louise on the way out to dance | A practice twirl

67

We never thought that he would have gone so early. His family, however, carries on his legacy of joy, sportsmanship, and the love of dance and music. Brian was a positive soul. Brian loved his brothers and sisters, even though distance made that they did not see each other as often as he would like. Christine and Kim remember and cherish their memories of Christmas' at Aunty Joan and Uncle Sam's, with gingerbread men and wonderful dinners and trips to Toronto to see Aunty Dorothy (Brian spoke highly of Dots). Christine and Kim live in the suburbs of Montreal and both have three children.

Kim and Chris

BIG sister
LITTLE sister

The wedding party with Louise parents and Walter and Joan (standing in for Olive.

Brian making the ceremony legal.

69

The Happy Couple

Twins - Douglas and Brian

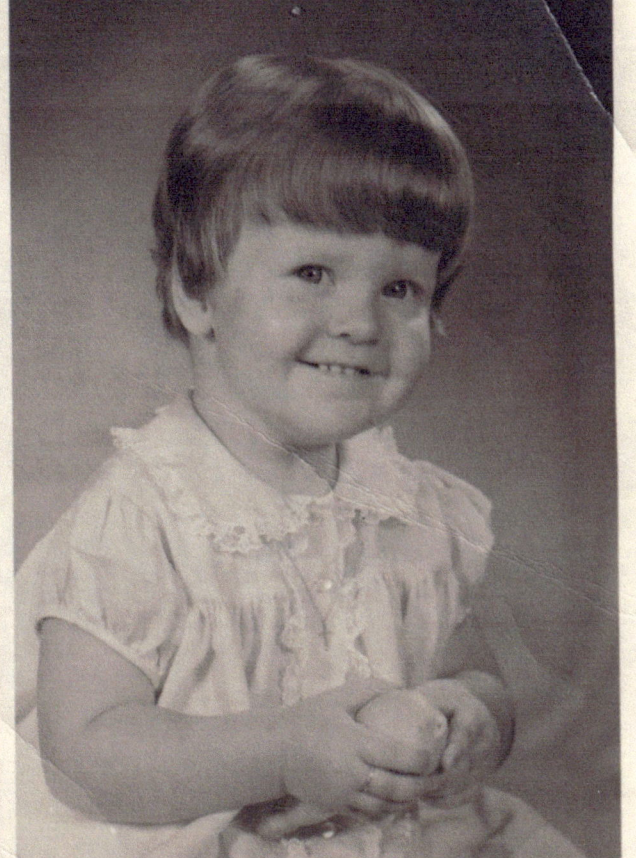

Douglas and Christine in Trinidad

Louise and Christine in Trinidad

71

Brian and his family with
Louise, Kim and Chris

- **Dorothy Esme Sheppard**
  1941–Living

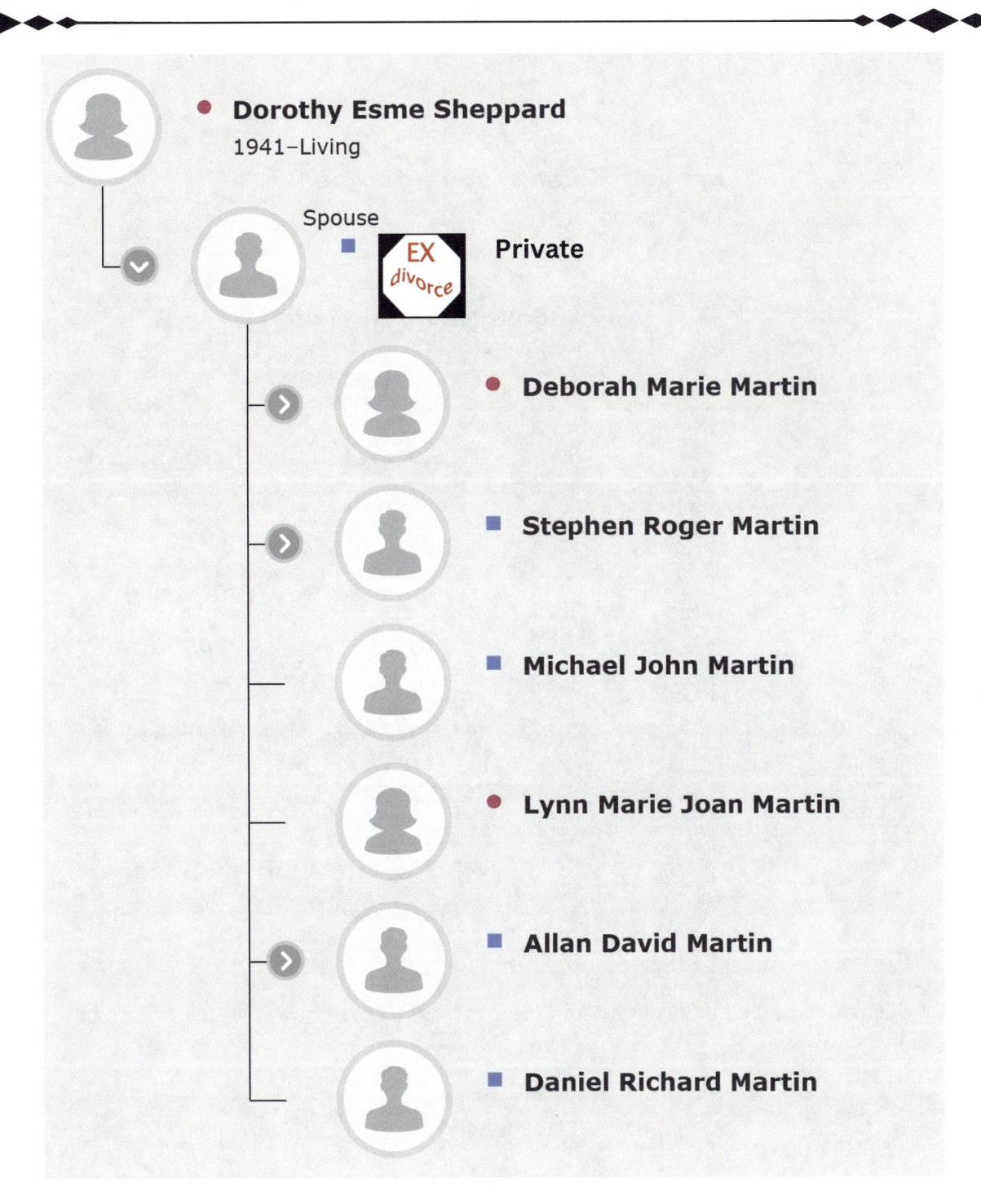

  Spouse ■ [EX divorce] **Private**

  - **Deborah Marie Martin**
  - ■ **Stephen Roger Martin**
  - ■ **Michael John Martin**
  - **Lynn Marie Joan Martin**
  - ■ **Allan David Martin**
  - ■ **Daniel Richard Martin**

During the Black Power Revolution, Dorothy left Trinidad and moved her family to Canada.

Kenneth Elliot Sheppard
1945–Living

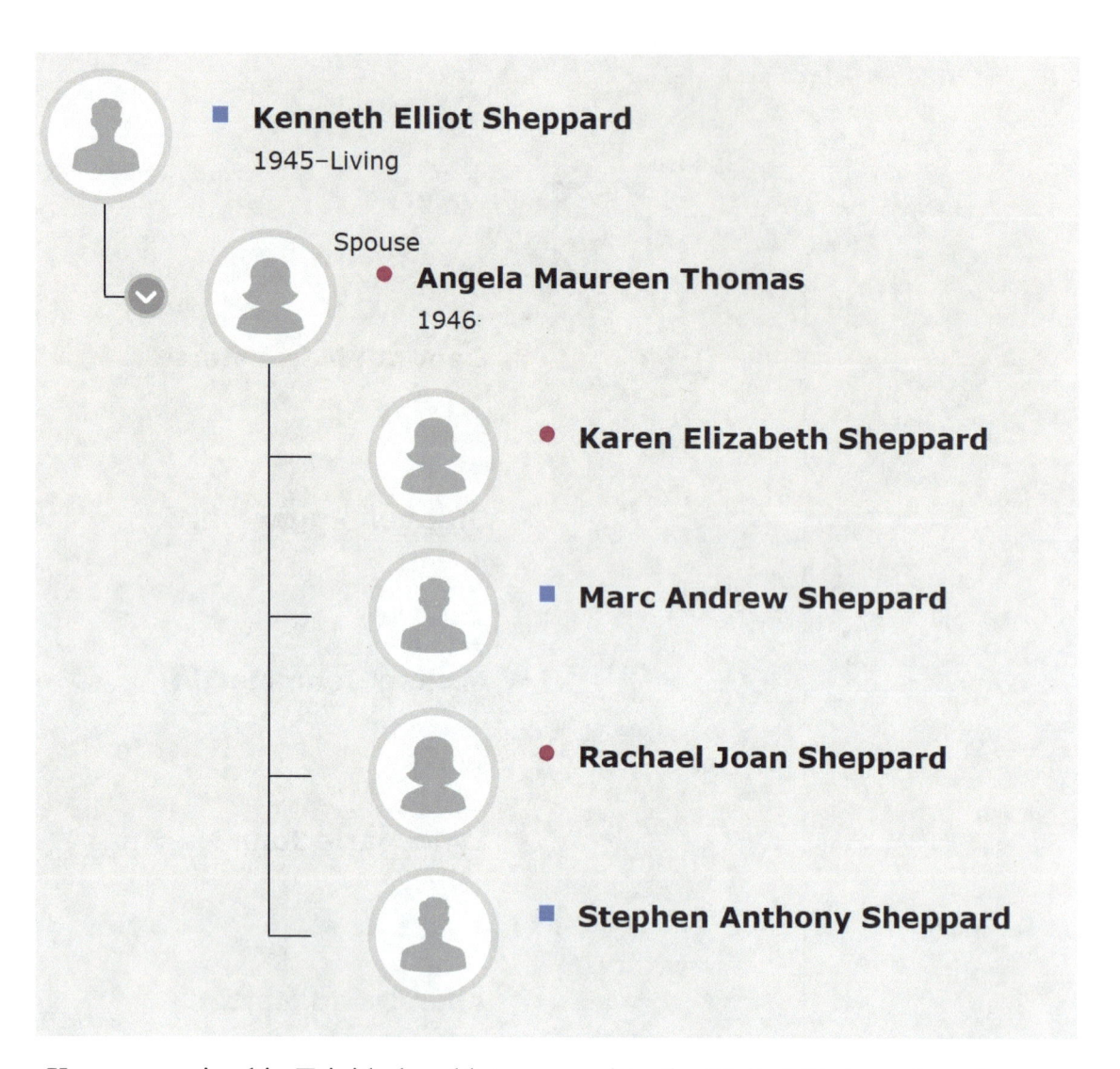

Spouse
Angela Maureen Thomas
1946-

Karen Elizabeth Sheppard

Marc Andrew Sheppard

Rachael Joan Sheppard

Stephen Anthony Sheppard

Kenny remained in Trinidad and later moved to the United States, where he lives now.

Generation Three Paternal

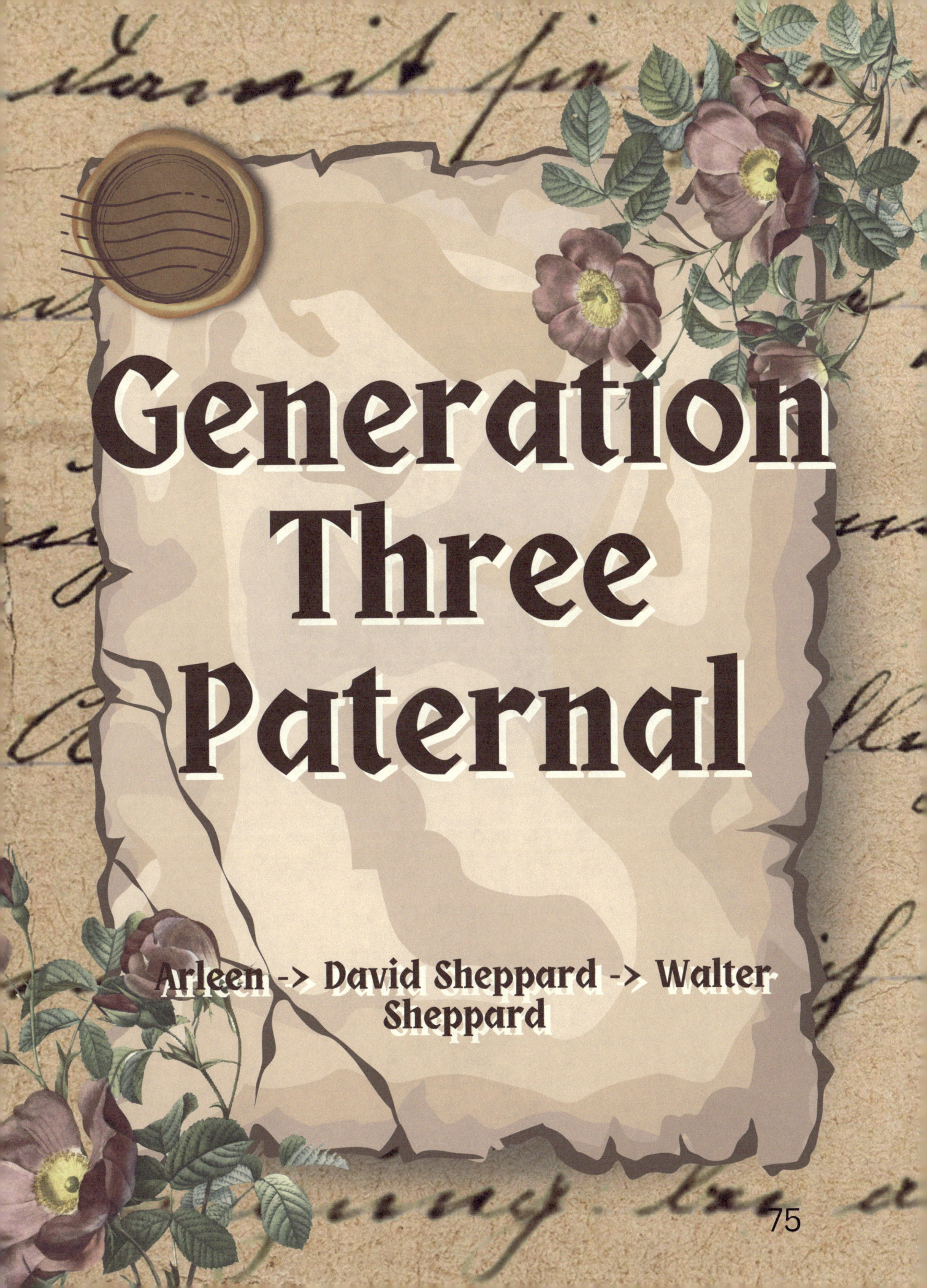

Arleen -> David Sheppard -> Walter Sheppard

HISTORY OF WALTER CYRIL SHEPPARD

QUICK FACTS:

BORN
PORT OF SPAIN, TRINIDAD

PARENTS
ARTHUR SHEPPARD
ADELINE ALSTON RICHARDS

CHILDREN
LOVING FATHER OF 12

Walter Cyril Sheppard

Walter Cyril Sheppard's mother, Adeline Richards, came to Trinidad from St. Vincent and the Grenadines. Her ancestry traced back to either the Netherlands or Denmark. His father, Arthur Sheppard, was born in the UK and passed away when Walter was newly married.

Walter was born on June 14, 1898, in Belmont, St. George, Trinidad and Tobago. He was one of eight children and one of three boys. The family was filled with aunts and grandmothers, and Walter and his brother grew up surrounded by strong, loving, and kind women. These remarkable women played a crucial role in shaping their character, encouraging them to grow in gentleness and kindness.

In about 1922, Walter married Olive Lyle Begg, and together they had twelve children, forming a loving and close-knit family. Tragically, Olive passed away in 1949 at the age of 45. Her death was a devastating blow to the family, especially to Walter, who lost his beloved wife.

Left to raise his children alone, Walter did not falter under the immense weight of this responsibility. Dorothy, his 11th child, commends him for his strength and resilience during such a challenging time. In contrast, family history reveals that Olive's father, James Begg, abandoned his four daughters after his wife died from complications during pregnancy, leaving them to be raised in different homes.

Despite the loss of his life partner, Walter managed to maintain a warm and loving home. At 51, he was still considered an eligible bachelor, but he never remarried, remaining loyal to Olive throughout his life. He successfully raised a family of vibrant, loving, and successful children. When interviewed, his surviving children described him as a peaceful, calm, stoic, placid, guileless, and dignified man—words that reflect the legacy of love and strength he imparted to his family.

Barbara, his 7th child, described Walter as the epitome of a perfect father. She never heard him speak in anger, use a bad word, or say anything derogatory about another person. Dorothy, his 11th child, proudly declared that Walter was someone she was proud to call her father. Kenny, his 12th child, said that nothing could ruffle him. When the boys were growing up, they often turned the side of the house into a cricket lane. It was common for the boys to break windows, but Kenny recalled that Walter never got upset. Instead, he would simply say, "Uh oh! I'll have to call Sammy to come fix the window." Sammy, the family caretaker, was often called upon to fix those broken windows.

David, his 6th child, does recall one instance when Walter got upset. Apparently, David had misbehaved so much that Walter, going against his usual peaceful nature, gave him "licks" (a spanking with a belt). David, ever the storyteller, assures everyone that the spanking was likely well deserved, though he cannot remember exactly what he did to earn it. For Walter, a man of calm and patience, to resort to spanking, it must have been something significant. Regardless of this rare incident, David shares the same admiration for his father as his siblings. He, too, considers Walter to have been a great and steadfast man.

Barbara and David both have fond memories around the family dinner table. David recalls that Walter, who worked at the Cable and Wireless company, used to send Morse code messages across the table, delighting the children with this unique skill. Barbara remembers how, when the family maid Caroline would serve dinner, if Walter got a pork chop, all the children would "fend" for the bone. Today, we'd call it "calling the bone." Walter would always give it to the child who called it first.

Unfortunately, Olive passed away in 1949 at the age of 45. This was a traumatic loss for the entire family, as they lost their beloved mother and Walter, his wife.

Walter was left to raise a household full of children on his own. Dorothy, his 11th child, praises him for not shirking under the great weight of this responsibility. This was in stark contrast to recent family history. James Begg, Olive's father, had left his four daughters when his wife passed away due to complications in pregnancy, but Walter didn't take the same route.

Although Walter didn't make a lot of money, the family was happy and managed to get by. Dorothy recalls that, despite their modest means, Walter still managed to take occasional trips to Australia, Canada, the U.S., or England. David remembers that when Richard got a job working in the oil fields, his first paycheck was more than Walter earned in a year. Yet, Walter somehow managed to raise 12 children on that honest salary. The family was rich in ways far beyond money.

David tells of Walter's rise to second in command at Cable and Wireless, a position that was the highest rank a colonial could achieve in a British company. Kenny, recalling when he started working there, remembers being impressed by how well-loved Walter was. He was beloved everywhere he went. Dorothy, returning from school at age 18, recalls a sea journey in 1959 from England to Port of Spain. She says that everyone aboard the ship came to love Walter, the gentle gentleman.

Cable and Wireless Offices

Barbara and David both recall that Walter had an incredible ability to add up three columns of figures simultaneously. Barbara also says that Walter was the smartest man she ever knew. Both Kenny and David remember that he was ambidextrous. When playing cricket in the homemade lane outside the house, Walter could bowl and bat with either hand, right or left.

Sundays were church days. David recalls the whole family attending church when Olive was alive, while Kenny remembers just him and his father going. Barbara and David also recall family picnics in the Savannah, watching cricket, horse races, and military formations.

Barbara remembers family outings to the beach, with Walter pacing along the shoreline, counting the children playing in the waters of Maracus or Mayaro. David's most vivid memories are from WW2. He recalls spending time with Walter at the Sailors and Soldiers club in Port of Spain during the early 1940s, where Walter befriended both a German submarine commander and a British Colonel. Though they didn't talk much, they enjoyed each other's company.

David was often asked to mix drinks for Walter and his friends whenever they were ready for another round. One story that stands out is about the German submarine commander who made his way into Port of Spain Bay and sank two British ships. Luckily, the bay was shallow, and the ships only sank a few feet.

The sub commander was able to escape the guarded bay because he spoke perfect English. He told the guard to shut the gate and prevent any other ships from leaving. The guard complied, and when questioned later, he explained that he followed the order because it was given in English. Eventually, news reached Trinidad that the German sub had been sunk in the Gulf of Mexico. David recalls Walter feeling saddened by the news. To him, the sub commander was a friend first, and a German second.

Walter and his wife Olive were also involved in supporting the war effort, even in the remote island of Trinidad. Barbara remembers watching the Harvest Scheme, a camp for Jewish refugees. These refugees had no idea where they would end up when they left Europe, but the island nation of Trinidad and Tobago welcomed them. The Sheppard family took in the Falkenstein family, a Jewish family of five who fled Nazi-occupied Germany.

The Falkensteins stayed with the Sheppards as they began rebuilding their lives and businesses. However, as the war continued, the refugees were forcibly relocated to camps and labeled "enemy aliens." David recalls visiting the camps with friends and joking about the lack of security, but the situation was still difficult for the Jewish families. Many of them emigrated from Trinidad after the war. There is a grave in the Mucurapo Cemetery in Port of Spain for a Karl Falkenstein. Could it be the same family?

The Jewish Section of the Mucurapo/Woodbrook Cemetary

Dorothy often recalled the image of Walter walking to work in his pressed suit, which evoked a sense of nobility and dignity. Pamela, David's late wife, frequently remarked on how much Walter resembled King George VI of England and even speculated that they might be distant cousins. Walter, like King George, was rarely seen without a cigarette in hand, as smoking was common in that era. Kenny and Dorothy both remembered how Walter's cigarettes often had a long ash, almost the length of the cigarette itself. This left an impression on Kenny, who fondly recalled Walter smoking his last cigarette of the day, flicking the long ash out of the window just before bed.

Barbara remembered her father's pious nature. One evening, while the family was playing Scrabble, someone played the word "RAP." Barbara, only eleven years old, asked if she could add an "E" to the word. Walter, with a few quiet "Ahem, Ahem, Ahem"s, made it clear that the game had come to an end. On another occasion, when Barbara came across the word "SYPHILIS" in a book and asked her father what it meant, Walter responded with the same "Ahem, Ahem, Ahem," signaling that it was a topic not to be discussed. At that moment, Barbara didn't understand the meaning, but she instinctively knew it was a book she shouldn't continue reading, and she put it down immediately.

Barbara also cherished the quiet moments spent sitting on the porch with her father, chatting until it was time for bed. One of her fondest memories was when the three stars of Christmas began to appear in the eastern sky. They would chat about the stars, enjoying those peaceful, special moments together.

Walter retired from Cable and Wireless at the age of 55, but due to the difficulty of finding a replacement, he continued working for another five years, retiring at 60. After his retirement, Walter spent time visiting his children in Trinidad, Canada, and the US, staying with each of them for a while. He lived with Dorothy and Kathleen in Canada for a period, and later, he stayed with Pat in Australia. He also visited his sister in England. While living with Dorothy in Canada, Walter was diagnosed with stage 4 colon cancer in May of 1974. Despite undergoing surgery, the doctors were unable to remove all of the cancer. He decided to visit Trinidad one last time and stayed at a nursing home on Benjamin Street in Port of Spain, near his granddaughter Kathy and her husband, Alred Plimmer.

Kenny, who worked in southern Trinidad at the time, made the effort to visit his father every evening, sometimes not returning home until late and repeating the journey the next day.

Walter eventually returned to Ontario, accompanied by his grandson, Paul Sheppard, Richard's son. He passed away in a hospital in Whitby, Ontario, on December 10, 1974.

SAM MARSHAL   **JOAN**   **WALTER**   **PAM**   **BRIAN**

AIRLINE MANIFEST FOR WALTER CYRIL SHEPPARD ENTERING THE USA IN TRANSIT TO CANADA IN 1961

New York State, Passenger and Crew Lists, 1917-1967 for Walter Cyril W Sheppard
A3998 - New York, 1957-1967 > 497

Family Name	Given Name	Initial	
SHEPPARD	WALTER CYRIL	W	S-163

Nationality (Citizenship): BRITISH
Passport Number: 73492
United States Address: IN TRANSIT TO CANADA
Airline & Flight or Vessel of Arrival: GADVE BOAC #95
Passenger Boarded At: TRINIDAD TWI
Permanent Address: 7 LUCKPUT ST, ST JAMES, TRINIDAD TWI
Birthdate: 14 JUNE 1898
Birthplace: TRINIDAD TWI
Visa Issued At: TRINIDAD TWI
Date Visa Issued: 3rd July 1959
Admitted: NEW YORK CITY, JUN 8 1961
Class: B-2, July 1, 1961

This Airline Manifest from New York State provides wonderful details about Walter Sheppard. It clarifies his birth place. There was confusion about his birthplace either being St. Vincent or Trinidad. These two documents prove that they were in Trinidad by 1897.

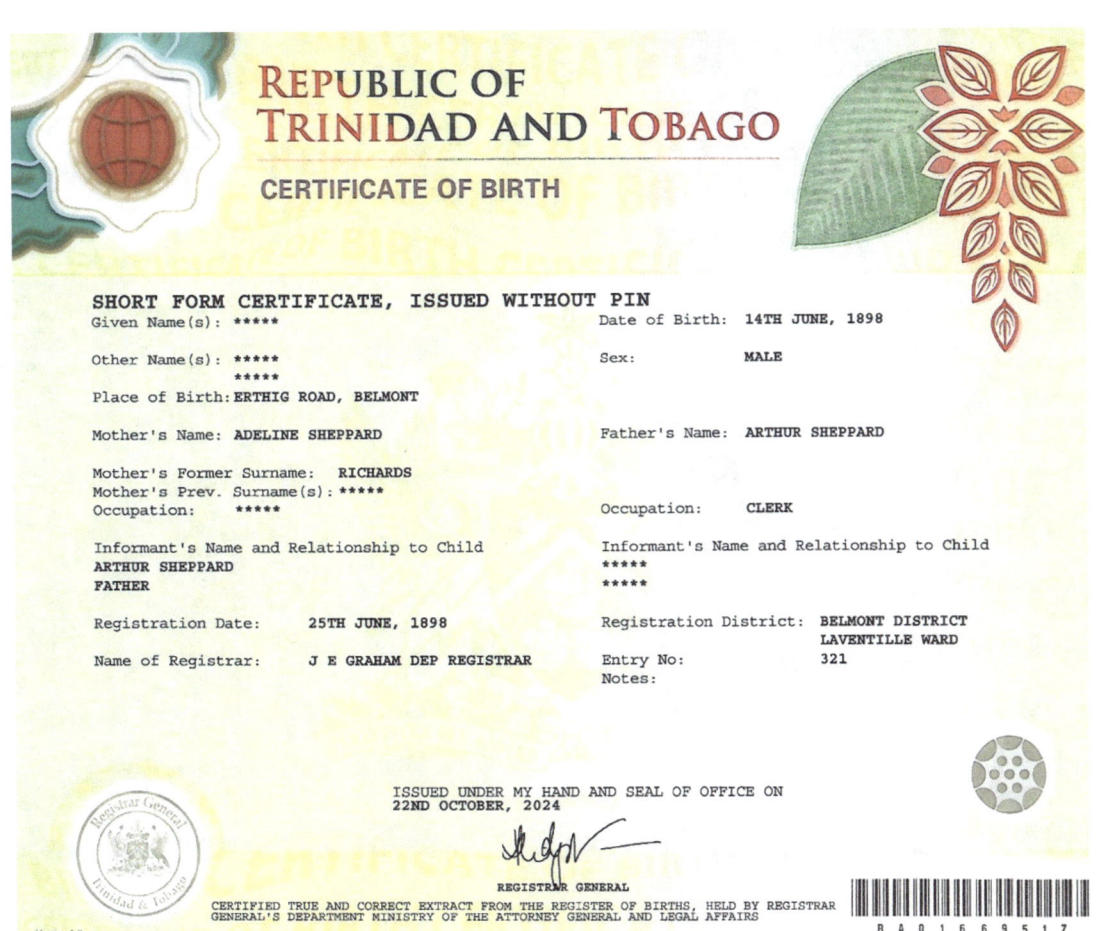

REPUBLIC OF TRINIDAD AND TOBAGO
CERTIFICATE OF BIRTH

SHORT FORM CERTIFICATE, ISSUED WITHOUT PIN

Given Name(s): *****
Other Name(s): *****
Place of Birth: ERTHIG ROAD, BELMONT
Mother's Name: ADELINE SHEPPARD
Mother's Former Surname: RICHARDS
Mother's Prev. Surname(s): *****
Occupation: *****
Informant's Name and Relationship to Child: ARTHUR SHEPPARD, FATHER
Registration Date: 25TH JUNE, 1898
Name of Registrar: J E GRAHAM DEP REGISTRAR

Date of Birth: 14TH JUNE, 1898
Sex: MALE
Father's Name: ARTHUR SHEPPARD
Occupation: CLERK
Informant's Name and Relationship to Child: *****
Registration District: BELMONT DISTRICT, LAVENTILLE WARD
Entry No: 321
Notes:

ISSUED UNDER MY HAND AND SEAL OF OFFICE ON 22ND OCTOBER, 2024

REGISTRAR GENERAL

CERTIFIED TRUE AND CORRECT EXTRACT FROM THE REGISTER OF BIRTHS, HELD BY REGISTRAR GENERAL'S DEPARTMENT MINISTRY OF THE ATTORNEY GENERAL AND LEGAL AFFAIRS

The name for Walter would have been added at his Baptism or Christening. We know this is Walter by the birthdate.

THE INTERNMENT OF THE ASHKENAZI JEWS OF TRINIDAD AND TOBAGO

The Ashkenazi Jews of Eastern Europe sought refuge from Nazi Germany in the Americas and eventually made their way to Trinidad and Tobago. These Jews who made Trinidad and Tobago their home were referred to as 'Calypso Jews'. In 1939, the calypsonian Gorilla sang "Jews in Trinidad", which chronicled the immigration of the Jews to the West Indies. He noted:

Tell me what you think of a dictator
Trampling the Jews like Adolph Hitler
Tumbling them out of Germany
Some running for refuge in the West Indies

However, by 1939 the British Government considered the approximately 600 Jews who made Trinidad their home, enemy aliens. The Jews therefore were to be placed in internment camps. An internment camp was a prison camp for enemy aliens or prisoners of war. The internment of the Jews took place in two phases. Phase One required all men and women 16 – 60 years in age to report to Police Headquarters where they were then transported to Nelson and Caledonia Island respectively. Phase Two was the internment of both men and women at Camp Rented in Trinidad. At Camp Rented the Jews, Germans (inclusive of captured crew from submarines), Austrians, Nazi Sympathizers and Japanese were interred. All those who were interred at Camp Rented were subject to the same regulations and comparatively their treatment was quite humane. Camp Rented was a prison camp which meant that its prisoners were subject to regular inspections and little access to individuals outside the camp. Privacy was non-existent since they were continuously monitored. Many suffered from depression and intense boredom. In 1943, some of the Jews were released from the camp but had to adhere to wartime constrictions such as being banned from driving cars or riding bicycles, they had to report to the nearest police station daily and they were under curfew from 8:00 PM to 6:00 AM. The period of Jewish internment in Trinidad and Tobago came to an end in January 1944 when Camp Rented closed its doors marking the end of an era in the history of the colony.

De Vertuil, Anthony. Edward Lanza and the Jews in Trinidad. Port of Spain: Litho Press, 2014. Print.

Rohlehr, Gordon. Calypso and Society in Pre-Independence Trinidad. Kingston: The University of West Indies Press, 1990. Print.

84

WORLD WAR II
THE TRINIDAD AND TOBAGO EXPERIENCE
THE BATTLE OF THE CARRIBEAN AND THE U-BOAT MENACE

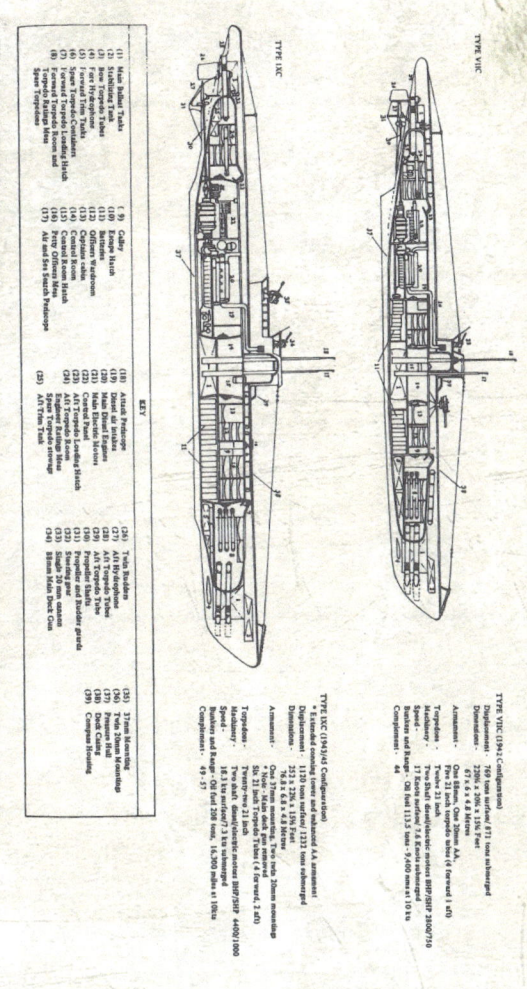

The Battle of the Caribbean (1941-1945) was a naval campaign during World War II. In this battle the German navy used U-Boats. The term U-Boat is derived from the German "Unterseeboot" which means 'undersea boat' which refers to all German navy submarines. The German naval operation in the Caribbean was codenamed "Operation NeuaInd." The period 1942 to 1943 was the most successful period for Caribbean German U-Boat operations in which a 150 mile strip around Trinidad suffered the greatest concentration of shipping losses experienced anywhere during World War II. The Growling Tiger in his 1939 calypso 'The Best Place is the United States" lamented the poor defensibility of Trinidad by saying,

I'll show you how we are targets for Germany

They can attack us from the north by the Caribbean Sea,

Ably supported by the Italians

With her ships and planes on the Atlantic Ocean

When it comes to the south, without any doubt

It's an easy thing to peep in the Dragon's Mouth

And then find our defence is rather slick

They can attack us on the West by the Pacific

The Growling Tiger's prediction came to fruition when in 1942, U-161, captained by Albrecht Achilles sailed into the Port of Spain Harbour and sank the 7400 ton American freighter, Mohikana and the British tanker, British Consul. On the 26th February 1942, U-156, captained by Werner Hartenstein sunk the oil tanker La Carriere south of the Monos Passage resulting in the loss of 16 Trinidadian lives. The German U-Boats had a successful Caribbean campaign, sinking 400 merchant ships, damaging 56 whilst only 17 U-Boats were sunk. The U-Boat menace was integral to Trinidad and Tobago's experience during the war.

Metzgen, Humphrey and John Graham. Caribbean Wars Untold: A Salute to the British West Indies. Kingston: University of the west Indies Press, 2007. Print.

Steele, Beverley A. Grenada in Wartime: The Tragic Loss of the Island Queen and Other Memories of World War II. Port of Spain: Paria Publishing Limited, 2011. Print.

Rohlehr, Gordon. Calypso and Society in Pre-Independence Trinidad. Kingston: The University of West Indies Press, 1990. Print.

Cross-section of a U-boat. (Gaylord Kelshall, The U-Boat War in the Caribbean [Shrewsbury, UK: Airlife, 1994])

Family Group Sheet for Walter Cyril Sheppard

Husband:		Walter Cyril Sheppard
	Birth:	14 Jun 1898 in Belmont, Saint George, Trinidad and Tobago
	Marriage:	14 Mar 1924 in Trinidad and Tobago, British West Indies
	Death:	11 Dec 1974 in Whitby, Ontario, Canada; Y
	Burial:	Whitby, Durham Regional Municipality, Ontario, Canada
	Father:	Arthur Sheppard
	Mother:	Adeline Alston Richards
Wife:		Olive Lyle Begg
	Birth:	05 May 1902 in Tobago, Trinidad and Tobago
	Death:	27 Jan 1949 in Port of Spain, Trinidad, W.I.
	Father:	James Bohill Begg
	Mother:	Kathleen Cunningham Patterson

Children:

1 M
- Name: Richard Walter Sheppard
- Birth: 08 Sep 1925 in Port of Spain, Trinidad and Tobago, British West Indies
- Marriage: 1951 in Port-of-Spain, Trinidad and Tobago
- Death: 14 Aug 2006 in Aberdeen, Aberdeen, Scotland; Y
- Spouse: Bianca Anne Nieves

2 F
- Name: Kathleen Lyle Sheppard
- Birth: 14 Sep 1926 in Port Of Spain, Trinidad
- Marriage: Jan 1945 in Port Of Spain, Trinidad
- Death: 03 Nov 2015 in London Ontario Canada; Y
- Burial: Ontario
- Spouse: Elliot Michael Gaston-Johnston

3 M
- Name: George Neville Sheppard
- Birth: 18 Oct 1927 in Port of Spain, Trinidad and Tobago, British West Indies
- Marriage: 09 Aug 1952 in Bogota, Colombia
- Death: 09 Dec 2008 in Saint Petersburg, Pinellas, Florida; Y
- Spouse: Maria Wilhelmina Johnson

4 F
- Name: Joan Daphne Mae Sheppard
- Birth: 26 May 1929 in Port of Spain, Trinidad and Tobago, British West Indies
- Marriage: 10 Sep 1949 in Port Of Spain, Trinidad
- Death: 28 May 2003 in Ontario, Canada; Death based on info from obituary: http://news.ourontario.ca/2455977/data?n=215
- Burial: Carleton, Ontario, Canada
- Spouse: Clement Wilroy Marshall

5 F
- Name: Patricia Myrna Sheppard
- Birth: 23 Sep 1930 in Port of Spain, Trinidad and Tobago, British West Indies
- Marriage: 21 Mar 1951 in Port Of Spain, Trinidad
- Death: 2017 in Brisbane, Queensland, Australia
- Spouse: John Frederick Torry

6 M	Name:	David Allan Sheppard	
	Birth:	20 Nov 1931 in Port of Spain, Trinidad and Tobago, British West Indies	
	Marriage:	16 Apr 1955 in Montreal, Canada	
	Death:	02 Aug 2022 in Lecanto, Citrus, Florida, United States	
	Spouse:	Teresa Pamela Audra Martin	
7 F	Name:	Barbara Ann Sheppard	
	Birth:	▓▓▓▓▓▓▓▓▓▓▓▓▓▓▓▓▓▓▓▓▓▓▓▓	
	Marriage:		
	Spouse:	Harvey Thurston Williams	
8 M	Name:	Michael Ernest Sheppard	
	Birth:	▓▓▓▓▓▓▓▓▓▓▓▓▓▓▓▓▓▓▓▓▓▓▓▓	
	Marriage:		
	Spouse:	Heather MacLean	
9 M	Name:	Brian Godfrey Sheppard	
	Birth:	15 May 1940 in Port of Spain, Trinidad and Tobago, British West Indies	
	Marriage:	01 Jul 1965 in Montreal, Canada	
	Death:	21 Nov 2002 in Île-de-Montréal, Quebec, Canada; Y	
	Spouse:	Louise Halley	
10 M	Name:	Douglas Elton Sheppard	
	Birth:	15 May 1940 in Port of Spain, Trinidad and Tobago, British West Indies	
	Death:	16 May 2004 in Toronto, York, Ontario, Canada; Y	
	Burial:	21 May 2004 in Toronto, York, Ontario, Canada	
11 F	Name:	Dorothy Esme Sheppard	
	Birth:	▓▓▓▓▓▓▓▓▓▓▓▓▓▓▓▓▓▓▓▓▓▓▓▓	
	Marriage:		
	Spouse:		
12 M	Name:	Kenneth Elliot Sheppard	
	Birth:	▓▓▓▓▓▓▓▓▓▓▓▓▓▓▓▓▓▓▓▓▓▓▓▓	
	Marriage:		
	Spouse:	Angela Maureen Thomas	

Notes:

THE SHEPPARDS

88

THE SHEPPARDS

Row 7 John Torry, Walter Sheppard

Row 6 Roland Pierre, Elliot Gaston Johnston

Row 5 George, Maria, Maria Bella and Ina

Row 4 Grandma Adeline, Isabel Johnson and Minnie Begg Pierre

Row 3 Pat Torry, Joan Marshall and Kathleen Gaston Johnston

Row 2 Yvonne Pierre, Isabel Johnson, and Mary Pierre

Row 1 Julia Gaston Johnston, Gail Marshall, Dorothy Sheppard, Kathy Gaston Johnston, Kenny Sheppard

90

Generation Three

Siblings of Walter Cyril Sheppard

- **Arthur Sheppard**
  1859–1925 • LZ4L-251

  Spouse
  - **Adeleline Richards**
    1878–Deceased • LZ4L-2RN

    - **Eloise Alston Sheppard**
      1894–Deceased • L15T-KR7

    - **Ina Muriel Sheppard**
      1896–Deceased • L15Y-SY6

    - **Walter Cyril Sheppard**
      1898–1974 • LKYG-98Q

    - **Denis Harvey Sheppard**
      1900–1919 • GX5W-DSJ

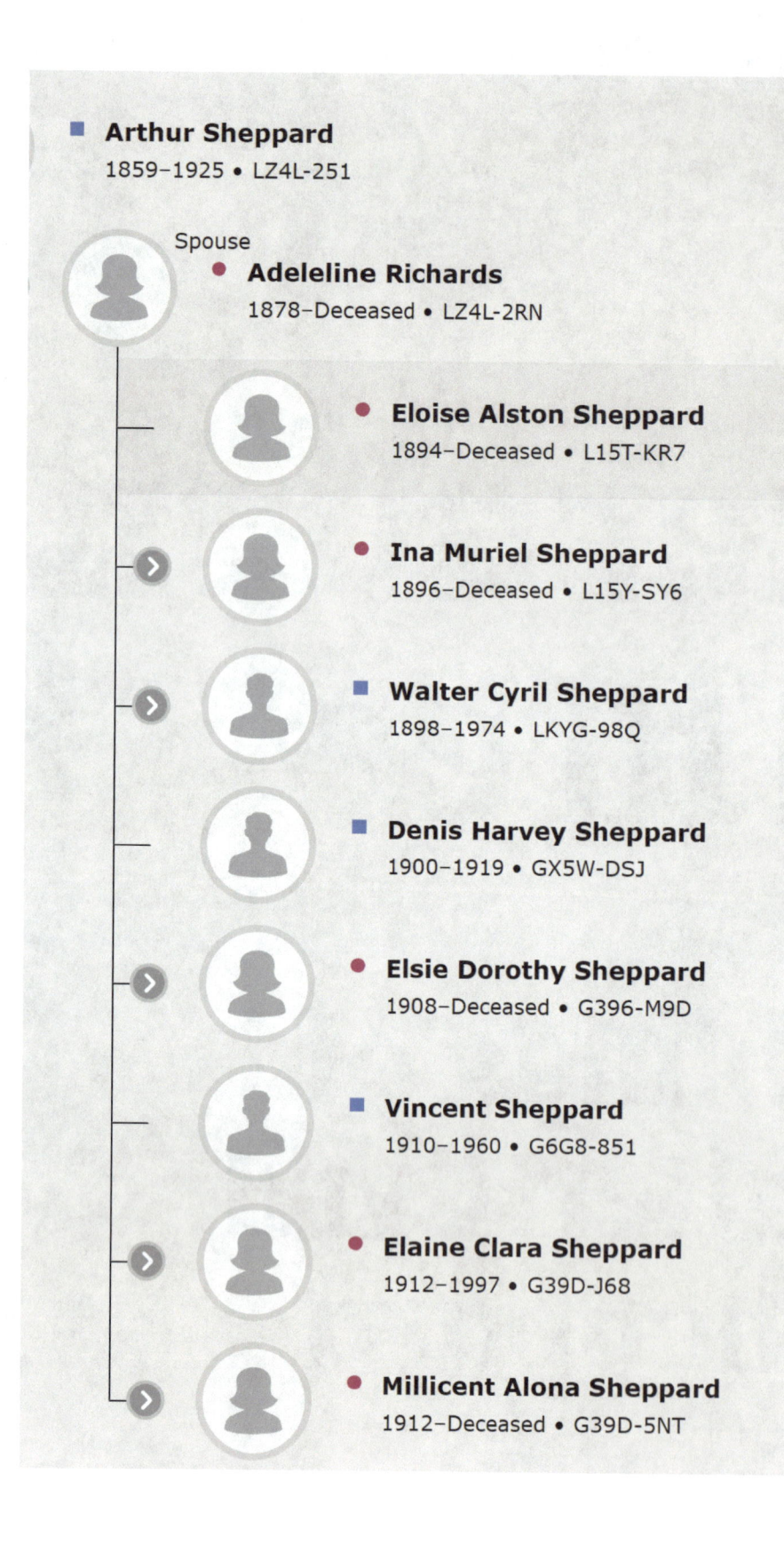

    - **Elsie Dorothy Sheppard**
      1908–Deceased • G396-M9D

    - **Vincent Sheppard**
      1910–1960 • G6G8-851

    - **Elaine Clara Sheppard**
      1912–1997 • G39D-J68

    - **Millicent Alona Sheppard**
      1912–Deceased • G39D-5NT

1. Eloise never married. No children

2. Ina's married (name) was O'Duffy. One child.

3. Walter married Olive Lyle Begg, 12 children survived past birth.

4. Denis never married. Died young, no children.

5. Elsie married Ralph Lindsey Harry. Number of children unknown

6. Vincent never married. No children

7. Elaine married William Taft for a brief period. No children.

8. Millicent married Kenneth Harvey. Number of children unknown.

Eloise Alston Sheppard

The only evidence of Eloise is a passenger manifest showing her traveling to Canada to visit family or friends.

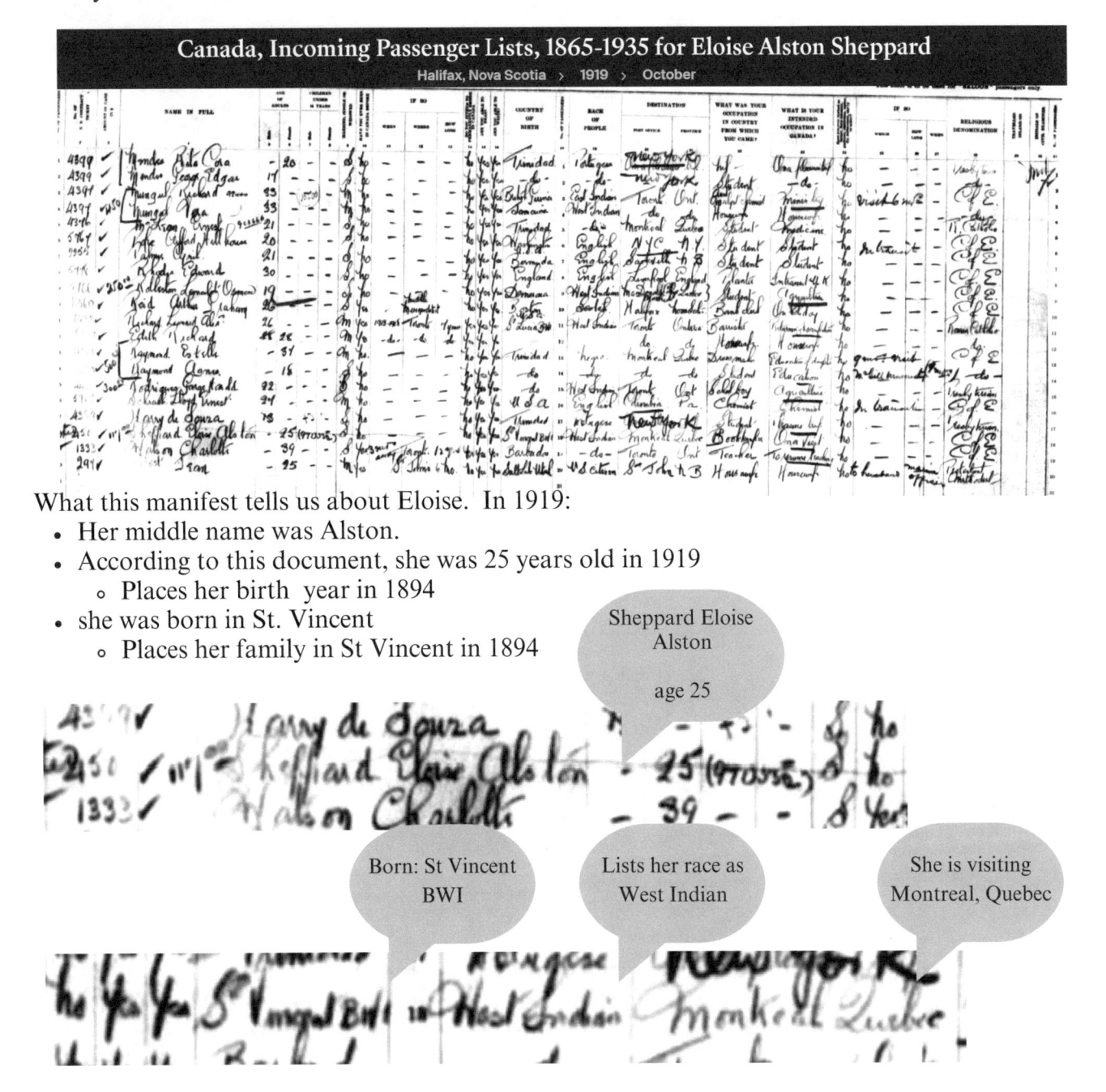

Canada, Incoming Passenger Lists, 1865-1935 for Eloise Alston Sheppard
Halifax, Nova Scotia > 1919 > October

What this manifest tells us about Eloise. In 1919:
- Her middle name was Alston.
- According to this document, she was 25 years old in 1919
  - Places her birth year in 1894
- she was born in St. Vincent
  - Places her family in St Vincent in 1894

- Sheppard Eloise Alston age 25
- Born: St Vincent BWI
- Lists her race as West Indian
- She is visiting Montreal, Quebec

The fact that we know that Eloise was born in St. Vincent is a big lead. By this we know that Arthur and Adeline were married in St. Vincent.

Ina Muriel Sheppard

REPUBLIC OF TRINIDAD AND TOBAGO

CERTIFICATE OF BIRTH

SHORT FORM CERTIFICATE, ISSUED WITHOUT PIN

Given Name(s): *****	Date of Birth: 18TH APRIL, 1897
Other Name(s): *****	Sex: FEMALE
Place of Birth: 10 DERT STREET, SOUTH	
Mother's Name: ADELINE SHEPPARD	Father's Name: ARTHUR SHEPPARD
Mother's Former Surname: RICHARDS	
Mother's Prev. Surname(s): *****	
Occupation: *****	Occupation: CLERK
Informant's Name and Relationship to Child ARTHUR SHEPPARD FATHER	Informant's Name and Relationship to Child ***** *****
Registration Date: 03RD MAY, 1897	Registration District: NORTH WESTERN DISTRICT OF PORT OF SPAIN
Name of Registrar: E JOHNSON	Entry No: 457
	Notes:

ISSUED UNDER MY HAND AND SEAL OF OFFICE ON 22ND OCTOBER, 2024

REGISTRAR GENERAL

CERTIFIED TRUE AND CORRECT EXTRACT FROM THE REGISTER OF BIRTHS, HELD BY REGISTRAR GENERAL'S DEPARTMENT MINISTRY OF THE ATTORNEY GENERAL AND LEGAL AFFAIRS

BA01669516

Important family History:

1. She was born in Trinidad
2. Based on her birth date, we know herp parents emigrated to Trinidad by 1897
3. Her father, Arthur, occupation was employed as a Clerk
    a. On Denis Sheppard's death certificate shows that Arthur worked in the Bonanza

Eloise and Ina

I called Eloise and Ina's nieces and nephew to ask about their memories of the two sisters. Barbara described them as lovely, kind, and sweet women. She never heard them argue or gossip, and she always remembered them as gentle and pleasant.

Eloise, who never married, was known for wearing long dresses, likely due to her condition. Some said she had swollen legs from elephantiasis, a disease caused by parasitic roundworms transmitted by mosquitoes, common in tropical regions. Despite this, Eloise did not let it slow her down. She worked as a bookkeeper in the office of Canning and Co., a major food importer in Port of Spain. Kathy Plimmer recalled attending a school that Eloise and Ina established at their home.

Barbara mentioned that Eloise was very devout, attending church every Sunday, often with a family named Spencer. David added that she attended a church called Ebeneezer, though there are several Ebeneezer churches in Port of Spain (Ebeneezer Seventh Day Adventist, Ebeneezer Baptist, Ebeneezer Presbyterian, and Ebeneezer Gospel Hall). The family followed different religious paths; Ina chose Catholicism, Millicent chose Anglican, and Walter, who raised his family in the Anglican faith, also attended Anglican services with all twelve of his children and his wife every Sunday.

Eloise did not like to travel, and there is only one record of her leaving Trinidad, dating back to 1919. Interestingly, that travel record shows Eloise was born in St. Vincent. Barbara shared a story of her granny making vanilla fudge and selling it at the Canning and Co. grocery store. As Eloise got older, Barbara would help stir the fudge pot.

David shared memories of making ice cream. He felt it was his primary job, and he recalled that no one ever offered him a break. He had to stir until the crank stiffened, making it nearly impossible to continue. He fondly remembered that Eloise, Ina, and Grannie (Adeleline) made the best ice cream, and he always got the first taste. David also recalled making a rich, dark fruitcake with rum every year. After he would stir the batter, Eloise would inspect it and ask him to stir it more until she was satisfied with the consistency. The kitchen was a place of many memories for David, always involving Eloise and Ina.

Though Eloise never married, and Ina was abandoned by her bigamist husband, the two sisters lived together for many years. Their bond was clearly deep, and their shared life in the kitchen and home was full of warmth and love.

Eloise and Ina worked together in the office of the grocery store and also in the kitchen, preparing for all the family events. In my estimation, they were truly great sisters, dedicated to each other and their family.

Eloise and Ina were the oldest children in their family. Eloise was born in St. Vincent, while Ina was the first child born in Trinidad. Walter, born in 1898, was the first male child. Then came Vincent, around 1901, followed by Denis, born in 1904.

The three youngest sisters were Elsie Dorothy, Elaine Clara, and Millicent Alona, born in 1910, 1911, and 1912, respectively. Like the older siblings, they did not remain in Trinidad. Elsie Dorothy married a government diplomat from Australia. Elaine Clara, a nurse, rose to the rank of Major in the U.S. Army and stayed in the U.S. Millicent Alona married a man from England, moved there, and started her family.

As for Vincent, also known as Uncle Winky, not much is known about him. He never married and lived with his sisters. It was reported that he struggled with alcoholism. After his death, it was said that he left a sum of money to Eloise and Ina.

Denis Harvey Sheppard

Denis Harvey Sheppard was lost to history for over a century. I stumbled across his obituary while researching more information about the Sheppards. In a report commissioned by Fleur Harvey, there was mention of a third brother, but no one knew his name or anything about his life. All I could find to document his existence was his obituary.

Barbara Williams remembered speaking to Walter Sheppard about a brother who had died, but she didn't know his name or any details about his birth or death. This obituary is the only record of Denis's short 15-year life. Welcome to the family, Denis.

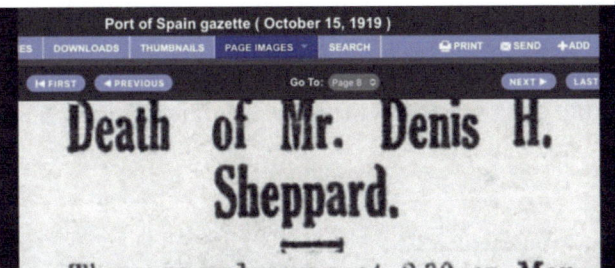

Port of Spain gazette (October 15, 1919)

Death of Mr. Denis H. Sheppard.

There passed away at 2.30 on Monday morning Denis H. Sheppard, youngest son of Mr. A. Sheppard of the Bonanza. A most promising and sturdy youth, he joined the local branch of the W. I. and P. Cable Co. in January last and continued making commendable progress at his work up to the time of his illness. To his parents, brothers, sisters and numerous relatives we offer our sympathy. The funeral took place the same evening at 5 p.m. from the house of mourning to St. Margaret's Church after which the body was interred in the family allotment. The large number of sympathetic followers bore full testimony to the esteem in which deceased was held. The principal mourners were Mr. & Mrs. Sheppard (parents), four sister and two brothers. The bearers were: Messrs. W. and V. Sheppard (brothers), H. and E. McCartney, P. Proudfoot and R. Sutherland. Among those present were Mr. and Mrs. R. McCartney, Mr. and Mrs. T. McCartney, Mr. and Mrs. E. McCartney, Mr. and Mrs. Talma, Miss A. Sheppard (aunt), Mr. and Mrs. Court and family, Mrs. E. Hinds, the Misses Wilson (3), Mrs. N. Hinds, Mr. R. Sutherland, Mr. G. Sutherland Mr. F. Sutherland, the Misses Sutherland (3), the Misses Bayne (3), the Misses Telfer (3), F. Hendy, the Misses Hendy (2), Mr. E. and C. Fifi, Mr. Peyreau, Mr. and Mrs. de Fague, Miss Murray, E. Bates, Miss J. Bates, Mrs. Agostini Miss Bell, Mrs. G. E. Slack, Mrs. and Miss Horne, R. Wells, E. Ghent, Miss O. Ghent, Miss D. Stanley, Miss E. Moniz, Miss S. Collier, Mrs and the Misses Winzey (2), V. F. Jardine, R. Richards, J. Campbell, Miss Wells, Mr. Gibbon, Mrs. R. Sutherland, Mrs. Spencer, E. Clarke, V. Donawa, Mrs. Grell and the Misses Grell (2), Mrs. and Miss Borde, Mr. and Mrs. Grosvenor, Mrs. Green, Miss Rousseau, Miss Swain, Mr. J. Harold Mr. W. Richards and Mr. V. Hutton.

Wreaths were sent by the following: Rev. and Mrs. G. F. Bourne, Mrs Raymond, G. Piggott, Mrs A. P. Spencer, Mr. and Mrs. Hinds, Mrs. R. A. Sutherland, Mrs. G. McCartney, Mr. and Mrs. Geo. E. Slack, Mrs. Attale, Mr. and Mrs. C. F. Agostini and family, Mr. and Mrs. Talma and family, Mr. and Mrs. Louis John and family, Mrs. Warner and family, the staff of the W.I. & P. Tel. Co., (Grenada), staff of Canning and Co., Miss I. Sheppard, Miss E. Sheppard (Canada), Mr. and Mrs. Sheppard, V. and W. Sheppard, staff of W.I. & P. Tel. Co., Mr. and Mrs. Peyrau, Miss Keane, Mr. and Mrs. Court and family Mr. and Mrs. Da Costa, Mr. and Mrs. R. McCartney and family, Mr. Sutherland and family, Mrs. and Miss McCartney and Mr. Percy Proudfoot.

Denis Harvey Sheppard
Obit Tidbits
Born: about 1904
Port of Spain, Trinidad
Died: 13 Oct 1919
in Port of Spain, Trinidad

T&T - Registar Search Results

. Denis H Sheppard/ Death year: 1919/ Search years 1918, 1919, 1920
District: Port of Spain. Cost US$15 – **Found: Denis Sheppard/ DOD 13th October, 1919/ Age 15 years/ Place where death occurred: Colonial Hospital, Port of Spain**

What did we learn?   No certificate ordered.

He was the youngest son of Arthur and Adeline. He worked at the Cable and Wireless company along with his brother He had a long illness before passing away. His father, Arthur, worked at The Bonanza.

What do we learn about his immediate family from his obituary?
Mr and Mrs A. Sheppard (parents)
Denis worked for Cable and Wireless before he died
W and V Sheppard (brothers)
Elosie, Ina, Millicent, Elsie, Elaine (sisters)
Miss A Sheppard (aunt)

What do we learn about his extended family from his obituary?
The last names are a who's who of relations as identified on the family tree done by Kelvin Pierre.

Acknowledgments.

Mr. and Mrs. Arthur Sheppard and family beg through this medium to thank all those who sent wreaths, letters of condolence or otherwise sympathised with them on the death of their son and brother Denis Harvey, and regret their inability to do so individually.

In this acknowledgement, we learn that Denis' middle name is Harvey. The previous article only used the initial H.

Also, I initially wondered what could have happened that would preclude them from thanking people personally. What I found out was that this was a common practice at the time.

Was Arthur sick at this point. His obit states he suffered from a long illness also

98

Elsie Dorothy Sheppard was born in 1910. She later dropped "Elsie" and became known simply as Dorothy. Dorothy married Ralph Lindsey Harry, who had a distinguished career as an ambassador in Australia. His life is well-documented, with detailed records available. The image below is from his Wikipedia page. Note: Although there is a section on his personal life, Dorothy and their children are not mentioned there.

Ralph Harry

Article Talk

From Wikipedia, the free encyclopedia

Ralph Lindsay Harry AC, CBE (10 March 1917 – 7 October 2002) was one of Australia's pioneer diplomats and intelligence specialists. He was recognised as a skilled diplomatic professional with a mastery of the traditional conventions and methods of diplomacy and politics. Having acted early in his career for three years as Director of the Australian Secret Intelligence Service, he was also known as an insightful intelligence analyst and cryptographer.[1]

Harry was the Acting Head of the Department of External Affairs and concluded his career as Australia's Ambassador to the United Nations. He made a lifelong emotional commitment to the promotion of the interests of Australia and the betterment of his fellow men and women through the promotion of international law and institutions. There was little he did or said that was not aimed in this direction.[1]

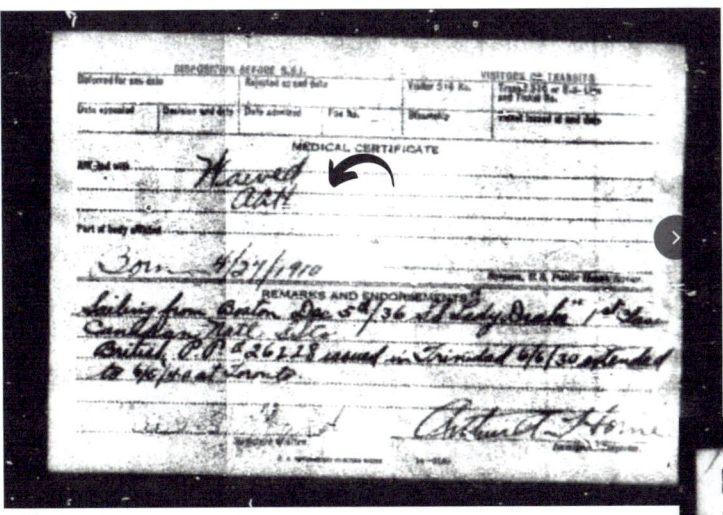

The immigration card from a trip Dorothy made to the US. It shows Dorothy's birthday as April 27, 1910

Elaine Clara Sheppard was born on February 2, 1911, and was the second of the three younger daughters in the family. The first record I found of her shows that she traveled to New York to study nursing. At that time, she was listed as 26 years old. Interestingly, she is also noted as being 20 years old on January 15, 1932, which may reflect the age recorded in official documents. Her reason for entering the United States was to study at Long Island College Hospital.

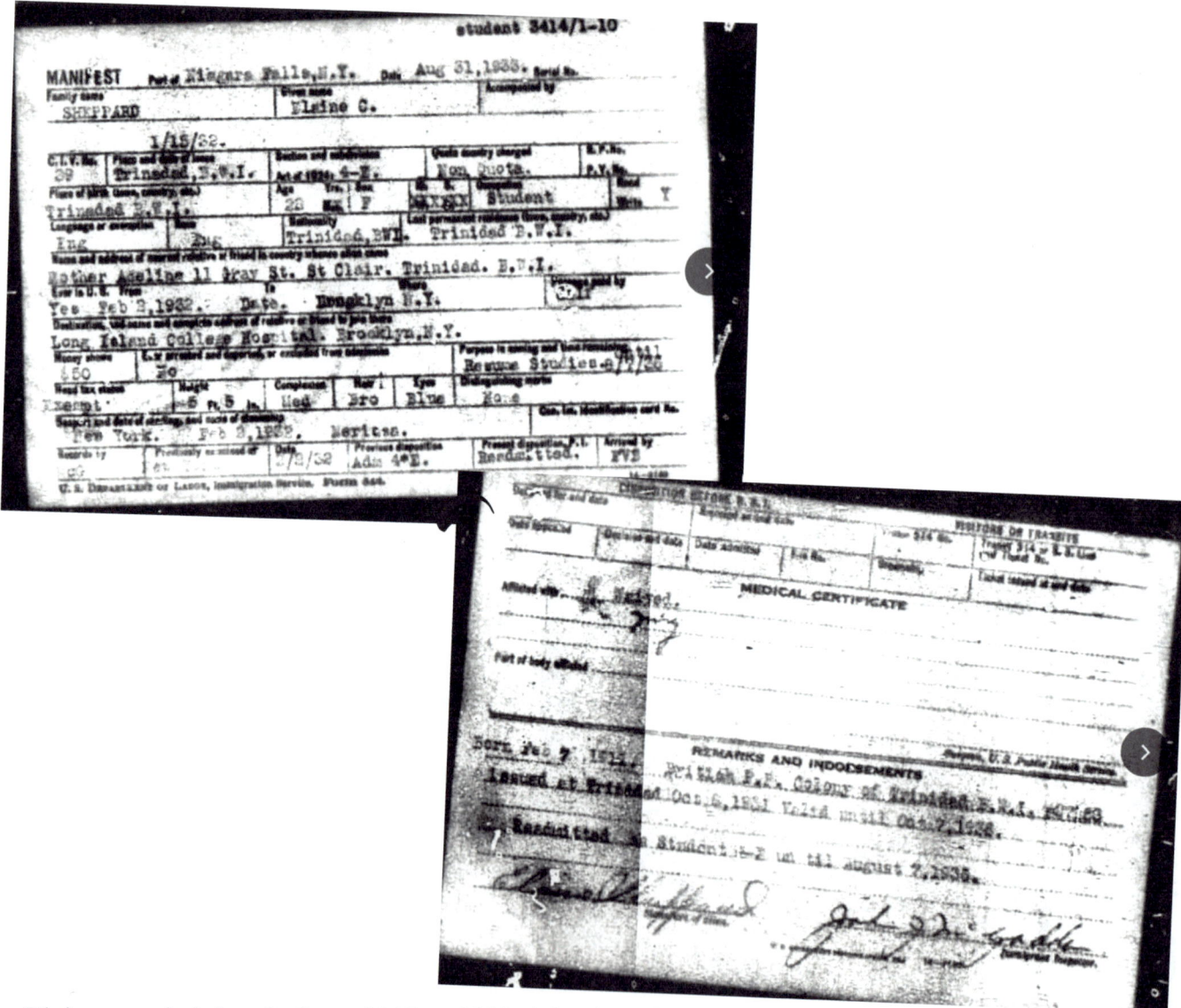

Elaine married shortly from 1945 to 1950. After her divorce, she went back to her maiden name, and lived until 1997.

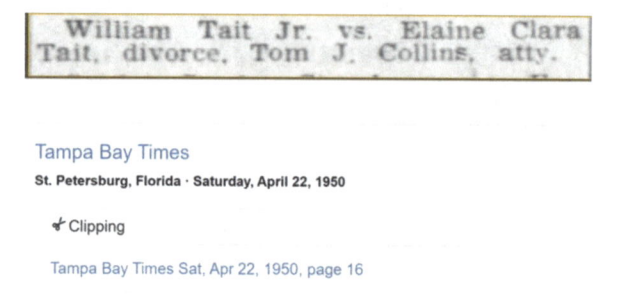

> William Tait Jr. vs. Elaine Clara Tait, divorce, Tom J. Collins, atty.

Tampa Bay Times
St. Petersburg, Florida · Saturday, April 22, 1950

Clipping

Tampa Bay Times Sat, Apr 22, 1950, page 16

Millicent "Tully" Alona Sheppard's birthplace has caused some confusion, but I would like to clarify that she was indeed born in Trinidad. A death notice from England, found in an Ancestry record, confirms her birth as Trinidad. While Eloise was the only sibling born in St. Vincent, both Arthur and Adeline were married there, which supports this detail.

Unfortunately, I do not have much additional information, as the Millicent Harvey (née Sheppard) family tree is private and tightly restricted. However, I do have a photo of a family gathering featuring Tully, which came from Pat's personal photo journal.

Generation Four Paternal

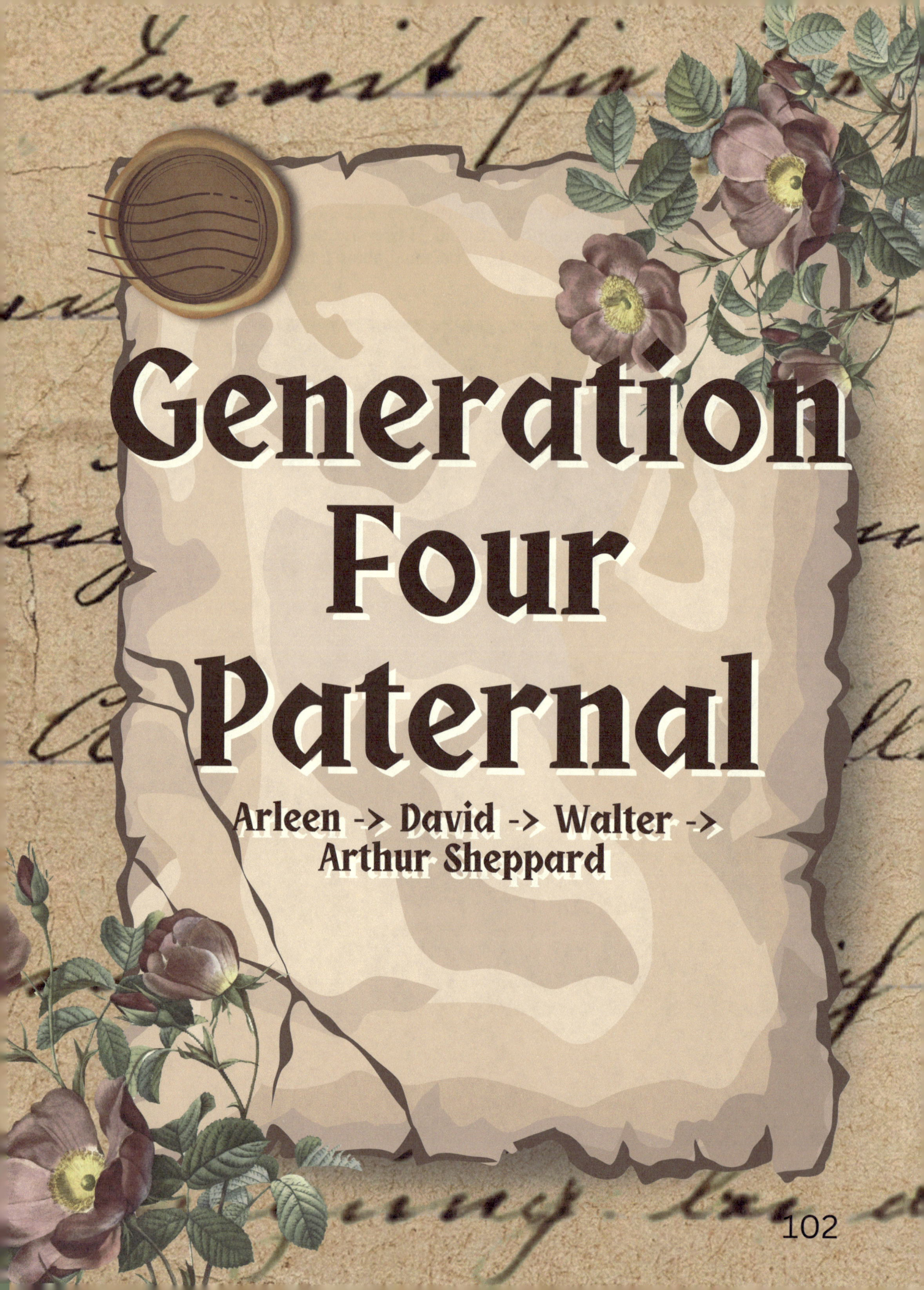

Arleen -> David -> Walter -> Arthur Sheppard

HISTORY OF ARTHUR SHEPPARD

QUICK FACTS:

BORN
UNITED KINGDOM

PARENTS
UNKNOWN

CHILDREN
3 Boys, 5 Girls

103

Arthur Sheppard - Obit

FUNERALS.

MR. A. SHEPPARD.

Mr. Arthur Sheppard died at his residence, No. 66 Belmont Circular Road, on Saturday after a long illness. He was born in England sixty-six years ago and after travelling among the various Islands settled in the Colony. He is survived by his wife, two sons and five daughters.

The funeral took place on Sunday afternoon to St. Margaret's Church, Belmont. A choral service was conducted by Rev. Canon H. A. Melville with Mr. M. Archbald presiding at the organ. When the bier entered the church, the choir sang hymn No. 264 "My God, My Father, While I Stray" which was followed by the chanting of Psalm 90 "Lord Thou hast been our refuge." The lesson was read and the congregation joined in singing hymn No. 184, "Rock of Ages," which brought the service to a close. The procession left the church to the strains of Chopin's Funeral March and continued to the Cemetery where the graveside rites were performed and the body interred.

The bearers were Messrs. W. and B. Sheppard (sons), A. and H. McCartney, Talma and E. McCartney.

The principal mourners were Mrs. A. Sheppard (wife), Misses Eloise Ina, Millicent, Elsie and Elaine Sheppard (daughters), Miss Adelle Sheppard (sister), Mr. Wilfred Richards (father-in-law) and Mrs. Walter Sheppard (daughter-in-law).

Other followers included Messrs. R. McCartney, H. McCartney, L. Walker, Masters C. Camps and S. Franco, G. Jackson, J. Algernon, Bates, Ellison, A. Richards, C. A. Hinds, J. Cook, Martin, W. Ferreira, C. Millan, F. Sutherland, T. A. Francois, L. Donawa, S. Wilson, D. Proudfoot, Cyril and Cecil Gittens, O. Telfer, D. Plimmer, C. S. Collier, Cozier, H. McClachlan, Barrow, G. Gordon, H. and D. de Souza, E. and R. Sutherland, W. Jackson, V. Hospedales, Oscar Edghill and Frank Edghill.

Mrs. R. McCartney, Mrs. Butler and the Misses Olga, Elaine, and Rita Butler, Mrs. Reece and Misses Reece (2), Mrs. Ghent, Mrs. Richards and Miss Richards, Mrs. Franco, Mrs. Luces and the Misses Luces (2), Miss May Marshall, Mrs. Anderson, Nurses Burnett, Todd and Francis, Mrs. R. Sutherland, Misses L. and V. Villaneuva, the Misses Cuthbert, (2), Misses B. and A. Rose, Miss Lynch, Miss Borne, Miss Pereira, Miss M. Bates, Miss Begg, Mrs. Ellison, Mrs. A. McCartney, Mrs. Talma, Miss G. Lynch, Mrs. Proudfoot and Miss Proudfoot, Mrs. A. Winsey, Miss Winsey, Mrs. J. Stalley, Miss L. Pujadas, Mrs. Hinds, Mrs. Cook and Miss Cook, Mrs. Flemming, Mrs. Martin and Miss Martin, Miss Joaquim, the Misses M., A., L. and D. Sutherland, Miss Seaton, Miss A. Henderson, Mrs. Court, the Misses Kitt-Kelly (2), Mrs. Sutherland, Miss O'Brien, Mrs. Bombard, Mrs. Collier, Mrs. D. Plimmer, Mrs. Cozier, Miss A. Montrichard, Misses I. and L. Castagne, Miss J. Lipez, Mrs. Bain, Mrs. Johnson and Miss S. Johnson.

Floral tributes were sent by Mrs. A. Sheppard (wife), Misses Eloise, Ina, Millicent, Elsie and Elaine Sheppard (daughters), Mr. V. Sheppard (snr), Walter and Olive (son and daughter-in-law), Mr. and Mrs. C. A. Hinds (sister), Maria and Clara (nieces), Mrs. Luces and family, Mr. C. Wears, Mrs. Francis and family, Mrs. Larien, Mr. and Mrs. J. Stalley and Miss Stalley, Mr. and Mrs. Court, Mr. and Mrs. Sutherland and family, Miss Bates, Mr. and Mrs. Talma and family.

Arthur Sheppard Obit Tidbits

Born: about 1859 (66 prior to death)
in England
Died: 19 July 1925
in Port of Spain, Trinidad

How did he get to Trinidad?
As a young man, Arthur traveled through the Caribbean. He started his family in St Vincent and finally settled in Port of Spain, Trinidad and Tobago

Who were his family members mentioned?
Mrs A Sheppard (wife)
W and B Sheppard (sons) The B is incorrect. It should be V, and appeared as V later in the obit.
Miss Adelle Sheppard (sister)
Eloise, Ina, Millicent, Elsie, Elaine (daughters)

Who were his family members mentioned? (continued)
Mr. Wilfred Richards (Father-in-law/ name should be William)
Mrs. W. Sheppard (daughter-in-law)
Mr C. A. Hinds (sister)
Clara and Maria (nieces)

Other relationships that can be inferred:
Mrs Anderson (grandmother of Olive Begg.)
Adeline Sheppard and Wilhelmina McCarthy are sisters whose maiden name is Richards.
Clara and Maria (nieces) based on placement in the obit, it is assumed that they were the daughters of Hinds.
Many other names listed in the obituary are relations,

Arthur worked at The Bonanza

Present Day Photo
66 Belmont Circular, Port of Spain, Trinidad

This photo is courtesy of the book, "The Caribbean in Sepia: A History in Photographs 1840-1900" by author Michael Ayre. This book is part of the National Archives of Trinidad and Tobago Reference Library.

The Bonanza

Founded by John H. Smith, the Bonanza was a mercantile store where dry-goods such as fabrics, ready-made clothing, accessories, toys, and furniture were sold. Over the years, it became a landmark in Port-of-Spain, known for its spacious interior that was brightly lit by skylights mounted on the ceiling. During that period, these skylights were referred to as "lantern roofs".

Generation FOUR

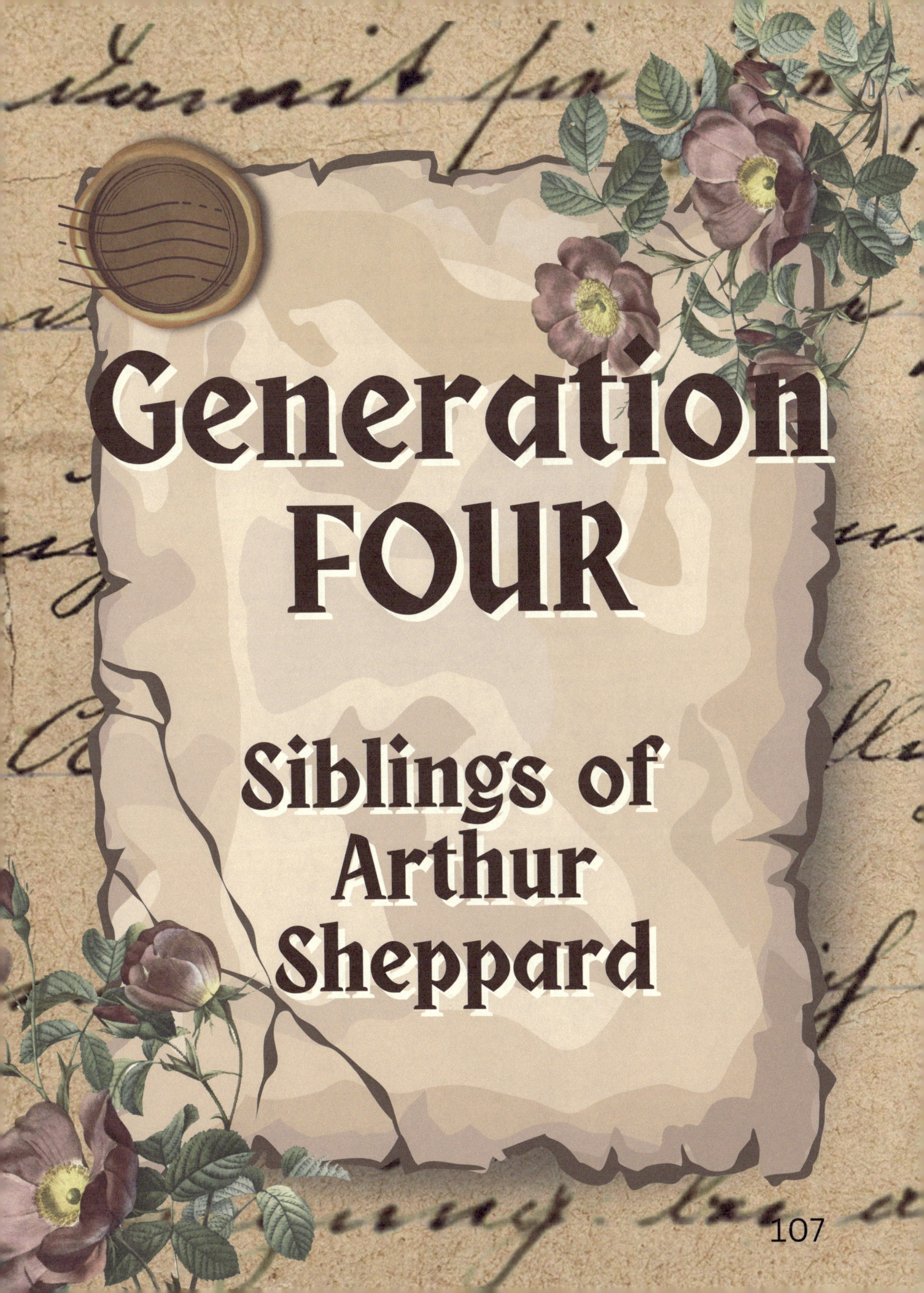

Siblings of Arthur Sheppard

Arthur Sheppard and Adeline Richards Children

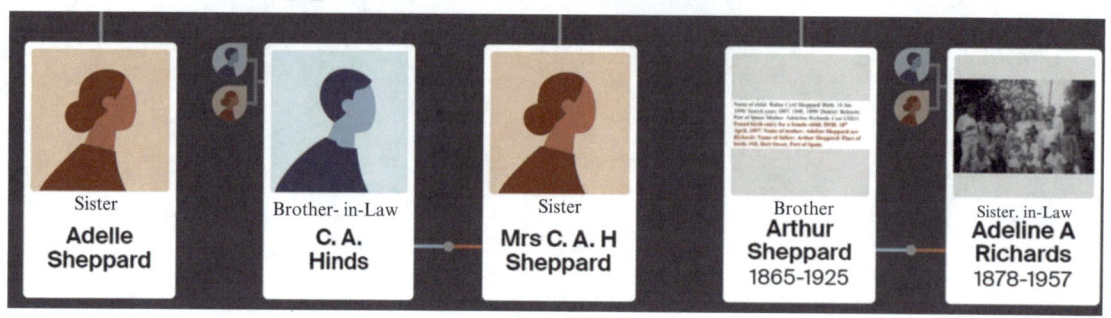

Sister	Brother-in-Law	Sister	Brother	Sister-in-Law
Adelle Sheppard	**C. A. Hinds**	**Mrs C. A. H Sheppard**	**Arthur Sheppard** 1865-1925	**Adeline A Richards** 1878-1957

These are the known siblings of Arthur Sheppard. Unfortunately, no additional genealogical information has been uncovered about them to date. Adelle, who was affectionately known as "Ole Auntie," was often heard playing the piano. David Sheppard recalled that she received a monthly stipend, which she eagerly anticipated. According to David, she would buy a pint of her favorite spirits and take a nip before bed each evening.

Generation Three Maternal

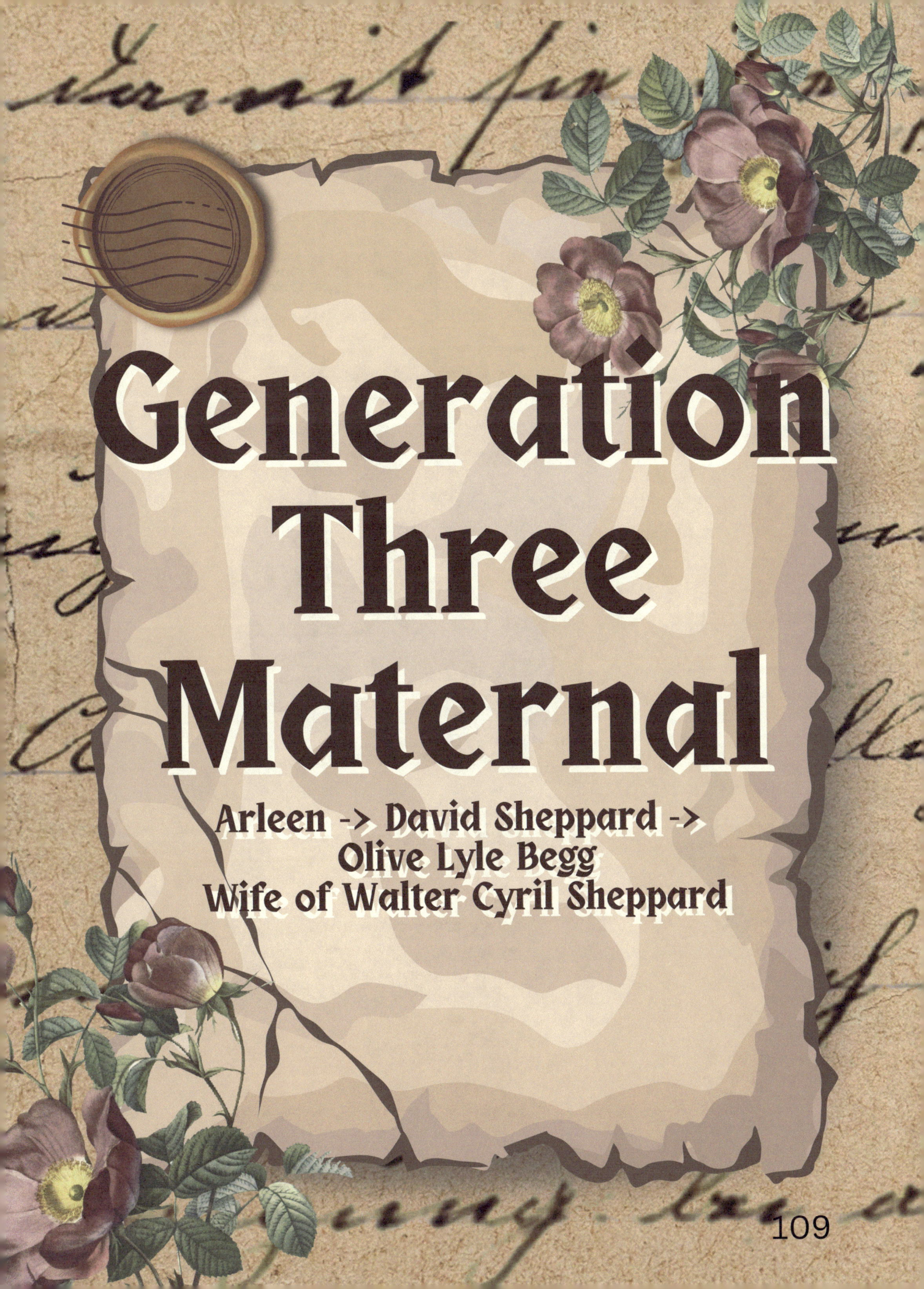

Arleen -> David Sheppard -> Olive Lyle Begg Wife of Walter Cyril Sheppard

HISTORY OF OLIVE LYLE BEGG

QUICK FACTS:

BORN
TOBAGO

PARENTS
JAMES BOWHILL BEGG
KATHLEEN CUNNINGHAM PATERSON

CHILDREN
LOVING MOTHER OF 12

Olive Lyle Seppard (nee Begg)

Kathleen Patterson died when the children were very small. They were split up, some going to Granny Anderson (Minnie Kirk). Olive went to Mummy Figeroux.

Barbara, her daughter, recalled a time before Olive passed away. The family went to Tobago to follow doctor's order for rest for Olive. She said Olive worked feeding and caring for the family the entire time. Shortly after, she passed away,

Olive Lyle Begg was born in Tobago on May 5, 1902, one of four daughters of James Bowhill Begg and Kathleen Patterson. She passed away on January 27, 1949

Olive married Walter Cyrll Sheppard on March 14, 1925, at the Church of St. Margaret's, Belmont (Anglican Church), Trinidad.
Olive's mother passed away when Olive was between five and ten years old. According to a document from Pat's photo journal, Olive and her sisters were placed with family and friends after their mother's death. Minnie Begg went to live with Minnie Anderson (relict Paterson; nee Kirk). Olive was sent to live with Mummy Figeroux. The whereabouts of Louise and Enid, however, remain unclear. James Begg, their father, left Tobago and the girls behind, severing ties with them until his later years when he returned and moved into the family home of Olive and Walter.

Despite these early hardships, Olive was known for her kindness and compassion. Her sisters went on to form their own families, but they remained close to each other throughout their lives.

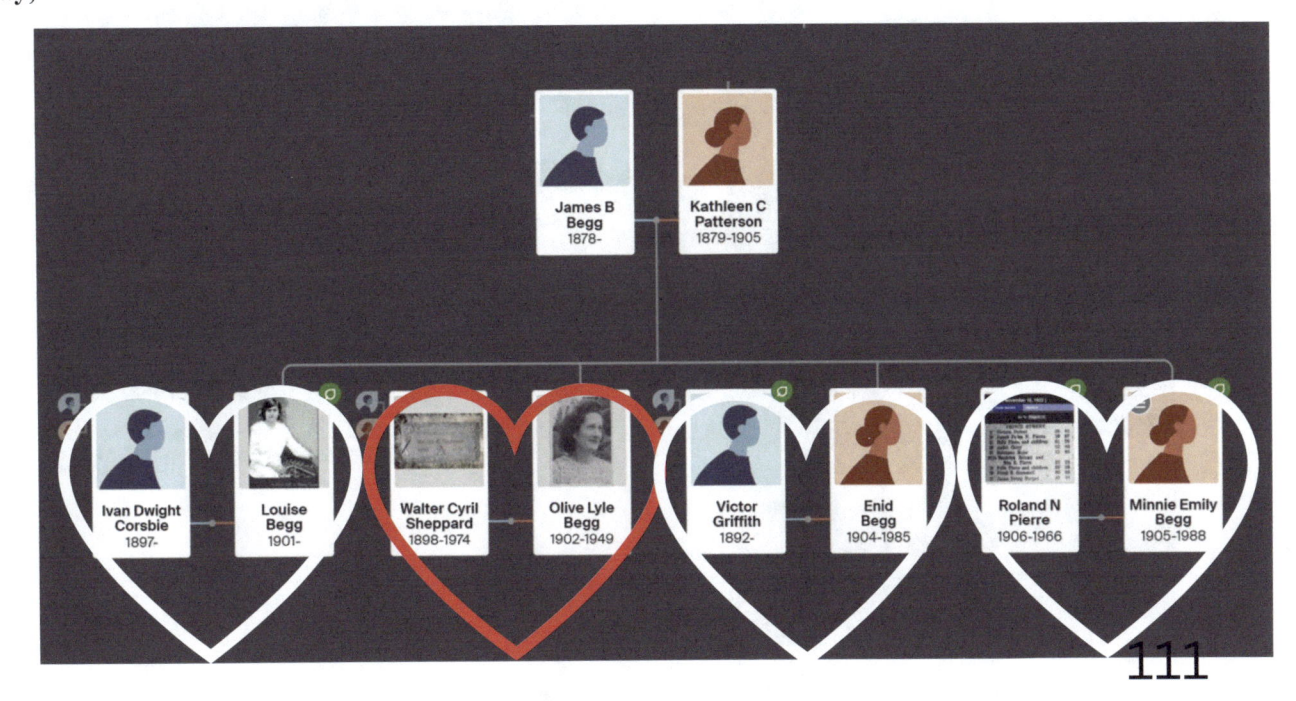

111

All who met Olive spoke of her generosity of spirit and kindness. During the Nazi occupation of Germany in the 1940s, a ship carrying Jewish refugees arrived in Port of Spain. Despite the Sheppard household already being full with young children and many mouths to feed, Olive made room for a family of Jewish refugees fleeing the war. This act of compassion was a testament to the generous nature of this great matriarch of the Sheppard family. It was not only Olive who embodied such kindness, but also her sisters, who shared in this noble spirit.

Olive is also remembered for never turning anyone away from the dinner table. If one of the children brought a friend home, she was often heard telling Caroline to add another cup of water to the pot to accommodate the extra guest. Though she passed away young, she left behind a great legacy and is still remembered and revered. One of her oldest grandchildren, Kathy Plimmer, shared, "Her spirit continues in her children, who all carry that same generous hospitality and love of family."

During World War II, Olive, along with several other mothers in Port of Spain, Trinidad, acted as chaperones at the American Soldiers' Dances. Only one of Olive's daughters, however, married an American sailor.

Olive enjoying the beach in her latter days

Death Certificate of Olive Lyle Begg

Uraemia - Uremia is a clinical condition associated with declining renal function and is characterized by fluid overload, electrolyte imbalances, metabolic abnormalities, and physiological changes. The term "uremia" literally means "urine in the blood," which develops most commonly in chronic and end-stage renal disease.

REPUBLIC OF TRINIDAD AND TOBAGO
CERTIFICATE OF DEATH

Name:	OLIVE LYLE SHEPPARD
Date of Death:	28TH JANUARY, 1949
Age:	46 YEAR(S)
Sex:	FEMALE
Rank/Profession:	*****
Informant Name:	H JODHAM
Informant Address:	4B TRAGARETE ROAD
Informant Description:	UNDERTAKER
Country of Birth:	TOBAGO
Place of Death:	7 LUCKPAT STREET
Cause of Death:	URAEMIA
Medical Examiner:	DR FREITAS
Registration Date:	29TH JANUARY, 1949
Registration District:	ST JAMES DISTRICT PORT OF SPAIN
Name of Registrar:	I SEARL
Entry No:	84
Notes:	

ISSUED UNDER MY HAND AND SEAL OF OFFICE ON 07TH FEBRUARY, 2024

REGISTRAR GENERAL

CERTIFIED TRUE AND CORRECT EXTRACT FROM THE REGISTER OF DEATHS, HELD BY REGISTRAR GENERAL'S DEPARTMENT MINISTRY OF THE ATTORNEY GENERAL AND LEGAL AFFAIRS

Generation Three

Siblings of Olive Lyle Begg

Louise Begg
1899–Deceased • L5JP-W1W

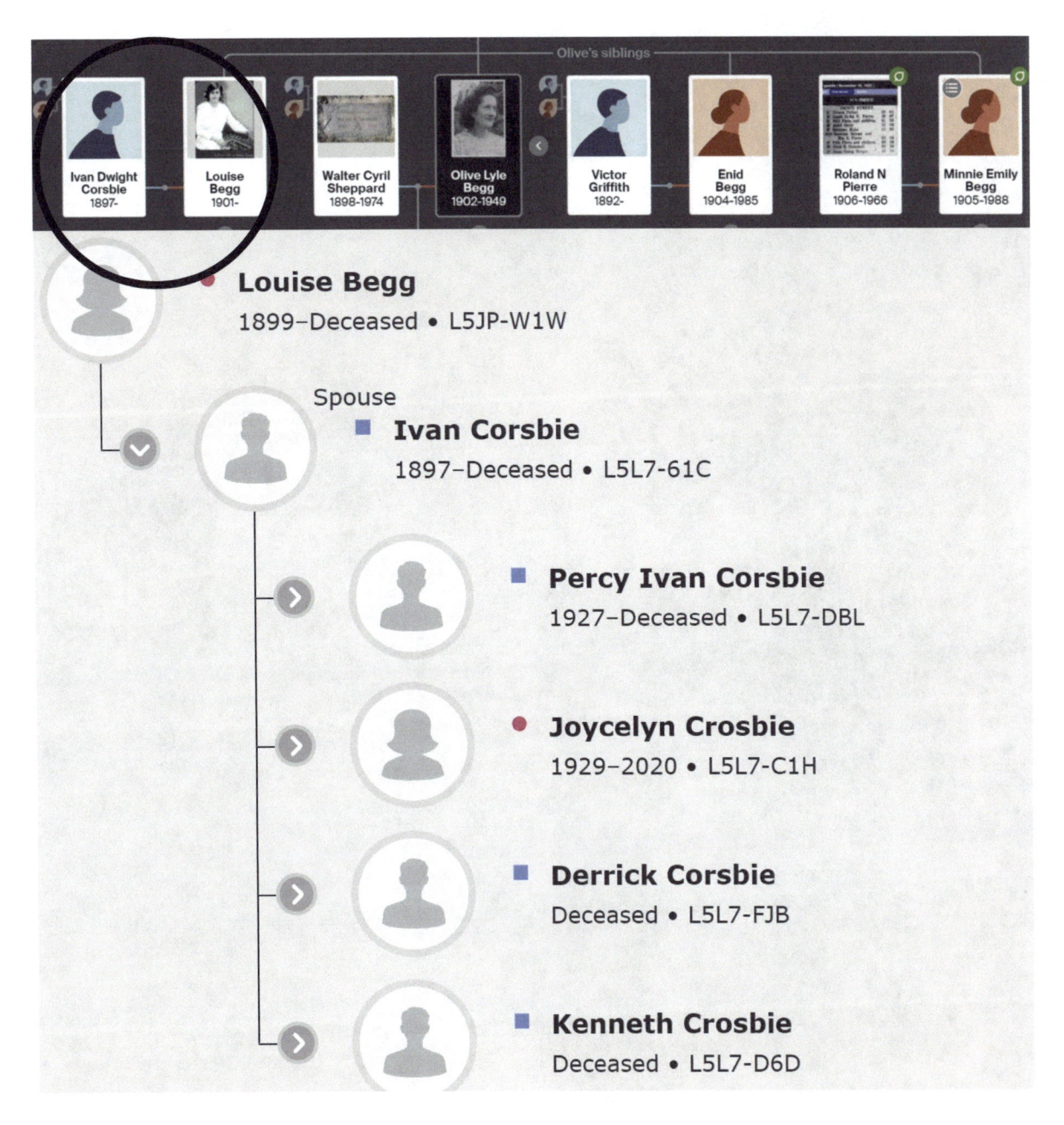

Spouse
Ivan Corsbie
1897–Deceased • L5L7-61C

Percy Ivan Corsbie
1927–Deceased • L5L7-DBL

Joycelyn Crosbie
1929–2020 • L5L7-C1H

Derrick Corsbie
Deceased • L5L7-FJB

Kenneth Crosbie
Deceased • L5L7-D6D

Louise Begg was born in Tobago and was the oldest of the four sisters. She married Ivan Corsbie and relocated to Guyana, where they raised their family. We have Kelvin's family history, which identifies Louise's children and grandchildren. This information is provided over the next three pages.

115

(20)

Ivan Corsbie m **Louise Begg**

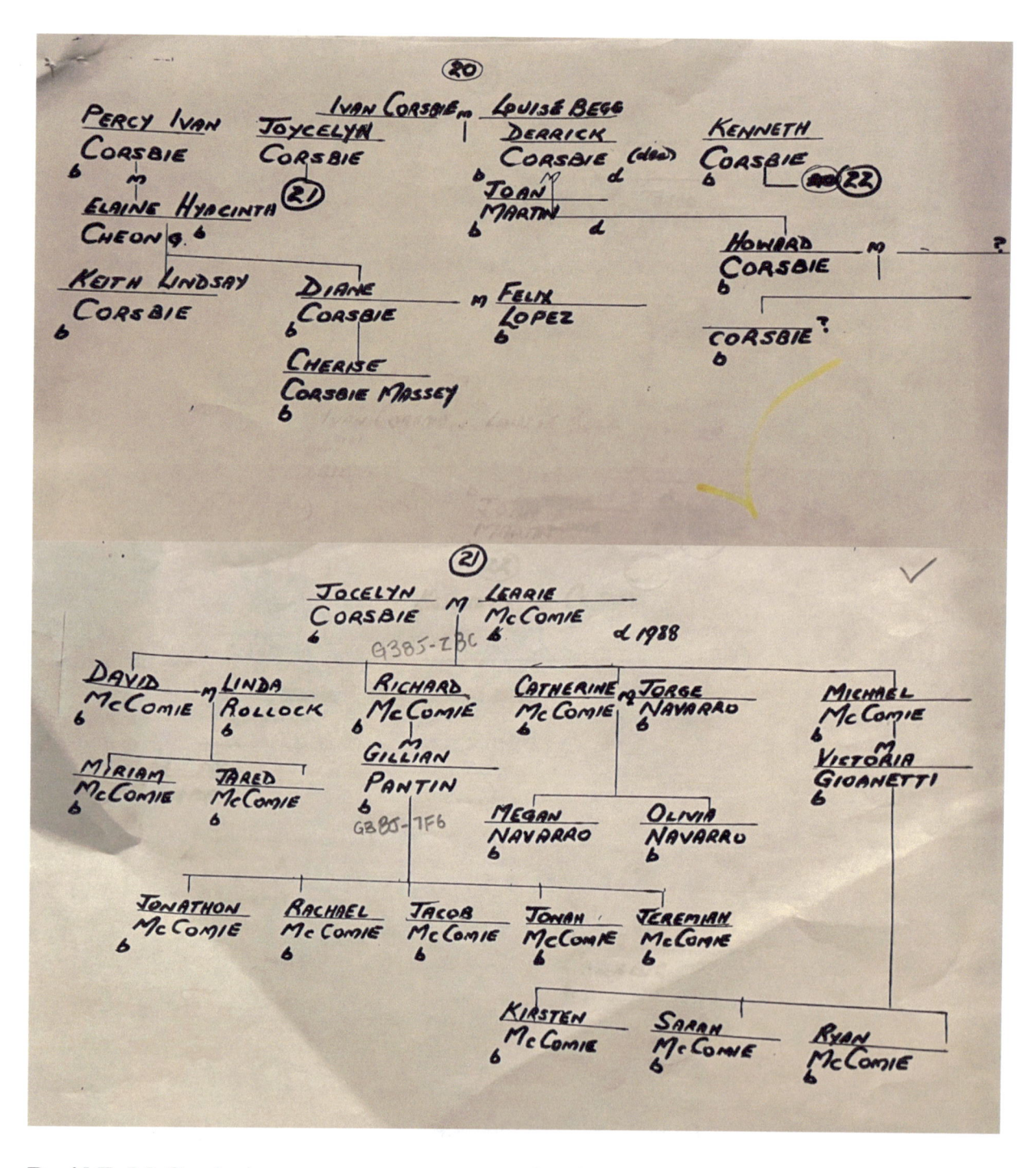

- **Percy Ivan Corsbie** b
  - m **Elaine Hyacinth Cheong** b
  - **Keith Lindsay Corsbie** b
- **Joycelyn Corsbie** (21)
- **Derrick Corsbie** (dec) b d
  - m **Joan Martin** b d
  - **Diane Corsbie** b — m **Felix Lopez** b
    - **Cherise Corsbie Massey** b
- **Kenneth Corsbie** b (22)
  - **Howard Corsbie** b — m ?
    - **_____ Corsbie** ? b

(21)

Jocelyn Corsbie b G385-ZBC m **Learie McComie** b d 1988

- **David McComie** b — m **Linda Rollock** b
  - **Miriam McComie** b
  - **Jared McComie** b
- **Richard McComie** b — m **Gillian Pantin** b G385-7F6
  - **Jonathon McComie** b
  - **Rachael McComie** b
  - **Jacob McComie** b
- **Catherine McComie** b — m **Jorge Navarro** b
  - **Megan Navarro** b
  - **Olivia Navarro** b
  - **Jonah McComie** b
  - **Jeremiah McComie** b
    - **Kirsten McComie** b
    - **Sarah McComie** b
    - **Ryan McComie** b
- **Michael McComie** b
  - m **Victoria Gioanetti** b

David E. McComie is our most recent contact for the Corsbie line and can be reached on our Facebook Group page, titled "Caribbean Genealogy Struggles".

(22)

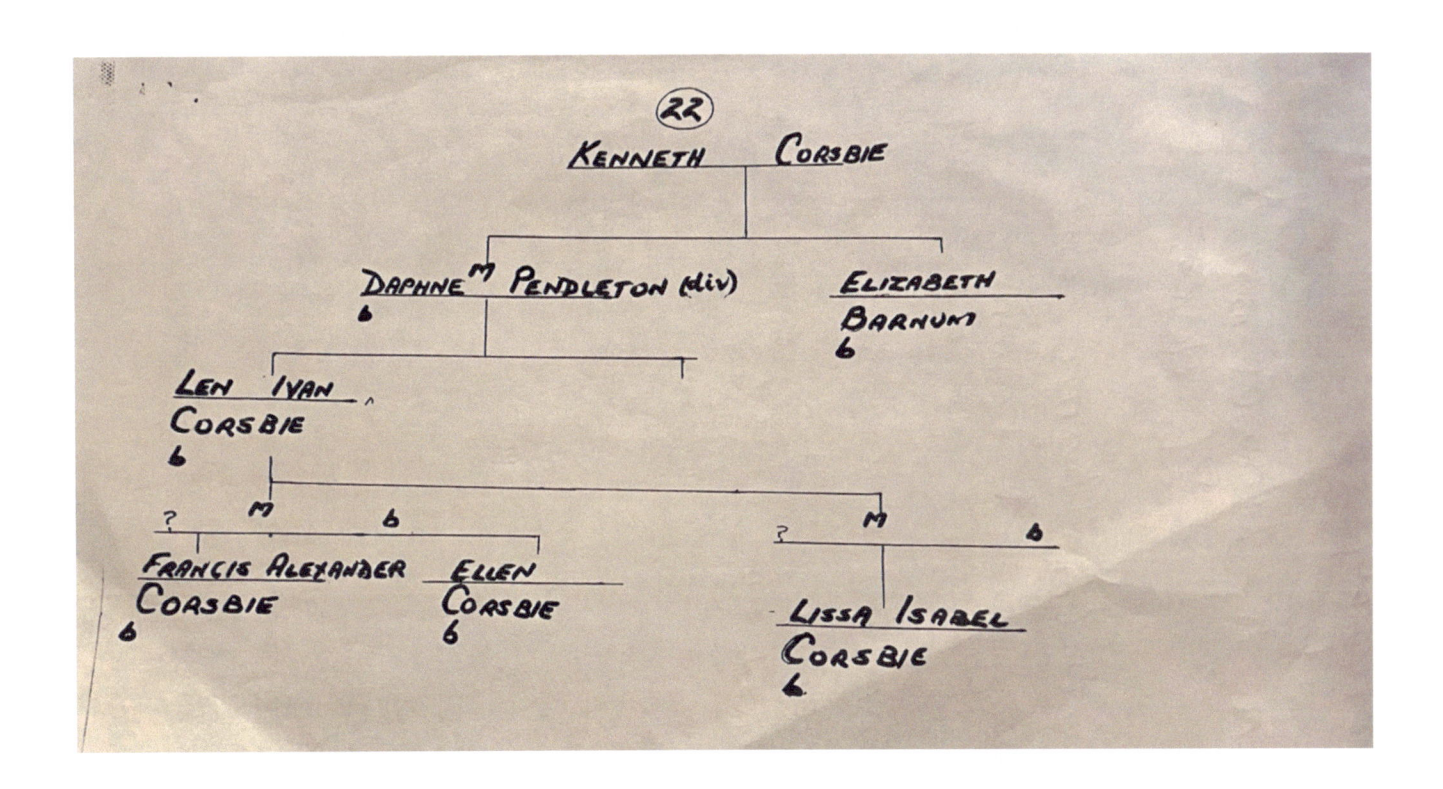

Kenneth Corsbie

- Daphne M Pendleton (div) b
- Elizabeth Barnum b

Children of Kenneth & Daphne:
- Len Ivan Corsbie b

Len Ivan Corsbie:
- ? M ? b — Francis Alexander Corsbie b, Ellen Corsbie b
- ? M ? b — Lissa Isabel Corsbie b

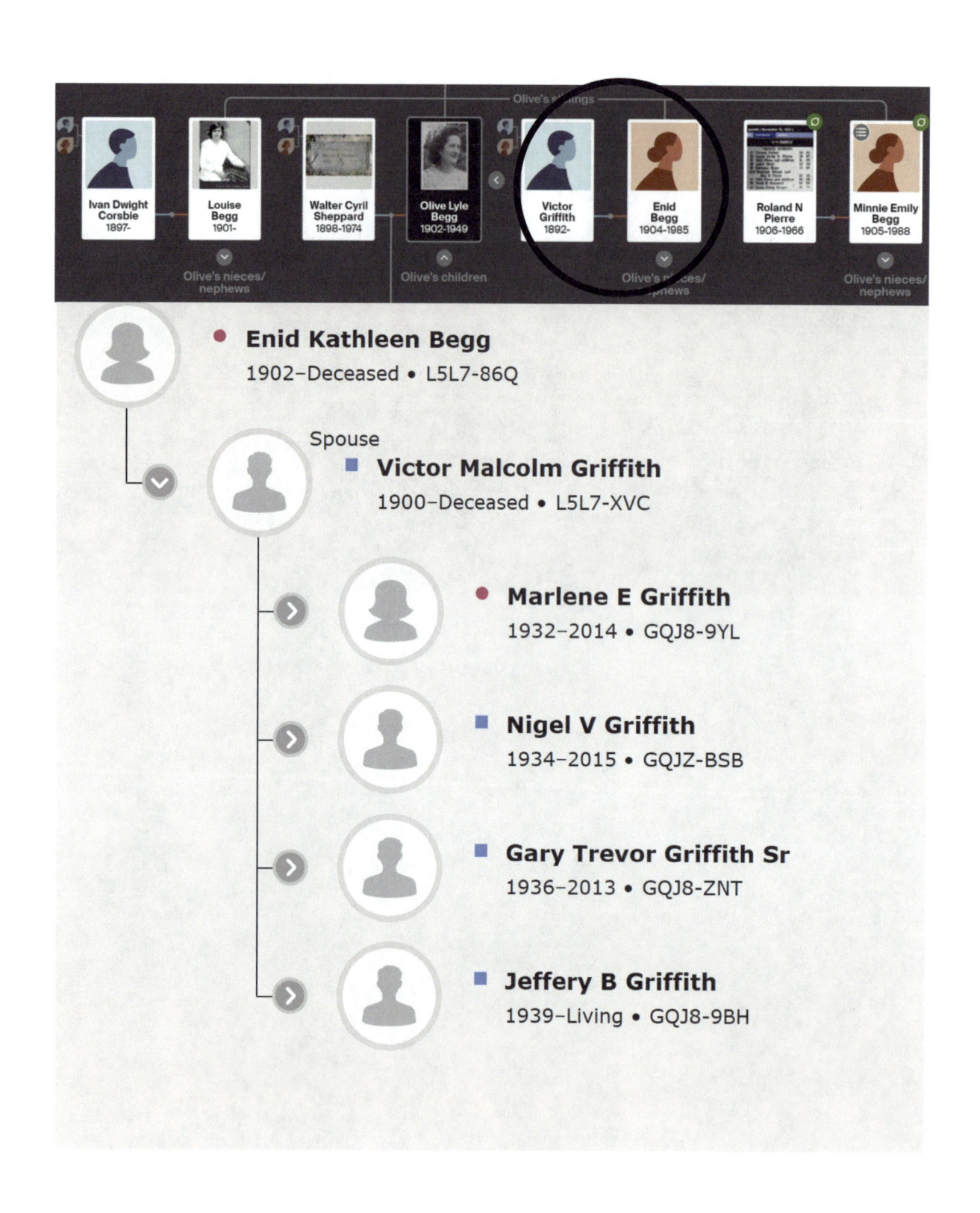

[Ivan Dwight Corsbie 1897-] [Louise Begg 1901-] [Walter Cyril Sheppard 1898-1974] [Olive Lyle Begg 1902-1949] [Victor Griffith 1892-] [Enid Begg 1904-1985] [Roland N Pierre 1906-1966] [Minnie Emily Begg 1905-1988]

- **Enid Kathleen Begg**
  1902–Deceased • L5L7-86Q

  Spouse
  - **Victor Malcolm Griffith**
    1900–Deceased • L5L7-XVC

    - **Marlene E Griffith**
      1932–2014 • GQJ8-9YL

    - **Nigel V Griffith**
      1934–2015 • GQJZ-BSB

    - **Gary Trevor Griffith Sr**
      1936–2013 • GQJ8-ZNT

    - **Jeffery B Griffith**
      1939–Living • GQJ8-9BH

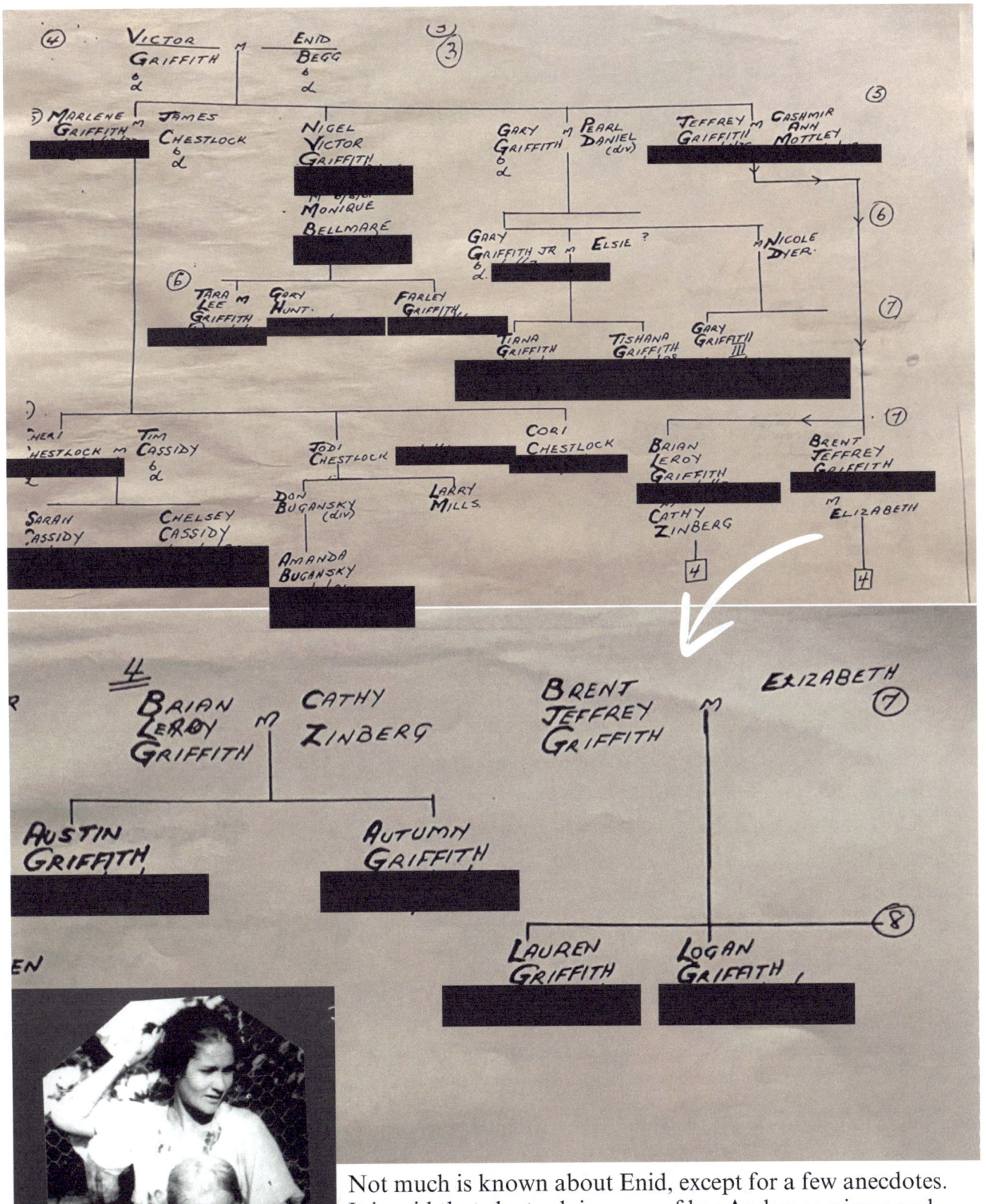

Not much is known about Enid, except for a few anecdotes. It is said that she took in some of her Anderson nieces and nephews who had lost both of their parents.

We also have an article written by cousin Alan De Montbrun about the life of Mary Olive Elizabeth Anderson. It includes information about living with the Griffith family.

Victor and Enid Griffith Family

Enid and Victor Griffith, the three Anderson children, two boys and a girl. The children in the front row are her children.

Mary Anderson was the granddaughter of Richard Benjamin Anderson,

Mary Olive Elizabeth Anderson was born in Auckland, New Zealand, on February 2nd, 1928. She was the first child of parents William Alfred Anderson and Olive May Ross. Two more children would soon follow, brothers Richard Benjamin Anderson on April 28, 1929 and Thorburn John Cunningham Anderson in 1930. Life for the young family would take a dramatic turn on January 22, 1931, when their mother, Olive, would die suddenly from appendicitis. This would leave William with the task of raising their three young children on his own.

William decided to return to the country of his birth, Tobago, where he hoped that his relatives there could assist him with raising his young family. The family packed up all their belongings and made the long sea voyage to the small island of Tobago on the other side of the world. Again, just a few years later, in 1935 tragedy would inflict another cruel blow on the family. William would die, leaving his three children as orphans.

The three Anderson children, Elizabeth (as she preferred to be called), Richard and Thorburn were sent to live in an orphanage in Trinidad, until through the intervention of distant relatives, Victor and Enid Griffith. Enid Griffith (nee Begg) was the granddaughter of Minnie Kirk and her first husband Dr Patterson and she was also left orphaned, or more precisely her mother died in childbirth and her father abandoned her at an early age.

120

The three Anderson children went to live with that family. The Griffiths also had four young children of their own, Marlene, Nigel, Gary and Jeffrey, so space was limited in their small home and the availability of food to feed all adequately was a continuous challenge. Nevertheless, it must have been a significant improvement on life at the local orphanage.

The Anderson boys, Richard and Thorburn however, yearned for the promise of a better life outside of the Griffith home and somehow, before they could even be considered young adults managed to find their way on to a ship to New Zealand. They would never return to Trinidad & Tobago. Elizabeth, now on her own without her younger brothers, found the courage to run away from the Griffith home and take refuge in a local convent in Port of Spain, where she would learn basic homemaking skills. It was sometime during this phase of her life that she met and fell for a young Alfred Hubert da Costa. The couple was married on October 28, 1945 at the St. Francis Roman Catholic Church in the north-east Port of Spain suburb of Belmont. Their first child, Margaret de Montbrun (our contributor's mother) was born soon after. Six more children, Michael, Noel, Anita, Christine, Joseph and Frank would follow in the next fourteen years.

In the 1960s and 70s, the granting of Independence in Trinidad and Tobago, and the rise of the Black Power movement prompted many families in Trinidad, in particular, to consider migration to Australia. Alfred, Elizabeth and children, Michael, Anita, Joseph and Frank da Costa would all eventually answer the call, and initially took up residence in Brisbane, Australia. Noel da Costa would choose another route and ultimately called Toronto, Canada his home. Margaret and Christine stayed in Trinidad & Tobago with their families.

Alfred da Costa succumbed to the effects of lung and throat cancer on December 3rd 1983 in Australia after a lifetime of smoking pipes. He would, however, summon the energy before his death to travel back to Trinidad and Tobago in 1982 to visit his family one last time. Elizabeth da Costa died at the Gold Coast Hospital of a heart attack on August 26, 1991 in Queensland, Australia. She was cremated and her ashes now held at the Allambe Memorial Park in Queensland, Australia. Both Albert and Elizabeth through their efforts and sacrifices have left an enduring legacy including twenty grandchildren and many more great-grandchildren that span several countries. Both persevered, notwithstanding the sternest of obstacles very early in their lives when many others would have faltered.

Article contributor: Alan De Montbrun
(descendant of Minnie Kirk and Richard Benjamin Anderson)

ENID BEGG BIRTH CERTIFICATE

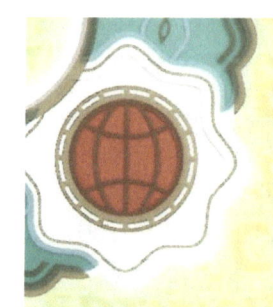

REPUBLIC OF TRINIDAD AND TOBAGO
CERTIFICATE OF BIRTH

SHORT FORM CERTIFICATE, ISSUED WITHOUT PIN

Given Name(s):	*****	Date of Birth:	20TH JANUARY, 1904
Other Name(s):	***** *****	Sex:	FEMALE
Place of Birth:	LOUIS D'OR		
Mother's Name:	KATHLEEN CUNNINGHAM	Father's Name:	JAMES BOWHILL BEGG
Mother's Former Surname:	PATTERSON		
Mother's Prev. Surname(s):	*****		
Occupation:	*****	Occupation:	PLANTER

Informant's Name and Relationship to Child
SAML T W CHARITY
SCHOOL MASTER

Informant's Name and Relationship to Child
*****
*****

Registration Date:	16TH FEBRUARY, 1904	Registration District:	WINWARD DISTRICT IN THE WARD OF TOBAGO
Name of Registrar:	S T W CHARITY	Entry No:	362
		Notes:	

ISSUED UNDER MY HAND AND SEAL OF OFFICE ON
23RD SEPTEMBER, 2022

REGISTRAR GENERAL

CERTIFIED TRUE AND CORRECT EXTRACT FROM THE REGISTER OF BIRTHS, HELD BY REGISTRAR GENERAL'S DEPARTMENT MINISTRY OF THE ATTORNEY GENERAL AND LEGAL AFFAIRS

BA01313740

Olive's siblings

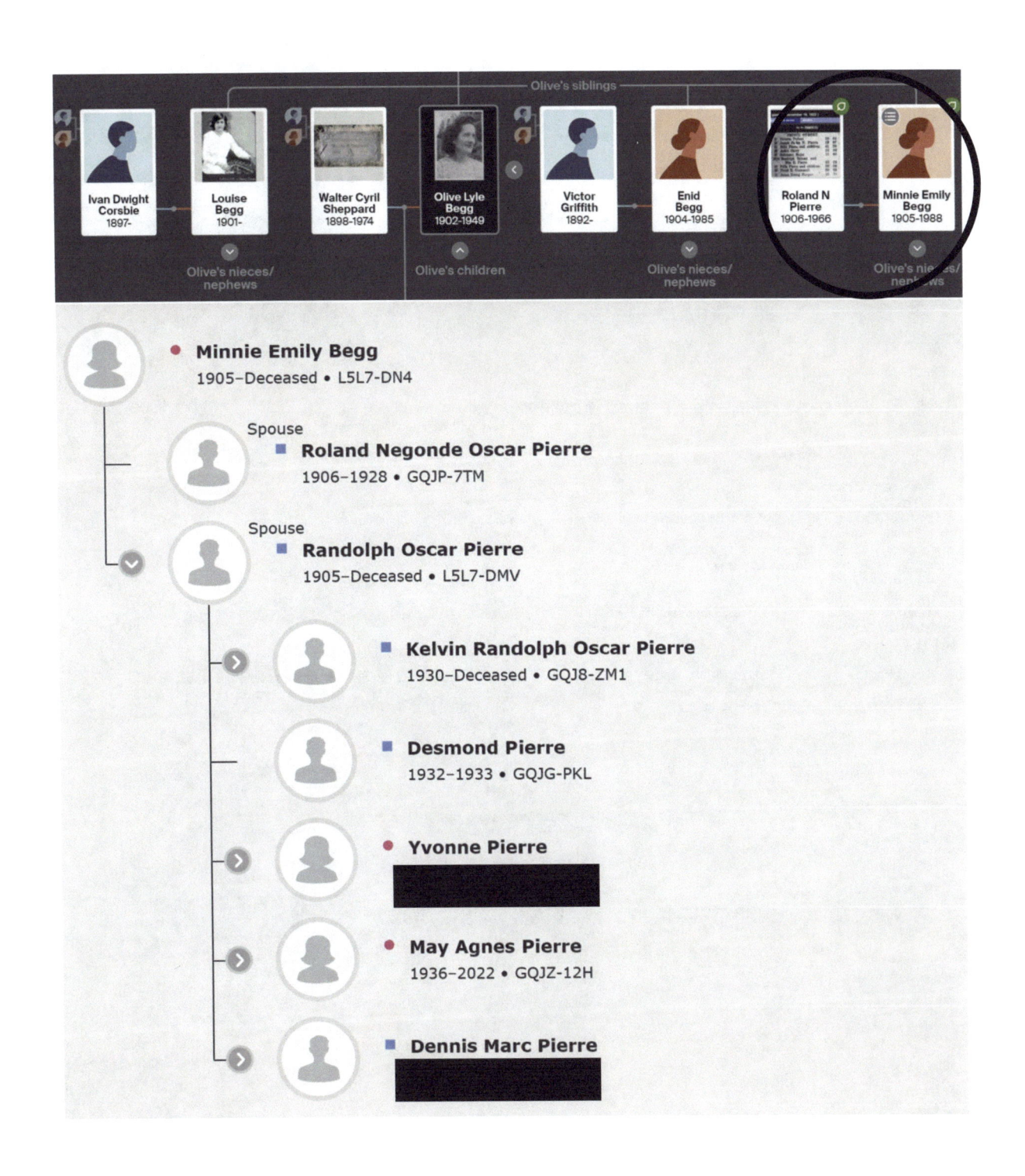

| Ivan Dwight Corsbie 1897- | Louise Begg 1901- | Walter Cyril Sheppard 1898-1974 | Olive Lyle Begg 1902-1949 | Victor Griffith 1892- | Enid Begg 1904-1985 | Roland N Pierre 1906-1966 | Minnie Emily Begg 1905-1988 |

- **Minnie Emily Begg**
  1905–Deceased • L5L7-DN4

  Spouse
  - **Roland Negonde Oscar Pierre**
    1906–1928 • GQJP-7TM

  Spouse
  - **Randolph Oscar Pierre**
    1905–Deceased • L5L7-DMV

    - **Kelvin Randolph Oscar Pierre**
      1930–Deceased • GQJ8-ZM1

    - **Desmond Pierre**
      1932–1933 • GQJG-PKL

    - **Yvonne Pierre**

    - **May Agnes Pierre**
      1936–2022 • GQJZ-12H

    - **Dennis Marc Pierre**

MINNIE BEGG BIRTH CERTIFICATE

REPUBLIC OF TRINIDAD AND TOBAGO
CERTIFICATE OF BIRTH

SHORT FORM CERTIFICATE, ISSUED WITHOUT PIN

Given Name(s): *****

Other Name(s): *****
*****

Place of Birth: ROXBORO BAY

Mother's Name: KATHLEEN CUNNINGHAM BEGG

Mother's Former Surname: PATTERSON
Mother's Prev. Surname(s): *****
Occupation: *****

Informant's Name and Relationship to Child
WILHELMINA SHEPHERD
TEACHER

Registration Date: 21ST JUNE, 1905

Name of Registrar: S T W CHARITY

Date of Birth: 27TH MAY, 1905

Sex: FEMALE

Father's Name: JAMES BOWHILL BEGG

Occupation: PLANTER

Informant's Name and Relationship to Child
*****
*****

Registration District: WINDWARD DISTRICT IN THE WARD OF TOBAGO
Entry No: 78
Notes:

ISSUED UNDER MY HAND AND SEAL OF OFFICE ON
23RD SEPTEMBER, 2022

REGISTRAR GENERAL

CERTIFIED TRUE AND CORRECT EXTRACT FROM THE REGISTER OF BIRTHS, HELD BY REGISTRAR GENERAL'S DEPARTMENT MINISTRY OF THE ATTORNEY GENERAL AND LEGAL AFFAIRS

B A 0 1 3 1 3 7 3 9

Oscar Pierre — m — Octavia Ferdiguer

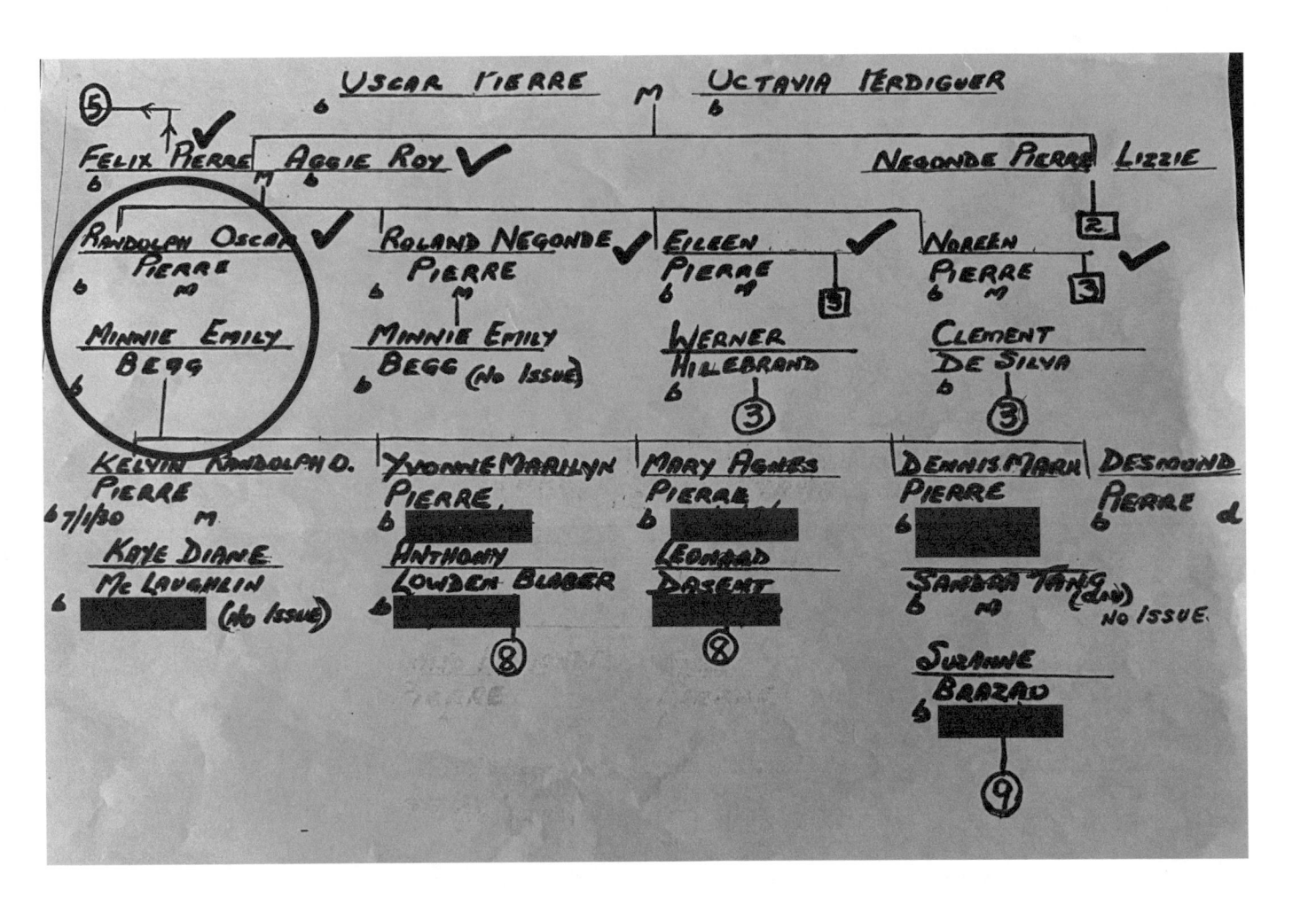

- ⑤ Felix Pierre ✓ — m — Aggie Roy ✓
- Negonde Pierre — Lizzie ②

Children of Felix Pierre & Aggie Roy:

| Randolph Oscar Pierre ✓ m Minnie Emily Begg | Roland Negonde Pierre ✓ m Minnie Emily Begg (No Issue) | Eileen Pierre ✓ m Werner Hillebrand ③ | Noreen Pierre ✓ m Clement De Silva ③ |

Next generation:

- Kelvin Randolph O. Pierre b 7/1/30 m Kaye Diane McLaughlin (No Issue)
- Yvonne Marilyn Pierre m Anthony Lowden Blaber ⑧
- Mary Agnes Pierre m Leonard Dasent ⑧
- Dennis Mark Pierre m Sandra Tang (div) No Issue; Suzanne Brazau ⑨
- Desmond Pierre d

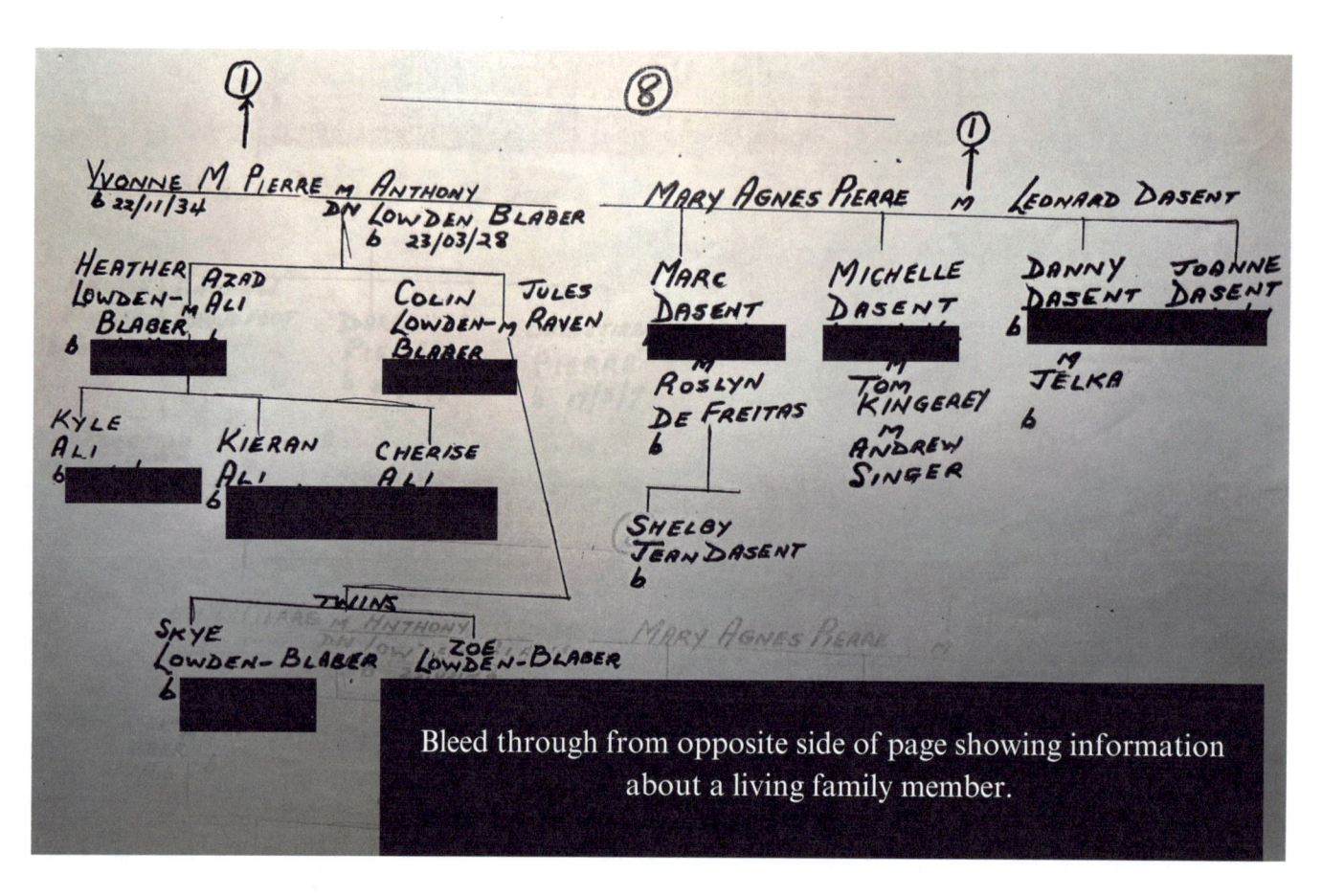

Chart 1 (from ①, ⑧)

Yvonne M Pierre b 22/11/34 m **Anthony D N Lowden Blaber** b 23/03/28

Children:
- **Heather Lowden-Blaber** m **Azad Ali**
  - Kyle Ali
  - Kieran Ali
  - Cherise Ali
- **Colin Lowden-Blaber** m **Jules Raven**
  - Twins: **Skye Lowden-Blaber** & **Zoe Lowden-Blaber**

Mary Agnes Pierre m **Leonard Dasent** (①)

Children:
- **Marc Dasent** m **Roslyn De Freitas**
  - Shelby Jean Dasent
- **Michelle Dasent** m **Tom Kingerey**, m **Andrew Singer**
- **Danny Dasent** m **Jelka**
- **Joanne Dasent**

Bleed through from opposite side of page showing information about a living family member.

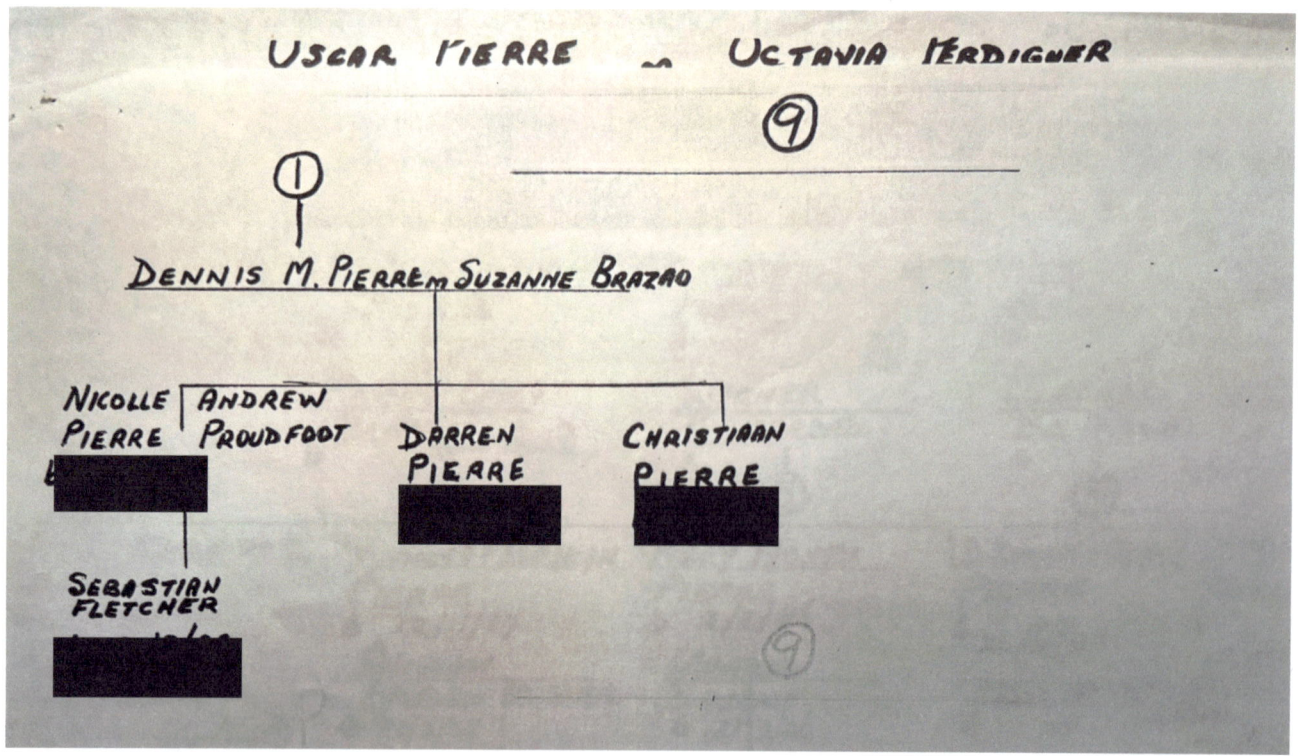

Chart 2

Oscar Pierre ~ **Octavia Herdigner** (⑨)

① **Dennis M. Pierre** m **Suzanne Brazao**

Children:
- **Nicolle Pierre** m **Andrew Proudfoot**
  - Sebastian Fletcher
- **Darren Pierre**
- **Christiaan Pierre**

MAGGIE or Minnie

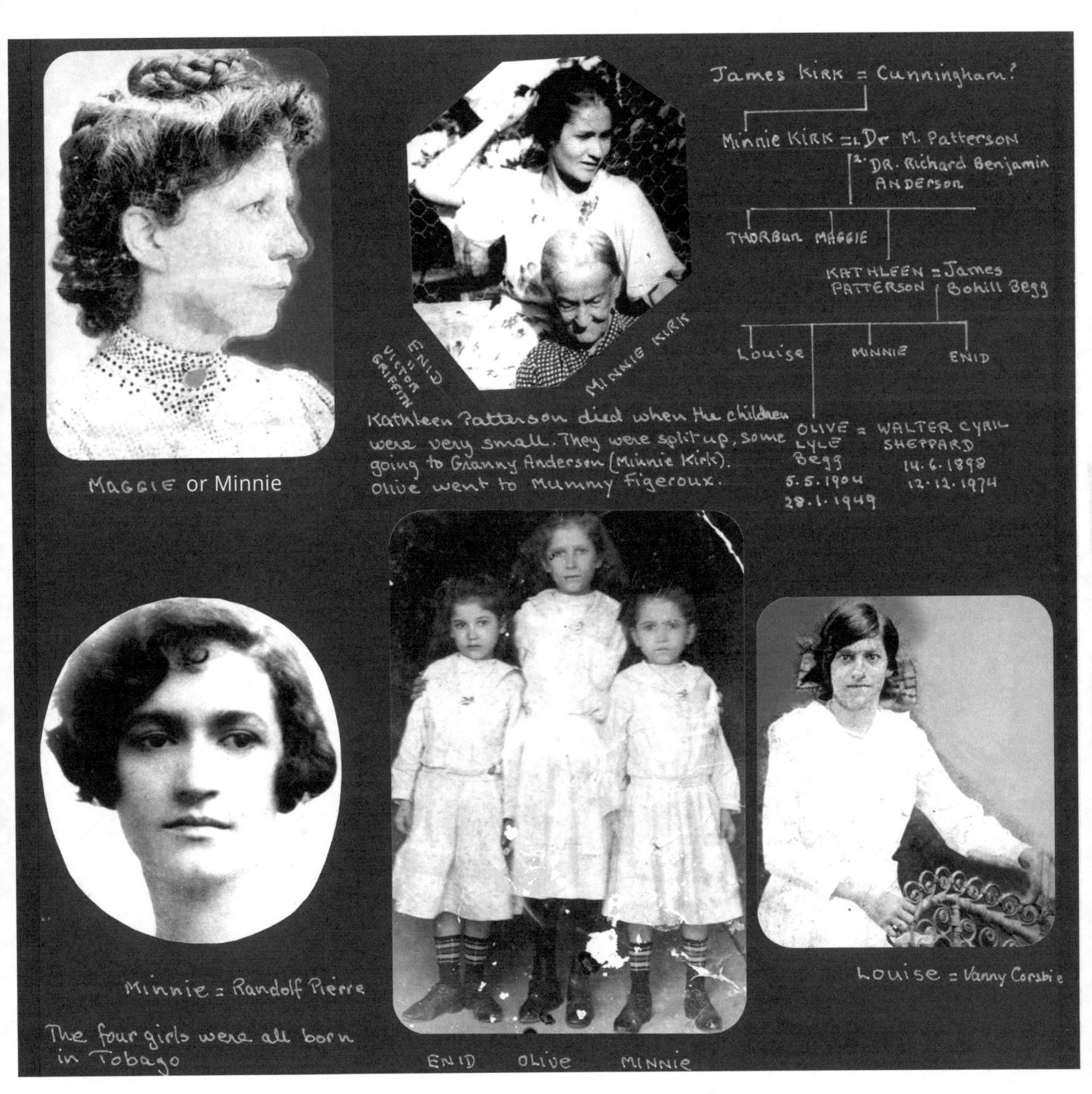

ENID / VICTOR GRIFFIN
MINNIE KIRK

James Kirk = Cunningham?
Minnie Kirk = 1. Dr. M. Patterson
            2. Dr. Richard Benjamin Anderson
   ├── THORBUN
   ├── MAGGIE
   └── KATHLEEN = James Bohill Begg
       PATTERSON
       ├── Louise
       ├── MINNIE
       └── ENID

OLIVE = WALTER CYRIL
LYLE   SHEPPARD
BEGG   14.6.1898
5.5.1904 12.12.1974
28.1.1949

Kathleen Patterson died when the children were very small. They were split up, some going to Granny Anderson (Minnie Kirk). Olive went to Mummy Figeroux.

Minnie = Randolf Pierre

The four girls were all born in Tobago

ENID   OLIVE   MINNIE

LOUISE = Vanny Corsbie

THE KIRK/BEGG SIDE

Generation Four++ Maternal

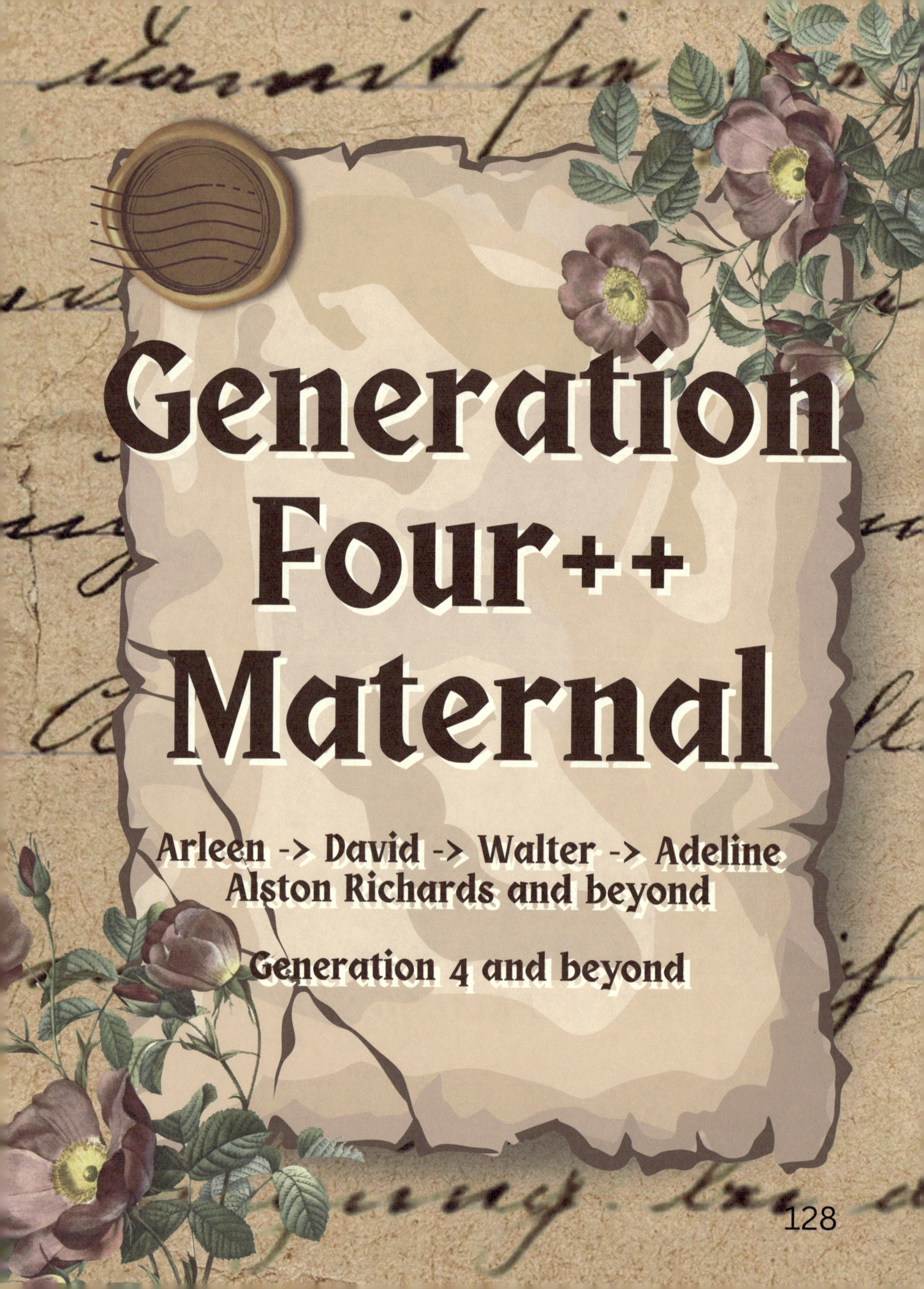

Arleen -> David -> Walter -> Adeline Alston Richards and beyond

Generation 4 and beyond

HISTORY OF ADELINE ALSTON RICHARDS

SABA WITH THE CLOUD

QUICK FACTS:

BORN
ST VINCENT

PARENTS
WILLIAM H RICHARDS
MOTHER UNKNOWN

CHILDREN

Adeline Alston Sheppard (nee Richards)

Not much is documented about the Richards family. Legend has it that their roots trace back to the Netherlands, specifically Amsterdam. The family chart below, kept by Pat Torry (daughter of Walter and Olive Sheppard), details the connection between William H. Richards and Walter and Olive Sheppard. According to the chart, Wilhelmina Arnold and Adeleline (spelled "Adeline" on her death certificate) are sisters. It also indicates that Arthur had a sister named Adelaide. This information is supported by an online genealogy at http://kingsleymccartney.com.

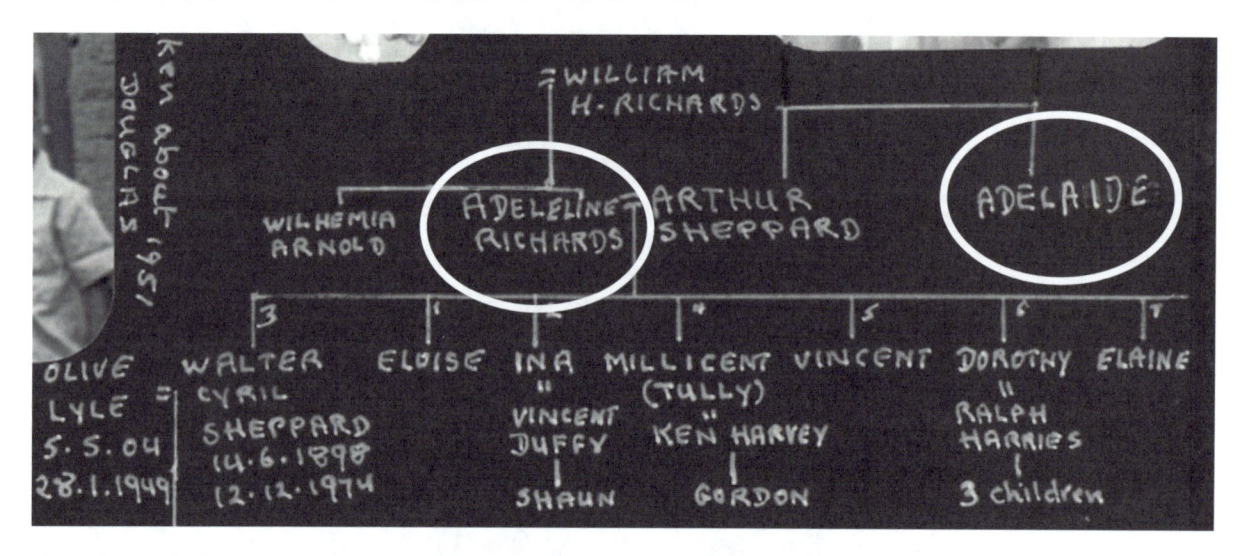

The chart below shows that Wilhelmina is the child of William H. Richards. Her brother is listed as Herbert E. Richards, with another profile marked as private. The space currently labeled as "Private" should be filled with Adeline Alston and John James Richards. Additionally, a few generations prior, Hercules Hazell and Elizabeth Simmons are noted. More information about them will be provided as it becomes available.

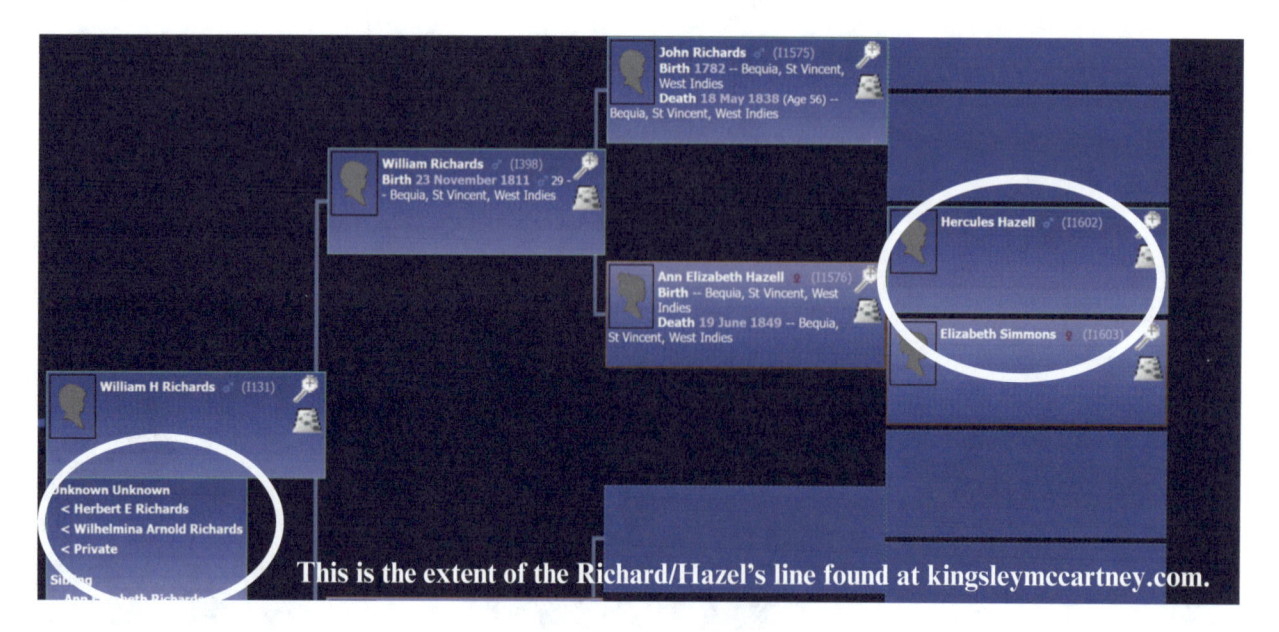

Wilhelmina Arnolds Richards

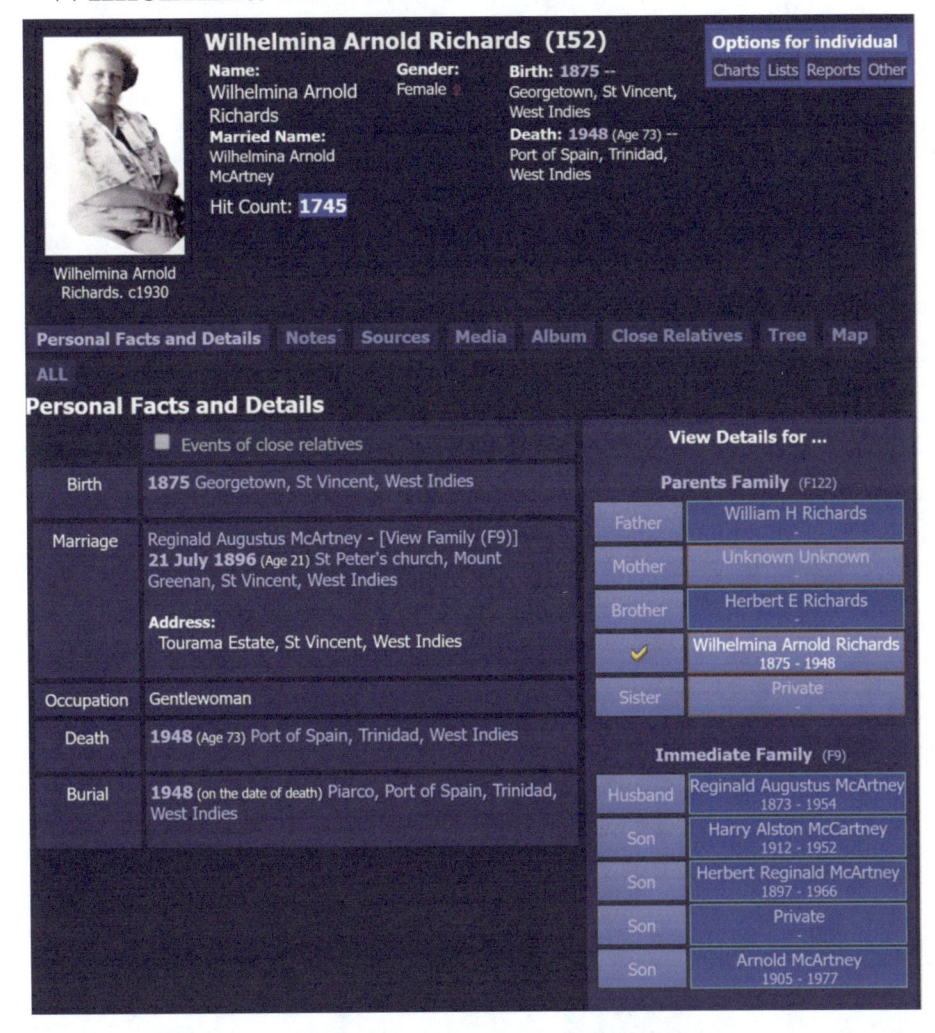

Wilhelmina Arnold Richards (I52)

Name: Wilhelmina Arnold Richards
Gender: Female
Birth: 1875 -- Georgetown, St Vincent, West Indies
Married Name: Wilhelmina Arnold McArtney
Death: 1948 (Age 73) -- Port of Spain, Trinidad, West Indies
Hit Count: 1745

Options for individual: Charts | Lists | Reports | Other

Wilhelmina Arnold Richards. c1930

Personal Facts and Details | Notes | Sources | Media | Album | Close Relatives | Tree | Map
ALL

Personal Facts and Details

☐ Events of close relatives

Birth	1875 Georgetown, St Vincent, West Indies
Marriage	Reginald Augustus McArtney - [View Family (F9)] 21 July 1896 (Age 21) St Peter's church, Mount Greenan, St Vincent, West Indies Address: Tourama Estate, St Vincent, West Indies
Occupation	Gentlewoman
Death	1948 (Age 73) Port of Spain, Trinidad, West Indies
Burial	1948 (on the date of death) Piarco, Port of Spain, Trinidad, West Indies

View Details for ...

Parents Family (F122)

Father	William H Richards
Mother	Unknown Unknown
Brother	Herbert E Richards
✓	Wilhelmina Arnold Richards 1875 - 1948
Sister	Private

Immediate Family (F9)

Husband	Reginald Augustus McArtney 1873 - 1954
Son	Harry Alston McCartney 1912 - 1952
Son	Herbert Reginald McArtney 1897 - 1966
Son	Private
Son	Arnold McArtney 1905 - 1977

Wilhelmina, the older sister of Adeline, was born and married in St. Vincent.

Her first child Herbert was born in St, Vincent and the youngest, Harry Alston was born in Trinidad.

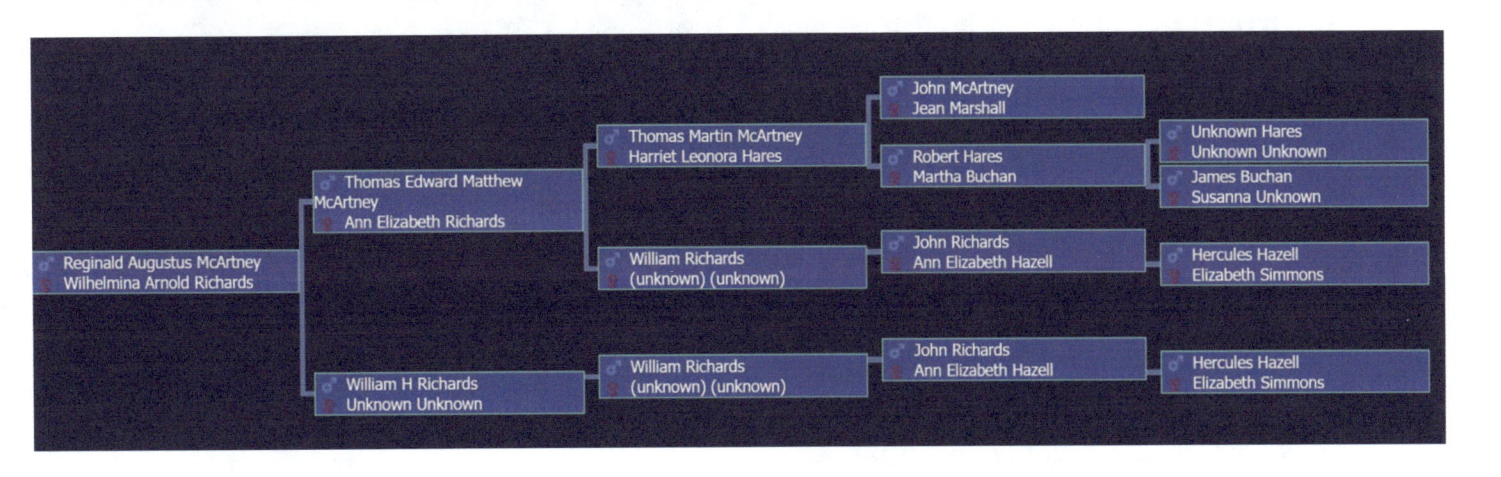

Reginald Augustus McArtney
Wilhelmina Arnold Richards

- Thomas Edward Matthew McArtney
  Ann Elizabeth Richards
  - Thomas Martin McArtney
    Harriet Leonora Hares
    - John McArtney
      Jean Marshall
    - Robert Hares
      Martha Buchan
      - Unknown Hares
        Unknown Unknown
      - James Buchan
        Susanna Unknown
  - William Richards
    (unknown) (unknown)
    - John Richards
      Ann Elizabeth Hazell
      - Hercules Hazell
        Elizabeth Simmons
- William H Richards
  Unknown Unknown
  - William Richards
    (unknown) (unknown)
    - John Richards
      Ann Elizabeth Hazell
      - Hercules Hazell
        Elizabeth Simmons

131

This article appeared in the Port of Spain Gazette 7 Aug 1932. It confirms the relationship between Wilhelmina, Mrs R. McArtney and Adeline. It also confirms the spelling of Adeline.

RICHARDS—On August 6, 1932, at 13 Fitt Street, William Richards, father of Mrs. R. McArtney and Mrs. Adeline Sheppard. Funeral this afternoon at 4.30 to St. Margaret's Church.

Additional family information for Herbert E. A Richards, brother of Adeline and Wilhelmina.

James J Richards was found and added to our family tree. As per usual, he was added and his supporting details were neglected and did not get uploaded. Currently, his details are lost, and the only thing that remains is the joy felt when he was found. Searches will continue to locate the supporting information.

In Loving Memory
- OF -
Herbert E Richards
Born 20th Oct. 1878
Died 6th Feb . 1919
Aged 41 Years

132

Richard's Migration from St. Vincent

In 1902, a volcanic eruption in St. Vincent and Martinique, likened to Pompeii, caused widespread devastation and loss of life. In its aftermath, some members of the Richards family, and possibly the Sheppards, migrated to Trinidad for safety. While it's unclear exactly who moved, Arthur and Adeline were likely already in Trinidad by the time of the disaster. "Ole Auntie," who kept a book referencing the eruption, shared a story with Barbara about the only known survivor—a man in a basement jail who was spared from the deadly gases. The people of St. Vincent, wrongly believing lava was the main threat, were unprepared for the ash and poisonous gases that killed tens of thousands. This tragedy left a lasting impact on the family, linking the Sheppards and Richards to this moment in history.

The Eruption of the Souffrier Mountains, in the Island of St Vincent at Midnight

Painted by Joseph Mallord William Turner in April, 1912.

It was from a Sketch taken at the time by Hugh P. Keane,

The Saint Vincent eruption of 6 May 1902 killed 1,680 people, just hours before the eruption of Mount Pelée on Martinique that killed 29,000. On St. Vincent, a further 600 people were injured or burned and some 4,000 were left homeless

PREFACE.

THE appalling catastrophe which visited the Islands of Martinique and St. Vincent, resulting in the destruction of many towns and nearly fifty thousand lives, horrified every part of the world. The heart of humanity shudders at every calamity which results in the sudden death of thousands of people.

Without warning, the terrible volcanic eruption overwhelmed the doomed cities. In the brief space of only a few minutes a large part of the Island of Martinique was turned into an unparalleled scene of devastation. Few persons escaped the horrible fate that swept a vast multitude to sudden death.

Mont Pelée, a great volcano long ago believed to be extinct, suddenly awoke from the sleep of ages. Out of the mouth of the treacherous crater, around which nestled the summer villas and the pretty homes of the wealthy French West Indian residents, suddenly belched forth smoke and flame. Then, like the discharge from a Titanic gun, the volcanic substances leaped thousands of feet into the air and from the awful cauldron's mouth poured down rivers of fire swallowing everything that lay in their path to the sea. Torrents of red-hot ashes and lava burned the country for miles around.

Mont Pelée, which had been quiet for half a century, gave the first indication of its fatal activity on Thursday, May 1, 1902, a week before the great eruption. Strange noises were heard on that day from the region of the mountain. At midnight of May 3, the volcano belched forth volumes of boiling mud. Disturbances were intermittent after that, doing little damage outside a radius of two miles, until Ascension Day, Thursday, May 8. At 7.50 o'clock on the morning of that day the people of St. Pierre heard a terrific explosion from the volcano. A volume of molten metal and lava was thrown off, enveloping the city and all the shipping in the harbor in one mighty flame. Simultaneously the tidal wave swept the roadstead.

With a single blast of the torrent of flame St. Pierre, covering an area of four miles by two, was on fire. By land and sea all was one seething mass of flame. Nothing escaped. Animal and vegetable life was snuffed out in a moment. Seventy-two hours after the disaster thousands of charred bodies were lying dead on the water front.

A relieving party from the French warship Suchet, on the afternoon of Thursday, the day of the disaster, went ashore. Her captain estimated the loss of life at 40,000, including Governor Mouttet and wife, the General commanding the troops, and one hundred soldiers, who were armed before the disaster to pacify the panic-stricken people and prevent looting.

Huge trees were torn up by their roots and laid flat, scarce one being left standing, and other indications showed that the wave of fire must have passed over this section of the island at extreme hurricane velocity. Every house in St. Pierre, not excepting those that were most solidly built of stone, is absolutely in ruins. The streets were piled twelve feet high in debris and hundreds of bodies could be seen in every direction.

It is known that many persons who sought refuge in the cathedral perished, but their bodies were scarcely visible, being covered with debris. The sites of the club, the bank, the bourse, the telegraph office and the principal shops—everywhere was the same scene of utter desolation and death.

The Island of St. Vincent was also shaken to its centre by a terrible convulsion of Mont Soufriere. Vast destruction in this island was caused by the raging eruption, and here alone more than two thousand persons lost their lives.

This work depicts the scenes following the deadly eruptions of Mont Pelée and Mont Soufriere, the frantic efforts of the inhabitants to escape their doom, the present appearance of the ruined cities and a full description and history of the Islands of Martinique and St. Vincent. It also narrates the magnificent uprising of people everywhere to afford relief to the survivors of the great catastrophe, including President Roosevelt's message to Congress recommending an appropriation of $500,000 by our Government.

CONTENTS.

INTRODUCTION . . . .

CHAPTER I.
APPALLING CALAMITY IN THE ISLANDS OF MARTINIQUE AND ST. VINCENT.—TRAGIC DEATH OF MANY THOUSANDS OF PEOPLE.—DESCRIPTION OF THE ISLANDS.—FRIGHTFUL SCENES OF DEVASTATION . . . .

CHAPTER II.
GRAPHIC ACCOUNTS OF THE GREAT DISASTER.—TRAGEDY COMPLETED IN THE BRIEF SPACE OF A FEW MINUTES.—DESPATCHES FROM UNITED STATES OFFICIALS.—VOLCANIC ISLANDS DESCRIBED.—URGENT APPEALS FOR HELP . . .

CHAPTER III.
MARTINIQUE CITY A HEAP OF SMOKING RUINS.—STREETS FILLED WITH CHARRED BODIES.—LARGE PORTIONS OF THE ISLAND ENGULFED WITH LAVA.—ST. VINCENT ALSO DEVASTATED.—RELIEF FOR THE SUFFERERS . . . . . .

CHAPTER IV.
AWFUL SCENE IN ST. PIERRE—WHOLE MOUNTAIN APPEARED TO BLOW UP.—SHIPS SWALLOWED BY AN ENORMOUS WAVE.—HARROWING TALES BY EYE-WITNESSES OF THE BURNED CITY . . . . . .

CHAPTER V.
PRESIDENT ROOSEVELT'S SPECIAL MESSAGE TO CONGRESS.—LARGE APPROPRIATION BY OUR GOVERNMENT FOR IMMEDIATE RELIEF OF THE SURVIVORS.—ADDITIONAL DETAILS OF THE TERRIBLE CALAMITY.—SCENES BAFFLING DESCRIPTION . . . . . .

https://www.loc.gov/item/02019281/t
another resources: https://www.loc.gov/resource/gdcmassbookdig.destructionofstp00morr/?sp=221&st=image&r=-0.263,0.78,1.442,0.748,0

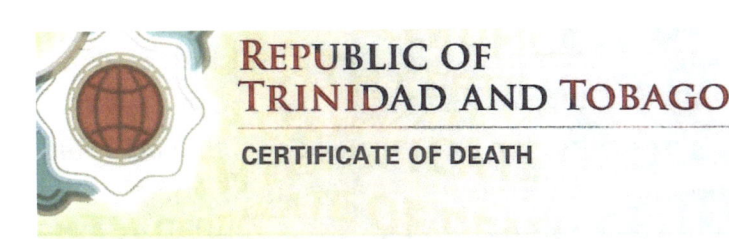

Death Certificates for Adeline Richards (nee Sheppard)

REPUBLIC OF TRINIDAD AND TOBAGO
CERTIFICATE OF DEATH

Name:	ADELINE ALSTON SHEPPARD	Date of Death:	13TH OCTOBER, 1957
Age:	85 YEAR(S)	Sex:	FEMALE
Rank/Profession:	*****		
Informant Name:	MC CLARENCE LALLA		
Informant Address:	4B TRAGARETTE ROAD		
Informant Description:	UNDERTAKER'S CLERK		
Country of Birth:	ST VINCENT		
Place of Death:	34 O'CONNOR STREET		
Cause of Death:	CORONARY THROMBOSIS, ARTERIOSCLEROSIS		

Medical Examiner: DR REID
Registration Date: 14TH OCTOBER, 1957
Registration District: NORTH WESTERN DISTRICT OF PORT OF SPAIN
Name of Registrar: S DUPREY
Entry No: 355
Notes:

ISSUED UNDER MY HAND AND SEAL OF OFFICE ON 08TH SEPTEMBER, 2022
REGISTRAR GENERAL

Death Certificates for William Richards (her father)

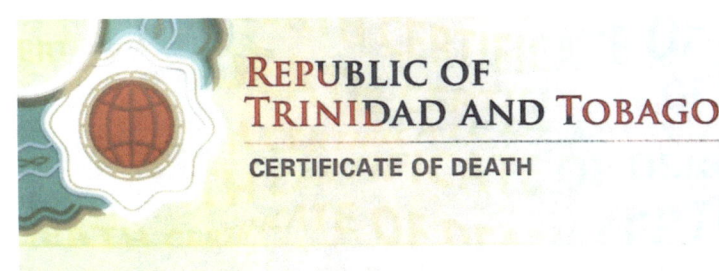

REPUBLIC OF TRINIDAD AND TOBAGO
CERTIFICATE OF DEATH

Name:	WILLIAM RICHARDS	Date of Death:	06TH AUGUST, 1932
Age:	84 YEAR(S)	Sex:	MALE
Rank/Profession:	ACCOUNTANT		
Informant Name:	CHARLES E ARMSTRONG		
Informant Address:	11 TRAGARETE ROAD		
Informant Description:	UNDERTAKER'S CLERK		
Country of Birth:	ST. VINCENT		
Place of Death:	CORNER OF FRENCH STREET AND TRAGARETE ROADS WOODBROOK		
Cause of Death:	AORTIC INCOMPETENCE, ARTERIOSCLEROSIS		

Medical Examiner: DR MC LEAN
Registration Date: 06TH AUGUST, 1932
Registration District: SOUTH WESTERN DISTRICT OF PORT OF SPAIN
Name of Registrar: E WILSON TELFER
Entry No: 267
Notes:

ISSUED UNDER MY HAND AND SEAL OF OFFICE ON 01ST MARCH, 2024
REGISTRAR GENERAL

CERTIFIED TRUE AND CORRECT EXTRACT FROM THE REGISTER OF DEATHS, HELD BY REGISTRAR GENERAL'S DEPARTMENT MINISTRY OF THE ATTORNEY GENERAL AND LEGAL AFFAIRS

This is the family tree showing the intersection between the Hazels and Richards of St. Vincent.

We've already determined from Arthur's obit that he traveled throughout the Islands and finally settled in Trinidad.

Based on Elosie's birth information, it appears that she was the only child born in St, Vincent.

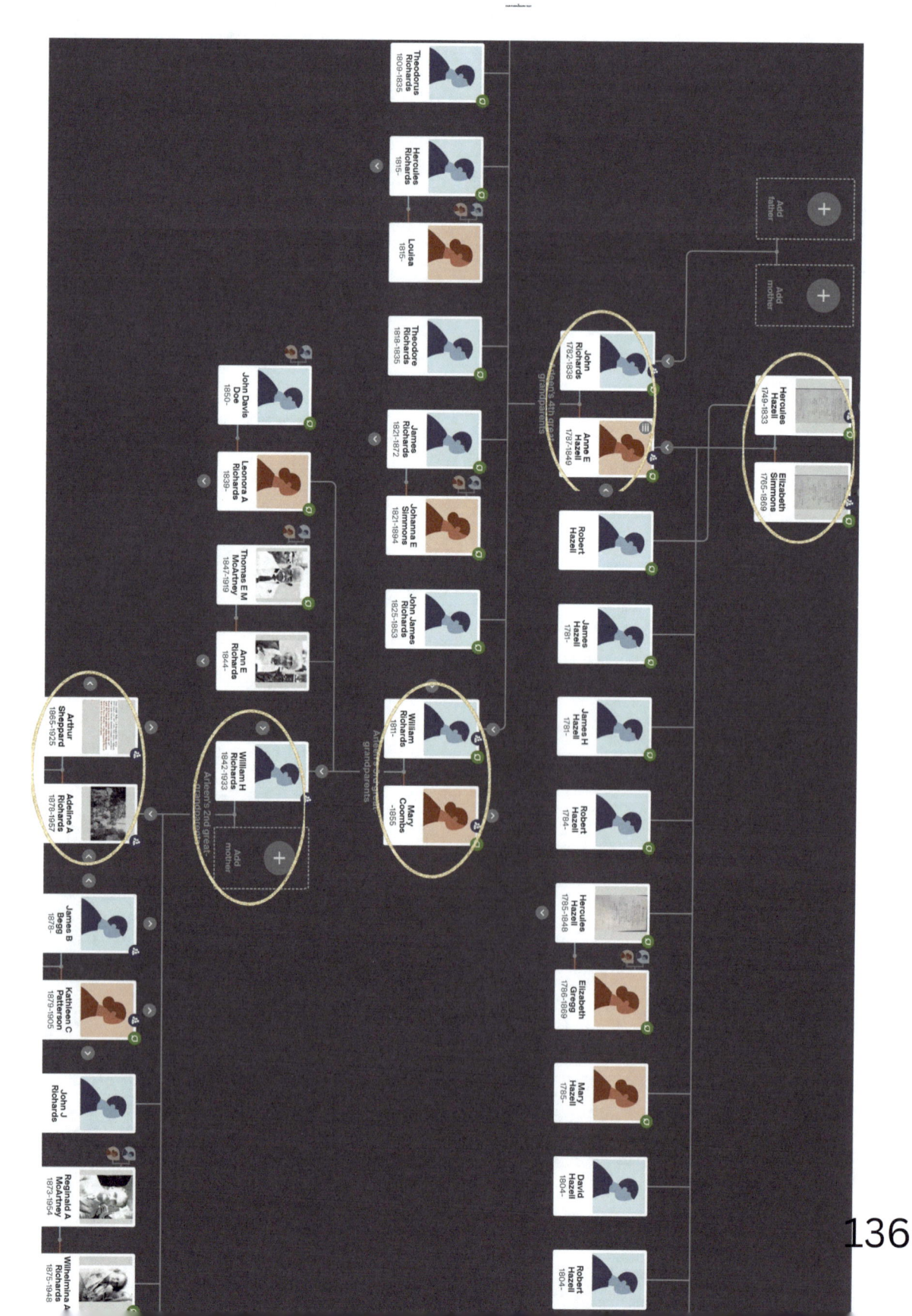

> HERCULES HAZELL.
> WHO DIED IN SEPTEMBER 1833.
> AT THE AGE OF 84 YEARS.
> AND ELIZABETH HIS WIFE.
> WERE AMONG THE EARLY SETTLERS
> IN THIS ISLAND.
>
> THEIR SON
> HERCULES HAZELL
> DIED IN SEPTEMBER 1848.
> AGED 63 YEARS.
> AND WITH HIS PARENTS
> IS BURIED IN THIS CHURCHYARD
>
> ELIZA HIS WIFE.
> DIED IN AUGUST 1869
> AGED 83 YEARS
> AND IS BURIED
> ST GEORGE'S CHURCHYARD, KINGSTOWN
>
> THIS TABLET
> IS ERECTED TO THEIR MEMORY
> BY JOHN H HAZELL

"We do not know which of the Hazel descendants were impacted by the volcano. However, we do know that Hercules and his son, Hercules, as well as John H. Hazel, died before the eruption. The Richards family, on the other hand, had already emigrated to Trinidad prior to the disaster."

"As noted on the following page, Hercules Hazell and Elizabeth Simmons were legends in the Caribbean. A story about them appears in the book Under the Perfume Tree, which is included in the next section. Before we dive into that, here is the headstone for Hercules Hazell, Elizabeth Hazell (née Simmons), their son Hercules Jr., and his wife Eliza. The headstone was erected by John H. (Hercules) Hazel. Ann Elizabeth Hazel married John Richards."

> In
> loving Memory of
> JOHN HERCULES HAZELL.
> WHO DIED
> AT THE ISLAND OF MUSTIQUE.
> 22ND NOVEMBER 1886.
> AND WAS BURIED AT
> ST GEORGES CATHEDRAL
> KINGSTOWN.
> AGED 70.
>
> THIS TRIBUTE IS ERECTED TO HIS MEMORY
> BY HIS BEREAVED AND SORROWING WIDOW.

John Hercules Hazel

1. This is a book and contains many short stories about life in the Caribbean.

2. I have tried to validate the story "Marooned by Pirates" against Saba history, to no avail.

3. There is a historical record of British troops being marooned on Saba in the 1600s.

4. It's an incredible love story. So I want this to be true. Especially since he is my 5th Great Grandfather.

"Hercules Hazell was a prominent figure in the shipbuilding industry and one of the oldest settlers of Bequia (pronounced Beckway).

Our Hazel line connects with the Richards family through the marriage of Ann Elizabeth Hazel and John Richards. Two stories about the Hazell family are featured in the book Under the Perfume Tree. These stories, titled Marooned by Pirates and Emancipation School, are retold by the author Peter Stone. Emancipation School touches on the experiences of enslaved people and the education provided to the freed members of society."

Hercules Hazell 1749-1833
5th great-grandfather
∨
Anne Elizabeth Hazell 1787-1849
Daughter of Hercules Hazell
∨
William Richards 1811-
Son of Anne Elizabeth Hazell
∨
William H Richards 1842-1933
Son of William Richards
∨
Adeline Alston Richards 1878-1957
Daughter of William H Richards
∨
Walter Cyril Sheppard 1898-1974
Son of Adeline Alston Richards
∨
David Allan Sheppard 1931-2022
Son of Walter Cyril Sheppard
∨
Arleen Lorraine Olive Marie Sheppard
You are the daughter of David Allan Sheppard

Marooned by Pirates

Peter Stone

After the European explorers came the European settlers. They did not have an easy time of it. Based on actual events, this extract from the family history **Ten Little Islands** *recreates the struggles of several pioneering Dutch and English families in the late 18th century. Bound for a new life in St Kitts, the emigrants' first experience of the Caribbean was to be chased by pirates and marooned on the sheer rock now known as Saba. Peter Stone, late of Trinidad & Tobago and a direct descendant of the heroic master craftsman Hercules Hassell, tells how the settlers eventually escaped the island; how they encountered free blacks, the slaver Zong and an abolitionist; and how Hassell came to establish the famous boat-building industry in Bequia.*

The Dutch merchantman *Van Dyck*, out of Rotterdam, was bound for Wilhelmstadt. There were Dutch passengers aboard and two English families picked up at Plymouth to be dropped off at St Kitts. These latter were Devon folk, the one family consisting of a schoolteacher named Simmons, his wife and two teenage children, a boy and a girl, and the other family a blacksmith, Henry Newton, his wife and infant son. The vessel had made the crossing in less than five weeks and was still going well when, rounding St Maarten, she acquired a tail. A sloop, flying no colours but mounting a cannon, had suddenly appeared from behind a headland as if intending to intercept. Thwarted in its intention by an adverse tide, the sloop had then fallen in behind and was following in the *Van Dyck's* wake. Clearly the pursuer was a privateer out for a prize.

By crowding on all sail Captain Huysmans was able slowly to draw away from the sloop, and as long as the wind held the *Van Dyck* was safe. But next morning found her becalmed and those aboard staring at a horizon empty save for the topgallants of the pirate just distinguishable above the haze astern. Now the smaller vessel would inexorably close the gap. The calm might last a week and if the sloop could come alongside and her crew of cut-throats board the merchantman, Captain Huysmans knew the women and children in his charge would not be spared.

*

The longboat was lowered, provisioned for a week and the oars manned by the four sturdiest of the ship's Dutch crew. The burliest of these, as petty officer in charge, was the ship's carpenter, Hercules Hassell, "Tiny" to his shipmates.

"Head south-south-west, Hassell," called the captain as the boat, laden to the gunnels, pushed off from the ship's side and pulled away. "My chart shows no land within rowing distance, but I see a tall cloud stationary there upon the horizon, which must mean an island within two days' row. God be with you."

"And with you, Meinheer," replied Hassell. "We'll pray for a wind before the sun rises once again on this comfortless sea."

All that day and the following night, with the male passengers taking spells at the oars along with the crew, the rowers headed south-south-west. At dawn the next day there was no cloud in view ahead of them, but where it had been there could now plainly be seen the more substantial shape of a mountain. Wearily they plied the oars, and slowly as the day progressed the mountain grew larger and more distinct. Above them seabirds circled in the blue. Occasionally a shoal of flying fish would start up at their approach and skim away across the sea surface, and once a pod of whales, their black shapes rising in turn to blow, crossed their bows too close for comfort. To help the rowers the passengers sang rowing songs, canticles and hymns.

Towards evening a breeze sprang up and, freshening, whipped the sea into white horses, speeding their progress to the land still some twenty miles off. Whether the wind had come in time to save the *Van Dyck*, they could not tell. Dawn of the third day found them seeking a landing place as they rowed along a forbidding coast of sheer cliffs. There was no sign of habitation anywhere and little vegetation that they could see on the bare, treeless slopes of the mountain. At one point they were encouraged by a thin stream of water cascading down from a cleft in the rocks high above them. At least there was fresh water to be had ashore.

They had gone about halfway round the island to the leeward side before they spotted a possible landing place. It was a steeply shelving strip of shingle beach, upon which the waves lapped gently and behind which the hill, though steep, seemed scalable. The cove, too open to provide shelter for boats in a storm, would serve as a starting-point for an exploration of what the voyagers now knew was a desert island, consisting of a solitary mountain rising abruptly out of the ocean.

They had escaped the horror of death at the hands of the pirates only to find themselves doomed to a life of privation in the most primitive conditions. From now on, it was clear, they would have to look to the sea to furnish their sustenance; but there, thank God, there was every sign of abundance. And there was so much to be thankful for. They had survived, and while there was life there was hope.

As the keel of the boat crunched on the shingle and the bowman, painter in hand, leapt onto the beach, cormorants from the surrounding rocks rose screaming a protest at the invasion of their sanctuary. Once ashore the emigrants knelt and gave thanks for their deliverance.

Having made the boat secure, Henry Newton, familiar with the cliffs of the south Devon coast, pioneered the easiest gradient upwards from the beach. Then the whole party, each carrying what he or she could bear of the boat's provisions, set off upwards in single file. Two hours later, some fifteen hundred feet above the beach, they came to the first level ground. It was an area of about three hundred acres, stretching between two spurs of the mountain. Beyond this a gully descended from the upper slopes, broadening lower down into a ravine with a stream beside which, sheltered from the storms, grew many shrubs and trees. They recognised clumps of bamboo, and also banana plants, many with bunches to be had for the picking. Calabash and guava trees grew in profusion, and a plant which they later discovered to be cassava. The ubiquitous coconut, however, had not been able to find a foothold anywhere on the rocky coastline.

On this plateau, with the main massif of the mountain still towering above them, they established their base and called it Bottom. The plateau itself was well grassed, and if they only had stock to graze it would make a good pasture. To the teenage children, David and Elizabeth Simmons, all this was the most exciting adventure and they roamed everywhere. They were still exploring the plateau when the heavens opened and drenched them with a sudden downpour. The tall cumulus which had been their guide from afar, rebuilt every day over the mountain, and with a shower every afternoon kept the island fresh and green. They had only to dam the gully just above the level of the plateau to obtain a permanent water source.

Excavating a rock pool in the gully produced a supply of boulders that were put to good use in the construction of a dry wall, as a windbreak against the prevailing easterly sweeping the plateau. The blacksmith Newton was delighted to recognise among the rocks the blood red of the iron ore haematite. While three men worked on the wall, Hassell put three others to cut branches from the trees of the ravine and to fashion them into rude shelters for their first night ashore.

That night, from the declination of the pole star, Hassell reckoned their new domain was seventeen and a half degrees north of the equator. Looking out from this mountain home under the starlit sky, the emigrants saw Christ's blood streaming in the western firmament and, far beyond the eastern horizon, the red glow of a ship on fire. The wind had freshened too late to save the *Van Dyck* from the maurauders. And the castaways' hearts went out to the captain and crew who had so generously arranged their escape.

In time the party, resourceful people all, learnt how to survive, even to flourish, in their new colony. Under the direction of Hassell, timber was selected from the trees of the valley, felled, rough-hewn with axes and built into huts, one per family, thatched with banana leaves. For the first three years they kept a huge beacon high on the mountain, ready to be lit at any hint of a sail on the empty expanse of sea around them. But in all that time the beacon was lit only twice, and on neither occasion did it attract the ship which in the night hastened past the smoking mountain as if it were a live volcano. The island was off the regular shipping route and stray vessels were all too wary of hidden reefs in these uncharted waters.

Eventually the castaways all became resigned to life on their mountain; all, that is, save one. Hassell. He knew that if the islanders were ever to make a decent life for themselves, they would need supplies of many kinds, but especially of livestock and the seeds for fruit and vegetables. To get these supplies they would have to trade, but to do that they would have to re-establish links with the outside world, and they would have to do this by their own efforts.

As to what they might trade, all they would have to offer in exchange for the bare necessities of life would be the products of their own handiwork, in particular Hassell's own. The island had iron ore in abundance, but as far as they knew was otherwise devoid of mineral resources. Sisal, however, grew everywhere. Elizabeth Simmons, a girl of lively intelligence, had recognised the plant, having once seen an illustration of its inflorescence in a botany book, and she knew that rope could be made from it. The women set to work with a will to harvest, dry and card the leaves into fibres and then plait them into rope. They found too, that one of the taller grasses could, by a similar process, be made into a coarse material like burlap or sackcloth, useful at a pinch for rough clothing and very serviceable sails. Meanwhile Newton extracted metal from the iron ore, and with an improvised anvil fashioned nails and even horseshoes. Hassell himself was a master craftsman, a shipwright, and knew how to build a boat. With a team of willing helpers, keenest of all the two flaxen-haired Simmons youngsters, he set up a boatyard and slipway. Elizabeth, now sweet seventeen, spent every day making herself useful in a dozen ways about the boatyard. Hassell found the dedication of his two willing apprentices greatly eased his labours and he began to notice that Elizabeth was growing very attractive. Elizabeth, privately, idolised the large, imperturbable man who always seemed to know what needed to be done and how to do it.

For his boat-building Hassell had chosen a design that he knew well, a six-metre Dutch drogher of proven seaworthiness, high-bowed, half-decked with a mast and cabin forward of midships, rowing position, an open cockpit astern and cutter-rigged sail. Designed to withstand North Sea gales, the boats, properly handled, could take a big sea.

When Hassell and his team had built six of these fishing boats and the wind stood fair for the Leeward Islands, he lashed the six boats together in line astern, five metres apart. The six cabins were laden with horseshoes for ballast and coils of new rope for trade. On each boat Hassell hoisted a makeshift lateen sail and, with David Simmons as mate in the aftermost vessel, he set off to the east, expecting to make landfall in St Kitts or Nevis. With him went all the hopes of the islanders and the heart of one fair maid. There could be no second chance, for Hassell's string of boats had used up the tiny island's entire stock of timber.

The mountain was still visible astern of them when a thick leaden pall crept out of the east and spread over the sky blotting out the sun, the wind turned northerly and ahead of them the sky became ominously black. High above, strange, udder-like clouds appeared. Hassell read the signs and could see they were heading straight into an advancing hurricane. In the mountainous waves blown up by such a wind the little flotilla would face certain destruction. Their only hope was to keep as far as they could away from the centre of the storm. Guessing the cyclone would track north, he turned due south and ran before the wind and the rising sea. There were, he reckoned, still some hours before the main force of the hurricane would strike. If in that time they could gain even fifty sea-miles to the south, it might be enough for them to escape the worst of it.

Not fifty, but some two hundred miles to the south they were swept by the gale-force winds and turbulent seas. When the rising sea caused his chain of boats to straggle out of line, David trailed a sea anchor from the sternmost and Hassell maintained just enough sail on the lead boat to tauten the ropes between them and so keep some semblance of his in-line formation.

At the height of the storm a British man-o'-war, scudding on bare poles before the wind, suddenly loomed out of a rain-squall dead astern and bore down on them, narrowly averting a collision by going hard to port at the last moment and passing them broadside on. The deck officers could be seen looking down with astonishment at the spectacle of young David on the crest of a mountainous wave, sodden to the skin, bailer in hand, vaulting precariously like a mountain goat from the bucking prow of one drogher into the ducking cockpit of the next. By timing his spring for the top of the rise, he ensured that the cockpit of the boat ahead was some feet below him.

On the poop of *HMS Thetis*, without waiting for an order, the keen-eyed midshipman sprang to the helm, wrested it from the bosun and twirled it rapidly.

"What are you at, Tom?" roared the Admiral. "You damn near ditched us. Straighten up, blast you."

"It's the boats, Uncle – we almost rammed 'em," Tom shouted back over the continuous uproar of the wind in the rigging.

Admiral Sir Alexander Cochrane did as his nephew bid him, looked down over the starboard beam, and saw Hassell's straggle of boats sliding past.

"Extraordinary! What are droghers doing here? They've no business to be out in this weather. Poor fellows! They'll never make it, I fear. But there's nothing we can do. Already we are leeward of 'em and there's no beating against this."

"I thought they were coping rather well, Uncle. Did you see the lad with the calabash hopping across?"

Tom Cochrane, more sanguine than his uncle, was serving with the flagship of the North America and West Indies

Squadron. They had a rendezvous with Nelson in Antigua, but had been forced by the hurricane to turn south. For three years *HMS Thetis* had patrolled the American coast from Nova Scotia to Florida and back again on the routine interception of contraband runners, with never a hint of action, and Tom was bored. He had come to know the ports of Halifax, Chesapeake Bay and Fort Lauderdale intimately. The port women didn't interest him; all he craved was a chance to show his mettle in a real naval action, preferably against the French, but any enemy was better than none. His heart had gone out to the half-naked lad, leaping gazelle-like between the droghers, and now again lost in the murk astern.

Hassell's string of droghers skirted the rim of the storm. After three days the wind abated and the sea subsided. Hassell and David, who were exhausted but by dint of David's continuous bailing still afloat, found themselves bobbing on a sunlit sea off a chain of green, palm-fringed islands stretching as far as the eye could see. They headed for the nearest one. And so Hassell first came to Bequia.

It's an ill wind ... Here now was a real haven, a deep, sheltered bay with a beach of gleaming white sand and, behind it, a thickly wooded hillside. Between the beachside coconut palms could be seen a single, palm-thatched dwelling, home presumably of the black fisherman who sat at his oars in the middle of the bay, holding a line over the side of his boat. In the stern of the boat sat a boy, his son perhaps, the two of them gazing apprehensively at the new arrivals and their sea train. Having decided that the strangers were not slave catchers, the fishermen hailed them across the water and Hassell replied in his Dutch-accented, Devonian brogue. Neither at first realised that the other was speaking English. The newcomers understood, however, the welcoming gesture which beckoned them ashore. Hassell and his mate beached the string of boats and homespun rope was less successful; it was coarse and lacked consistency and the finished appearance of the manufactured article. But Hassell knew it was not lacking in strength, and rather than sell it cheaply he kept it for his own use.

With the money he received for his boats he bought copper nails, screws and fittings, canvas, sailmaker's needles and twine, an axe, a saw, a file, a marlin spike, oakum and a caulking iron, and several kegs of hardtack and salted beef. In the sixth boat he returned to Bequia to build a vessel large enough to transport all the inhabitants of the island mountain to Bequia and re-establish the colony in that more friendly island. The fisherman, his wife and son were at present the only inhabitants of Bequia. They were Maroons who some years before had escaped in a stolen rowing boat from St Vincent.

On the foreshore Hassell built a slipway and on it mounted a cradle. Within six months, working sixteen hours a day, David and he had completed the keel and hull of a fifty-cubit schooner. Another three months and the masts had been stepped and the hull decked. A year after he started, the *Esmeralda*, displacing some thirty tons, had been launched by the fisherman's wife and a bottle of rum. Rigged and equipped and provisioned, she rode at her moorings in the bay ready for her maiden voyage. Her shiny pitch-black hull and homespun cordage gave her a distinctive appearance. She looked every inch a tramp. François and Twan made up the crew.

The *Esmeralda* called first in Kingstown to register. The office of Registrar-General had just been created under a new ordnance. A happy-go-lucky young man called Charlie had been appointed to it, his only qualification being an elegant copperplate hand. Charlie had set himself up with a table and chair and a stack of empty ledgers and official forms in the corner of a warehouse on the quayside. He sat there all day ready to register anything, from a birth, marriage or death to a title deed, patent or trademark, or even a cow if requested. He thought of his registers as in a race with each other. Births were well ahead of the field; a long way behind came deaths; and then a poor third came marriages. The rest were non-starters. Until Hassell turned up Charlie had never registered a ship and wasn't at all sure how to do it. Confronted with the applicant in person and the prescribed fee of half-a-crown, Charlie seized an empty ledger, wrote "Register of Ships" in large flowing capitals at the top of the first page, and then below that, Number One, Tuesday, November 11th, 1791. He got everything right except the name of the owner, which he spelt Hazell. After the boat-builder had left, Charlie, judging by Hassell's command of English, entered his nationality as British. This was how the entry appeared in the Royal Gazette, the official monthly publication that served St Vincent as its only newspaper. To Vincentians thereafter Hassell was Hazell and, with the ownership of a British Registered vessel, an honorary Briton. It was all the same to him.

When the news got around that he was headed north, he was asked to deliver a cargo of ground provisions to Roseau in Dominica and to drop off some passengers there. In Roseau, the northbound *Esmeralda* loaded limes, lemons and other citrus for Basseterre, St Kitts. The voyage was proving more profitable than Hassell had expected. In Basseterre he bought livestock and poultry and headed due west.

Some fifteen months after he had last seen the mountain, Hassell recognised the cloud that had first taken him there and, with the wind behind him, he that evening anchored off the same shingle beach on which he had first set foot so long before. This time the whole population, having seen his sail from afar, and Elizabeth having guessed who it was heading straight for them, had come down to the shore to greet him. All except Elizabeth had given the two mariners up for lost in the great hurricane that had struck the mountain soon after their departure.

But his great plans to take them all back to Bequia had a mixed reception. In his absence there had been changes. The island and its little settlement had been officially discovered. More than four years earlier, under cover of darkness, the captain and crew of the *Van Dyck* had themselves escaped the pirates in the ship's remaining boat and, rowing east, had made land on St Kitts. But it had been more than a year before the captain had got back to Holland and reported to the authorities, and another two years before the Dutch government could be stirred into taking some action to discover the fate of the missing passengers, and then another before the navy despatched a frigate to search for survivors.

Cruising off the island mountain, the frigate lookout had seen smoke arising from halfway up the mountain, and closer inspection through a spyglass had revealed the little settlement of Bottom. The frigate captain planted a flagstaff at Bottom, named the island Saba, after Sheba's ancient realm, claimed it for the Dutch and hoisted the Dutch flag. In an age when contending fleets were ranging the Caribbean, history does not record that any other power thought it worthwhile to dispute the Dutch claim.

Two of the settlers had accepted the frigate captain's offer of a passage with him back to Holland. Most of them, however, found the equable climate of Saba much to their liking. Austere as the life might be, they had grown accustomed to it. Henry Newton who, as a boy, had known all the bays and inlets round Plymouth Sound, preferred the life of the sea to the toil of the forge, and with his wife's agreement was content to stay. Later he established a foundry for ships' anchors and found his product much in demand, especially in Bequia. Mr and Mrs Simmons would have gone with the frigate, but Elizabeth, now a young woman, inexplicably declined to accompany them, saying she would wait for her brother's return. And so it was that only the Simmons family left Saba with Hassell on the *Esmeralda*, and they sailed with him only as far as St Kitts.

*

The sea was calm. Long after the others had turned in, Hassell and Elizabeth sat together at the helm through the moonlit Caribbean night, and dawn found them miles off course. The same afternoon the *Esmeralda* docked alongside the Basseterre quayside. At the far end of the quay, the *Zong*, a larger vessel, was tied up. From the stench that wafted their way from time to time, she was clearly a slaver whose cargo was even now being auctioned off to a group of eager buyers, the slaves having been bathed and spruced before being offered for sale. To François, *Esmeralda*'s bosun, it was an all too familiar scene and he deemed it prudent to stay out of sight lest the crew of the *Zong* should mistake him for one of their cargo.

Later, when the crowd had dispersed and the quay was deserted except for the unsaleable remnants of the auction, François ventured ashore and along towards the *Zong* through the discarded humanity of the sick and crippled, all those unable to stand up to be sold and now abandoned by the slavers to their fate. He was astonished to hear himself hailed by a young woman in his own West African dialect. She was sitting up with her back to a cask nursing one leg, her ankle horribly swollen. He went up and spoke to her, discovering that, like himself, she was an Ibo and came from a village not far from his own. Her name was Mbala. Like all the slaves she had suffered cruelly from the three-month voyage in the hold of the slaver, and was worn and emaciated but, apart from her ankle, in surprisingly good physical condition. Left to herself she would certainly die and become carrion for the vultures circling overhead. François helped her up onto her good leg and half-carried her back to the *Esmeralda*.

The next day Hassell agreed that Mbala might come with them back to Bequia once she had been seen by a doctor. The doctor diagnosed a severe sprain and prescribed complete rest. They were casting off when a gentleman unseasonably garbed in a frock coat and top hat appeared on the quay beside the *Esmeralda*, carrying a portmanteau. He hailed Hassell with, "Are you going to Nevis?"

"We can do," replied Hassell. "The fare is ten dollars, come aboard."

During the next two hours they learnt that their passenger was a Mr Wedgwood, maker of chinaware, who was visiting St Kitts and Nevis on behalf of the Anti-Slavery Society. He had witnessed the *Zong* auction and was still seething with indignation at the inhumanity of it. He did not recognise Mbala as one of the unsold remnants. When he was told her story, Wedgwood assured them all that the matter would be raised in the British House of Commons by their spokesman, William Wilberforce. Their society was gaining ground with every year that passed, with the object of abolishing the nefarious trade.

Mbala spent the voyage on deck refusing to go below. By the time they reached Bequia she was able to hobble up the beach. In three months' time her ankle was as good as new, and in three years she and Twan were married according to Ibo rites.

Hassell and Elizabeth were married in the Anglican Church in Basseterre and returned to Bequia as Mr and Mrs Hazell. They remained on the little island for the rest of their lives, as Hercules applied all his skills to developing the most successful schooner-building industry in the Caribbean. Simmons the schoolteacher took a post as head of a government secondary school in St Kitts and David became skipper of the *Esmeralda*, plying for many years up and down the Windward and Leeward Islands.

The *Esmeralda* became a familiar sight in all the ports of the islands, her masts always readily distinguishable by their shrouds amidst the forest of masts along any quayside. She was known throughout the islands as "The Shaggy Lady". In 1806 the southbound *Esmeralda* ran into some heavy weather, and under the stress of the motion an expectant woman passenger who had boarded in Dominica started labour. Mrs Warner hadn't been due for another ten days, by which time she should have been safely in married quarters with the regiment in Trinidad to which her husband, Major Warner, had been posted. There was no other woman aboard. David kept on as much sail as he dared in the hope of getting his passenger to a midwife in St Vincent but it was not to be. In the event, Charles Warner, future Attorney-General of Trinidad, was born at sea off St Vincent. Ten years later David, weekending in Basseterre with his parents, met and fell in love with a visiting schoolteacher. Having married her, he handed the *Esmeralda* over to his first mate Twan, and set himself up as a shipping agent in St Kitts.

A year after their marriage Elizabeth bore her husband their first son, Robert Hazell, who was to grow into a strapping lad. Robert learnt the shipwright's craft from Hercules, becoming as skilled a woodworker as his father. His brother, young Hercules, preferred the life on the ocean wave and his youth was spent plying between the islands as a Royal Mail packet, the only link of the smaller islands with the outside world.

On Hassell's retirement, Robert took over and continued the business of building and selling schooners for the island trade.

List of Male Slaves belonging to Hercules Hazell Junior

Names	Colour	Employment	Age	Country
William	Negro	Sailor	20	Creole
Thomas	Do.	Invalid	85	Do.
Providence	Do.	Fisherman	21	Do.

List of Female Slaves belonging to Hercules Hazell Junior

| Caroline | Negro | Washer | 20 | African |
| Christianna | Do. | Cook | 35 | Do. |

The Total Number of Slaves belonging to H. Hazell Junr. is Five
Sworn 11th September 1817
by Hercules Hazell Junr.

Caribbean Slavery Rears It's Ugly Head

It's true; our Family members were slaveholders.

1833–34 No More Slave Trade
Great Britain passes the Slavery Abolition Act in 1833. The law, which took effect in 1834, abolished slavery in most British colonies, freeing more than 800,000 enslaved Africans in the Caribbean and South Africa as well as a small number in Canada.

1834-1837 Apprenticeship Period
The British government decided to begin to free the slaves through apprenticeship. The British decided they would try apprenticeship before the total emancipation of the slaves to see if this system of more gradual change worked. Apprenticeship was a form of wage labor because ex-slaves were paid for their labor, but it was not completely free because they were obligated to work for a specified set of hours and for a specified person. Although this situation was better than total slavery, it still was not total freedom.

1838 Emancipation
The British government decided to begin to Still, once apprenticeship began, education on the island began to flourish. During apprenticeship, and after emancipation finally became a reality, education was a priority for the ex-enslaved.

Interesting Details of the Slave Roll Above:
The males were Creole, and the females were African.
Thomas was an Invalid at 85 years old.
William and Providence jobs were as a Sailor and Fisherman respectively.

"The next page features a story about John H. Hazell and his work at the Emancipation School. This marks the end of the Hazel line for this book. There is a wealth of information available about the family in Bequia, and the family tree includes more names than listed here. For further research, try a simple Google search or explore online family history trees. Interestingly, actor Chris Pratt is our 13th cousin, tracing his lineage further up our ancestral line."

Emancipation School

John Hazell

Following its settlement by Europeans, the island of Bequia flourished, and so did the Dutch-English descendants of Hercules Hassell, the hero of the preceding account. In his brief autobiography **The Life of John H Hazell**, *Hassell's grandson, who was to serve as Speaker and later President of the Legislative Assembly, Assistant Justice of the Supreme Court and member of Queen Victoria's Privy Council, sketches a contemporary view of the developing society in this tiny island during the early 19th century. The following extract touches on Hazell's own role in the process of Emancipation, as a 12-year-old charged with educating the "benighted Africans"; he betrays an attitude towards Bequia's slaves that is in marked contrast to the romanticised views attributed to his grandfather.*

The 29th day of March, 1817, was the all-important day which ushered me into existence. My parents, poor but honest and respectable citizens, lived in an obscure little fishing village in the island of Bequia, the principal of the Grenadines, under the Government of St Vincent. At the time I chronicle Bequia boasted of a church of its own, with a full-blown rector, two resident medical practitioners, a stipendiary magistrate, and a church clerk and schoolmaster, besides several resident proprietors who, with the managers of estates, their families and a few respectable mechanics and mariners, constituted the Society of the Island, among whom my parents held a respectable position.

My father, the younger Hercules Hazell, not caring to follow in the footsteps of his respected parent – "who was a designer of marine craft, vulgarly called a 'shipbuilder'" – but having imbibed in his infancy a love for the element for which his paterfamilias designed his craft, became a seafaring man. Having purchased for himself a tiny craft of about thirty tons, he took to trading intercolonially, and engaged his craft frequently in HM Mail service. In those days we were not favoured with bi-monthly visits from the Royal Mail Company's steamers, but were only honoured with a monthly mail, conveyed to Barbados by a gun brig, and intercolonially by small sailing craft.

While in this service – not a very lucrative one – my father would be often from home for months, and my mother, an industrious old soul, kept house and brought up a large family, of whom I am the third son and fourth child, as best she could, by sending out to the villagers, in such quantities as would best suit their wants, the commodities my father would from time to time bring home from foreign parts. Our neighbours quaintly termed these commodities "the importations". These "importations" not being on a very extensive scale rendered it necessary for the observance of the strictest economy in the management of our household and family affairs, and required that each member of the family should be early trained to the system of self-support, there being no prospects of an endowment fund being established in our family.

Elder brothers, as a rule, are the most favoured individuals in a family and so it was in mine, if the fact of our firstborn brother's being placed at a private school in Kingstown, the seat of Government, can be considered, as we all looked upon it then, as an act of grace and favour. We younger ones served an educational apprenticeship under a very old lady with a large pair of spectacles on her nasal organ and a huge bunch of keys and scissors suspended at her side, "the usual ornament of housekeepers in those days." She taught us the Lord's Prayer and the Ten Commandments in the vulgar tongue, and the alphabet, and to write "BA ba" in large black letters, and impressed each lesson upon the juvenile mind, or rather back, with a three-pronged leathern strap, which had grown black from age, but not rusty from want of use.

After serving our apprenticeship at this model school we were placed at the parish school to finish up our education! I may consider myself, however, the most fortunate of my brothers in that respect, as just at the time I had to finish my scholastic attainments my mother's brother was appointed to the dignity of clerk of the church, catechist and schoolmaster. This threefold office was rendered necessary by the action and philanthropy of the Anti-slavery Society, Bishop Coleridge considering it advisable to send forth to the slaves, "in imitation of John the Baptist preparing the way for the coming of the Saviour", catechists to prepare the way for the coming of emancipation, whose duty it was to teach the old as well as young their prayers and catechism.

At that time I had the good luck to be the head boy in the school, and no doubt continued to be so as much from my being the nephew of the schoolmaster and, therefore, more at his service and command, as from any superior attainments I possessed! Be that as it may, however, I had the good fortune, not that I considered it so at the time, to be selected by him to accompany him on his daily visits to the benighted Africans to teach them their duty to the Master of their souls and Creator of their bodies, so as to fit them to become masters of themselves.

These visits were usually performed in the mornings between six and eight, when the whole gang were supposed to be mustered in the factory to receive a lecture, hear prayers read, and be taught their prayers and catechism. My name being John, the reader may easily imagine me, a boy of twelve or thirteen, comparing myself to John the Baptist, when walking two or three miles in the morning by six o'clock, and for an hour or more drilling the Lord's Prayer and the Creed into the craniums of half-savage Africans.

I would not have it understood, however, that I objected to this sort of work, as my uncle was very kind, and I always reaped more than compensation for the assistance I rendered him in the attention shown to me by him, and the pains he took in endeavouring to impart to me as much of the knowledge he possessed as I was capable of acquiring. After a time I looked on this work as a privilege, as it seemed to give me a status among my schoolfellows as well as my scholars, of which I was not a little proud, and I gradually began to consider myself a dominic of the first order.

Having obtained the permission of my mother, I established a night school for adults, mainly for the purpose of teaching them their prayers, which they seemed anxious to learn. It must not, however, be supposed that this sacrifice of time in a boy of thirteen was from philanthropy. I may, perhaps, be entitled to take credit for a tinge of such feeling, but there were little contributions of fruit, eggs, and occasionally a fowl, which served as a stimulus and incentive to teaching, and were found very useful as aids to housekeeping.

I must not be considered egotistical in thus minutely describing, as I will be found to do, the various ways in which I sought to aid myself, or endeavoured to aid my parents in supporting me. My object in writing this memoir is to teach my children and grandchildren, should it be their lot to have to make their way in the world, how their father battled from his childhood, and how by dint of industry he succeeded, under God's blessing, to an honourable position among his fellowmen. If, on the other hand, my descendants are saved the toil and trouble of battling with fortune, as their father has had to do, to obtain his daily bread through his own exertions, then that they may learn to respect the honest and industrious person, however humble his position, and, if it is in their power, to encourage and help him with their countenance and support.

I undoubtedly must from nature have been imbued with a spirit of industry, and a very strong feeling of that kind of independence which makes one shrink from relying on another for aid of any kind, as I have lively recollections of assisting at tailoring my own clothes, helping to make bread for the household, and obtaining my boots or shoes by teaching the village shoemaker to read and write, while I myself was at school.

When I was fourteen my uncle, for some reason that I cannot now recollect, nor is it important for me to do so, resigned the appointment of clerk of the church, and for three months I was duly installed as acting clerk, having on two or three occasions previously performed this important duty when my uncle, from sickness or absence, was unable to do so. I thus received the first salaried pay I ever earned from the public treasury, through the hands of George Hartley Esq, treasurer, with no little pride. Having done so, my active mind did not allow me to remain a schoolboy much longer.

I made one or two voyages with my father in his sloop *Messenger*, having been still fourteen years old when, in 1831, I had assisted at the repairs of this vessel, working as an apprentice at the ship carpenter's trade. My father taking charge of his sloop and returning to his occupation at sea, I accompanied him. But I proved a very bad sailor, and suffered so much from seasickness that, after a voyage to St Thomas and one to Barbados, I sought and obtained employment in the grocery and liquor store of Alexander Glass Esq, a Jewish Scotchman, whom I served until the early part of 1834. I then sought and obtained employment in the lumber and provision business of Adam Skelly Esq, a Scotch merchant and dealer in estates' supplies, whom I served to the day of his death, in 1840. I finally closed his business in 1841. Having accomplished this I commenced my own career in business, of which I will write hereafter.

Generation Four++ Paternal

Arleen -> David -> Olive -> James Bowhill Begg and beyond

HISTORY OF JAMES BOWHILL BEGG

Alexander Begg 1850-
2nd great-grandfather
∨
James Bohill Begg 1878-
Son of Alexander Begg
∨
Olive Lyle Begg 1902-1949
Daughter of James Bohill Begg
∨
David Allan Sheppard 1931-2022
Son of Olive Lyle Begg
∨
Arleen Lorraine Olive Marie Sheppard
You are the daughter of David Allan Sheppard

QUICK FACTS:

BORN
TOBAGO

PARENTS
FATHER - ALEXANDER BEGG
EMILY GRACE GORDON BOWHILL

CHILDREN
CHRISSEE, WM HUGH, JOHN GERALD, JAS BOWHILL

JAMES BOWHILL BEGG

"There is limited information about James Bowhill Begg, mostly family lore and two inconsequential newspaper articles. However, the Begg family history in Trinidad is primarily centered around Toco, where a large contingent of Beggs resides, and many are likely related. James Bowhill Begg married Kathleen Cunningham Paterson, but their marriage was short-lived. After Kathleen's early death due to complications from her pregnancy with their youngest daughter, Minnie Emily, James left his daughters with family and friends. His departure also led to the estrangement of the Begg family from the girls during their formative years. The girls lost touch with their aunts, uncles, and extended family, including grandparents, who were all part of James's exodus.

Barbara Williams recalls either visiting or hearing about Aunt Chrisse in Tobago, remembering her as having died young. The other Begg brothers settled in Toco, the nearest port to Tobago. They claimed work as engineers, and both William Begg and James Begg (Uncle Jimmy) worked on the road between Toco and Port of Spain. A street, Begg Lane, was named in their honor in Trinidad.

Cousin Kathleen Green has traced parental matches for Emily Grace Gordon Bowhill. While I don't have verified sources for this information, I'm including it because Kathy has corroborated this connection through her DNA. Though I'm not well-versed in DNA research, I trust Kathy's findings."

I asked on our Facebook Group, *Caribbean Genealogy Struggles* "Has anyone heard about a road in Toco named Begg Trace?" The following is a conversation with cousin, Kathy Green about the road.

Note: Toco is the most northern part of Trinidad and the closest point to Tobago. Toco was also the headquarters for the Begg brothers and their families.

Kathy Green
Yes I do. According to my mom Jean (Begg) de Silva it's in Toco, Trinidad. The road or trace (a small road) is named after Gerald and James Begg who worked building the roads in that area. My mom said that Gerald lived in the area where the road is situated.

1y   Like   Reply

Arleen Sheppard Froemming Author Admin +2
Kathy Green James Begg my Great grandfather, James?

1y   Like   Reply

Kathy Green
Arleen Sheppard Froemming yes.

1y   Like   Reply

Kathy Green
Arleen Sheppard Froemming don't know if James or as my mum called him Uncle Jimmy married again not sure how long he lived there. But I do believe that Gerald had at least one child. My mum's brother Harold also lived with them.

1y   Like   Reply

Arleen Sheppard Froemming Author Admin +2
Kathy Green thank you for even having a inkling about this. Many thoughts scrambling about my brain. As far as I know, James died a bit before his granddaughter, Olive died. So I think it's somewhere in the 1940s. My dad had vivid memories of him and if the approximate time he died.

1y   Like   Reply

Kathy Green
Arleen Sheppard Froemming it's such a pity no one thought to write all this down. Would have been lovely if they told us all this.

Roads Crews building roadways in Trinidad

164

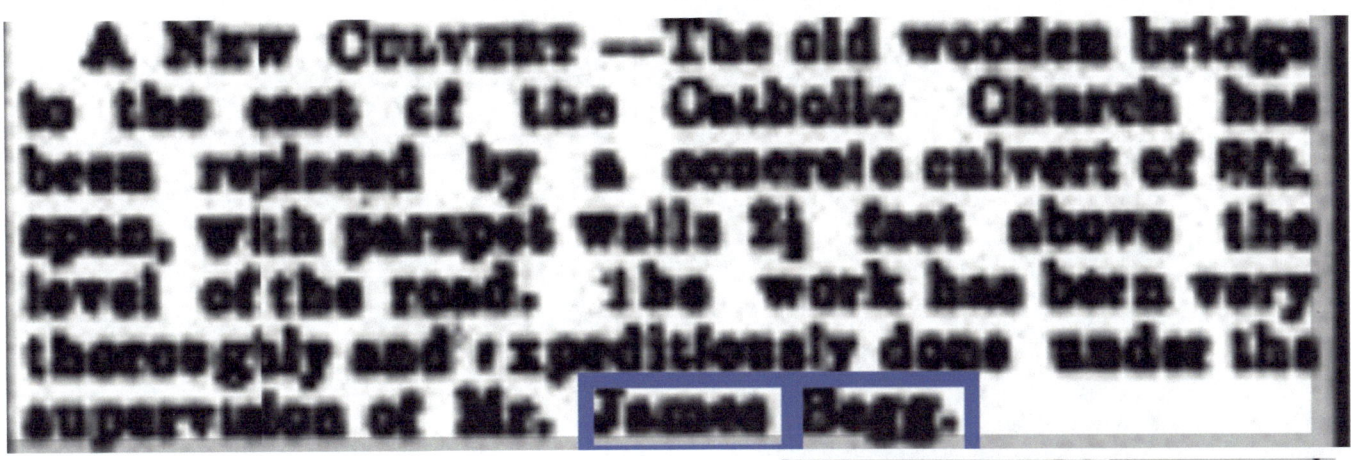

A NEW CULVERT.—The old wooden bridge to the east of the Catholic Church has been replaced by a concrete culvert of 8ft. span, with parapet walls 2½ feet above the level of the road. The work has been very thoroughly and expeditiously done under the supervision of Mr. James Begg.

Transcription

A New Culvert -- The old wooden bridge to the east of the Catholic Church has been replaced by a concrete culvert of 8ft span, with parapet walls of 2 1/2 feet above the level of the road. The work has been very thoroughly and expeditiously done under the supervision of Mr. James Begg

TOCO.

FUNERAL OF MR. JOHN A PATIENCE.

It is with regret that we announce the death of Mr. John A. Patience, proprietor of San Souci, son of Mr. George Patience of Toco, proprietor. The deceased, who was much beloved by his relatives and friends, fell ill at San Souci only a few days ago and was taken in a hammock to his father's residence, where Dr. Inniss was called in, but despite all that could be done he passed away on Friday afternoon at the early age of 23 years after only six days' illness. The funeral took place on Saturday afternoon from his father's house to the Mission R. C. Church, where the last rites were performed by the Rev. Father Pinard, acting parish priest of Toco. The procession then went to the cemetery, where the body was interred.

The following were the bearers:— Messrs. J. E. Joseph, Jas. Begg, Lewis Magloire, Henry Monsegue, William Sargeant (jun.) and Ederic Charles.

The following were the chief mourners: Mr. George Patience, Master Geo. Patience, Miss Jessie Patience, Miss Louisa Patience and the Misses Comissiong (4).

Among those who followed were Messrs. A. Monsegue, William Sargeant, P. C. Simeon, Abraham Samerson, Shalto Archibald, Ernest Archbard, W. H. Hislop, Michael David, Edward Legeri, Sixto de la Rosa, F. Figaro, Lewis E. Richardson, F. A. Agge, L. B. Hilaire, P. R. Coker, Mrs. M. N. Monsegue, Mrs. Bruce, Mrs. Samerson, Mrs. Comissiong Misses Hadaway, Magloire, Sargeant, Elce, Monsegue, Mrs. Archbard, Misses Pierre, Archbard (2), Borde (2), Thomas (2) and others.

Wreaths were sent by many friends.

Generation Four

Parents of
James Bowhill Begg

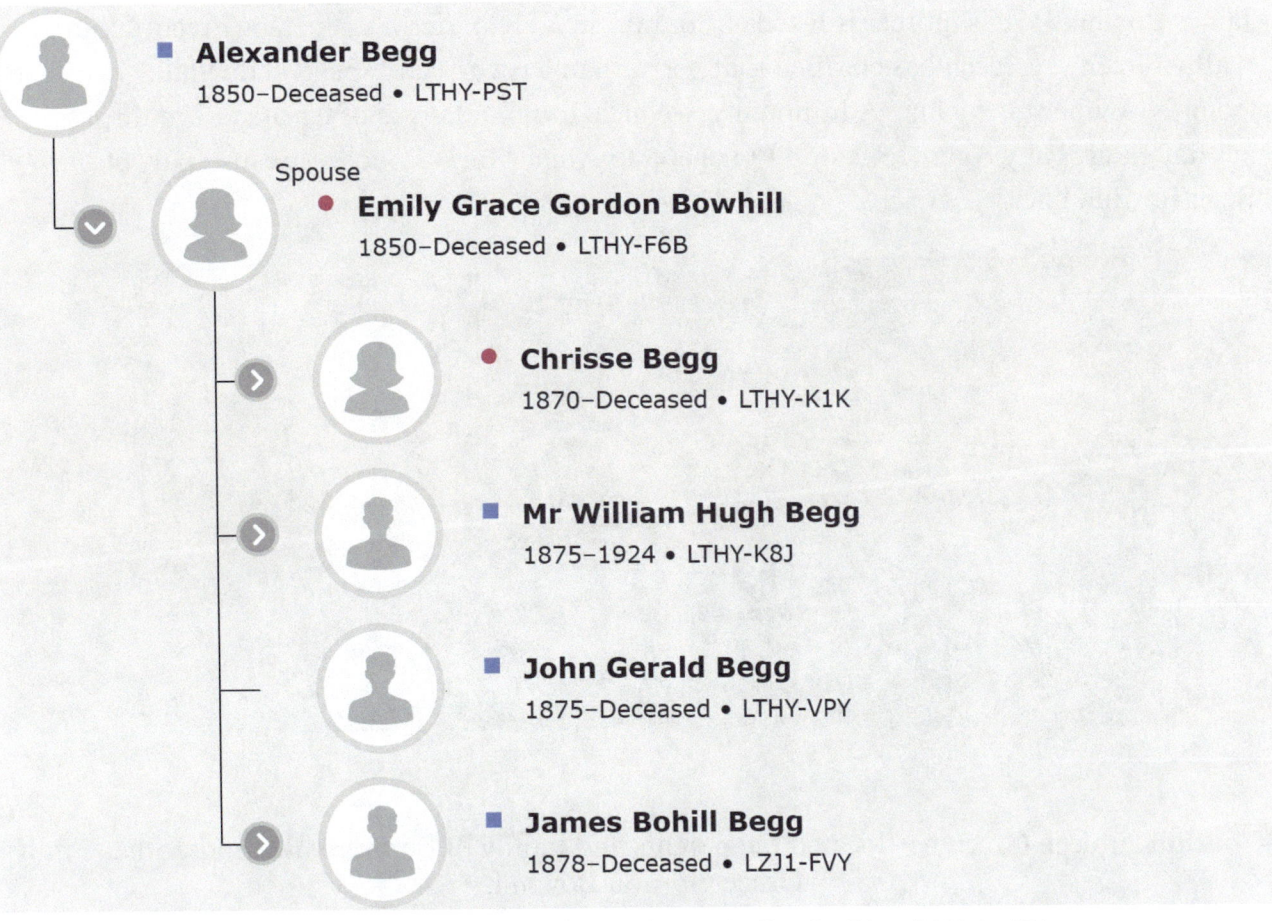

- **Alexander Begg**
  1850–Deceased • LTHY-PST

  Spouse
  - **Emily Grace Gordon Bowhill**
    1850–Deceased • LTHY-F6B

    - **Chrisse Begg**
      1870–Deceased • LTHY-K1K

    - **Mr William Hugh Begg**
      1875–1924 • LTHY-K8J

    - **John Gerald Begg**
      1875–Deceased • LTHY-VPY

    - **James Bohill Begg**
      1878–Deceased • LZJ1-FVY

1. Alexander Hugh Begg b: ABT 1850 in Scotland, United Kingdom. d: Deceased on Kings Bay, Tobago, Trinidad and Tobago.
+ Emily Grace Gordon Bowhill b: 1853 in Tobago West Indies. m: ABT 1870 in Scotland, United Kingdom. d: Deceased.
   2. Chrisse Begg b: 06 Jan 1868 on Studly Bay, Tobago, Tobago, Trinidad and Tobago. d: 1940 in Tobago, Trinidad and Tobago; age: 71.
   + George Agard b: Scotland. m: 1898. d: Deceased.
      3. Ruby A Agard b: 26 OCT 1892. d: JAN 1976; age: 83.
      + Nicholas T Pouchet b: Trinidad and Tobago. d: Deceased.
      3. James Agard b: ABT 1900. d: 1975; age: 75.
      3. Chrissie Agard b: Abt. 1900 on Studley Bay, Tobago, Trinidad and Tobago. d: Deceased.
      3. George Agard d: ABT 1980.
   2. William Hugh Begg b: Abt. 1875 in scotland. d: 1924 in Trinidad and Tobago; age: 49.
   + Sarah Minty b: 22 APR 1895 in Tobago. m: Tobago, Trinidad and Tobago. d: 1982 in Trinidad and Tobago; age: 86.
      3. Grace Emelda Begg b: 14 APR 1919 in Sangre Grande, Trinidad. d: 4 JUL 1997 in Barataria, Trinidad; age: 78.
      3. Harold Hugh Begg b: ABT 1920 in Tobago, Trinidad and Tobago. d: ABT 1952 in Tobago, Trinidad and Tobago; age: 32.
      + Gwendoline Mapp b: 12 AUG 1920 in Tobago, Trinidad and Tobago. d: 23 JAN 2011 in Westerville, Franklin, Ohio, United States of America; age: 90.
      3. Jean Geraldine Begg b: 10 AUG 1922 in Trinidad and Tobago. d: 11 Jun 2000 in Trinidad and Tobago; age: 77.
      + Ralph Gerald de Silva b: 8 MAR 1910 in Trinidad and Tobago. d: 1 AUG 2006 in Trinidad and Tobago; age: 96.
      3. Neville Begg b: 1924 in Trinidad and Tobago. d: 1985 in Trinidad and Tobago; age: 61.
   2. John Gerald Begg b: ABT 1875 in Scotland. d: ABT 1936 in Trinidad and Tobago; age: 61.
+ Gwendoline Mapp b: 12 Aug 1920 in Tobago, Trinidad and Tobago. d: 23 Jan 2011 in Westerville, Franklin, Ohio, United States of America; age: 90.
      3. Arnim John Begg b: 1936. d: july 2, 2008; age: 72.
   2. James Bowhill Begg b: Abt. 1878 in Tobago, British West Indies. d: Deceased in Port of Spain, Trinidad and Tobago, British West Indies.
+ Kathleen Cunningham Patterson b: 1879. m: 10 Nov 1900 in The Whim, Tobago, Trinidad and Tobago. d: 1905 in Roxborough, Tobago, Trinidad and Tobago; age: 26.
      3. Louise Begg b: 1901 in Tobago, Trinidad and Tobago. d: Deceased in Guyana.
      + Ivan Dwight Corsbie b: ABT 1897 in British Guiana. m: 1917 in Trinidad. d: Deceased in British Guiana.
      3. Olive Lyle Begg b: 5 MAY 1902 in Tobago, Trinidad and Tobago. d: 27 Jan 1949 in Port of Spain, Trinidad, W.I.; age: 46.
      + Walter Cyril Sheppard b: 14 JUN 1898 in Belmont, Saint George, Trinidad and Tobago. m: 14 Mar 1924 in Trinidad and Tobago, British West Indies. d: 11 DEC 1974 in Whitby, Ontario, Canada; age: 76.
      3. Enid Kathleen Begg b: 20 Jan 1904 in Louis D'Or, Tobago, Trinidad and Tobago, British West Indies. d: 07 Jan 1985 in Port of Spain, Trinidad and Tobago; age: 80.
      + Victor Malcolm Griffith b: 23 JUL 1892 in Port of Spain, Trinidad and Tobago. m: 29 Jun 1929 in Trinidad and Tobago, British West Indies. d: Deceased in USA.
      3. Minnie Emily Begg b: 27 May 1905 in Roxborough, Tobago, Trinidad and Tobago, British West Indies. d: 1988 in Australia; age: 82.
      + Randolph Oscar Pierre b: ABT 1905. m: 29 Jun 1929 in Trinidad and Tobago, British West Indies. d: Deceased.
      + Roland Negonde Pierre b: ABT 1906. d: 31 AUG 1966; age: 60.

James Bowhill Begg's mother is listed as "Bohill" in Kelvin Pierre's genealogy record, but Kathy Green's research has clarified that her surname is correctly spelled "Bowhill." Kathy is from the William Begg line. Additionally, we have found relatives of Chrisse Begg through her daughter Ruby Agard. Sheldon Pouchet and Anna Maria Pouchet are also part of our Begg/Bowhill line.

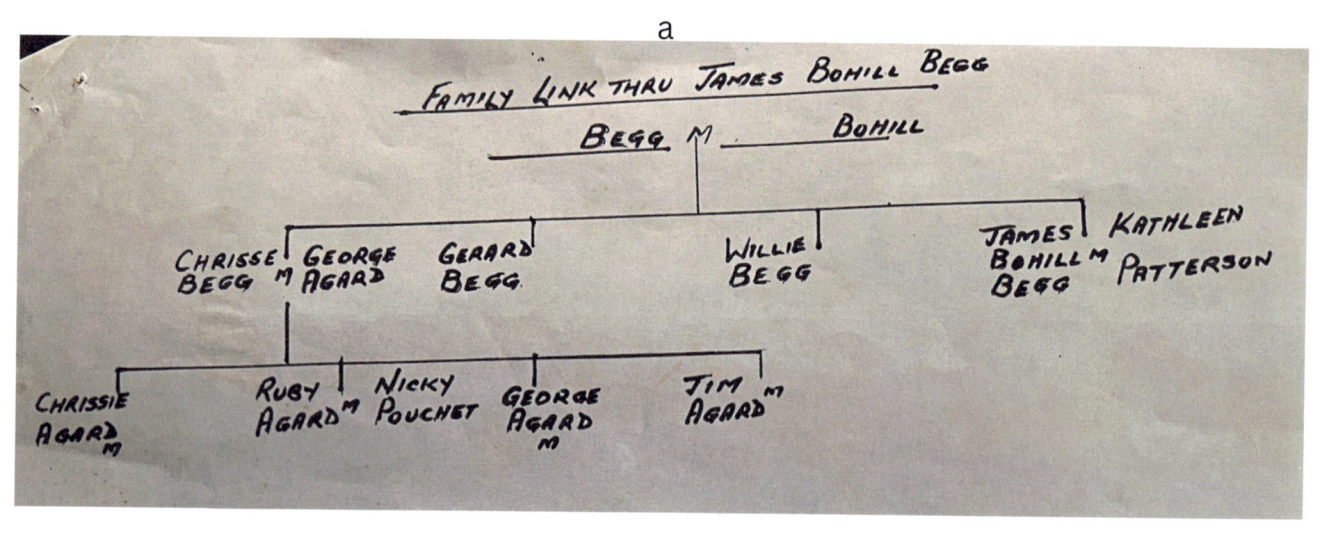

Cousin Kathleen Green has located the parents and family of our mutual grandmother Emily Grace Gordon Bowhill.

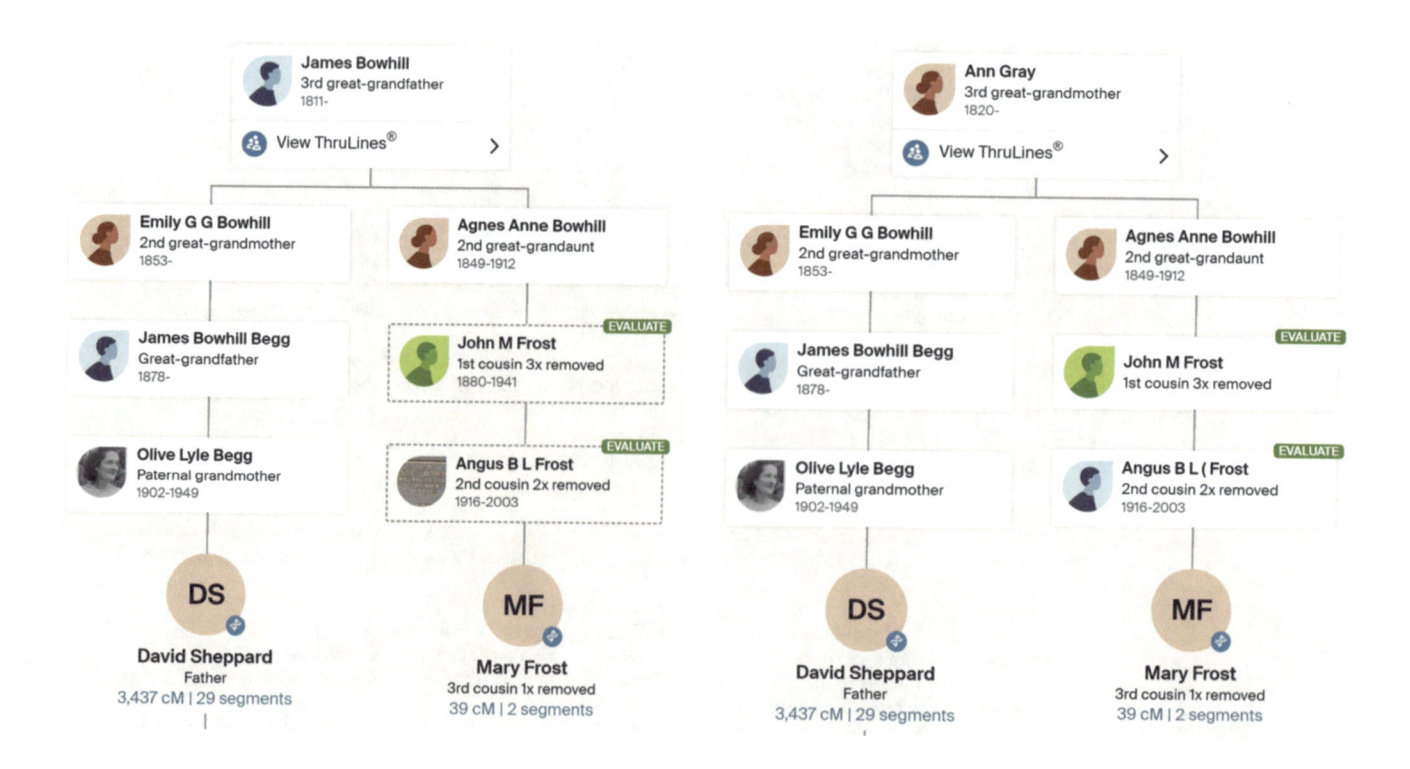

	Name:	Emily Grace Gordon Bowhill
	Birth:	1853 in Tobago West Indies.
	Spouse:	Alexander Hugh Begg
	Death:	Deceased.
	Father:	James Bowhill
	Mother:	Ann Gray

	Spouse:	Alexander Hugh Begg
	Birth:	ABT 1850 in Scotland, United Kingdom.
	Marriage:	ABT 1870 in Scotland, United Kingdom.
	Death:	Deceased on Kings Bay, Tobago, Trinidad and Tobago.
	Father:	John Begg
	Mother:	Agnes Houston

Children of Emily Grace Gordon Bowhill and Alexander Hugh Begg: 4

	Name:	Chrisse Begg
	Birth:	06 Jan 1868 on Studly Bay, Tobago, Tobago, Trinidad and Tobago.
	Spouse:	George Agard Marriage: 1898.
	Death:	1940 in Tobago, Trinidad and Tobago; age: 71.

	Name:	William Hugh Begg
	Birth:	Abt. 1875 in scotland.
	Spouse:	Sarah Minty Marriage: Tobago, Trinidad and Tobago.
	Death:	1924 in Trinidad and Tobago; age: 49.

	Name:	John Gerald Begg
	Birth:	ABT 1875 in Scotland.
	Spouse:	Gwendoline Mapp
	Death:	ABT 1936 in Trinidad and Tobago; age: 61.

	Name:	James Bowhill Begg
	Birth:	Abt. 1878 in Tobago, British West Indies.
	Spouse:	Kathleen Cunningham Patterson Marriage: 10 Nov 1900 in The Whim, Tobago, Trinidad and Tobago.
	Death:	Deceased in Port of Spain, Trinidad and Tobago, British West Indies.

Kathy Green has done an outstanding job tracing our Begg line, including tracking down our grandmother, her sisters, and their spouses. I nominate Kathy as our expert on the Begg line. As she continues her research, we hope to learn even more. My goal for each family line is to trace it back to Europe. We've succeeded with two lines so far, and our next goal is to trace the Begg line back to Scotland.

From Kathy's findings, we know that four Bowhill sisters were born in Tobago and sent to school in Scotland with the intention of finding suitable husbands. The four sisters married as follows:
- Emily Grace Gordon Bowhill married Alexander Begg (our line)
- Elizabeth Walker Bowhill married George Mason from the UK
- Annie Bulman Bowhill married Matthew Bell Crooks from Tobago
- Agnes Anne Bowhill married Andrew Roy

Agnes Anne's daughter, Agnes Roy, married Felix Pierre, and their two sons both married Minnie Begg. Agnes also married Clarence Frost.

Minnie Begg (Olive's sister) was the granddaughter of Emily Grace Gordon Bowhill and married the grandson of Emily's sister, Agnes. This is where genealogy gets complex! For example, Anita DeCosta Martin is both my aunt and cousin, as we're related in multiple ways. We are not the first family to navigate such complicated relationships. Enjoy the lyrics to a song about this very topic!

I'm My Own Grandpa
Song by Willie Nelson

… Now, many many years ago
When I was twenty three
I was married to a widow
Who was pretty as could be
… This widow had a grown-up daughter
Had hair of red
My father fell in love with her
And soon the two were wed
… This made my dad my son-in-law
And changed my very life
My daughter was my mother
'Cause she was my father's wife
… To complicate the matters
Even though it brought me joy
I soon became the father
Of a bouncing baby boy
… My little baby then became
A brother-in-law to dad
And so became my uncle
Though it made me very sad
… For if he was my uncle
That also made him the brother
Of the widow's grown-up daughter
Who, of course, was my step-mother
… I'm my own grandpa
I'm my own grandpa
It sounds funny I know
But it really is so
I'm my own grandpa

… My father's wife then had a son
That kept them on the run
And he became my grandchild
For he was my daughter's son
… My wife is now my mother's mother
And it makes me blue
Because, she is my wife
She's my grandmother too
… I'm my own grandpa
I'm my own grandpa
It sounds funny I know
But it really is so
I'm my own grandpa
… Now, if my wife is my grandmother
Then, I am her grandchild
And every time I think of it
It nearly drives me wild
… For now I have become
The strangest case you ever saw
As husband of my grandmother
I am my own grandpa
… I'm my own grandpa
I'm my own grandpa
It sounds funny I know
But it really is so
I'm my own grandpa
… I'm my own grandpa
I'm my own grandpa
It sounds funny I know
But it really is so
I'm my own grandpa

Generation Four Maternal

Arleen -> David -> Olive -> Kathleen Cunningham Paterson

HISTORY OF KATHLEEN CUNNINGHAM PATERSON

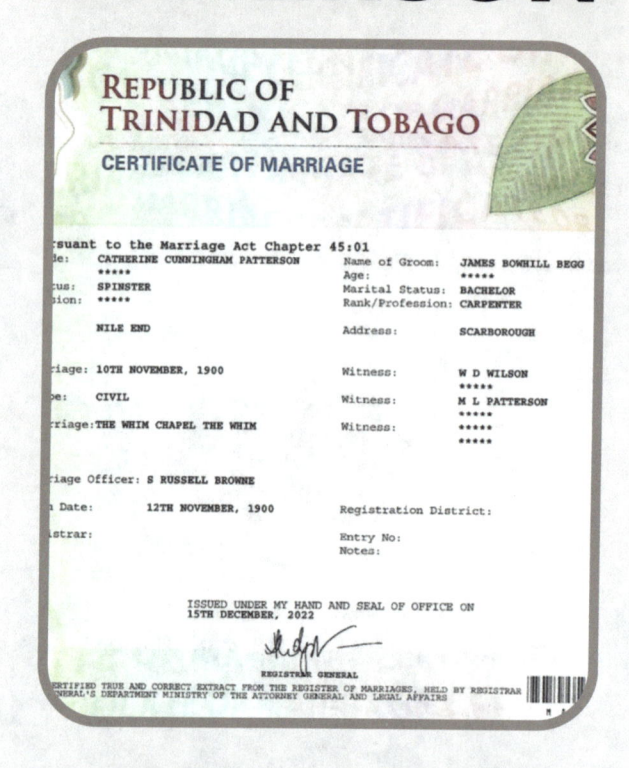

QUICK FACTS:

BORN
TOBAGO

PARENTS
JAMES PATERSON, ESQ
MINNIE KIRK

CHILDREN
LOUISE BEGG
OLIVE BEGG
ENID BEGG
MINNIE BEGG

KATHLEEN CUNNINGHAM PATERSON (NEE BEGG)

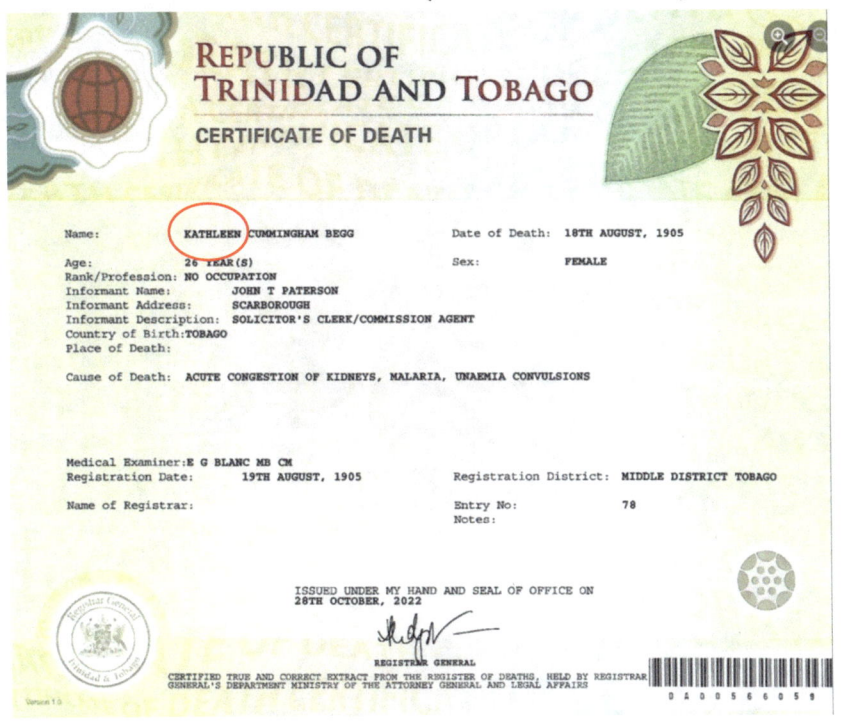

[Certificate of Death, Republic of Trinidad and Tobago, for Kathleen Cunningham Begg, Date of Death: 18th August, 1905, Age: 26 years, Sex: Female, No Occupation, Informant: John T Paterson, Scarborough, Solicitor's Clerk/Commission Agent, Country of Birth: Tobago, Cause of Death: Acute Congestion of Kidneys, Malaria, Unaemia Convulsions, Medical Examiner: E G Blanc MB CM, Registration Date: 19th August, 1905, Registration District: Middle District Tobago, Entry No: 78]

CATHERINE CUNNINGHAM PATERSON

[Certificate of Marriage, Republic of Trinidad and Tobago, Name of Bride: Catherine Cunningham Patterson, Marital Status: Spinster, Address: Nile End; Name of Groom: James Bowhill Begg, Marital Status: Bachelor, Rank/Profession: Carpenter, Address: Scarborough, Date of Marriage: 10th November, 1900, Marriage Type: Civil, Place of Marriage: The Whim Chapel The Whim, Witnesses: W D Wilson, M L Patterson, Marriage Officer: S Russell Browne, Registration Date: 12th November, 1900]

1. **Death Certificate:** Name is listed as Kathleen.
2. **Marriage Certificate:** Her name is listed as Catherine.

Kathleen passed away at a young age, but in her short life, she gave birth to four daughters: Louise, Olive, Enid, and Minnie. Minnie was her last child, and postpartum complications contributed to Kathleen's death. Her kidneys failed—both she and her daughter Olive passed away from similar health issues. Kathleen died due to complications from childbirth, while Olive's health deteriorated after multiple pregnancies, which took a toll on her body.

Kathleen's mother, Minnie Kirk, lived in Scarborough and was married to a doctor. As Kathleen's health worsened after Minnie's birth, her husband, James, took her in an open-air boat to Scarborough to be with her family, where she continued to deteriorate.

Kathleen's illness was exacerbated by the conditions in the boat, which contributed to her death

After her passing, James left Tobago and moved to Toco, where he was welcomed by his relatives. The four young girls were separated and sent to live with friends and family members, including Grandma Anderson, and with family friend, Mama Figeroux.

Generation Four

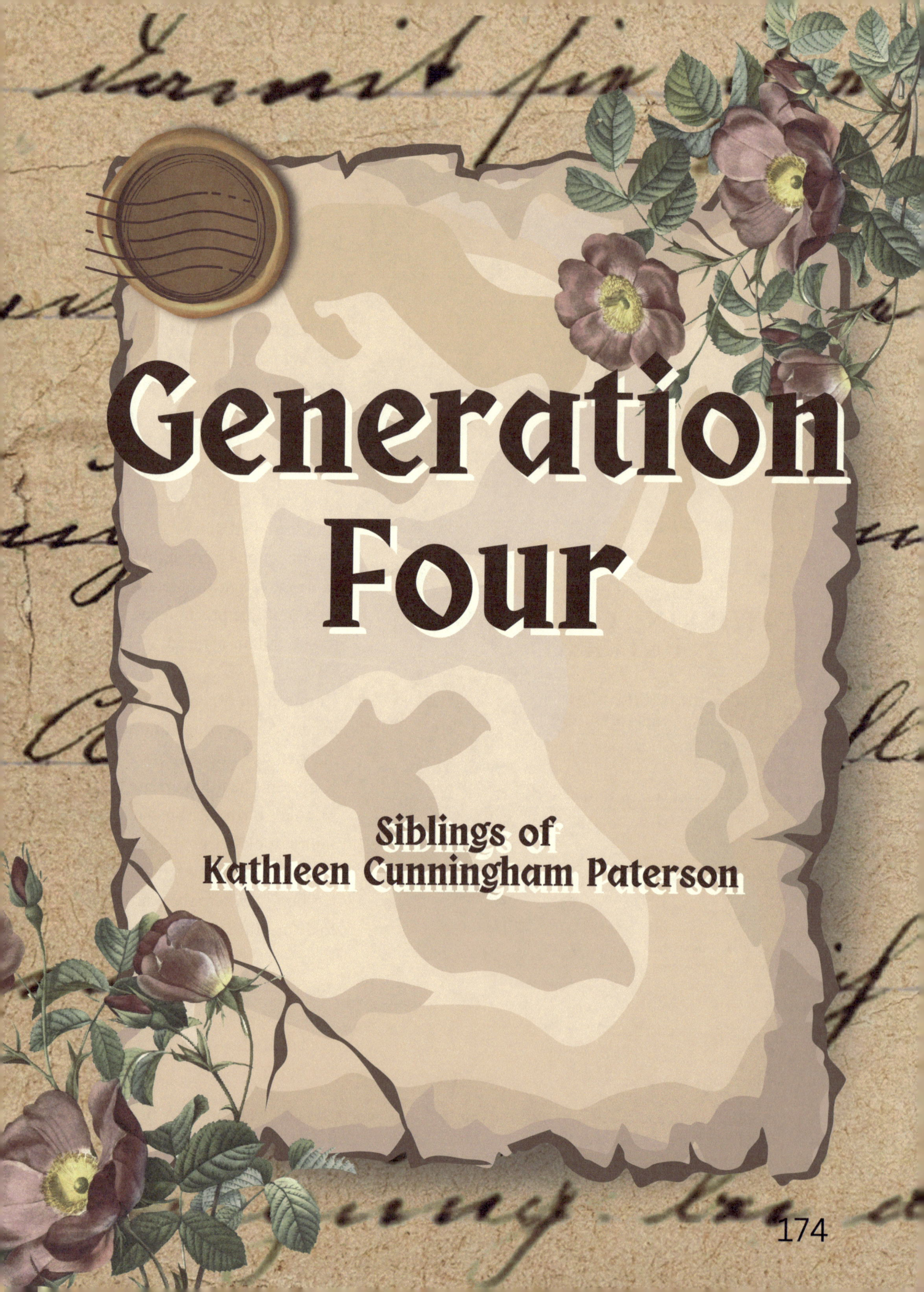

Siblings of
Kathleen Cunningham Paterson

James Thorburn frequently appears in newspapers regarding a lawsuit against his mother's family over a stolen inheritance, specifically related to Minnie's inheritance.

George moved to Scotland to live with his grandmother before his 9th birthday and lived there until his death in 1929. Little is known about **Margaret**, except for information in Kelvin Pierre's family history, which mentions that she went to Canada with her brother James Thorburn.

Kathleen has been discussed in earlier pages.

Children of Minnie Kirk and James Paterson: 4

Name:	James Thorburn Paterson	
Birth:	about 1872 in Tobago, Trinidad and Tobago.	
Death:	Deceased in Canada.	

Name:	George Cundel Kirk Paterson	
Birth:	About 1874 in Trinidad and Tobago, British West Indies.	
Death:	4 November 1929 in Kilmarnock, Ayrshire, Scotland; age: 55.	

Name:	Margaret Patterson	
Birth:	Abt. 1875 in Tobago, Trinidad and Tobago.	
Death:	Deceased.	

Name:	Kathleen Cunningham Patterson	
Birth:	1879.	
Spouse:	James Bowhill Begg Marriage: 10 Nov 1900 in The Whim, Tobago, Trinidad and Tobago.	
Death:	1905 in Roxborough, Tobago, Trinidad and Tobago; age: 26.	

Children of Minnie Kirk and Richard Benjamin Anderson F.R.C.S: 2

William was mentioned in his daughter's Mary Olive Elizabeth Anderson's history.

Arthur is usually mentioned as an appendage to William Alfred. They were twins and made decisions as a unit. Arthur was more than likely his middle name.

Name:	William Alfred Anderson	
Birth:	21 JUL 1884 in Orange Grove, Middle District, Tobago, Trinidad and Tobago.	
Spouse:	Olive May Ross Rossieire Marriage: 1926 in New Zealand.	
Death:	1935; age: 50.	

Name:	Arthur Anderson	
Birth:	21 JUL 1884 in Orange Grove, Middle District, Tobago, Trinidad and Tobago.	
Death:	1948; age: 63.	

On a copy of a birth certificate for one of the twin boys (the specific twin is not known), it was common practice at the time to name children during their baptism or christening. The name will be provided in the following pages. What is important to note is that Minnie Kirk is also known as Mary Kirk.

The birth certificate for William Alfred or Arthur's Anderson's birth certificate

HH No 43604

033412

REPUBLIC OF TRINIDAD AND TOBAGO 1884 BIRTH IN THE Middle District Tobago Ward

No.	When Born	Name (if any)	Sex	Name and Surname of Father	Name and Maiden name of Mother	Rank or Profession of Father	Signature, description and residence of Informant	When registered	Signature of Registrar	Baptismal name if added after registration of Birth	Number of house or locality where born
393	21st July	—	Boy	Richard Benjamin Anderson	Mary Kirk née Patterson	F.R.C.S England	Richard Benjamin Anderson Tobago	4th Aug.	Tho M. Sealy Registrar	—	Orange Grove

I, [illegible] AUTHORISED BY [illegible] Registrar General of Trinidad and Tobago do certify that the above is a true and correct copy of the
Entry No. 393 Vol. entered at Page 66 Register of Births for the year 1884

In Witness whereof I have hereunto set my Hand and affixed my Seal of Office this 17th day of August in the year of Our Lord, One Thousand Nine Hundred and ninety two

S N——
Registrar General

SUPPORTING DOCUMENTATION TO SIBLING'S OF KATHLEEN CUNNINGHAM PAT(T)ERSON.

THE MIRROR TUESDAY FEBRUARY 27 1906

APPLICATION.

Mr J T Paterson applied for permission to sue (1) James Kirk, at No 9, George street, Port-of-Spain, and (2) Edmund Nelson, at Tocoo, Trinidad, out of this jurisdiction, for debts contracted in Tobago. The application was granted.

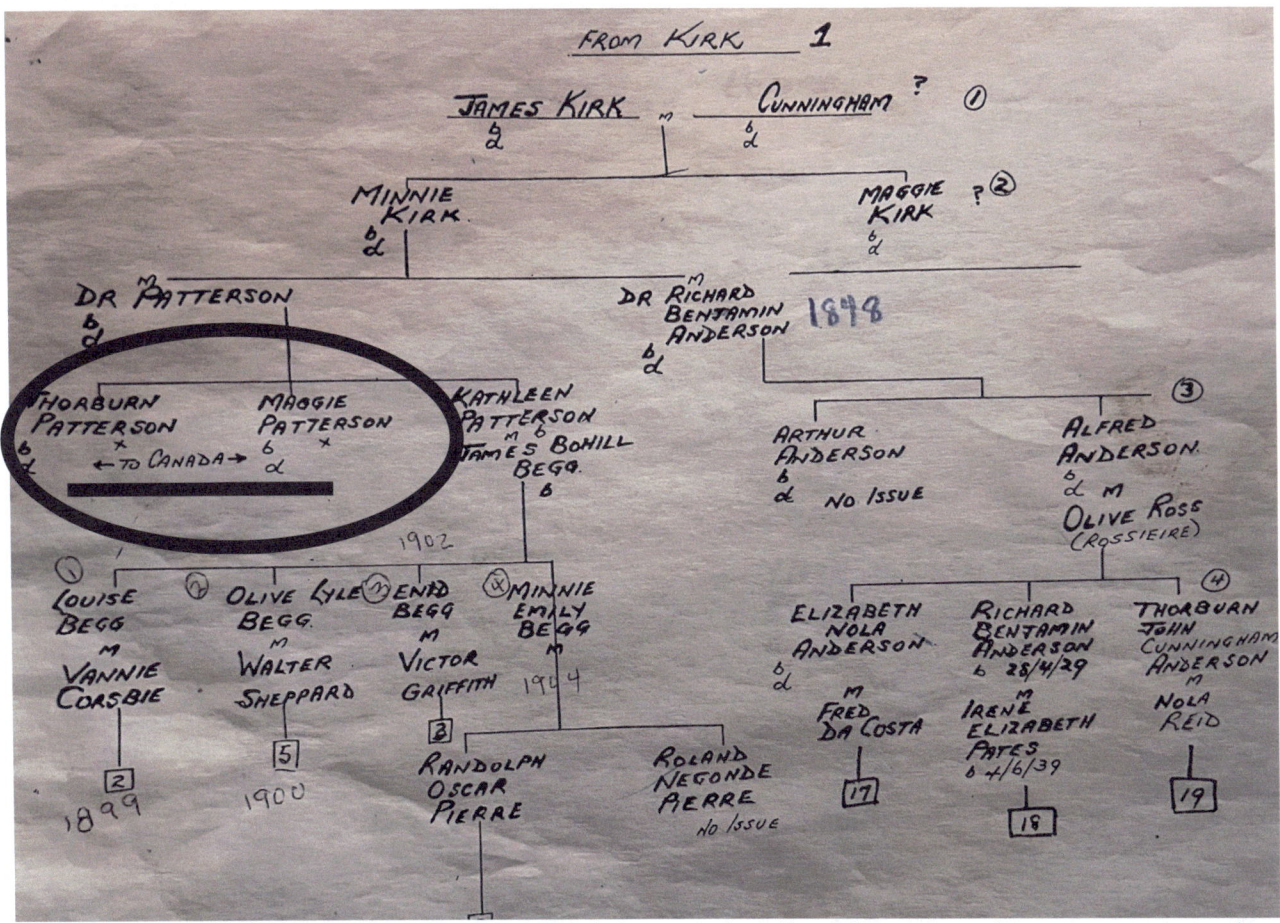

Note: Many of our relatives' names in Kelvin's records reflect the names they were commonly called, which differ from official records. For example, James Thorburn Patterson (son of James Paterson) was known as "Thorburn," and Margaret was referred to as "Maggie." Additionally, George was not known in Tobago, as he was living in Scotland at the time. Also, Dr. Patterson was actually James Paterson (with one 'T'), Esq., making him an attorney, not a doctor.

George Cundel Kirk Paterson

This is one of the most exciting records I've been able to locate, second only to the Gruny Family line. It provides valuable insight, though it also raises more questions, especially regarding one of Minnie Kirk's marriages. Additionally, the absence of this record in Kelvin Pierre's work is curious.

The record pertains to Kathleen Cunningham Paterson's brother, George Cundel Kirk Paterson, born around 1874 to James Paterson and Minnie Kirk. This single record offers information about our family in Scotland, as well as a few generations beyond George.

As with previous records, his death record reveals even more details.

Record Transcription: 1929 Deaths in the Parish Kilmarnock in the County of Ayr
George Cundel Kirk Paterson   Law Clerk (Retired)   (Single)
1929 November fourth 9 h. 0 m. PM. The Infirmary
(usual address) 6 Glebe Road Kilmarnock
m male   age 55
Father: James Paterson, Plantation Manager (Deceased)
   Mother: Minnie Paterson afterwards Anderson, M.S (Maiden Surname) Kirk
Cause of Death: Chronic Interstitial; Chronic Alcoholism
This record implies that Minnie was alive in 1929.

George provides us with additional information via two census'

178

This is the first census in which George appears, at the age of 9. It shows that he was living with his grandparents, John Patterson and Margaret Thorburn. We don't have any information on why George did not stay with his family in Tobago. He was in Scotland from a young age, living with his grandparents until his death in 1929 at the age of 55.

It appears George may have been the first or second child born to James Paterson and Minnie Kirk. In subsequent censuses, he is listed as a law clerk, later retiring. There is evidence suggesting he may have served in the army, but this has yet to be verified. Additionally, his aunts, Mary and Barbara, played an important role in his life, as he lived with them for the duration of his life.

Record Transcription:

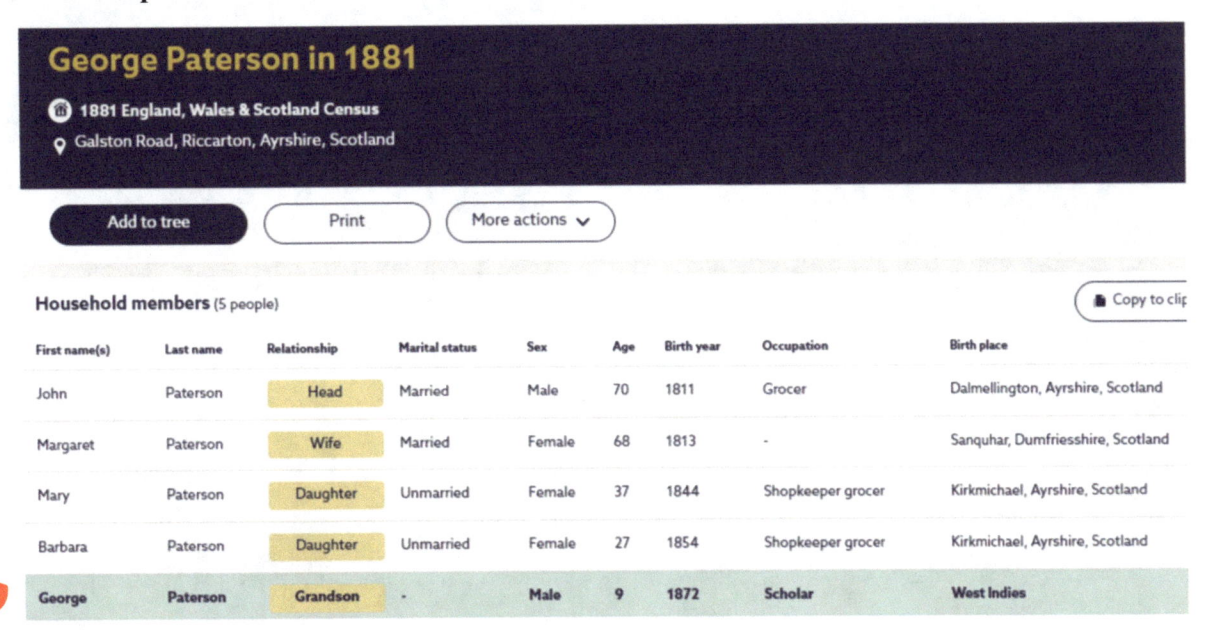

George Paterson in 1881

1881 England, Wales & Scotland Census
Galston Road, Riccarton, Ayrshire, Scotland

Household members (5 people)

First name(s)	Last name	Relationship	Marital status	Sex	Age	Birth year	Occupation	Birth place
John	Paterson	Head	Married	Male	70	1811	Grocer	Dalmellington, Ayrshire, Scotland
Margaret	Paterson	Wife	Married	Female	68	1813	-	Sanquhar, Dumfriesshire, Scotland
Mary	Paterson	Daughter	Unmarried	Female	37	1844	Shopkeeper grocer	Kirkmichael, Ayrshire, Scotland
Barbara	Paterson	Daughter	Unmarried	Female	27	1854	Shopkeeper grocer	Kirkmichael, Ayrshire, Scotland
George	Paterson	Grandson	-	Male	9	1872	Scholar	West Indies

Generation Four++

Arleen Sheppard -> David Sheppard -> Olive Lyle Begg -> Kathleen Cunningham Paterson -> James Paterson and Minnie/Mary Kirk

HISTORY OF JAMES PATERSON

QUICK FACTS:

BORN
IRELAND

PARENTS
JOHN PATERSON
MARGARET THORBURN

CHILDREN
4 KNOWN CHILDREN

181

James Patterson birth record. He is the only child in the family born in Ireland. The genealogist stated that it was common for families to travel back and forth. There is a parrell in my life. I was the only child born in Trinidad. My brother younger than me, and my sister, older were both born in Montreal Canada.

Name:	James Patterson	Date of Birth:	05-Oct-1843
		Date of Baptism:	23-Oct-1843
Address:	Newtown Barry	Parish/District:	Bunclody
Gender:	Male	County	Co. Wexford
		Denomination:	Church Of Ireland
Father:	John Patterson	Mother:	Margaret Patterson
Occupation:	Saoyer		
Sponsor 1 / Informant 1:	N R	Sponsor 2 / Informant 2:	N R
	Notes:		
	JOHN LE ARCHDALL		

Church Baptism Record

It seems like James Paterson's life is somewhat elusive in the historical records, but the 1851 Census gives us a crucial glimpse into his early years. Here's a brief summary of the information based on what you've shared:

- James Paterson's Census Record (1851): This is the only known record of him before his marriage to Minnie Kirk. He would have been around 8 years old in 1851.
- Marriage to Minnie Kirk: After his appearance in the 1851 Census, the next major record is his marriage to Minnie Kirk, which may have occurred in the late 1860s.
- Son George's Death Record: James is also listed on his son George's death record, providing another point of reference for his life.

Given the lack of records between the census and later events, it's likely that James' life details, like his activities in Tobago or his professional life, are either lost to time or were not thoroughly documented in accessible records. However, the fact that we know he was a key figure in Tobago's governance and his legal work as a lawyer helps paint a picture of his adult life, even if more specifics are still unknown.

THE PATTERSON SIDE

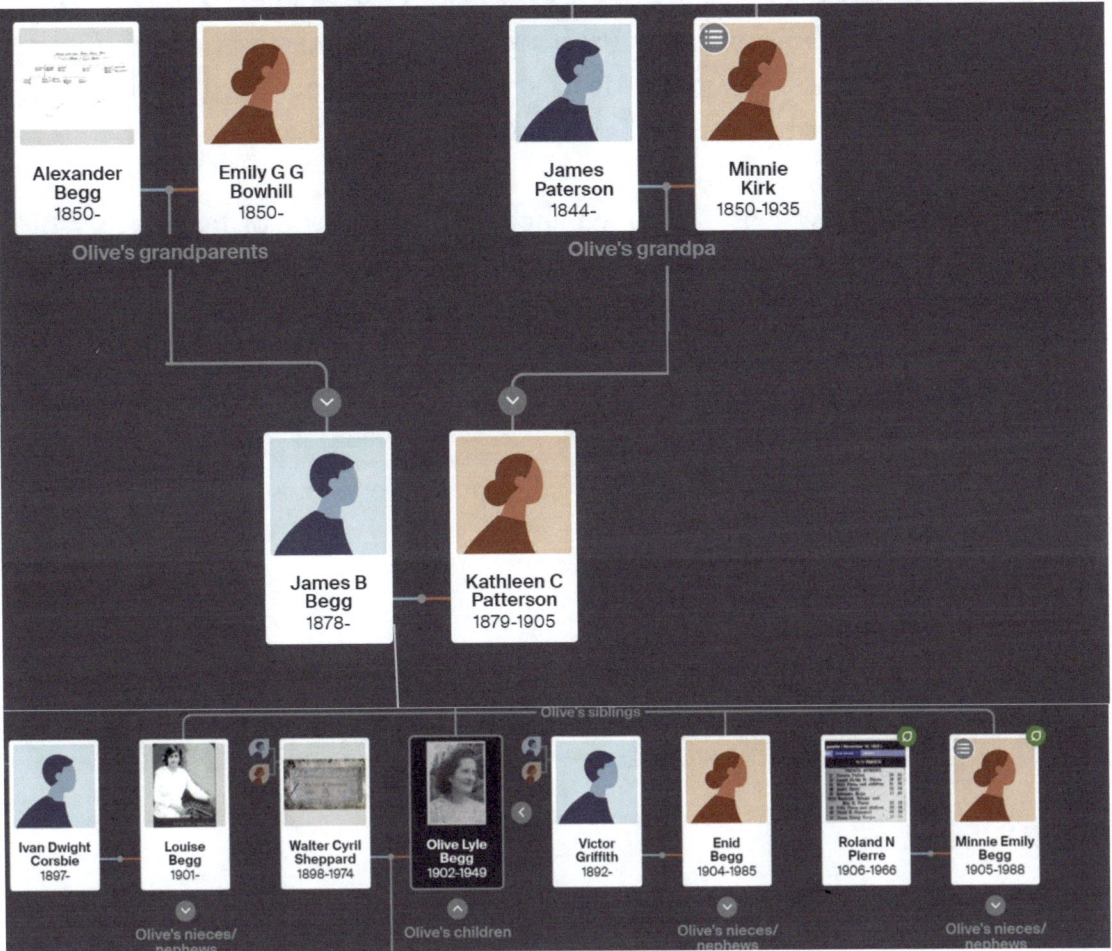

Alexander Begg 1850–
Emily G G Bowhill 1850–
Olive's grandparents

James Paterson 1844–
Minnie Kirk 1850–1935
Olive's grandpa

James B Begg 1878–
Kathleen C Patterson 1879–1905

Olive's siblings

Ivan Dwight Corsbie 1897–
Louise Begg 1901–
Walter Cyril Sheppard 1898–1974
Olive Lyle Begg 1902–1949
Victor Griffith 1892–
Enid Begg 1904–1985
Roland N Pierre 1906–1966
Minnie Emily Begg 1905–1988

Olive's nieces/nephews — *Olive's children* — *Olive's nieces/nephews* — *Olive's nieces/nephews*

James Paterson - Minnie's First Husband

The only information available on James Paterson comes from his marriage notice in British newspapers, his name on his son George's death record, and several mentions in the Tobago Gazette. These sources describe his government role and voting record.

George's appearance in a few censuses helped uncover the identities of James Paterson's parents and grandparents. Family lore had listed his profession as a doctor, but he was actually a lawyer. It was common at the time for lawyers to manage estates, particularly crown lands, which were often overseen by managers hired from Europe, particularly Scotland, due to the landowners' absence from the estate.

This article, published in January 1871, appeared in newspapers in Scotland, England, and across the Caribbean colonies.

> On the 14th ult., at St. Paul's, De La Ford, Tobago, W.I., by the Rev. J. N. Roach, James Paterson Esq., to Minnie, youngest daughter of the Hon. James Kirk sen., of that island.

TRANSCRIPTION:

On the 14th ult. (Previous month which would have been Dec 1870) at St. Paul's, De La Ford, (Delaford). Tobago W.I. by the Rev. J. N. Roach, James Paterson Esp., to Minnie Kirk, youngest daughter of the Hon. James Kirk sen. of that Island.

Record Transcription: 1929 Deaths in the Parish Kilmarnock in the County of Ayr

George Cundel Kirk Paterson   Law Clerk   (Retired)   (Single)
1929 November fourth 9 h. 0 m. PM. The Infirmary
(usual address) 6 Glebe Road Kilmarnock
m = male   age 55

* Father: James Paterson, Plantation Manager (Deceased)
* Mother: Minnie Paterson afterwards Anderson, M.S (Maiden Surname) Kirk
Cause of Death: Chronic Interstitial; Chronic Alcoholism

JOHN PATERSON

The names of John Paterson's parents, Alexander Paterson and Mary Stewart, are found on his death record. A wealth of information is available on platforms like Ancestry.com and FamilySearch.org. Anyone interested in continuing the research on this family may find additional details through these resources.

Record Transcription: 1884 Deaths in the District of Riccarton in the County of Ayr
John Paterson   Licensed Grocer (married to Margaret Thorburn)
1884 November Third 3 h. 0 m. PM. Galston Road, Hurlford
m = male   age 75
Father: Alexander Paterson, Stone Mason (Deceased)
Mother: Mary Paterson, M.S (Maiden Surname) Stewart (Deceased)
Cause of Death: Cardiac; Long Standing, General Anasarca Two Months
Informant: Alexander Paterson, son

NOTE:

Anasarca is a medical condition that leads to general swelling of the whole body. It happens when your body tissues retain too much fluid due to several reasons. It differs from other types of edema that affect one or two parts of the body. The condition is also known as extreme generalized edema or massive edema. When it happens, it's usually as a result of a severe underlying condition or organ damage.

This is the transcription of John Paterson's death memorial at Kirkmichael Cemetery in Ayrshire. It shows the death date of two of his children, Thomas and Jane. We have them confirmed, as well as James, Barbara and Mary. There are more children that we are trying to add pending source confirmation.

First name(s)	John
Last name	Paterson
Birth year	1809
Birth date	? ? 1809
Age	75
Death year	1884
Death date	03 Nov 1884
Inscription	Erected by JOHN PATERSON to the memory of his son THOMAS d. 06/ Jun / 1860 aged 20 y Also of his daughter JANE d. 13/ Feb / 1862 aged 12 y 3 m Also JOHN PATERSON d. 03/ Nov / 1884 aged 75 y, a loving husband and affectionate father Also of his wife MARGARET THORBURN d. Hurlford 06/ Jun / 1894 aged 82 y
Cemetery	Kirkmichael Cemetery
Place	Kirkmichael
County	Ayrshire
Country	Scotland
Record set	Scotland Monumental Inscriptions
Category	Birth, Marriage, Death & Parish Records
Subcategory	Parish Burials
Collections from	Great Britain, Scotland

John Paterson's parents are Alexander Paterson and Mary Stewart.

Here (1800, Dalmellington) is the marriage of Alexander Paterson and Mary Stewart. I have not been able to trace a death record for either of these two.

1800 PATERSON, ALEXANDER (Old Parish Registers Marriages 586/ Dalmellington) Page 380 of 434
©Crown copyright, National Records of Scotland. Image was generated at 26 March 2024 14:16

July 19th Alexander Paterson in this Parish and Mary Stewart in the Parish of Straiton Registrate this Day for Proclamation of Banns in order to marriage

1800 PATERSON, ALEXANDER (Old Parish Registers Marriages 617/ Straiton) Page 342 of 370
©Crown copyright, National Records of Scotland. Image was generated at 26 March 2024 14:19

ued upon the 29 July ... Paterson Alexander Paterson in parish of Dalmellington & Stewart and Mary Stewart in this parish after public proclamation were married upon the 25th July

Margaret Paterson (nee Thorburn)

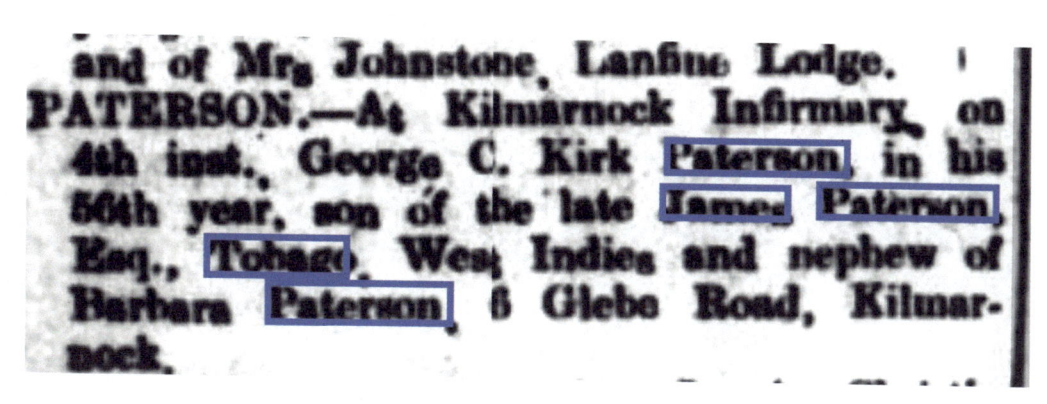

...and of Mrs Johnstone, Lanfine Lodge.
PATERSON.—At Kilmarnock Infirmary, on 4th inst., George C. Kirk Paterson, in his 56th year, son of the late James Paterson Esq., Tobago, West Indies and nephew of Barbara Paterson, 6 Glebe Road, Kilmarnock.

Because we were able to find George Cundell Kirk Paterson, we were able to locate his extended family in Scotland.

John Paterson and Margaret Thorburn Marriage Bann - a declaration of Marriage for the parents of James Paterson.

Patterson   John Patterson and Margaret Thorburn both of
Thorburn   this Parish after Public Proclamation were married
            on the 20th Dec 1833

Transcript of Margaret's record

First name(s)	Margaret	Country	Scotland
Last name	Thorburn	Archive reference	OPR 617/2
Marriage year	1833	Item	2
Marriage date	20 Dec 1833	Year range	1820-1854
Residence	Straiton	Page	45
Spouse's first name	John	Record set	Scotland, Parish Marriages & Banns 1561-1893
Spouse's last name	Patterson	Category	Birth, Marriage & Death (Parish Registers)
Spouse's residence	Straiton	Subcategory	Parish Marriages
Place	Straiton	Collections from	Great Britain, Scotland
County	Ayrshire		

1851 and 1861 Census Transcription

Household members (8 people)

First name(s)	Last name	Relationship	Marital status	Sex	Age	Birth year	Occupation	Birth place
John	Paterson	Head	Married	Male	42	1809	Sawyer	Dalmellington, Ayrshire, Scotland
Margaret	Paterson	Wife	Married	Female	40	1811	Sawyers wife	Sanquhar, Dumfriesshire, Scotland
Thomas	Paterson	Son	Unmarried	Male	11	1840	Scholar	Kirkmichael, Ayrshire, Scotland
Mary	Paterson	Daughter	-	Female	9	1842	Scholar	Kirkmichael, Ayrshire, Scotland
James	Paterson	-	-	Male	7	1844	Scholar	Ireland
Janet	Paterson	-	-	Female	4	1847	Scholar	Kirkmichael, Ayrshire, Scotland
Jean	Paterson	-	-	Female	1	1850	-	Kirkmichael, Ayrshire, Scotland
Margaret	McCaul	Mother-in-law	Widow	Female	76	1775	-	Lanarkshire, Scotland

Here are John and Margaret Paterson, with four daughters but no son on the 1861 census.

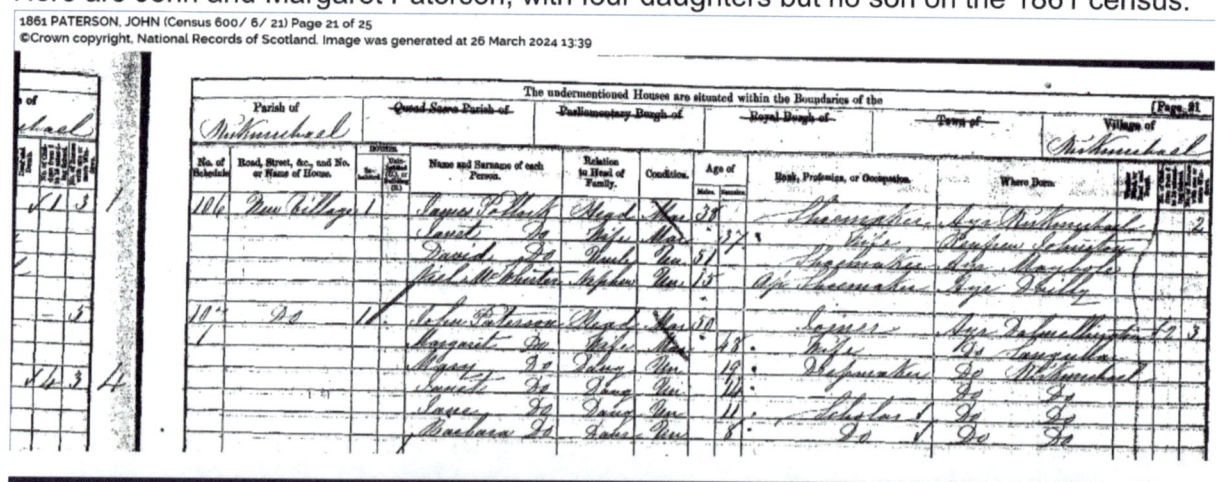

1861 PATERSON, JOHN (Census 600/ 6/ 21) Page 21 of 25
©Crown copyright, National Records of Scotland. Image was generated at 26 March 2024 13:39

John Paterson in 1861

1861 England, Wales & Scotland Census

New Village, Kirkmichael(Ayr), Kirkmichael, Ayrshire, Scotland

Household members (6 people)

First name(s)	Last name	Relationship	Marital status	Sex	Age	Birth year	Occupation	Birth place
John	Paterson	Head	Married	Male	50	1811	Joiner	Dalmellington, Ayrshire, Scotland
Margaret	Paterson	Wife	Married	Female	48	1813	Wife	Sanquhar, Ayrshire, Scotland
Mary	Paterson	Daughter	Unmarried	Female	19	1842	Dressmaker	Kirkmichael, Ayrshire, Scotland
Janet	Paterson	Daughter	Unmarried	Female	14	1847	-	Kirkmichael, Ayrshire, Scotland
Jane	Paterson	Daughter	Unmarried	Female	11	1850	Scholar	Kirkmichael, Ayrshire, Scotland
Barbara	Paterson	Daughter	Unmarried	Female	8	1853	Scholar	Kirkmichael, Ayrshire, Scotland

VALUATION ROLL for the COUNTY of AYR (Kyle District) for the Year 1885-1886.

This is a valuation roll for the purpose of taxation, showing that Margaret Thorburn, later Paterson, James' mother, was an occupant of a shop on Galston Road. I have been unable to pinpoint the exact location of the shop, but a strong possibility is the Galston Co-operative, located at Location 13. On the 1861 Census, the daughters of John and Margaret, Mary and Barbara, were listed as dressmakers. Since the Co-op began with multiple shops, it's possible that the daughters started in that trade and presented their parents with the opportunity to switch from being a Sawyer and later a Joiner to a Licensed Grocer. While this is a plausible theory, it cannot be confirmed.

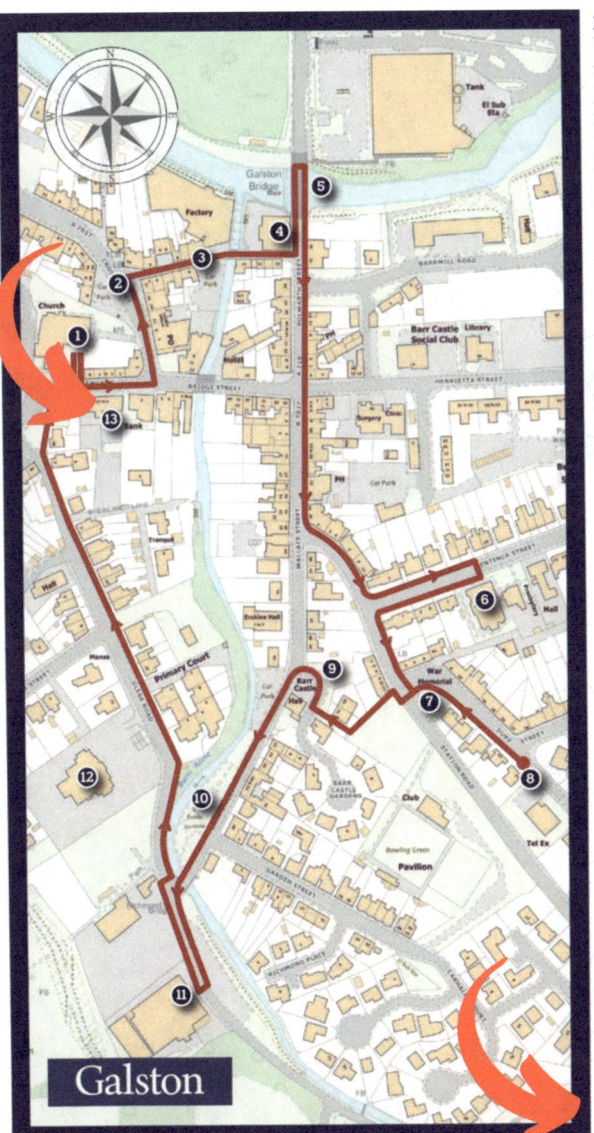

Location 1: Parish Church
Leave the side gate of the church in Brewland Street and walk to the corner past the cafe and turn left. Continue past the front gate of the church to

Location 2: The Cross
Cross over the pedestrian crossing outside the butcher's shop and enter

Location 3: Church Lane
Continue along Church Lane and at the end, where it meets Polwarth Street turn left to the front of

Location 4: Brown's Institute
Continue to the left and reach, at the top of the rise,

Location 5: The Muckle Bridge
Retrace your steps and continue along Polwarth Street toward the Four Corners, cross to the left at the Pedestrian Crossing to Henrietta Street and then right to the crossing for Wallace Street. Walk along Wallace Street past the chemist and the Wee Train Public House and bear left into Station Road. At the first corner, turn left into Bentinck Street and walk along to

Location 6: St Sophia's Church
Retrace your route to Station Road and at the corner turn left walk on uphill to the corner with Duke Street and in front is

Location 7: The War Memorial
From the War Memorial turn right along Duke Street to the corner with Belvedere View. This brings you to

Location 8: Once the site of the Railway Station
Turn around and go back to the War Memorial. Cross the street, look both ways carefully, and go down the lane at the side of the vacant plot of land. [The infants school, Barr School once stood there.] At the bottom turn right and follow the path bearing to the right. This leads to

Location 9: The Barr Castle
Cross carefully to the car park side and turn left along Barr Street. Halfway along on the grassy area on the right is

Location 10: The Mining Memorial
Continue along Barr Street to the bridge and turn left into Cemetery Road. A short distance along on the right is

Location 11: Grant's Factory
Turn round and walk back along the pavement in Cemetery Road to the bridge. Cross straight over and walk forward up the hill beside the Burnawn and into Glebe Road. At the top of the slope and once round the corner is

Location 12: Once the site of two schools, the Higher Grade on the left and the Primary on the right
Continue on down Glebe Road on the right hand pavement, bear to the right at the bottom and then turn right opposite Dunblane Gardens. This brings you to

Location 13: The Old Co-operative building
You are now back where you started, opposite the side gate of the church

13 The Co-operative

A Co-operative is where a group of businesses trade together for the mutual benefit for all. Commonly this includes distributing a share of profits according to purchases through a scheme which became to be known as 'the divi'. It is thought that one of the first Cooperative groups in the world was the Fenwick Weavers' Society formed in Fenwick in 1761 to sell discounted oatmeal to local workers. The first modern Co-op was founded in 1844 by the Rochdale Society of Equitable Pioneers. Mostly weavers they set up their own store to sell food they otherwise could not afford.

In 1901 the Central Premises of the Co-operative Society opened in Brewland Street. Retail shops on the ground floor included a drapery, hosiery, shoe repairs, tailoring, grocers, fishmonger, house furnishing and a bank. Upper floors accommodated dressmakers and a cobblers workshops, also a bank, the Board Room and a hall with kitchen facilities. Many functions indeed weddings took place in the Co-operative Hall. The Co-op logo of a beehive can be identified on the front of the building.

There were four other branches of the Co-op in town, one shop issued the society's token in lieu of money which could be used to pay for coal. None of these Co-op shops remain, the branch in Brewland Street is now flats. However Galston does have a modern branch of the Co-op sited at its northern outskirts..

189

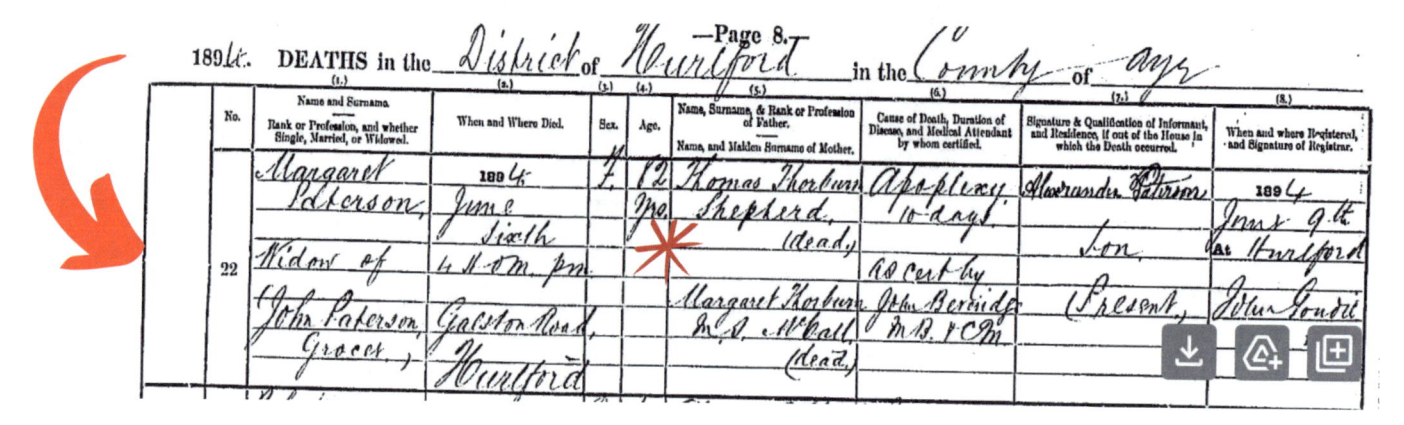

1894 DEATHS in the District of Hurlford in the County of Ayr —Page 8.—

No.	Name and Surname, Rank or Profession, and whether Single, Married, or Widowed	When and Where Died	Sex	Age	Name, Surname, & Rank or Profession of Father. Name, and Maiden Surname of Mother.	Cause of Death, Duration of Disease, and Medical Attendant by whom certified	Signature & Qualification of Informant, and Residence, if out of the House in which the Death occurred	When and where Registered, and Signature of Registrar
22	Margaret Paterson, Widow of John Paterson, Grocer	1894 June Sixth 4 h 0 m. pm Galston Road, Hurlford	F	82	Thomas Thorburn Shepherd (dead) *Margaret Thorburn M.S. McCall (dead)	Apoplexy 10 days as cert by John Berridge M.B. & CM	Alexander Paterson Son (Present)	1894 June 9th At Hurlford John Goudi

Record Transcription: 1894 Deaths in the District of Hurlford in the County of Ayr
Name: Margaret Paterson Widow of (John Paterson, grocer)
1894 June Sixth 4 h. 0 m. PM. Galston Road, Hurlford
F = Female   age 82 years
✳ Father: Thomas Thorburn, Shepherd (Dead)
✳ Mother: Margaret   M.S (Maiden Surname) McCall (Dead)
Cause of Death: Apoplexy 10 days
Informant: Alexander Paterson, son

Thomas Thorburn 1783–Deceased GFPY-2WZ
Margaret McCall 1789–Deceased GFPY-PF8
John Paterson 1808–1884 K8X7-8TQ
Margaret Thorburn 1809–1894 KHL7-NZB

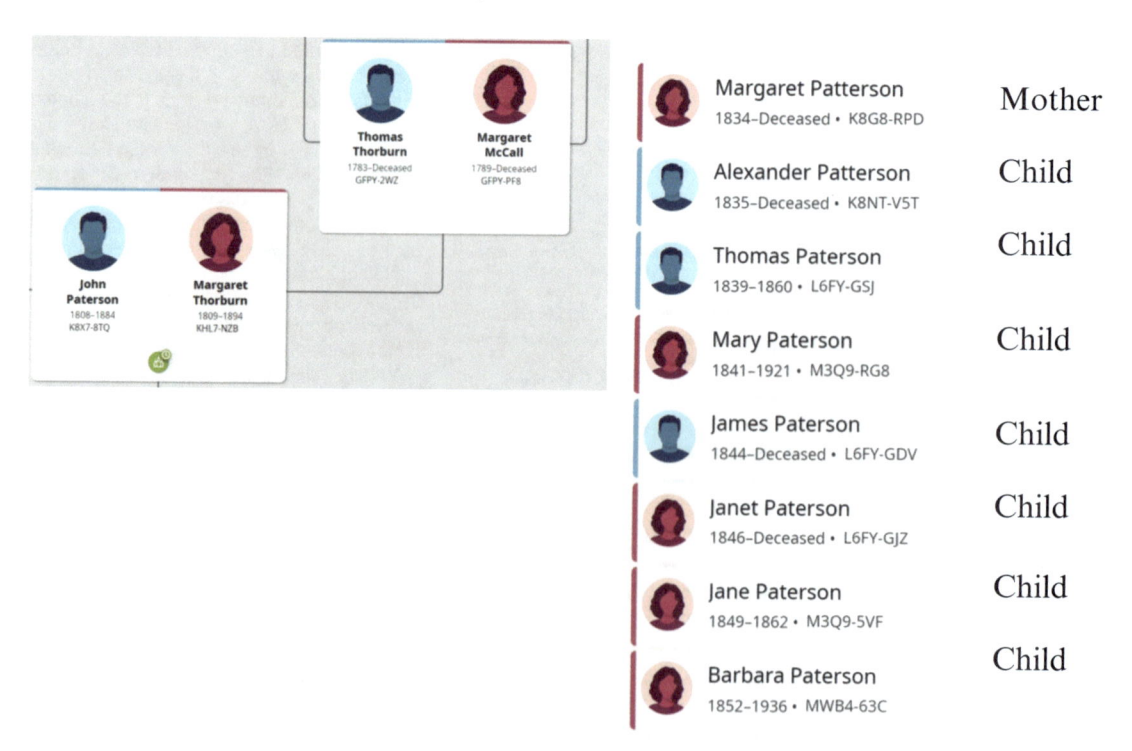

Margaret Patterson 1834–Deceased • K8G8-RPD	Mother	
Alexander Patterson 1835–Deceased • K8NT-V5T	Child	
Thomas Paterson 1839–1860 • L6FY-GSJ	Child	
Mary Paterson 1841–1921 • M3Q9-RG8	Child	
James Paterson 1844–Deceased • L6FY-GDV	Child	
Janet Paterson 1846–Deceased • L6FY-GJZ	Child	
Jane Paterson 1849–1862 • M3Q9-5VF	Child	
Barbara Paterson 1852–1936 • MWB4-63C	Child	

Alexander Paterson
Mary Stewart
parentage

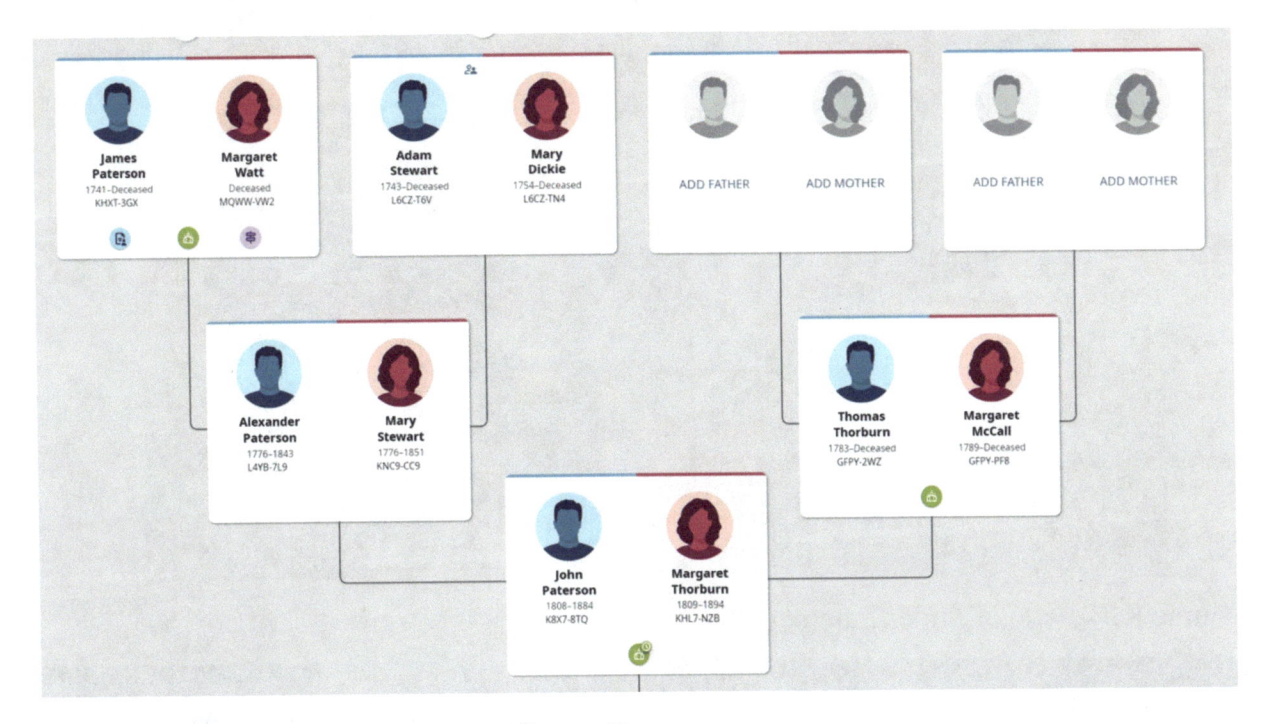

James Paterson

This mini tree shows James Paterson's father, John, along with his parents and grandparents, as well as Margaret Thorburn's parents. John's father, Alexander, and Mary's parents are listed. However, James Paterson's maternal grandparents, Thomas Thorburn and Margaret McCall, don't have their parents listed, but I believe they should be easy to locate.

Memorial for James's Sister and Son. There are siblings, but more research is required to locate them and their families.

IN LOVING MEMORY OF BARBARA PATERSON DIED 10 SEP. 1936 AGED 84 YEARS "Sleeping"

ALSO ... HER NEPHEW GEORGE KIRK PATERSON

Minnie Kirk, wife of James Paterson

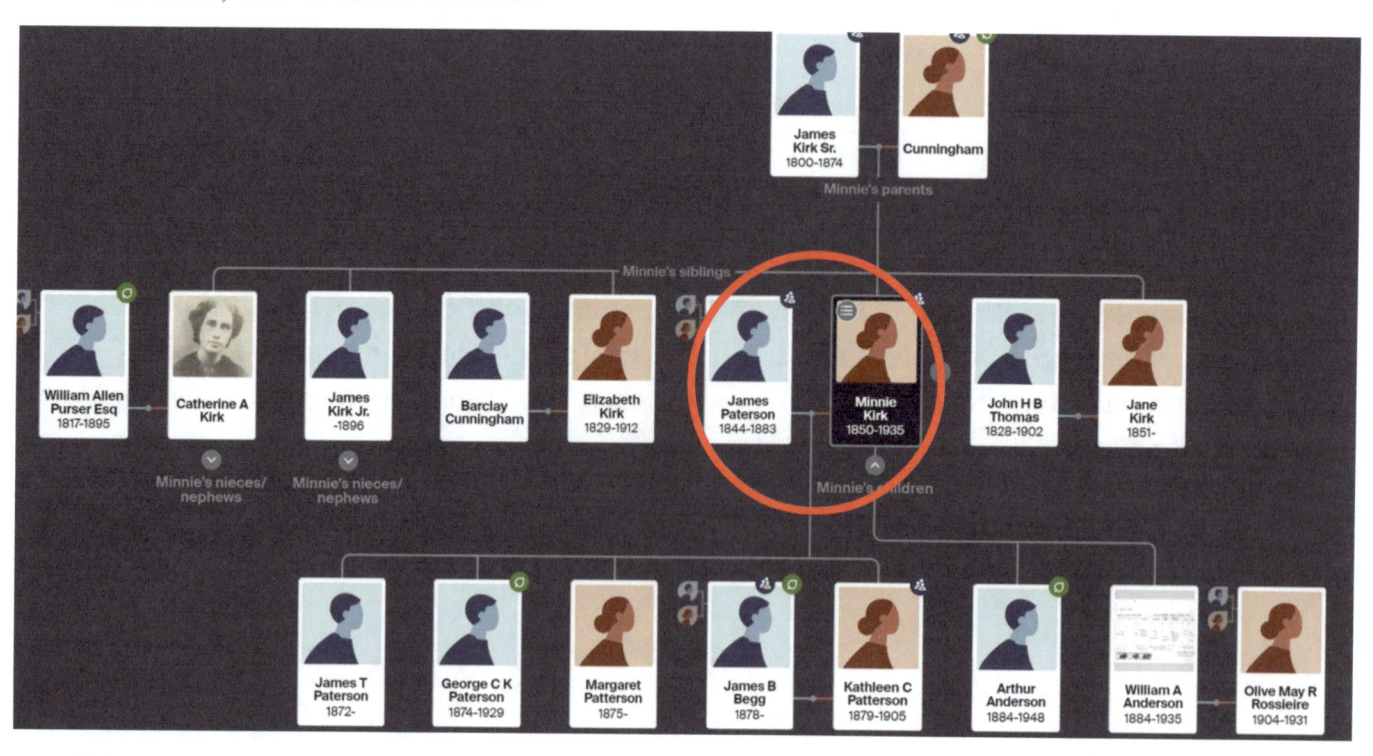

NOTE: *Minnie's first husband, James Paterson, passed as soon as 1883 or before. Her second husband, Richard Benjamin Anderson's family information will be addressed in the next section.*

192

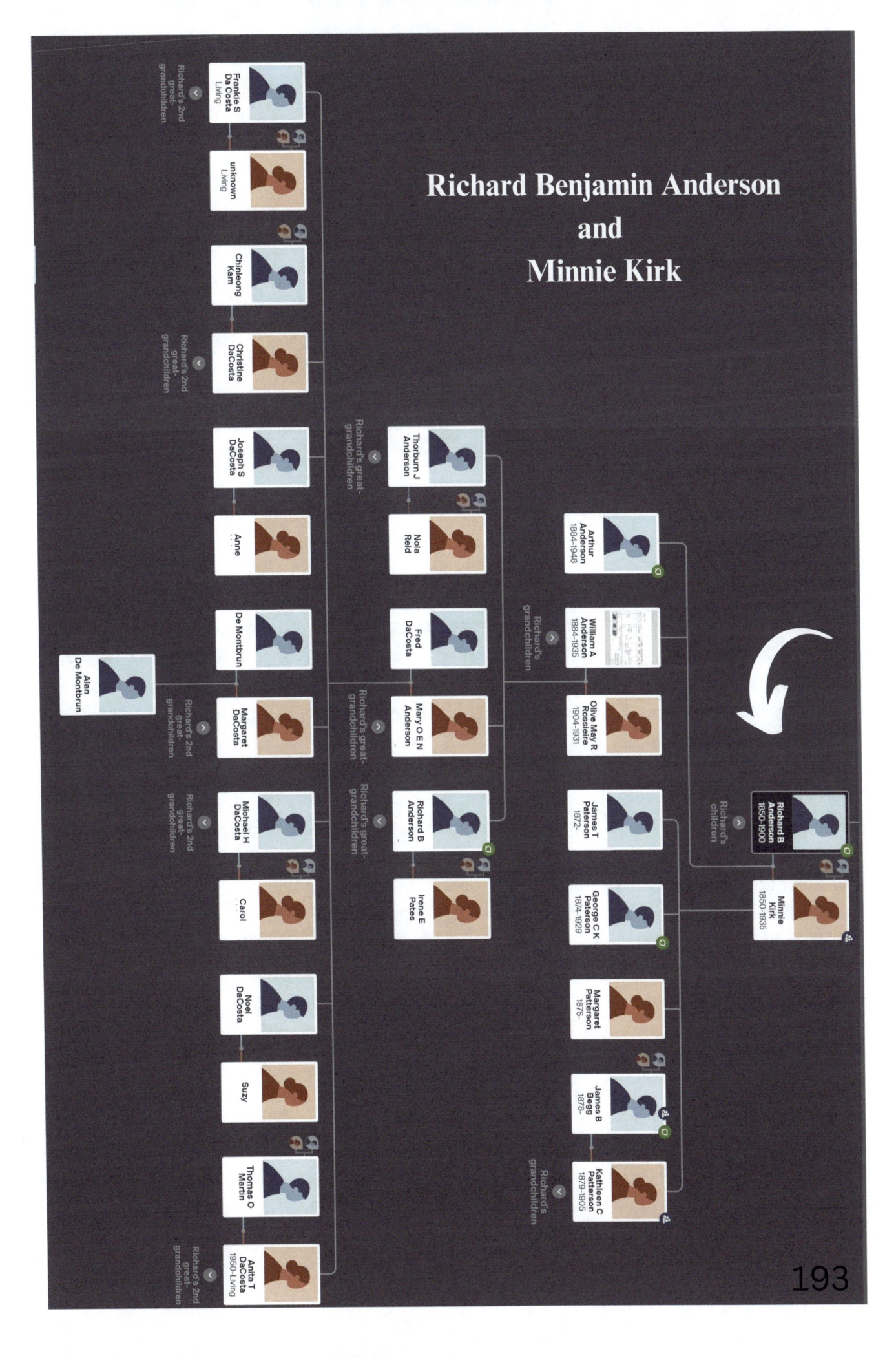

Richard Benjamin Anderson and Minnie Kirk

193

Dr. Richard B. Anderson, F.R.C.S.E

(https://www.encyclopedia.com/history/encyclopedias-almanacs-transcripts-and-maps/belmanna-riots#:~:text=The%20Belmanna%20Riots%2C%20which%20took,the%20English%2Dspeaking%20West%20Indies).

Fellowship of the Royal Colleges of Surgeons of England (FRCSE) is a professional qualification to practice as a senior surgeon in Ireland or the United Kingdom.

Dr. Richard B. Anderson + Minnie Kirk = William Alfred Anderson = Mary Olive Elizabeth Anderson = Da Costa Family. I realize that the DaCosta name is new to some members of the family, but this is one of the primary family that came out of the union of Dr. Richard Anderson and Minnie Kirk. This union would be the step family to the Minnie Kirk and James Paterson union.

This story about Richard Benjamin Anderson was written by his Great Great Grandson, Alan De Montbrun.

Dr. Richard Benjamin Anderson was an extraordinary man who like the Icarus persona of Greek mythology, rapidly rose higher in prestige than many, only to come crashing down in the most dramatic fashion. Unlike Icarus, however, his story did not climax with his collapse, rather it would become the place where his true life narrative would commence. Dr. Anderson would ultimately rise from the ashes of his medical career, and begin a prolonged battle that would consume the rest of his life.

He was born in Billinghay, Lincolnshire, England, one of the three sons of English-born Dr. William Anderson and his Scottish wife, Charlotte Anderson (nee Goode). He followed in his father's footsteps into the medical profession, and he became a distinguished student and prizeman at the St. Mary's Hospital Medical School in England, which he entered in 1866, and in which he became Prosector of Anatomy in 1867. After completing the double qualification of College and Hall in 1869, and taking the Fellowship of the Royal College of Surgeons of England (F.R.C.S.E.) in 1873. He proceeded to the West Indies, where he would join his brother Dr. James G. Anderson who was a Colonial Surgeon on the island of Tobago, and where he would practice until 1891, holding several Government appointments and ultimately becoming a Justice of the Peace for the island.

He became enamoured with Minnie Patterson (nee Kirk), widow of James Patterson, and mother of three young children, Thorburn, Maggie and Kathleen Patterson. They were soon married in 1882, and twin sons, William and Arthur, were born on July 21, 1884 in Orange Grove, Tobago. It was around this time that Dr. Anderson became the owner of a 400-acre cocoa plantation in

Castara, Tobago. With his investment in the plantation, his interest in the politics of his adopted island would grow, and by 1889, he was elevated to act as a Member of the Legislature of the island. It seemed at that time that the doctor was on the fast track to an outstanding medical and political career in the British territory. But everything the young Dr. Anderson had so feverishly built was only just about to come crashing down.

In the same year (1889), he was consulted by a native woman suffering from necrosis of the lower jaw. The patient and her husband were troublesome and Dr. Anderson refused to administer his medical attention. Litigation quickly followed, and Anderson was finally imprisoned by Justice Gorrie and Justice Cook for fourteen days in default of finding bail. As his medical career lay in ruins before him,

Dr. Anderson refused to capitulate, and in 1891 travelled to London to raise a court action against the judgement in Tobago. He successfully obtained a verdict in his favour with 500 pounds in damages against Mr. Justice Cook (Justice Gorrie had since passed away). On Justice Cook's appeal, Lord Esher decided that action could not be taken against a judge for an act done in his judicial capacity, and refused to honour the damages brought by the former judgement, though, he did confirm the London verdict. The disappointment of the ruling would fuel a passion that would consume the balance of Dr. Anderson's life which was spent in a campaign against the wrongs and injustices done to the medical profession.

Outside of his many court battles, Dr. R.B. Anderson was a lover of the English game of cricket, and became one of the main organizers behind the first English cricket team to visit the West Indies on tour in 1894-95. Lord Alan de Montbrun Stamford, together with N. Lubbock, Dr. Anderson and Lord Hawke, coordinated the arrangements and selected the team. It was hoped that Lord Hawke would tour as captain, but in his absence, R.S. Lucas led the party. The team left Southampton on the Medway, and arrived in Barbados on January 28. Other fixtures followed with visits to Antigua, St. Kitts, St. Lucia, St. Vincent, Trinidad, Demerara and Jamaica. This first tour would lead to many more tours over the coming decades to follow. To this day, English cricket tours of the West Indies continue to be a sporting highlight in every island they visit.

On November 7, 1900, Dr. Anderson, perhaps due to some extent to the pressures of his labours as a reformer, suffered the first symptoms of a failing heart, which was temporarily relieved by treatment. On November 8, 1900 however, he succumbed to a second attack at his 32 Montague Place home in London, England at the relatively young age of fifty-two. He was interred at the Lambeth Cemetery, near Balham in England dying as a martyr for the cause of medical reform. Despite the misgivings of his many critics regarding his methods, no one could sincerely doubt Dr. Anderson's absolute honesty of purpose and his desire to serve his profession according to his beliefs. He died alone in his small flat, with no loving family around him to ease his passing, unequivocally proving his fidelity to his cause by giving up to it all dearest to him, including his own life.

A Few More Tidbits about Dr. Richard Benjamin Anderson and His Brother J Goodridge Anderson

.In order to understand this next portion of information about Richard Benjamin Anderson and to some degree, his brother, J. Goodridge Anderson, we need to set up the conditions und understand a bit about the Belmanna riots in Tobago in 1876.

The following article written by Angelo Bissessarsingh, Historian / Researcher (2012) provides us with an insight into what led to the linking of Trinidad and Tobago. It sets up the stage to understand what happened in Tobago. Then I can address, the brothers.

The Roxborough Militia 1877

We sometimes forget that before 1889 Tobago was a separate colony from Trinidad, and therefore it was responsible for its own affairs. A planter militia existed from 1770 as a control mechanism against slave uprisings. Every white male over 21 was required to join the militia, which carried ranks and uniforms. Tobago is an island which preserved its West African heritage against the onslaught of chattel slavery, and its people were little inclined to put up with the oppressions of colonialism.

Meanwhile, in 1854 all British Troops on the island of Tobago were recalled and they were replaced by a scanty force of a Militia. In 1876 unrest erupted on a cocoa estate near Roxborough where our great great great grandfather, James Kirk lived before he died in 1874. The manager of the estate was attacked and chased into the high woods where he was never seen again. The estate house was also burnt to the ground. As disorder spread, the five policemen led by Corporal Belmana intervened to restore peace once again. Belmana , however, a Barbadian was not popular since he was considered a bully. A scuffle broke out between the few police officers and the rioters during which it was alleged that a civilian was shot.

This further aggravated the rioters. The mob went berserk and the police retaliated. The mob had succeeded in getting hold of Bellmana. He was badly beaten and mutilated. A woman called "TI Piggi", due to her appearance was said to have gorged out his eyes and then stabbed him. The corpse was then burnt. Reid was found in hiding, dragged out and badly beaten. The other policemen were also assaulted, stripped and humiliated barricading themselves in their station.

Surrounding the building the mob threatened to burn down the station if Belmana was not handed over. Corporal Reid to ensure his safety lowered himself through some gaps in the floorboards and hid himself under the edifice. Tobago was thrown into a state of anarchy. A frantic message was dispatched by boat to Barbados where the Royal Navy had a fleet of warships.

For a week the rioters were in control, until a warship was sighted. Using tact its captain sent a boat ashore with an emissary who thanked the rioters for "keeping the peace", and not destroying public property. He invited the rioters aboard the ship to be decorated by the Captain for their services rendered. The rioters fell for the ploy and began boarding the ship by the dozens. When the captain was satisfied the ship could hold no more the insurrectionists were clapped with iron and taken to Scarborough to stand trial.

Due to this insurrection the colonial authorities, realized that Tobago, which was already weakened state due to recession and unrest, had to be allied to another colony. This led to the political linking of Tobago to Trinidad in 1889. The riot also led to the strengthening of the Militia in Tobago which from 1887 had a detachment in Roxborough . The new Militia included many blacks since the colonial authorities realized that integration of locals was a more sensible alternative to curbing violence in the island. The Tobago Militia lasted until 1913 when it was disbanded for the last time. (Photo:Roxborough Militia 1877).
— with Angelo Bissessarsingh.

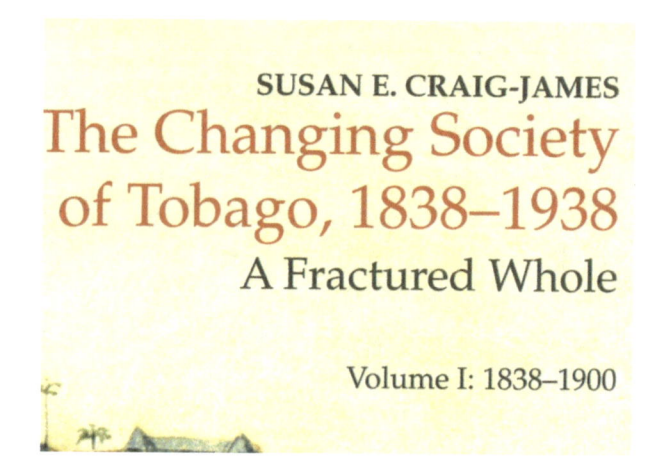

SUSAN E. CRAIG-JAMES
The Changing Society of Tobago, 1838–1938
A Fractured Whole

Volume I: 1838–1900

The fifth combustible element (of the Belmanna Riots in Tobago) in the situation was Dr. Richard Benjamin Anderson (1847-1900), a physician, surgeon and Fellow of the Royal College of Surgeons. He and his brother, Dr. James Goodridge Anderson, also a physician, arrived in Tobago in 1874. By 1876 the Andersons were notorious for charging extortionate fees. The newspapers reported on their high fees as a cause of the Belmanna riots of 1876, and they had to flee from the Windward District to Scarborough for safety during the uprising...

... 1877 Richard Anderson was appointed District Medical Officer (DMO) in District No. 1, which included Scarborough; and the Anderson brothers also became lessees of Castara Estate, which they bought in 1880. They displayed a remarkable penchant for litigation, and took clients to court for trifling sums owed. In 1878 alone, Richard brought 80 such cases before the courts.

Between 1880 and 1882, three petitions, signed by people of all walks of life, asked for neither brother to be a DMO, because of their rough manners and high fees. Richard Anderson was therefore confined to being the Colonial Surgeon, with responsibility for the Scarborough hospital. With his brother he conducted a lucrative private practice. Sir William Robinson, then Governor of the Windward Islands, commented privately to Edward Wingfield at the Colonial Office: I have no confidence in these Andersons, they are a hard & grinding lot.

In 1881 the Andersons owned the only chemist's shop in Scarborough, as part of their dry goods merchant house, trading under the ironic name of Goodridge and Good. As the only chemists in Scarborough, Goodridge and Good enjoyed a monopoly over the importing of medical drugs. As Colonial Surgeon, Richard Anderson prescribed and supplied drugs from his own dispensary at the Government's expense. By 1882 the Andersons had increased their holdings in Tobago, having leased Grafton Estate and become part-owners of The Dawn, a steam vessel.

When the authorities investigated Richard Anderson's business connections, he denied that his involvement in Goodridge and Good was prejudicial to his office. He agreed that the rates charged by his firm for drugs were too high by half, but stated that theirs were the most reasonable uncontracted rates in the West Indies or probably in the world! At length, under pressure, he agreed on 6 October 1882 to withdraw from Goodridge and Good, but the medical practice in partnership continued.

In 1883 the Royal Commission enquiring on the public revenue, debts and liabilities of some of the British Caribbean colonies reported that the Tobago hospital under Anderson's care was the worst in the BWI. To justify himself, Anderson wrote reports totaling 420 pages, in which he blamed the Government for lack of funds and cooperation.

By then, the London officials were tired of the contentious correspondence to which he was prone. Sydney Olivier described him as 'a wrongheaded & cantankerous man', and Lord Derby, the Secretary of State, as 'self important and touchy in the extreme'. They began to anticipate, in Wingfield's words, that 'we may have to consider ... getting rid of Mr Anderson from the service.' After Anderson took two women to court for fees more than twice the official rates in 1883, he was carefully watched with a view to his dismissal. Again, his 'hard and inequitable spirit' received comment, this time from Dr. Carrington, the Administrator.

But the Colonial Office hesitated to transfer Anderson, because they thought his appointment elsewhere would be unjust to any recipient colony. However, Sir Walter J. Sendall, the Governor-in-Chief, was asked '(privately) to find out what he would take' to be sent elsewhere."

The Colonial Office finally had to remove Anderson from office when he refused to visit Jane Dryce, also known as Blacky Mamby, although she was in labour and having fits. Dryce, aged 19, died a miserably agonizing death in childbirth at Lambeau on 2 December 1885. Her mother, Sarah Mamby, had walked over 20 miles to find the DMOs without success, since two of 'them were out of their districts. Though she returned several times to plead, and undertook to pay little by little as was customary, Anderson demanded that people with cash guarantee his payment before he visited Dryce.

The News, commenting on Anderson's 'shameful and heartless brutality' and his 'surpassing heartlessness', called for his dismissal. All Tobago was incensed. The inquest found that Anderson had 'acted with great inhumanity in not attending her—more especially as he had attended her on a previous occasion and had been paid for his services." The only redeeming features of Anderson's career in Tobago were his activities as secretary to the Commission for the Colonial and Indian Exhibition held in London in 1886, and his energetic service on the planning committee for Queen Victoria's Jubilee in 1887. The post of Colonial Surgeon was abolished in 1886. Anderson was granted abolition allowance, but the London officials decided that he should not be employed elsewhere." This is the unhappy record of Anderson's public service before 1888 when his brother died.

HISTORY OF MINNIE KIRK

QUICK FACTS:

BORN
TOBAGO

PARENTS
JAMES KIRK
[UNKNOWN CUNNINGHAM

CHILDREN
AT LEAST 6

200

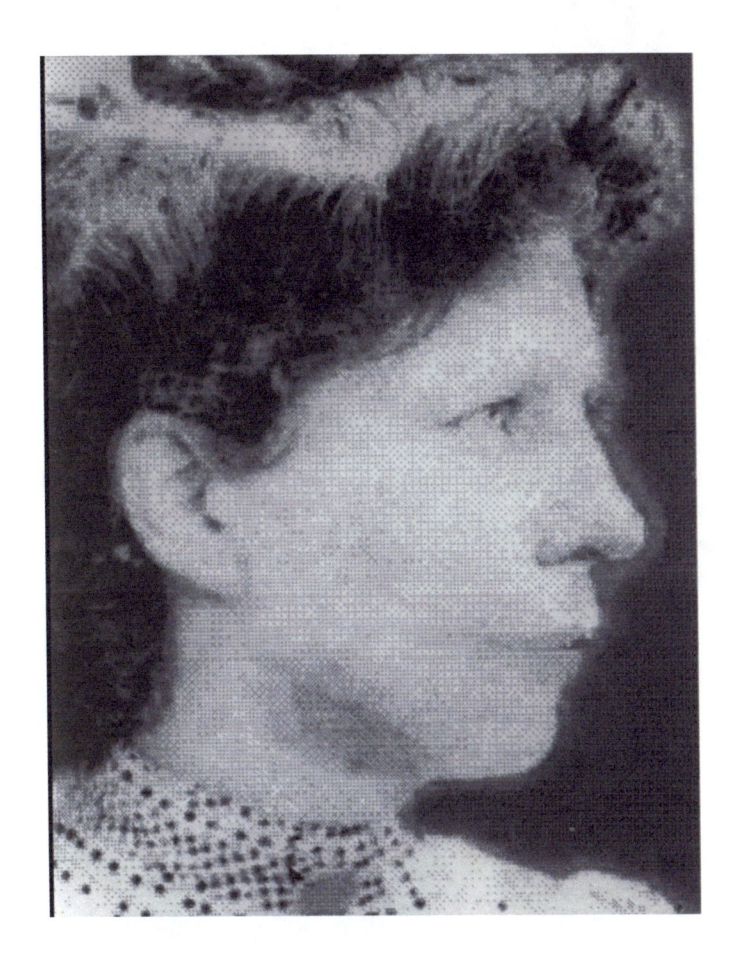

Minnie Kirk a Brief Introduction

Born: Approximately 1850
Died: December 25, 1989

Minnie was married to James Paterson, deceased, then Richard Benjamin Anderson.

Born the youngest child of James Kirk, Sr. **Her siblings** were: James Kirk, Jr. Catherine, Elizabeth, Jane.

Children with James Paterson
Kathleen Cunningham Paterson
James Thorburn Paterson
George Cundel Kirk Paterson
Margaret Paterson (???)no substantiated source available

Children with Richard Benjamin Anderson
Twins, William Alfred, and Arthur Anderson

Date - Approx.	Milestone Event
1850	Birth - Tobago
1870	Marriage to James Paterson
1882	Death of James Paterson
1883	Marriage to Richard Benjamin Anderson
1884	Birth of Twins
1900	Death of Richard Benjamin Anderson
1935	Death of Minnie

ALL ABOUT MINNIE

Minnie Kirk - There has been some mention that this photo is Maggie. She is listed as Minnie's daughter on the Sheppard (Paterson) records. On the Anderson side, she is identified as Minnie herself.

Minnie Kirk and her Granddaughter, Enid. Our information shows that Enid went to live with Grandma Anderson (Minnie Kirk) when she was a child.

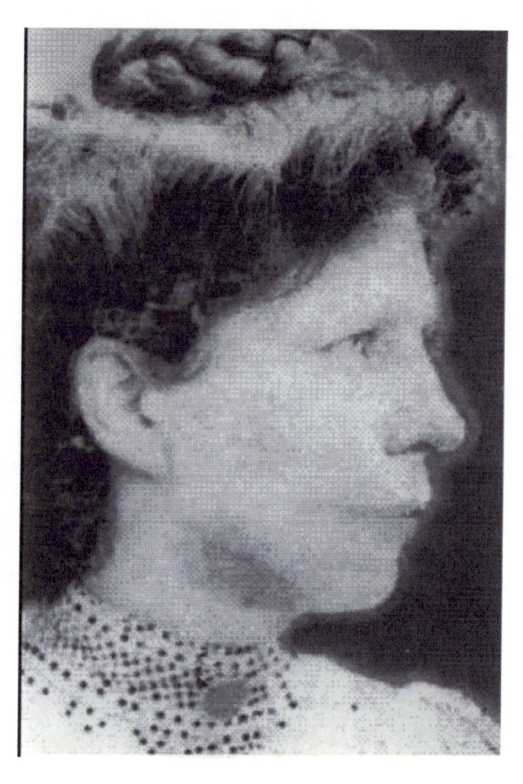

A random family of estate owners or managers in Tobago. This was how they would have dressed and the clothes they would have worn from the time of our ancestors in Tobago. This is very likely to be the manner in which Minnie lived.

The 1867 Paris Exposition tThe London Crystal Palace   Finsbury Squate

Where Minnie walked

A Letter from Catherine's son by her first marriage:
James Frederick Witz wrote his mother, Catherine, about an encounter with their Aunt Minnie. He wrote his letter, July 15, 1867 from Finsbury Square

My dear Mamma
As the time has come round again for writing I will tell you what news I have: the first is that Louis & myself went to the Crystal Palace about a fortnight ago with aunt Minnie & she told us that she was going to the Paris Exhibition and when she returned would take us to the Crystal Palace a second time as it was so crowded when we went with her before because it was considered a grand day.

The Crystal Palace

Opened 1851, Relocated in 1854. It stood until it was destroyed by fire on an evening in 1936

A Grand Day is a special day in English law when the courts are not in session.

The Exposition Universelle of 1867, better known in English as the 1867 Paris Exposition, was a world's fair held in Paris, France, from April 1 to November 3, 1867. There were 50,226 exhibitors, with 15,055 from France and its colonies, 6,176 from Great Britain and Ireland, 703 from the United States, and a small contingent from Canada.
What is particularly interesting is that Minnie attended the 1867 Expo. One hundred years later, I was able to attend Montreal's Expo '67, as it was called. I attended with my family and Grandpa Walter Sheppard, Minnie's grandson. It was a surreal and beautiful moment to realize that I, as his granddaughter, was following in the footsteps of my ancestor. The connection between these two Expos felt like a lovely synergy.

100 Years Later - Montreal's Expo 67

France | Great Britain | USA
USSR | Quebec | Japan
Canadian Tree Board | India | Ontario

The participating countries were:

Africa

Algeria, Cameroun, Chad, Congo, Côte d'Ivoire, Ethiopia, Gabon, Ghana, Kenya, Madagascar, Morocco, Mauritius, Niger, Rwanda, Senegal, Tanzania, Togo, Tunisia, Uganda, and the United Arab Republic (Egypt);

Asia

Burma, Ceylon, China (Taiwan), Korea, Kuwait, India, Iran, Israel, Japan, and Thailand;

Australia

Europe

Austria, Belgium, Czechoslovakia, Denmark, Finland, France, Federal Republic of Germany, Greece, Iceland, Italy, Monaco, the Netherlands, Norway, Sweden, Switzerland, United Kingdom, the USSR, and Yugoslavia;

South America

Guyana and Venezuela;

North America & Central America

Barbados, Canada, Cuba, Grenada, Haiti, Jamaica, Mexico, Trinidad and Tobago, and the United States.

1967 Montreal

Official Expo 67 Logo

Expo '67 - Theme: Man and his World

- **Du Pont Auditorium of Canada**: The philosophy and scientific content of theme exhibits were presented and emphasized in this 372 seat hall.[26]
- **Habitat 67**
- **Labyrinth**
- **Man and his Health**
- **Man in the Community**
- **Man the Explorer**: Man, his Planet and Space; Man and Life; Man and the Oceans; Man and the Polar Regions
- **Man the Creator**: The Gallery of Fine Arts; Contemporary Sculpture; Industrial Design; Photography.
- **Man the Producer**: Resources for Man; Man in Control; Progress.
- **Man the Provider**

Pamela Sheppard, (nee Martin) and Brent Sheppard at Expo 67 in front a Man the Explorer; Man and the Polar Regions; and Man and the Oceans exhibits. Summer 1967.

The American Pavilion

Pam, Brent, Carol and Arleen (looking toward Pam) Fall 1967

My father, David Sheppard, worked for Nelson Stud Welding during the construction of the Montreal Expo '67. He was the salesman responsible for the bridge that provided access to the island where Expo '67 was held. He also supplied the stud welding parts and systems for the construction of the American Pavilion.

Generation Four++

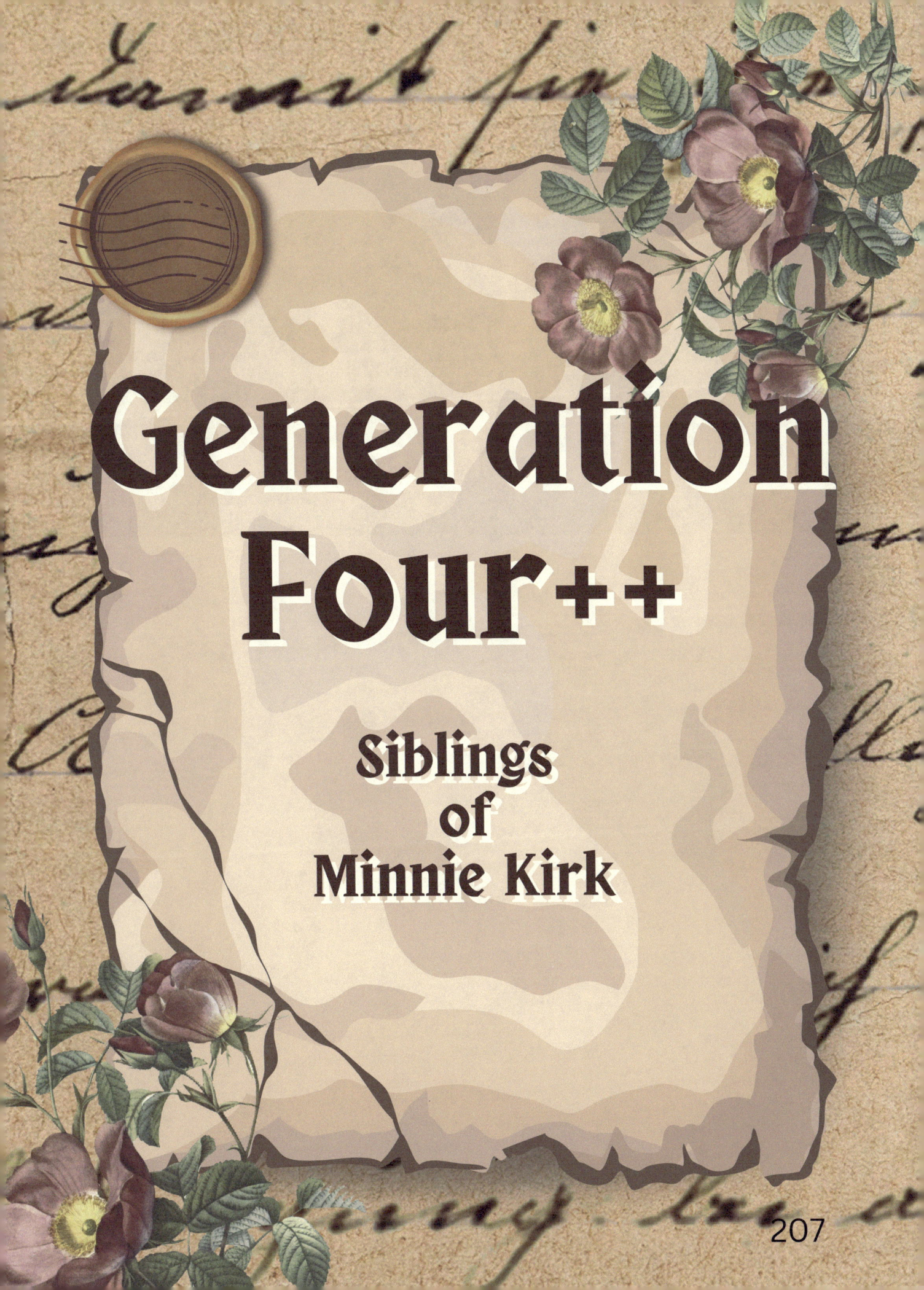

Siblings of Minnie Kirk

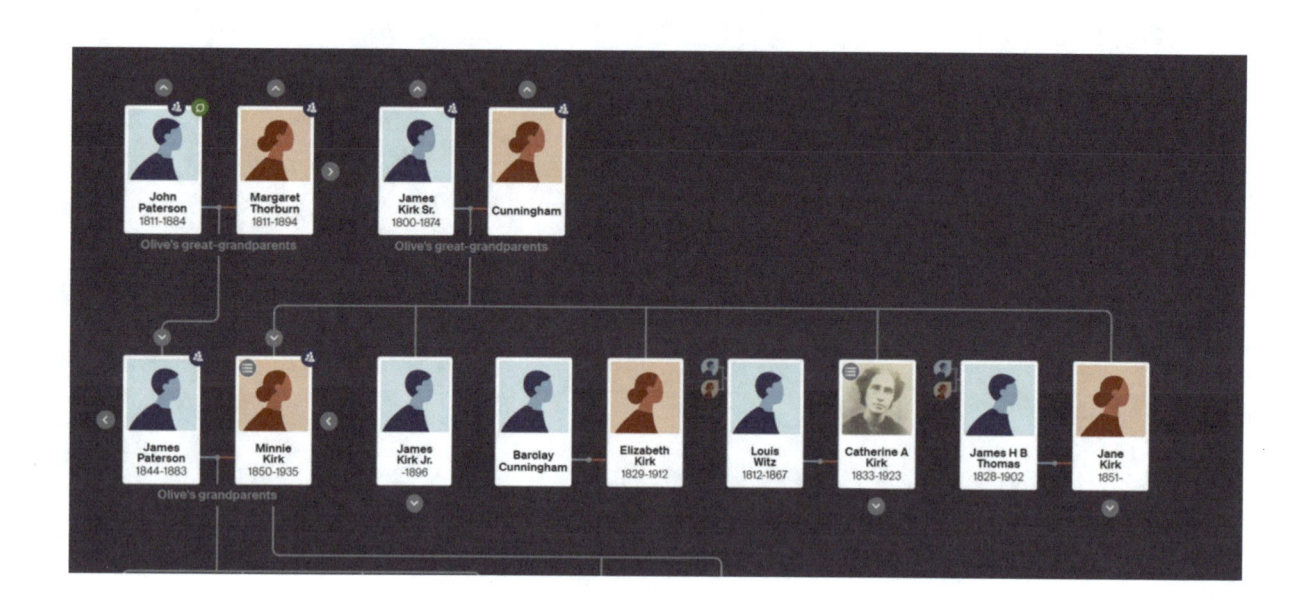

Olive's great-grandparents: John Paterson (1811-1884), Margaret Thorburn (1811-1894)

Olive's great-grandparents: James Kirk Sr. (1800-1874), Cunningham

Olive's grandparents: James Paterson (1844-1883), Minnie Kirk (1850-1935)

James Kirk Jr. (-1896), Barclay Cunningham, Elizabeth Kirk (1829-1912), Louis Witz (1812-1867), Catherine A Kirk (1833-1923), James H B Thomas (1828-1902), Jane Kirk (1851-)

Jane Kirk's Husband and Son

DEATH.—Mr. James Henry Barker Thomas, J.P., died in Scarborough on Monday, 31st March, having completed his seventy-fourth year on the 8th March. Mr. Thomas was a native of Grenada, and came to Tobago when he was eighteen. His energy and perseverance brought him to the front rank in Tobago society. He married Miss Jane Kirk, daughter of the late President Kirk, by whom he had thirteen children—nine sons and four daughters—six of whom (three sons and three daughters) survive him. Mr. Thomas owned Kendal Place, Belle Garden, Sion Hill and Florida estates, all of which went out of his hands during the sugar crisis. He was attorney for the large sugar estate Messrs. Thomas Reid and Sons London, and he continued to enjoy their confidence until the fall of sugar compelled those gentlemen to withdraw their business from Tobago. Mr. Thomas was a master carpenter of ability. He built St. Mary's Anglican Church and Plymouth Anglican Church, besides several other buildings. He was quiet and unassuming in character. By his death, another "living history" has

End of Article missing.

Minnie Kirk's sister Jane. was married to James Henry Barker Thomas. They had 13 children - 9 sons and four daughter. 6 children survive to 1902 - 3 sons and 3 daughters

James Barclay Thomas was the son of James Henry Baker Thomas and Jane Kirk.
Article appeared in the Mirror (Trinidad & Tobago) - Monday 05 September 1907
James was alive when his father died. He was one of the 3 sons who was alive when his father died. Four short years later he died as he and his career and positions on the island were starting to take off.

A FATAL FALL.

On Thursday, September 5, whilst Mr. James Barclay Thomas was returning from the Government Stock Farm, his horse slipped with him twice at the Bay, and the second time he was thrown over the horse's head, the animal falling on him. He was taken up by some people who ran to his assistance and taken to a house near by, bleeding profusely through the mouth and nose. Dr Blanc was telephoned for, and he replied, ordering him to be taken to the hospital with all possible haste. No time was lost in removing him, and with prompt medical aid consciousness was restored after some time. It was quite evident that he could not survive the shock very long, and although medical skill succeeded in lengthening out the time, the end came on Sunday morning, September 8, at the early age of 35. He was buried the same afternoon at the Wesleyan Cemetery at the Scotch Kirk by the Rev. G. Earle, Wesleyan Minister, at 5 o'clock Mr. Thomas was one of those friendly, unostentatious unassuming characters rarely met with in these small communities, hence the large funeral procession which followed his remains to their last resting place, borne by the principal master carpenters in Scarborough, he having been a master carpenter himself. He was appointed Government foreman carpenter previous to the death of Mr. Clarke, and the late Bishop Hayes appointed him carpenter for the Anglican Church in Tobago. During his appointment he built the Les Coteaux Anglican church, and also sealed the St. Andrew's Anglican church, Scarborough, on the eve of his receiving an appointment from the Governor. As Government foreman carpenter he built the new Roxborough Police Station, and received the thanks and congratulations of Colonel Brake and Mr. Hitchins. Mr. Thomas was from the old aristocracy of Tobago, his father being the late James Henry Barker Thomas, proprietor of Kendall Place estate and his mother Miss Kirk, daughter of the late President Kirk. The late Mrs. Elliot was his paternal aunt. Much sorrow is expressed on all sides for his sorrowing mother, his young widow, and his other relatives who have been thrown so suddenly into such grief. The certificate of death issued by Dr Blanc says the unfortunate young man died of "acute traumatic meningitis."

Elizabeth Kirk

Mirror (Trinidad & Tobago) July 19, 1912

DEATH OF MRS. E. CUNNINGHAM.

One of the oldest and much respected landmarks of Tobago was removed in the death of Mrs Elizabeth Cunningham on Thursday, July 11, at her late residence at "Highland".

The deceased was the daughter of the late James Kirk, at one time President of Tobago in the early sixties of the last century and owner of the Roxborough estate. She was born in 1829 and was the relict of the late Barclay Cunningham, who was at one time chief clerk in the Colonial Secretary's Office in Tobago, in the last century. Mrs Cunningham had a very brief illness which she bore with all christian courage, and despite the tender care of her relations she succumbed to an attack of dysentery, the malady which is very prevalent just now in this ward. She left two sisters, Mrs Purser, relict of the late Dr Purser, and Mrs Anderson, relict of the late Dr Anderson for whom much sympathy is felt.

The funeral took place at 4.30 p.m on Friday, July 12, to the Moriah Moravian Church and was very largely attended. Mrs Cunningham was an Anglican all her life, but was a great supporter of the Moravian Church. A very solemn ceremony was performed by Rev T L Clemens. The other ministers present were the Revs W T Allen, W Charles and Ross. Mrs T L Clemens presided at the organ and as the corpse entered the church the Dead March in Saul was played.

The bearers were Messrs Thomas Joseph, George Agard, A John, G Hamilton, T Edwards and D Catto.

Among the followers were Messrs William McCall, Jas Baird, C Armstrong representing G D Hatt (merchant) and W Patterson.

Letters of condolence were sent by Messrs D McGillivray, John Isaac and G D Hatt.

Minnie Kirk's sister, Elizabeth, was married to Barclay Cunningham. She was born in Tobago in 1829. Died at 83 years old.

Catherine Anne Kirk

Catherine was the most photographed and with pictures still existing. We are fortunate to have records, photos and stories about her and her family.

Catherine Kirk a young woman

Catherine the Matriarch

Catherine Anne Kirk
Born: 1833
Died: 1923
Married to Louis Witz
Widowed in 1867
Married to William Allen Purser
Widowed in 1895

At some point after William passed away, Catherine, with some of her family, moved to Ireland.

However by the time she passed away in 1923 at Steeple Bumpstead, Essex

Catherine with Her Children and Grand Children

A Tale of Catherine's Two Husbands

Catherine was reputed to have said, "My first husband was a worldly man, my second husband was a Godly man."

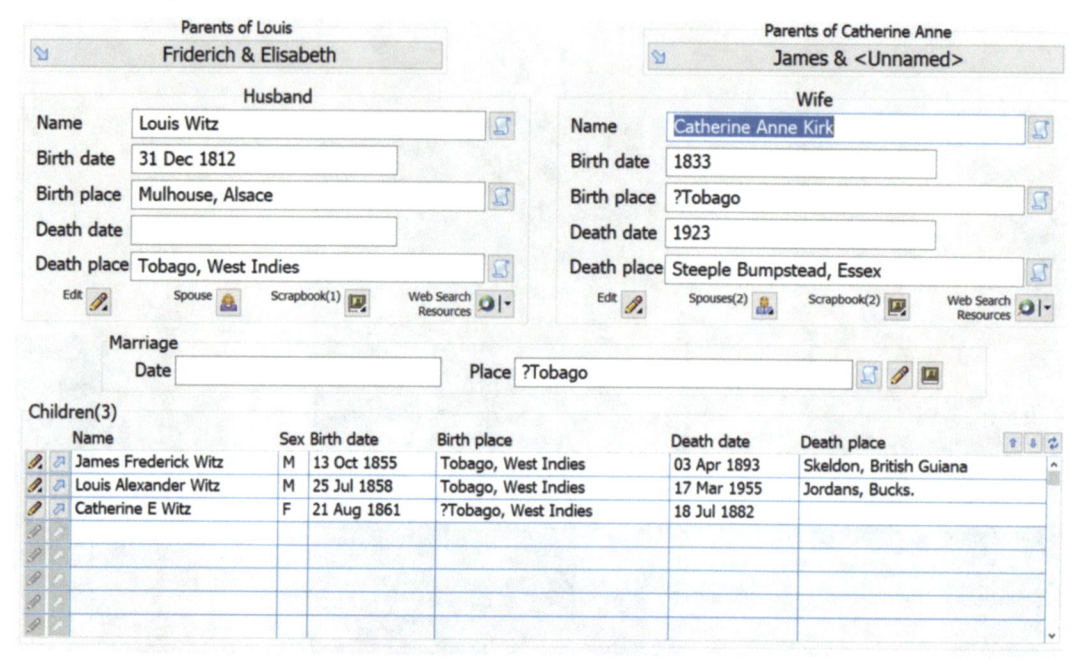

Parents of Louis: Friderich & Elisabeth
Parents of Catherine Anne: James & <Unnamed>

Husband
- Name: Louis Witz
- Birth date: 31 Dec 1812
- Birth place: Mulhouse, Alsace
- Death date:
- Death place: Tobago, West Indies

Wife
- Name: Catherine Anne Kirk
- Birth date: 1833
- Birth place: ?Tobago
- Death date: 1923
- Death place: Steeple Bumpstead, Essex

Marriage
- Date:
- Place: ?Tobago

Children(3)

Name	Sex	Birth date	Birth place	Death date	Death place
James Frederick Witz	M	13 Oct 1855	Tobago, West Indies	03 Apr 1893	Skeldon, British Guiana
Louis Alexander Witz	M	25 Jul 1858	Tobago, West Indies	17 Mar 1955	Jordans, Bucks.
Catherine E Witz	F	21 Aug 1861	?Tobago, West Indies	18 Jul 1882	

Louis Witz was an estate manager and owner.

Parents of William Allen: John Secundus & Sarah
Parents of Catherine Anne: James & <Unnamed>

Husband
- Name: William Allen Purser
- Birth date: 09 Apr 1817
- Birth place:
- Death date: 09 Apr 1895
- Death place: Babylon Island, Tobago, West Indies

Wife
- Name: Catherine Anne Kirk
- Birth date: 1833
- Birth place: ?Tobago
- Death date: 1923
- Death place: Steeple Bumpstead, Essex

Marriage
- Date: 04 Feb 1868
- Place: Tobago, West Indies

Children(3)

Name	Sex	Birth date	Birth place	Death date	Death place
John James Purser	M	17 Feb 1872	Tobago, West Indies	1962	
Lyle Sarah Purser	F	10 Dec 1873	?Tobago, West Indies	20 Sep 1876	?Tobago, West Indies
Lydmar Moline Purser	M	06 Oct 1875	Tobago, West Indies	14 Mar 1964	Truro, Cornwall

William Purser was a doctor who happen to attend to many of our ancestors.

On the next page, the Article about Dr. William Purser's life is shown here in its totality. It was written by Jesma McFarlane. Dr Purser is not a direct ancestor, but his wife is my 2xs great aunt. There are a few corrects, but they are listed at the end.

The Untold Story of Dr William Allen Purser, Tobago (1817 – 1895)
by Researcher & Author : Jesma Mc Farlane.

William Purser was born on April 9,1817 and came to Tobago in 1853 when he was about 36 yrs. old. He was a physician, a Licentiate of the Royal College of Surgeons (LRCSI), Ireland. He was interred at the Moriah Moravian cemetery. On his tomb seen above is the following epitaph:

Dr. Purser was married to Catherine Anne Witz on February 10 1868, He was 50 years old, a surgeon, a bachelor, and lived in a house overlooking the Moriah Broadplace junction (his home was called Babylon (3). Catherine Anne was 34 years old, a widow, a proprietress of an estate, and lived at Woodlands. Catherine's maiden name was Kirk and she is described as the relict of the late Louis Wite (2) of Woodlands. William and Catherine were married in the United Brethren church of Moriah (now known as the Moriah Moravian church). One of the witnesses was James Kirk senior. William and Catherine had 4 children, Dr John James Purser, Lydmar Moline Purser, Catherine Anne Purser and Lyle Sarah Purser(5a).

"In Affectionate Remembrance
of
William Allen Purser LRCSI.
Born April 9, 1817.
Departed April 12th, 1895.
For over forty years he
laboured in this island
doing good to soul and body.
Always abounding in the work
of the Lord.
1 Cor XV 58."(1)

Dr. Purser was an Irish Physician, educated at Trinity College, Ireland and came to Tobago in1853. He was an accomplished musician and engaged in many religious activities including lay preacher. By 1855 he was active in the Methodist school in Castara teaching the elder of the children the elements of music and singing. In 1856, Purser was giving weekly singing lessons to the children and young people of Montgomery, while training a children's choir at Moriah. Members of the Church of England, especially at Plymouth and Les Coteaux came under his influence, and he was officially appointed a Reader in that denomination.

By September 1857, Purser formed a large class at Moriah and included among his contributions was as conductor to a 100-voice choir who sang Handel's Messiah at Fort King George, Scarborough, Tobago.

In January 1876, a Board of Education drawn from each denomination in Tobago was formed. Dr William A. Purser, Rev. J.L. Hasting and C.A. Berkeley represented the Moravian church; Rev. Henry Hutson, Charles F. Cadiz and H.L. Byng from the Church of England; and Rev Charles Buzza, James H. Keens and Duncan McGillivray from the Methodist Church.

In 1887, Dr Purser had a semi-theatrical troupe at Moriah. He kept up his ministry of music until his death in 1895.**(4)**:

In the burial register he was #450, class command unattached, buried on April 13, 1895 (4 days after his death). His number in the record was 1049 and he was the 251st male. He was buried by Theodor L. Clemens. In the remarks column was written "Israelite indeed! Revs Turpin and Giterribe? Read lessons**(5b)**. Influenza (was the cause of death"). In the year Purser died there were 2 other influenza deaths in May.

It is interesting to note that from 1777 to 1846 in the death records there were deaths from dysentery, most occurring in the months of July and August. From July 1912 to Nov. 1913 a notable amount of dysentery deaths.
Other areas of interest was that when Dr. Purser died probate was granted to Louis Alexander Witz in Dublin.

SPECULATIONS

· James Kirk was the acting Governor of Tobago in 1856. He also owned Woodlands estate at one time. He was possible **the brother (1)** of Catherine Anne Kirk whose age is given as 34 years at marriage in 1868. It can be estimated **her birth year to be 1834 and was 22 years old (2)** when her **brother (1)** was Governor Her profession on her marriage certificate is given as Proprietress of an estate. In1884 Purser was allegedly suspended from his duties as (District Medical Officer) DMO, Justice of the Peace and member of the Board of Education, for assisting his wife's brother, James Kirk, who was suspected of embezzling public funds to leave Tobago.**(a)**

PERSPECTIVES

The Moravian church has a tradition of cleaning graves and placing flowers on them at easter time. As a child growing up in the Moravian church I joined the tradition after my father died in
"Perhaps one of the most prolific sources of error in contemporary thinking rises precisely from the popular habit of lifting history out of its proper context, and bending it to the values of another age and day."**(6)** I say this because it appears as though there were no choirs in existence and no reference to them. I believe that Dr. Purser with his experience simply built on what was already present.
I am speculating that maybe Dr. Purser's migration to Tobago was due to the great famine in Ireland in the 1840's when about a million Irish migrated.

SOURCES

a Craig, Susan. 2008. "The Changing Society of Tobago, 1838-1938. A fractured Whole. Vol. 1).

11 Corinthians XV 58 states "Therefore, my beloved brethren, be ye stedfast, unmoveable, always abounding in the work of the Lord, for as much as ye know that your labour is not in vain in the Lord."

2 There must have been some connection between Catherine Anne and Louis Alexander Witz who was granted probate of Dr. Purser's estate. Catherine was referred to as the relict of the late Louis Wite (the name Wite and Witz seems to have been interchangeable and relict = widow) of Woodlands. The name Witz is probably of German origin.

3 The area is still referred to as Babylon

4 Susan E. Craig-James. 2016. "What Mean These Stones?" St. Andrews Heritage Trust.

5a No. 1049 in the Burial Register, Moravian Church, Moriah, Tobago, West Indies
The expression "Israelite Indeed" was drawn from Gospel of John 1:47. Verses 46 – 48 are instructive." Verse 47 states "Jesus saw Nathanael coming to him, and saith of him, Behold an Israelite indeed, in whom is no guile."

5b Marriage Register , Moravian Church, Moriah, Tobago, West Indies. 1840-1883

6 Laurens Van Der Post. 1958. "The Lost World of the Kalahari." Penguin Books

Wiki Tree – where Genealogist collaborate.

ACKNOWLEDGEMENTS

There are persons who contributed to this document that I must mention. Chief among them is *Reverend Roberts* of the Moriah Moravian Church for allowing me access to valuable church records. The *Reverend Canon Leroy Lyon*s on religious directions. *Shirley Taylor, Joy Lyons, Cheryl Lee Kim, Jessa McFarlane* for their input in terms of critical comments and *Glenda Blackman Anthony* for accompanying me on church and cemetery research.

The Tomb of William Allen Purser in the Moriah Moravian Church Cemetery, Tobago, West Indies

CLARIFICATIONS *by Arleen Froemming*

There are corrections to this article. This is due to confusion between James Kirk, SR and James Kirk, JR.

(1) James Kirk, SR was the acting governor in 1956 and was Catherine's father. She was born in 1833, therefore she was 23 when her father became the acting governor. He died in 1874 in Tobago.

James Kirk, Jr., Catherine's brother, was the party found guilty of 3 counts of embezzlement. He is the one that William was censured for allegedly helping escape prosecution.

(2) Catherine was born in 1833 in Tobago.

(3) Catherine was the mother of Louis Alexander Witz.

James Kirk, Jr

James Kirk, Jr's life is as a puzzle. We can piece his life together bit by bit by articles and registers where he appears. However, understanding them and what they mean can only be assumed.

Kirk, James
10 years
Scarboro

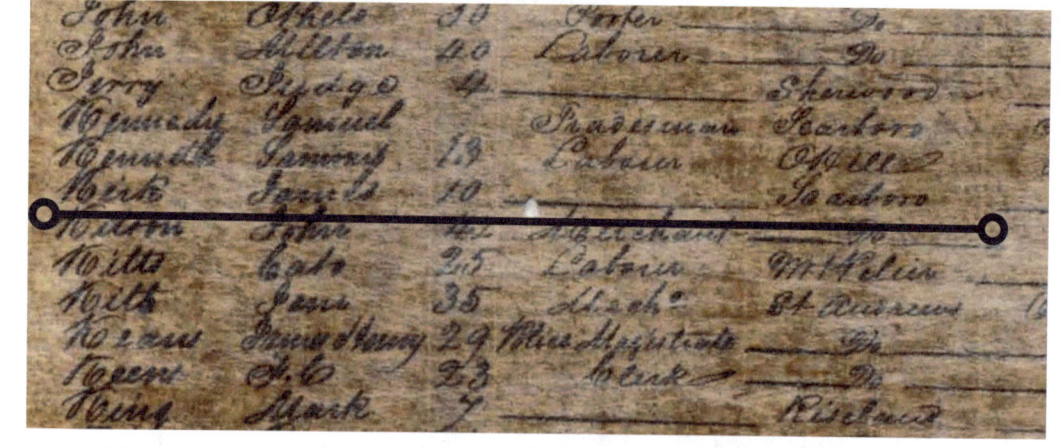

The first record of James Kirk Jr. appears on the Tobago Census for St. Andrew between 1839 and 1841. His birth year can be inferred as between 1828 and 1831. In the same census, a Jane Kirk is listed as being 2 1/2 years old in another parish. If she was his sister, it suggests they had different maternal parents.

It's important to note that learning about their mothers through traditional means is difficult, as records before 1892 in Tobago have not been digitized.

Next, I'd like to present a few pieces of evidence regarding James Kirk Sr.'s life, which help paint a picture of his son's (James Kirk Jr.) life. In 1844, James Kirk Sr. applied for convalescence leave and was granted it. He traveled to South Florida, then to New York, and eventually to the UK. While in the UK, he attended the Ween and Breadalbane Cattle Show, where he was seated in a position of honor.

Another piece of evidence comes from an 1847 advertisement in various newspapers across the colonies. The ad promoted the High School of Glasgow, and James Kirk was listed as a contact for the school in Tobago. This meant that anyone in Tobago seeking an endorsement to attend the prestigious school could reach out to him. Scots who had made their fortunes in the West Indies often sought such prestigious schools for their children.

Many Scots who went to Tobago or other sugar plantation islands sought to elevate their status by sending their children to such schools or returning to Scotland with enough wealth to build an estate. I believe James Kirk Sr. may have accomplished at least one of these goals, possibly for his only son.

Here is part of the advertisement that described the mission of the High School of Glasgow in educating young men. I believe James Kirk Sr. may have brought his son, James Kirk Jr., to Scotland in 1844 during his convalescence tour to enroll him at this school. It's possible that James Jr. graduated from in 1847, the same year the ad appeared.

Glasgow Courier *May 27, 1847*

Page 3 of 4   Article: Liverpool, Farber, r

> ...Grounds of Dalbeth, can receive, on TUESDAY, 1st June, a few additional Pupils, from eight to sixteen years of age, to be prepared for the UNIVERSITIES, the MILITARY COLLEGES, or COMMERCIAL PURSUITS. Young Gentlemen requiring peculiar attention may be educated entirely at Dalbeth; but in ordinary cases, the boys are taught on a system which unites the discipline and emulation of a Public School, with the advantages of Private Study under a Clergyman and a Cambridge Graduate in Honours, both resident in the House. The domestic arrangements are superintended by an English Lady; and the Pupils (chiefly from England) are treated in every respect as members of the family, and trained to the usages of good society.

There is a possibility that the James Kirk mentioned in this article could be James Kirk Jr. (JR) rather than James Kirk Sr. (SR) as the Tobago representative. For this to be the case, JR would have had to have obtained his law degree upon graduating. While James Kirk Sr.'s name was styled with "Honorable James Kirk," this ad refers to James Kirk, Esq. This could apply to either of them, meaning the individual in question could be my great-great-great-grandfather (GGGGrandfather) or my 2nd great-uncle.

Glasgow Courier - Thursday 27 May 1847   Page 3 of 4

Public domain

Location	Representative
Kingston, Jamaica	Messrs. Scott, Leaycraft & Co.
Madras	Rev. Mr. Bowie.
Malta	G. M. Pullis, Esq.
Manilla	Messrs. Ker, M'Micking & Co.
Mauritius	Messrs. Richardson, Mood & Co.
Melbourne	Messrs. Pullar, Porter & Co.
Montreal	Messrs. Pollok, Gilmour & Co.
Nevis	Messrs. A. Linnington & Co.
New-Orleans	Messrs. Lowe & Pattison.
New-York	Messrs. Buchanan, Harris & Co.
Point-de-Galle	John Black, Esq.
Porto Rico	William Orr, Esq.
Singapore	Messrs. Syme & Co. ❤️❤️
Sydney	Messrs. R. How & Co.
St. John, N.P.	Messrs. M'Bride & Kerr.
Toronto	Walter Macfarlane, Esq.
Tobago	James Kirk, Esq.
Trinidad	Messrs. Losh, Spiers & Co.

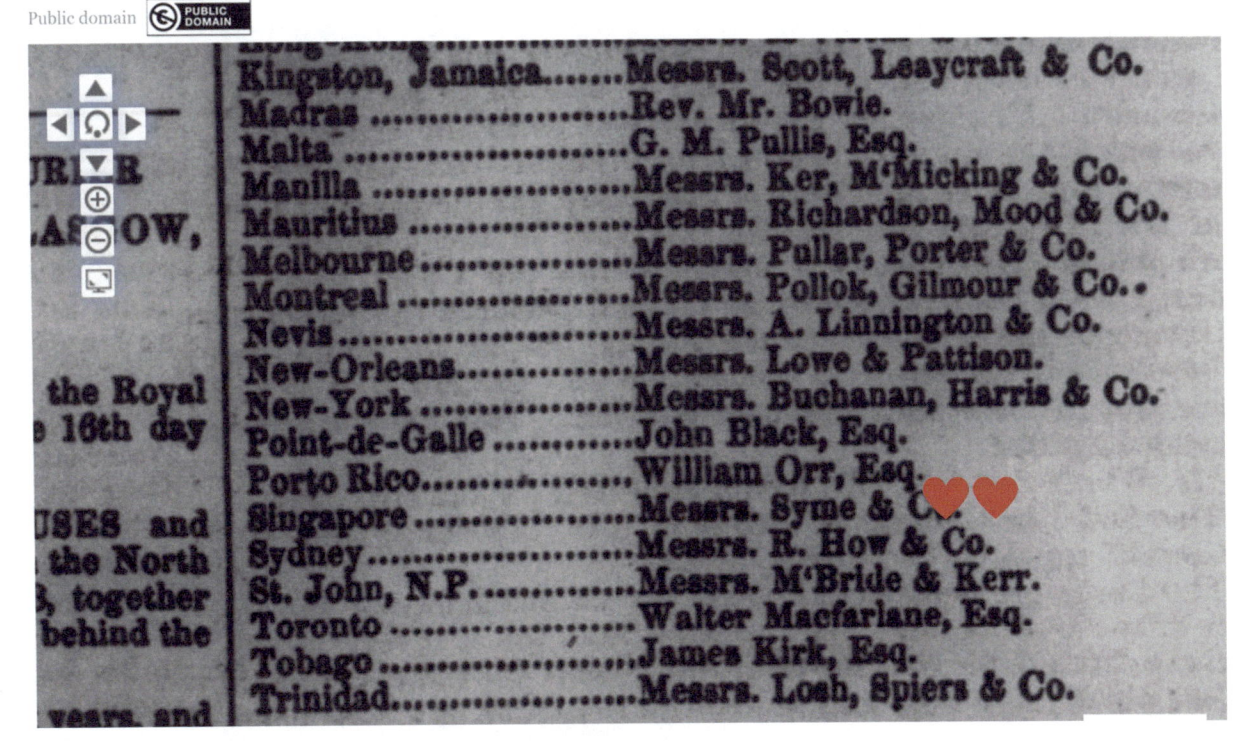

Here we will see his just a few of various appointments by the Queen Victoria of England to James Kirk, JR.

The Colonies and India, 09 February 1883

Official Appointments.—The Queen has been pleased to appoint Alfred Peach Hensman, Esq., to be Attorney-General of the Colony of Western Australia. The Queen has been pleased to appoint James Kirk, Esq., to be a member of the Executive Council of the Island of Tobago. The Queen has been pleased to appoint the Rev. Ernest Graham Ingham, M.A., to be ordained and consecrated Bishop of the See of Sierra Leone. The Earl of Derby has appointed Mr. H. W. Just, of the Colonial Office, to be his Assistant Private Secretary.

The London Gazette, 06 November, 1870

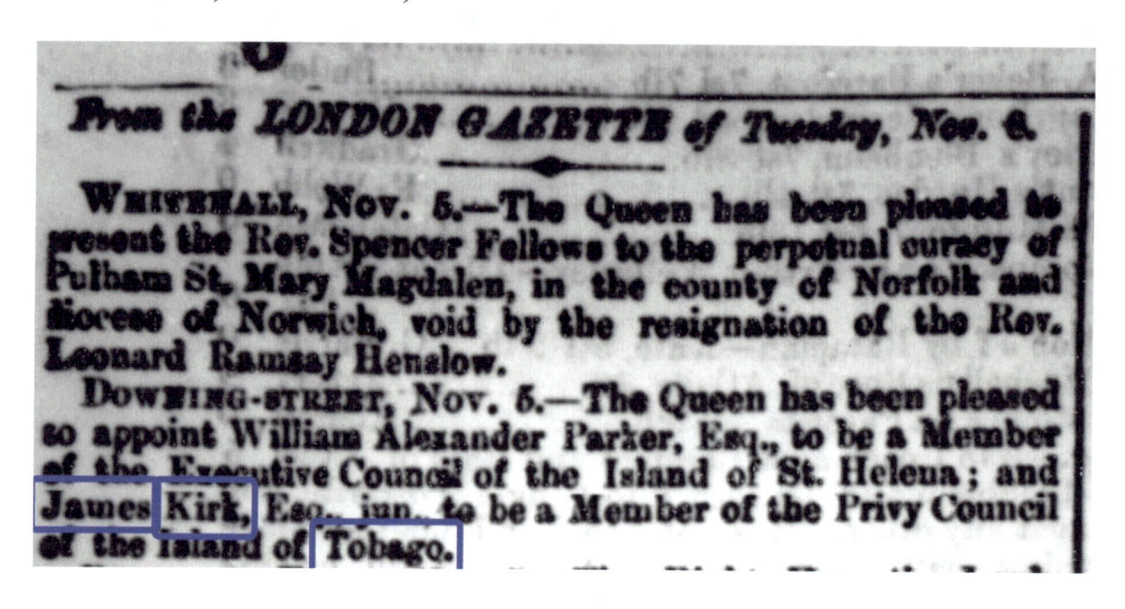

From the LONDON GAZETTE of Tuesday, Nov. 8.

WHITEHALL, Nov. 5.—The Queen has been pleased to present the Rev. Spencer Fellows to the perpetual curacy of Pulham St. Mary Magdalen, in the county of Norfolk and diocese of Norwich, void by the resignation of the Rev. Leonard Ramsay Henslow.

DOWNING-STREET, Nov. 5.—The Queen has been pleased to appoint William Alexander Parker, Esq., to be a Member of the Executive Council of the Island of St. Helena; and James Kirk, Esq., jun., to be a Member of the Privy Council of the Island of Tobago.

THE YORKSHIRE POST AND LEEDS INTELLIGENCER, WEDNESDAY, FEBRUARY 7, 1883.

OFFICIAL APPOINTMENTS.

Last night's *Gazette* announces that the Queen has been pleased to appoint Mr Alfred Peach Hensman to be Attorney-General of the colony of Western Australia; Mr James Kirk to be a member of the Executive Council of the island of Tobago; and the Rev. Ernest Graham Ingham, M.A., to be ordained and consecrated Bishop of the see of Sierra Leone.

Here are a few more appointments for James Kirk, Jr.

THOM'S
IRISH ALMANAC
AND
OFFICIAL DIRECTORY
OF THE
UNITED KINGDOM OF GREAT BRITAIN AND IRELAND;
FOR THE YEAR
1873.

James Kirk SR
Privy Council

This article for 1873 is noteworthy because James Kirk SR and James Kirk JR are both appointed to leadership positions for Tobago. Which at this time was independent. Trinidad and Tobago merged to one nation in government in 1892.

This is also curious because according to Seniors obituary when he died in 1874, he was reported to be suffering from a condition that left him paralyzed for 4 years before surrendered to the disease.

James Kirk JR, Coroner

TOBAGO.

This island is situated in 11° 9' N. lat., and 60° 1 W. long., 18 miles north-east of Trinidad. It is 3 miles long, and from 6 to 12 broad, and its area is 9 square miles. Population in 1871, 17,054. The government consists of a Lieutenant-Governor (subordinate to the Governor-in-Chief of the Windward Islands and Barbados), a Privy Council, Legislative Council, and House of Assembly, the latter consisting of 16 Members elected by the several parishes. Revenue, 1871, £14,270 Expenditure, £10,387. Value of Imports, 1871, £66,378 of Exports, consisting chiefly of Sugar, Rum, and Molasses, £95,310. Total tonnage of vessels entered and cleared in 1871, 8,233 tons.

Lieutenant-Governor, Chancellor, and Ordinary, His Excellency HERBERT TAYLOR USSHER, C.M.G., (1872), Scarborough, £1,300
Colonial Secretary, S. H. Hill, esq., £200 and fees

PRIVY COUNCIL.
The Lieutenant-Governor.

Hon. James Kirk, sen. | Hon. Dougald Yeates
Hon. James Henry Keens | Hon. Chas. A. Berkeley
Hon. Robert Gordon | Hon. Thomas Miller Sealy
Hon. Charles F. Cadiz

Clerk, S. H. Hill, esq.

EXECUTIVE COMMITTEE.
Hon. Robert Gordon | Hon. T. M. Sealy.
Hon. Charles F. Cadiz

Secretary, S. H. Hill, esq.

LEGISLATIVE COUNCIL.
(7 Members.)
Clerk, S. H. Hill, esq

LEGISLATIVE ASSEMBLY (16 members).
Speaker, Hon. Robert Crooks.
Clerk of Assembly, William Desvignes, esq.

CIVIL ESTABLISHMENT.
Treasurer, Charles A. Berkeley, esq., £350
Revenue Officers, Henry Francis and Joseph Worall, esqrs.
Postmaster, James Hamilton, esq., £60
Harbour-master, William Yeates, esq.
Inspector-General of Police, Robert Crooks, esq., £250
Government Engineer and Surveyor, R.W. M'Eachnie,
Inspector of Roads, R. W. Mackachnie, £200

JUDICIAL ESTABLISHMENT.
Chief Justice and Judge of Vice-Admiralty Court a Commr. of Incumbered Estates Court, Hon. Joseph K. Wattley, £700 and fees
Attorney-General, Hon. Charles F. Cadiz, £250
Provost-Marshal, Robert Crooks, esq., £200
Stipendiary Magistrates, Dougald Yeates, Samuel Ferdinand Titzek, and S. J. Fraser, esqrs, £200 each
Coroners, Robert Gordon, Dougald Yeates, Samuel F. Tit James M'Call, James Kirk, jun., and S. J. Fraser, esqrs

ECCLESIASTICAL ESTABLISHMENT.
Rectors, Rev. Henry Hutson, Rev. S. Bradshaw (act.), £320

219

James Kirk, Jr., in 1872, was appointed to the Legislative Council in Tobago in a Special Session. He was also appointed as Justice of the Peace and Inland Revenue officer.

THE TOBAGO GAZETTE.

SCARBOROUGH, FRIDAY, SEPTEMBER 27, 1872. [No. 39.]

TOBAGO

SPECIAL SESSION

OF THE

HONORABLE HOUSE OF LEGISLATIVE COUNCIL.

To JAMES KIRK the Younger Esquire—GREETING

WHEREAS a vacancy has occurred in our Legislative Council and we deem it expedient and proper to fill such vacancy NOW KNOW YE that having especial trust and con-

THE TOBAGO GAZETTE.

fidence in your ability integrity and fidelity We summon and command you the said James Kirk the younger that laying aside all excuses you be and appear in our said Council as soon as our said Council shall meet then and there to advise with our Governor and Councillors upon the Public affairs and business of our said Island and to give us your counsel therein and in this you are not to fail as you will answer the contrary at your peril.

Witness our trusty and well beloved Cornelius Hendericksen Kortright Esquire Lieutenant Governor in and over our Island of Tobago and its Dependencies Chancellor Ordinary and Vice-Admiral of the same.

Dated at the Court House in Scarborough this sixth day of August 1872 and in the thirty-sixth year of Our Reign

By His Excellency's Command,

SAMUEL H. HILL

Colonial Secretary.

Here we will see his just a few of various appointments by the Queen Victoria of England to James Kirk, JR.

The London Gazette, 06 November, 1870

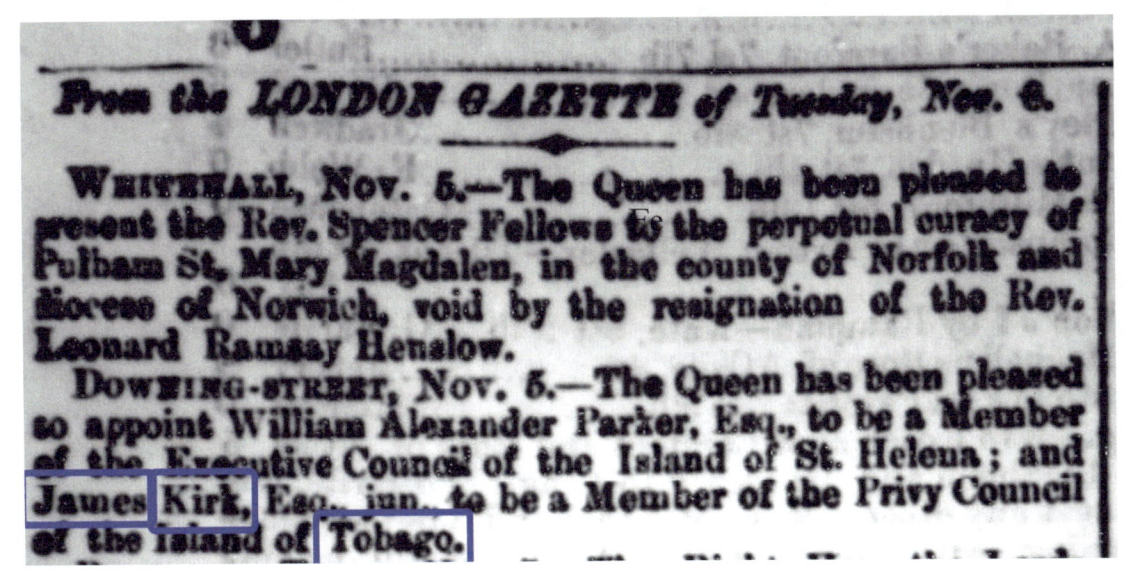

From the LONDON GAZETTE of Tuesday, Nov. 6.

WHITEHALL, Nov. 5.—The Queen has been pleased to present the Rev. Spencer Fellows to the perpetual curacy of Pulham St. Mary Magdalen, in the county of Norfolk and diocese of Norwich, void by the resignation of the Rev. Leonard Ramsay Henslow.

DOWNING-STREET, Nov. 5.—The Queen has been pleased to appoint William Alexander Parker, Esq., to be a Member of the Executive Council of the Island of St. Helena; and James Kirk, Esq., jun. to be a Member of the Privy Council of the Island of Tobago.

The Morning Herald - April 1, 1863 - This is James Kirk Sr.

DOWNING-STREET, MARCH 28.—The Queen has been pleased to appoint the Right. Rev. William Walrong Jackson, D.D., Lord Bishop of Antigua, to be a Member of the Legislative Council of the Island of Antigua. Her Majesty has also been pleased to appoint James Kirk, Esq., to be a Member of the Privy Council of the Island of Tobago; Joseph Goodman, Esq., to be a Member of the Legislative Council of the Island of Saint Lucia; John Stevenson Grant, Esq., to be a Member of the Legislative Council of the Bahama Islands; and Copeland James Stamers, Esq., to be a Member of the Legislative Council of the Turks and Caicos Islands.

KIRK, JAMES.—Inspector of police and inland revenue, Tobago.
KIRK, SIR JOHN, M.D., K.C.M.G. (1881), C.M.G. (1879).—Her Majesty's political agent and consul-general at Zanzibar.
KIRKE, HENRY.—Graduated at Oxford, B.A., 1863. M.A. 1866. B C.L. 1866. Called to the bar

These are the most significant appointments of James Kirk JR, and will shape generations of Kirks to come.

In order to present that information, we must present the events of SR's life.

⟵⟶

We will pause on James Kirk Jr. for now. There is a very tangled web that arises after James Kirk Sr.'s life. Our goal is to explain, in part, how all of this knowledge about our family line was completely lost. I hope to be able to address this in a logical and clear manner in the future..

⟵⟶

KIRK SR TO TOBAGO IN 1825

The Honorable James Kirk, Senior

James Kirk was born in Dumfries, Scotland on or about 1800. He remained there until approximately 1825 when he relocated to Tobago, West Indies as an Indentured Servant. The details of Senior's life are gathered from his Obituary:

The Colonist BMDs - 1874

THE COLONIST MONDAY APRIL 6 1874 P 2 COL 3

KIRK -At Roxborough, Tobago, on 21st March, after suffering for four years from an attack of paralysis, which kept him confined to his bed during that period, the Hon. James Kirk, senior, aged 74 years.

Standard *May 6, 1874*

There is no way that we can talk about James Kirk and avoid talking about his participation in Estates and Plantations funded by Slavery.

DEATH OF THE HON. JAMES KIRK.—In our obituary of to-day will be found recorded the death of the Hon. James Kirk, senior, at Roxborough, Tobago. The deceased gentleman, says a Tobago journal, who was a native of Dumfries (Scotland), was the oldest European inhabitant of the colony, having been resident there for over 49 years. He was of most active and energetic habits, was the representative there of many influential gentlemen in England, and became himself the proprietor of several estates in the colony. He was the senior member of her Majesty's Privy Council, and administered the Government on four different occasions. The esteem in which the deceased gentleman was held by the whole community was evinced by the large and numerous assembly who attended at Roxborough, some of whom had come a distance of 25 miles, to pay the last tribute of respect to his memory. The cortege consisted of gentlemen of all positions and from all parts of the Island, besides a large concourse of labourers, &c., from the various estates, who had been recipients of his bounty. He leaves a large family, and also a large circle of friends and acquaintances, to mourn their loss.

The esteem in which he was held is notable and evidenced by inclusion of a large concourse of Laborers. The large family he left behind appears to be mostly lost. We were able to uncover a few details about the family with the articles that written about in obituaries.

Indented by Lord William Robert Keith Douglas

JJames Kirk was born around 1800 in Scotland. He was indentured to Lord William Robert Keith Douglas and served on his properties in Tobago from 1825 to 1828.

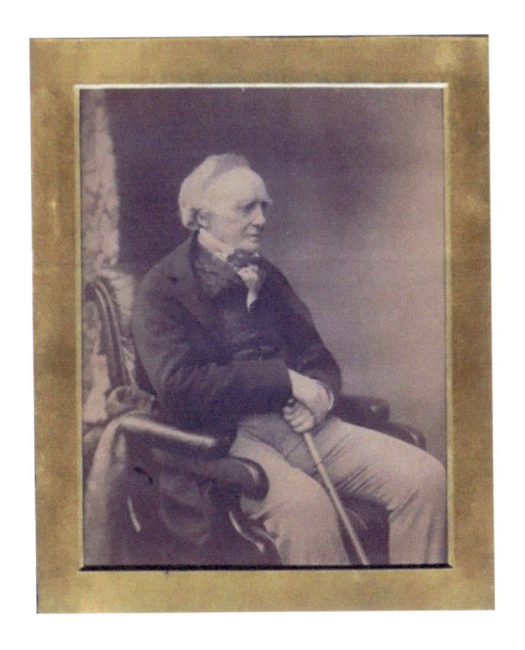

Lord Douglas married Elizabeth Irvine, the daughter of Walter Irvine of Tobago. Upon their marriage, Lord Douglas inherited the properties left to Elizabeth by her father. James Kirk was initially hired through an Indenture Agreement to work on these estates. However, the specific position James began with on the estates is not known.

In later texts, newspaper articles, magazines, and books, James Kirk begins to be referred to as the "Honorable James Kirk" and also as "James Kirk, Esq." It is unclear whether James became a lawyer after his period of indenture or if he already possessed those skills before coming to Tobago from Scotland.

Speculation

Kirk must have had some skills before he left Scotland in 1825, as a 25-year-old man. Clearly, he was educated, as evidenced by his impeccable penmanship. It is highly plausible that Kirk already had an advanced education and may have been a solicitor in Scotland, or he could have served a three-year clerk apprenticeship, which was required to become an attorney. The Kirk's indenture could have been to serve as a clerk for three years and then become an attorney.

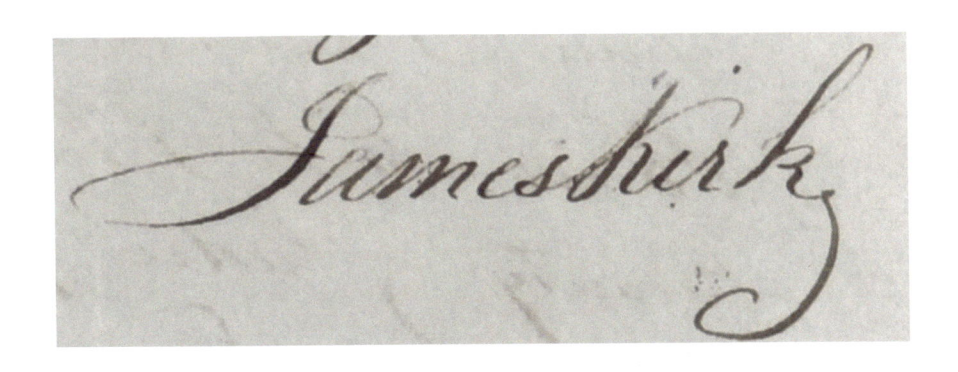

James Kirk Signature

KIRK
APPOINTMENTS &
ACCOLADES

While he was in he held many appointments, including to the British Privy Council for several years. Appointments and reappointments. Such as:

The London Gazette.
Published by Authority.
Numb. 22695.
FRIDAY, JANUARY 2, 1863.

There are several appointments, but this example will suffice.
if someone would like to see more, you can go to https://dloc.com/ and search "James Kirk" and add "Tobago"
You will get upwards of 2700 hits and many tell the story of James Kirk to pick through.

Downing Street, March 2ᵈ, 1863.
The Queen has been pleased to appoint the Right Reverend William Walrong Jackson, D.D., Lord Bishop of Antigua, to be a Member of the Legislative Council of the Island of Antigua.
Her Majesty has also been pleased to appoint James Kirk, Esq., to be a Member of the Privy Council of the Island of Tobago; Joseph Goodman, Esq., to be a Member of the Legislative Council of the Island of Saint Lucia; John Stevenson Grant, Esq., to be a Member of the Legislative Council of the Bahama Islands; and Copeland James Stamers, Esq., to be a Member of the Legislative Council of the Turks and Caicos Islands.

He served as the interim President of Tobago at least twice, in 1856 and again from 1864 to 1865. His obituary mentions that he served four terms as Administrator, as he was the senior member of the Privy Council. This is confirmed by several notices of his appointment to the Privy Council.

In addition to his administrative work, he was an artist and naturalist. He is credited with naming many of the birds found on the island. One of the birds he identified is called a "Kirkie" in his honor. He also named Pigeon Point in Tobago after the large flock of birds that roosted there. He authored a book titled List of Birds in Tobago, which is housed, though not displayed, in The London Museum. Additionally, he has entries in Types-Specimens of Birds in the British Museum (Natural History).

Perthshire Courier October 24, 1844

The first recorded mention of James Kirk in the newspaper occurs on October 24, 1844, in Scotland, where he attended the Ween and Breadalbane Cattle Show. He was listed as an attendee, seated closely to the left of the chairperson of the event. The mention of his seating position near the chair may have been intended to highlight his honor or importance at the show.

KENMORE.
The Weem and Breadalbane Cattle Show was held here upon Thursday the 17th instant, and, upon the whole, was not only equal in point of numbers to most of the former ones, but decidedly superior as regards the quality of the stock exhibited—particularly black-faced sheep. In the latter class, indeed, so great was the general merit of the stock brought forward, that the Judges had considerable difficulty in awarding some of the premiums. From the general appearance of the stock, as well as the encreased competition with black cattle amongst the lower class of tenants, the great benefits of this competition in such a district must be very obvious; and deserves the warmest encouragement both from proprietors and tenants. A number of gentlemen, farmers, and others interested, sat down to dinner, in Walker's Inn, at four o'clock. The chair was occupied by John S. Menzies, Esq. of Chesthill (in the absence of the Marquis of Breadalbane), supported on the right by Capt. Houston Stewart, R.N., Captain Mackenzie, E.I.C.S.,; on the left by Robert Robertson, Esq., yr. of Auchleeks, James Kirk, Esq. of Tobago, &c. Alexander Stewart, Esq. of Duneaves, John Campbell, Esq. of Garrows, Angus Macdonald, Esq., banker, Callander, Robert Peter, Esq., banker, Aberfeldy, Messrs Charles Stewart, Duneaves, Menzies, Auch, Sinclair of Inverhaggarry, &c., &c., were present.— J. F. Wyllie, Esq., Bolfracks, and Archibald Campbell, Esq., Camserney Cottage, acted as croupiers. The party spent a highly pleasant evening—the wit and humour emanating from the vicinity of the chair literally keeping the table in

KIRK AND JARDINE

Contemporary of Sir William Jardine

James Kirk met Sir William Jardine when he was a young man. During a hunting expedition, Kirk provided bearers to assist with the hunt. Afterward, he was tasked with delivering some specimens that had been shot during the trip. Upon arrival at the residence of the 7th Baronet, Sir William Jardine was not home, but his wife, Lady Jardine, was there. She took James on a tour of Jardine's Natural History Museum.

This encounter sparked James Kirk's passion for Ornithology. When he reintroduced himself to Sir William Jardine, he reminded him of their first meeting and proceeded to share details about the birds he had observed on the islands. For Jardine, this was like winning the lottery, and it marked the beginning of a professional relationship that lasted over three decades.

We have access to all of the letters James Kirk wrote to Jardine, and most of them focus on birds. However, a few of the letters provide personal details, and some are particularly interesting for their reactions to changes in labor following the end of slavery, banking issues, and the emancipation of enslaved people.

Jardine was a co-founder of the Berwickshire Naturalists' Club, and contributed to the founding of the Ray. He was "keenly addicted to field-sports, and a master equally of the rod and the gun". While ornithology was his main passion, he also studied ichthyology, botany and geology. His book on fossil burrows and traces, the Ichnology of Annandale, included fossils from his ancestral estate. He was the first to coin the term ichnology, and this was the first book written on the subject. His private natural history museum and library are said to have been the finest in Britain and displayed many of James Kirk's birds.

-- WIKIPEDIA

James Kirk the Introductory Letter to Sir William Jardine - page 1

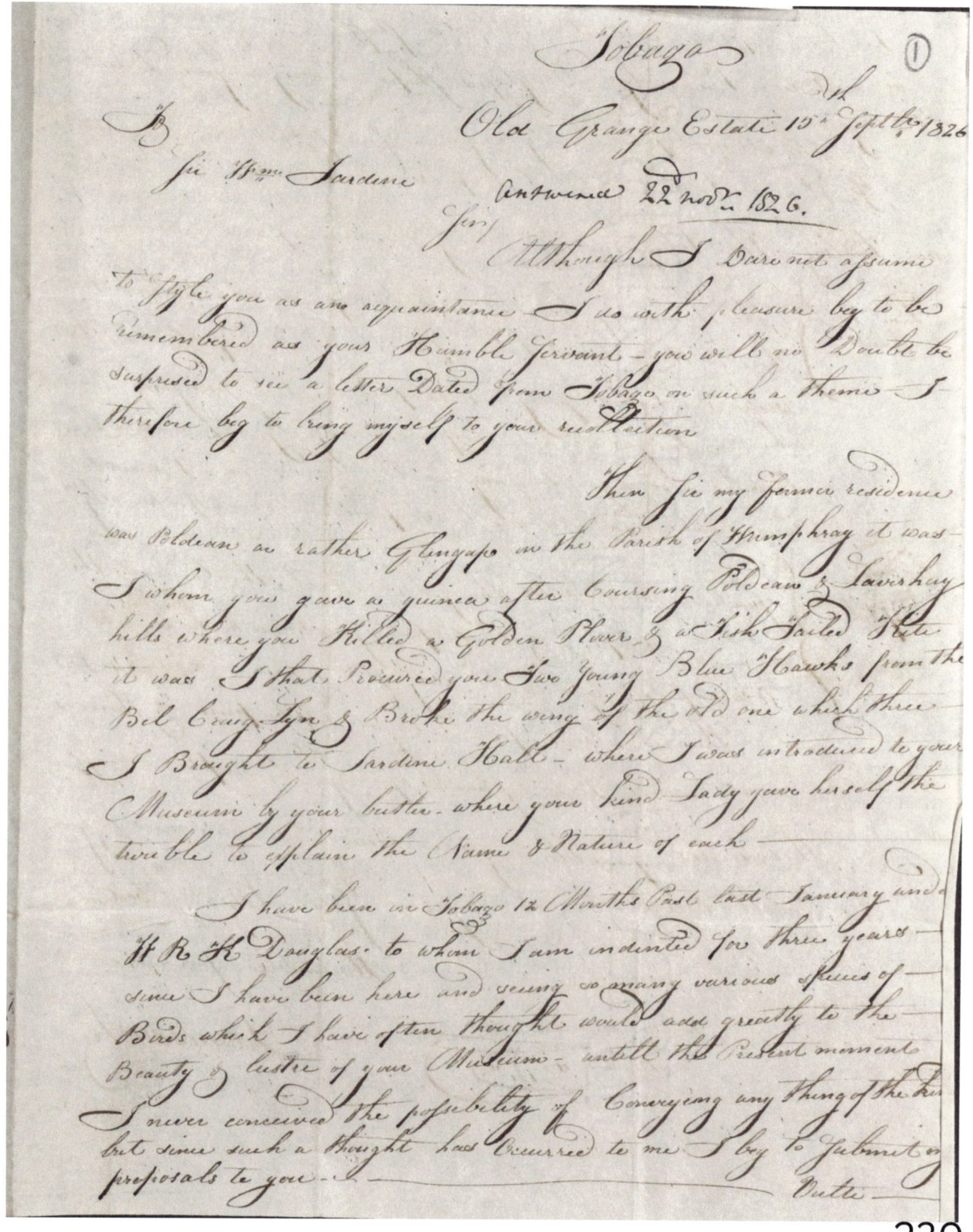

Tobago
Old Grange Estate 15th Septbr 1826

Sir Wm Jardine
Answered 22 novr 1826.

Sir,
Although I Dare not assume to style you as an acquaintance I do with pleasure beg to be remembered as your Humble Servant — you will no Doubt be surprised to see a letter Dated from Tobago on such a theme I therefore beg to bring myself to your recollection

Then Sir my former residence was Poldean or rather Glengape in the Parish of Humphray it was I whom you gave a guinea after Coursing Poldean & Lavershay hills where you Killed a Golden Plover & a Fish Tailed Kite it was I that Procured you Two Young Blue Hawks from the Bel Craig Lyn & Broke the wing of the old one which three I Brought to Jardine Hall — where I was introduced to your Museum by your butler — where your kind Lady gave herself the trouble to explain the Name & Nature of each —

I have been in Tobago 12 Months Past last January under H R H Douglas to whom I am indebted for three years since I have been here and seeing so many various species of Birds which I have often thought would add greatly to the Beauty & lustre of your Museum — untill the Present moment I never conceived the possibility of Conveying any thing of the kind but since such a thought has Occurred to me I beg to Submit my proposals to you —

But

Letter Transcription - Page 1

Tobago
Old Granger Estate 15 Sept 1826

To
Sir Wm. Jardine

Sir,

Although I dare not assume
to style you as acquaintance. I do with pleasure beg to be
remembered as your Humble Servant - you will no doubt be
surprised to see a later dated from Tobago on such a theme. I
therefore beg to bring myself to your recollection.

Then sir my former residence
was Poldean or rather Glencaple in the parish of Wamphray. It was
I whom you gave a Guinea after coursing Poldean or Laverhay
hills where you killed a Golden Plover or a fishtailed kite.
it was I that procured young blue hawks from the
Bel Craig Lyn and Broke the wing of the old which three
I brought to Jardine Hall - where I was introduced to your
Museum by your butler - where your kind Lady gave herself the
trouble to explain the name and nature of each.

I have been in Tobago 12 months past last January and
William Robert Keith Douglas to whom I am indented for three years.
Since I have been here seeing do many various species of
Birds which I have often thought would add greatly to the
Beauty and luster of your Museum - until the Present moments
I never concerned the profibility of Conveying any thing of the kind
but since such a thought had occurred to me I beg to submit my
proposal to you.

Notable on Page 1

- Scottish Places are named. These could be where James Kirk's family may be located.
- James Kirk was indented to Lord William Robert Keith Douglas
- Gives us the date when James Kirk arrived in Tobago - Jan 25, 1825
- Tells us that he had been to Jardine's Museum in Scotland

Introductory Letter to Sir William Jardine - page 2

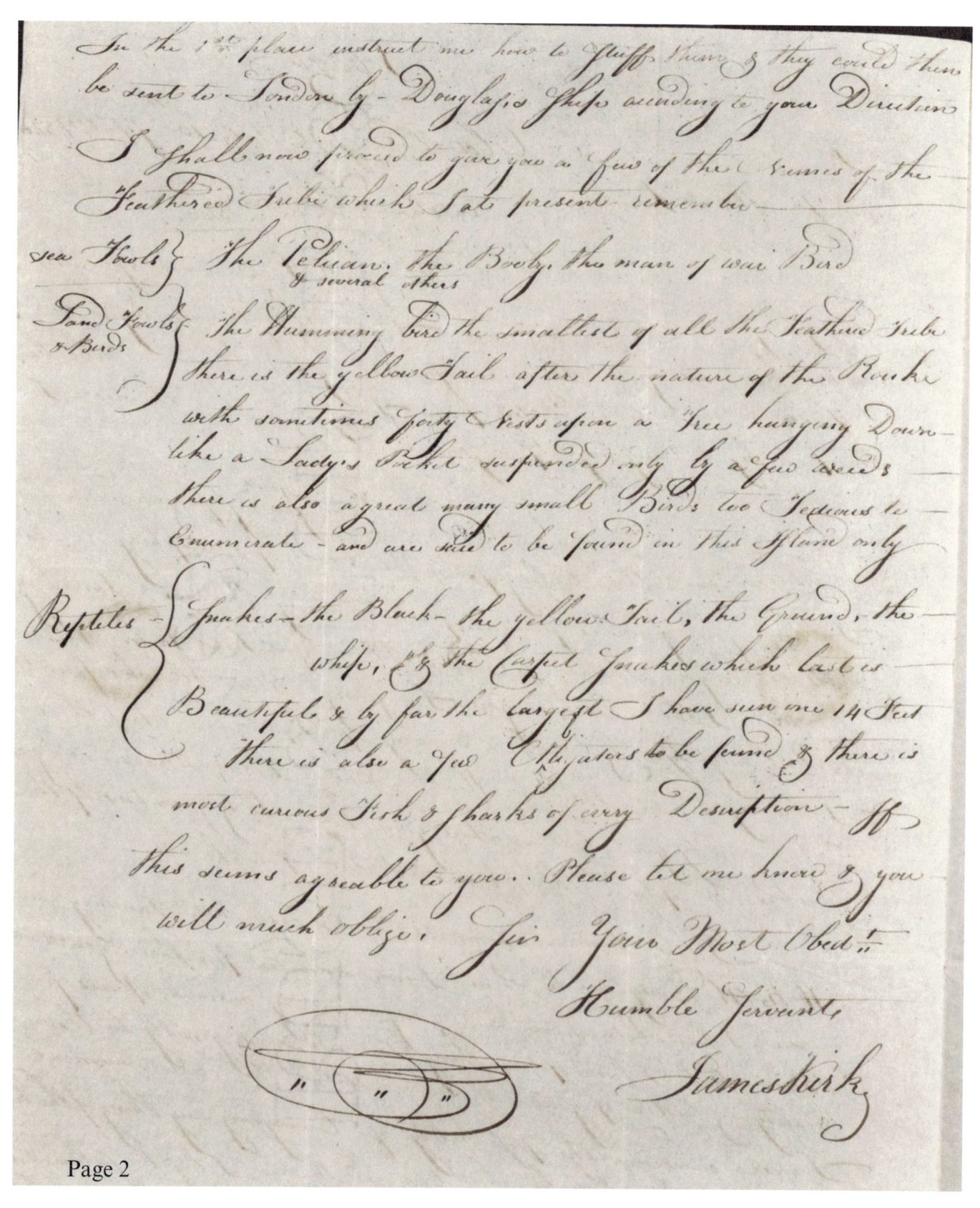

In the 1st place instruct me how to stuff them & they could then be sent to London by Douglas's Ship according to your Direction

I shall now proceed to give you a few of the names of the Feathered Tribe which I at present remember

Sea Fowls } The Pelican, the Booby, the man of war Bird & several others

Land Fowls & Birds } The Humming bird the smallest of all the Feathered Tribe there is the yellow Tail after the nature of the Rook with sometimes forty Nests upon a Tree hanging Down like a Lady's Pocket suspended only by a few weeds there is also a great many small Birds too Tedious to Enumerate — and are said to be found in this Island only

Reptiles } Snakes — the Black — the yellow Tail, the Ground, the whip, & the Carpet Snakes which last is Beautiful & by far the largest I have seen one 14 Feet There is also a few Alligators to be found & there is most curious Fish & Sharks of every Description — If this seems agreeable to you. Please let me know & you will much oblige. Sir Your Most Obedt.

Humble Servant,

James Kirk

Letter Transcription - Page 2

In the first place instruct me on how to stuff them and they could then be shipped to London by Douglas's ship according to your direction.
I shall now proceed to give you a few of the
Feathered Tribes which at personal remember.

Sea Fowls } The Pelican and Booby birds, the man of war Birds and several others.

Land Fowl } The humming bird, the smallest of the feathered Tribe.
or Birds. There is the yellow tail after the nature of the (illegible) with sometime 40 nests upon a tree hanging down like a Lady's Pocket suspended only by a few weeds. There is also a great many small birds to tedious to enumerate and are said to be found in this Island only.

Reptiles } Snakes - the black - the yellow tail - the ground (?), the white and the carpet snakes which last is Beautiful and by far the largest. I have seen one 14 feet there is also a few Alligators to be found and there is most curious Fish and sharks of every description.

If this seems agreeable to you, please let me know and you I
will much oblige. Sir your Most Obedient
and Humble Servant

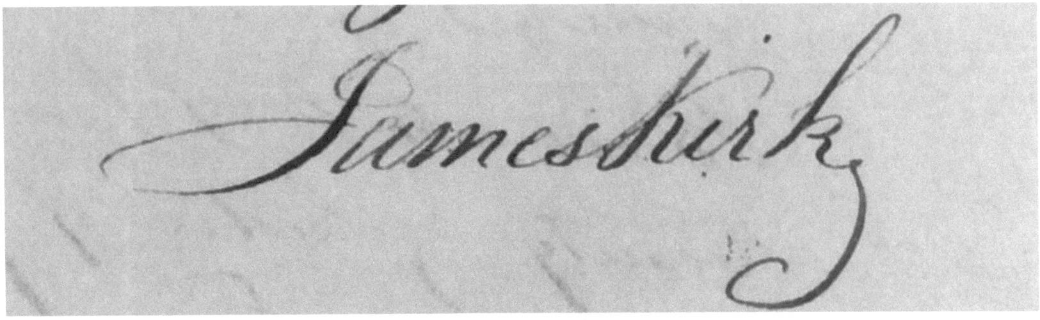

Notable on Page 2

- Kirk felt he needed instruction on how to prepare stuffed birds for Jardine.
- Kirk teased Jardine by sending information about the fauna of Tobago
- Jardine responded to the letter almost immediately, He responded and dispatched his reply on 22 November 1826

KIRK

LETTER SUMMARIES

JARDINE

This next section delves into the letters James Kirk wrote to Sir William Jardine. The majority of these letters focus on the flora and fauna of Tobago, particularly its avian life.

In the following sections, I have included summaries of all the letters provided by The National Records of Scotland. While most of the letters pertain to natural history, a few contain glimpses into Kirk's personal life. These "little gems" have been highlighted to draw attention to any relevant details about James Kirk, Sr.'s life.

Unfortunately, none of Jardine's replies have been preserved. Given Kirk's meticulous nature, it is likely that he would have kept these responses well-organized and categorized. However, it is believed that they were lost in the Hurricane of 1847, which likely destroyed much of his personal archive.

Kirk to Jardine - Letter Summaries pg 1

[NAS Catalogue - browse - details of record (nrscotland.gov.uk)](#)

	GB
Repository code	234
Organisation	NAS
Repository	National Records of Scotland
Reference	GD472/122
Title	Letters to Sir William Jardine chiefly from James Kirk, Tobago concerning the natural history and related phenomena of the Island and other associated matters
Dates	Sep 1826-Mar 1829
Access status	Open
Description	Comprising

15 September 1826. James Kirk, Old Grange Estate, Tobago to Sir William Jardine, Jardinehall. Reminds him of their previous acquaintance, tells Jardine that he has been in Tobago '12 months past last January' under HRK Douglas 'to whom I am indented for 3 years'. Describes various birds and reptiles on the Island 'which I have often thought would add greatly to the Beauty & lustre of your Museum'. Suggests that specimens be sent to Britain 'by Douglas's ship'. (Endorsed: 'Answered 22nd November 1826').

2 April 1827. James Kirk, Betsey's Hope, Tobago to Sir William Jardine, Jardinehall. Mentions that he has been 'five months in a convalescent state' and, because of this, has 'removed to the windward of the Island'. Describes attempts at taxidermy and has engaged a servant 'who promises Perfection if I will allow him to take out the entrails and so Dry the specimen in an oven'. Tells him that snakes can be obtained with 'no Difficulty' adding that 'I think I can get the necessary ingredients in the Island for the preservation of the skins'. Hopes that Jardine will send him 'a Double-Barreled Fowling Piece' (Endorsed: 'Answered 28 May 1827').

21 November 1827. James Kirk, Glamorgan Estate, Tobago to Sir William Jardine, Jardinehall. Has received Jardine's letter of 28 May and will send specimens. 'I have formed an acquaintance with a gentleman who is a professed Naturalist' and another 'who has upwards of 100 Birds', but who 'speaks of 2 Dollars each' for them.

Mentions difficulties in obtaining undamaged specimens 'from want of proper ammunition' and problems in preserving and packing 'large animals'. Notes some of his recent acquisitions: a 'Carpet Snake 9 feet long ... a wild dog (resembling a fox) ...

Kirk to Jardine - Letter Summaries pg 2

a Man 'O' War bird 7 feet 3 betwixt the tips of the wings' and others. Mentions he is now manager of the Glamorgan Estates 'and will have more leisure than I have had hitherto'. Requests further items for taxidermy as postscript.

10 May 1828. James Kirk, Tobago to Sir William Jardine, Jardinehall. Discusses latest requisitions of specimens and problems in their preservation, treatment or packing 'I have had a great many specimens spoilt lately from ants and mice'. Gives details of his employment 'with £130 stg per annum'. Lists specimens which were enclosed with letter 'This letter accompanies a Box of Birds sent by the Brig Acastra'.

£130 in 1828 equals £17,217.54 today which equals $22,097.42 US Dollars

31 July 1828. James Kirk, Tobago to Sir William Jardine, Jardinehall. Encloses further specimens with the bearer, Mr Lang, whom he hopes Jardine will show 'specimens of Natural History'. Adds that Lang will visit his native Aberdeen before returning to Tobago 'in January next' (Endorsed: 'answered 10 Nov'r 1828').

25 October 1828. William Laing, Aberdeen to Sir William Jardine, Jardinehall sending the specimens and Kirk's letter (of 31 July) with apologies that he could not deliver them personally as his time was 'very limited'. Adds that 'Mr Kirk is a very fine & promising young man and giving every satisfaction to those he is connected with in the Island' (Endorsed: 'answered 10 Nov'r 1828').

4 March 1829. James Kirk, Glamorgan Estate, Tobago to Sir William Jardine, Jardinehall. Discusses specimens sent and informs him 'I am giving up the stuffing for a short time and confining myself entirely to shooting'. Hopes to procure nests and eggs as requested.

Level File
Extent 7 items

NAS Catalogue - browse - details of record (nrscotland.gov.uk)

Reference GD472/123
Title Correspondence and reports on the natural history of Tobago sent by James Kirk to Sir William Jardine
Dates Apr 1832-May 1839
Access status Open

Kirk to Jardine Letter Summaries pg 3

Description Comprising

13 April 1832. James Kirk, Betsey's Hope Estate, Tobago to Sir William Jardine, Jardinehall. Apologises for the break in their correspondence 'having laid all your letters before me bearing Dates 28th May 1827, 1st Sept 1828 & 10th Novbr 1828'. Details the 'last barrell' of specimens he sent in August 1829, adding 'I regret to say [I] have never heard of their receipt'. Mentions other specimens going astray by being 'seized in the London Docks' and suggests this is what has happened. Hopes to renew their friendship and business arrangements. Adds 'I intend to visit Scotland in a few years' (Endorsed: 'answered 6 June 1832').

19 August 1832. James Kirk, Betsey's Hope Estate, Tobago to Sir William Jardine, Jardinehall. A detailed description of the 78 bird specimens which accompanied the letter (Endorsed: 'Answered 2nd December 1832').

[-] September 1832. James Kirk, Betsey's Hope Estate, Tobago to Sir William Jardine, Jardinehall. An addition to previous letter, itemising specimens 79-90 sent separately.

1 March 1833. James Kirk, Betsey's Hope Estate, Tobago to Sir William Jardine, Jardinehall. Thanks him for edition of American Ornothology. Adds, 'I am doubling my dilligence in the pursuit of Birds. I have again got upwards of one hundred on hand'. Mentions his observations on the annual and departure of migrating birds, particularly the habits of the Ruby Topas Humming Bird and the 'Night Hawke of Tobago'.

14 August 1833. James Kirk, Betsey's Hope Estate, Tobago to Sir William Jardine, Jardinehall. Concerns a physical description and habits of many of the species he has sent.

15 August 1833. Last to last. Continues list and description of specimens. Adds that 'there are not many land Birds peculiar of this Island which you have not had'.

12 June 1834. James Kirk, Roxburgh Estate, Tobago to Sir William Jardine. Sends further birds with Mr McLellan 'who leaves this for Scotland'. Notes from Jardine's preface to 'the 2nd Volume on Hummingbirds & C' that he must have received the consignment dispatched in August 1833. Discusses whether the 'Tobago Bird' and Hirsutus are the same or two species. Adds that he has now left his 'old residence for promotion' and is now the sole agent for Captain Houston Stewart RN.

6 December 1836. James Kirk, Roxburgh Estate, Tobago to Sir William Jardine, Jardinehall. 'I find in reference to my letterbook that my list to you is as far back as 12th June 1834'. Acknowledges receipt of 10 volumes of The Naturalists Library and other books. Notes that he has

New Estate is Roxborough
RN = Royal Navy

See Estate Manager for Captain Houston Steward, RN (Royal Navy)

Kirk to Jardine Letter Summaries pg 4

been so busy the 'last two years with other duties as to leave no business for the ornothological department'. Informs Jardine of recently acquired specimens - the Daitu or Auhinga and a Hercules Beetle.

17 April 1837. James Kirk, Roxburgh Estate, Tobago to Sir William Jardine, Jardinehall. Concerns the collection and dispatch of animal, rather than bird, specimens. Adds 'I am just commencing a collection of Fishes & Insects but still be at a loss how to describe or keep a list of our numerous specimens, many of the smaller birds having been so little attended to'.

2 December 1837. James Kirk, Roxburgh Estate, Tobago to Sir William Jardine, Jardinehall. 'I find that my list to you was as far back as 17th April'. Apologises for the 'great many promises not yet fulfilled' concerning specimens noted in this last letter. 'I have been busily employed ever since receipt of your Books on Entomology with that fascinating study. I have made a large collection of our Island Butterfiles, Beetles, Moths & C'. Details the Island's varied insect life, reasons for delay in sending specimens and damaged caused to delicate insects in preparation, storage and transit. (Endorsed: 'Ans'd 31 Jan'y').

25 April 1838. James Kirk, Roxburgh Estates, Tobago to Sir William Jardine, Jardinehall. Concerns the immediate dispatch of '57 Birds skins and several Hundred Butterflies, Moths, Beetles and Birds Eggs' aboard the Mary Ann of Leith (Endorsed: Ans'd 26th July').

4 October 1838. James Kirk, Roxburgh Estate, Tobago to Sir William Jardine, Jardinehall. Concerns his growing interest and knowledge in entomology. The finding of some specimens still aboard the Mary Ann on its return from Scotland and Kirk's increasing workload 'consequent upon the late change which has taken place in the conditions of our labouring population' which has prevented him from pursuing 'matters connected with Nat. History'. (Endorsed: 'Ans'd 25 December 1838').

22 March 1839. James Kirk, Roxburgh Estate, Tobago to Sir William Jardine, Jardinehall. Concerns his observations of the breeding and resting habits of the Crotophaga and the fact that his observations are at odds with those of 'Mr Swainson's writings'. Details the hunting and dietry habits of the Prioritus. Adds that 'the influence of Government of late with our labouring population has altogether unsettled their minds so that no steady labor can be depended upon - our local laws have been disallowed the Governor and legislature at variance and the Negros opinion of Independence is that it cannot be exhibited without impudence'.

4 May 1839. James Kirk, Roxburgh Estate, Tobago to Sir

Kirk to Jardine
Letter Summaries pg 5

	William Jardine, Jardinehall. Concerns a consignment of bird and other specimens sent 'in spirits'.
Level	File
Extent	14 items

[NAS Catalogue - browse - details of record (nrscotland.gov.uk)](#)

Reference	GD472/124
Title	Letters from James Kirk to Sir William Jardine, copy correspondence, reports and illustrations by or concerning Kirk and the fauna of the Island of Tobago
Dates	1838-1843
Access status	Open

Description

Comprising

23 July 1840. James Kirk, Roxburgh, Tobago to Sir William Jardine, Jardinehall. Encloses 'a small Box of Birds, Skins, Nests and Eggs' with annotated list. Bemoanes the fact that the Mary Ann will load for London instead of Leith' in future.

11 September 1841. James Kirk, Roxburgh Estate, Tobago to Sir William Jardine, Jardinehall. Concerns his recent illness, a 'sever attack of cold', followed by a 'Bileous' fever - the effects of which lingers about me'. Has applied for leave of absence for convalescence 'in England', will leave 'for the southern states of America' in April and travel from there to New York before getting a passage to Britain. Will meet with Jardine and discuss his (Jardine's) proposed book 'Synopsis and Zoology of Tobago'. Discusses other ornothological species and specimens.

(Copy correspondence) 9 and 20 February 1843. Colonial Secretary/Lieut. Governor General of Tobago to James Kirk. Thanks him for his contribution to the 'report' on Tobago.

Report on the Island of Tobago, in the form of questions and answers with an 'annexed description of the Hills, Rivers, Roads, Forests and general condition of the land' by 'the Honorable James Kirk a Member of Her Majesties Council and a resident in the Colony for twenty years', 14 January 1843.

Memorandum of Butterflies, Moths and Beetles forwarded to Sir William Jardine on the Mary Ann, April 1838.

Essay or article on the Crotophaga or 'Reed Bill provincially "Old Wife" and the Paroquit' or Trogon Mexicinus, n.d.

Kirk to Jardine
Letter Summaries pg 6

anything to say and nearly as less to send' to Jardine. Mentions the recent occurrance of 'large numbers' of nocturnal moths of which he has collected in 'great variety'. Lists the few samples he has acquired.

18 August 1845. James Kirk, Roxburgh Estate, Tobago to Sir William Jardine, Jardinehall. Concerns enclosed samples of 'blossoms, shells and seeds'. Discusses the flower of the Cogwood in detail and other matters.

20 August 1845. Mr McStein, Port Morant, Jamaica to Sir William Jardine, Jardinehall. Concerning the dispatch of specimens to Britain. Discusses the collection of 'land shells' and their rarity. 'I am continually about the woods and have frequent excursions with the Curator of the Botanical Gardens'. Notes the requisition of various birds, the Purple Humming Bird and 'Rain Cuckoo' among others. Mentions the excellence of the (sugar) crop 'We made 604 H'h'ds besides 200 puncheons Rum - which is the largest crop we have made for sixteen years past'.

23 September 1845. James Ewing (?), Glasgow to Sir William Jardine, Jardinehall. Informs him that specimens sent in the Nina by Kirk were to hand and that his parcel for Tobago would be despatched.

6 August 1846. W Denning, Falmouth, Jamaica to Sir William Jardine, Jardinehall. Discusses the bird life of the Carribbean in detail, enclosed specimens of birds and a 'List of the birds collected by myself in Cuba and Jamaica amounting in all to about 200 specimens' which he forwarded to 'Dr A. Smith'. Adds that he has 'paid a good deal of attention to every branch of Jamaican Natural History and have forwarded numerous birds, insects and reptiles to the Fort Pitt Museum' ... before this reaches Jardinehall I may probably be on my way to England to take charge of the Fort Pitt Museum which has been kindly offered to me by Dr A Smith'.

5 September 1846. James Kirk, Roxburgh [Estate], Tobago to Sir William Jardine, Jardinehall. Thanks him for copy of Jardine's manuscript of Ornothology of the Island of Tobago sent for inspection and comments. Asks him for 'something new in the West Indies, namely four dozen pairs of Lockerby Clogs' of various sizes.

19 November 1846. James Kirk, Roxburgh, Tobago to Sir William Jardine, Jardinehall. Concerns the identification of bird species, the re-employment of the 'young man who formerly stuffed birds for me' and other matters.

Level	File
Extent	11 items

Kirk to Jardine Letter Summaries pg 7

Reference GD472/126

Title Letters from James Kirk, Tobago to Sir William Jardine, Jardinehall concerning the wildlife, particularly the ornithology of Tobago, and related matters

Dates Feb 1847-Jun 1849 NAS Catalogue - browse - details of record (nrscotland.gov.uk) NAS Catalogue - browse - details of record (nrscotland.gov.uk)

Access status Open

Description Comprising

18 February 1847. James Kirk, Tobago to Sir William Jardine, [Jardinehall]. Concerns his taming of a 'Cockrico', the need for clogs for the negroes and other matters.

19 March 1847. James Kirk, Roxburgh, Tobago to Sir William Jardine, Jardinehall. Concerns the dispatch of three live 'Cockricos' to Jardinehall 'one of the males is very tame indeed he is rather troublesome by the liberties he takes in entering the House leaping upon the Tables, Sideboard & C he roosts upon the trees at large in the flower garden'. Discusses diet and habits of the birds; adds 'he is very bold and pugnacious and has on several occasions attacked a little negro child!'.

3 April 1847. James Kirk, Tobago to Sir William Jardine, Jardinehall. Discusses the 'Cockricos' prospective diet in Britain and his forthcoming visit to Trinidad, Guina and Barbados. Regrets Sir Robert Schornbugh's departure without visiting 'some others of our Islands when he was in Barbados'.

7 December 1847. James Kirk, Tobago to Sir William Jardine, Jardinehall. Informs him of the 'violent hurricane with which it pleased God to afflict us on the 17th Octr last - it carried Roxburgh House right before it and everything in it'. Details description of damage but adds 'strange to say 7 human beings escaped without a broken bone'. Bemoans the loss of many of his natural history books 'upwards of 240 volumes, all gone!'.

20 February 1848. James Kirk, Tobago to Sir William Jardine, Jardinehall. Relates to the rebuilding and repair operations to the estate 'what with the losses by the hurricane the failure of our only Bank, the unrenumerating price of W[est] I[ndian] Produce in the British Market and the want of specie to pay our labourers have all but brought things to a stand still'. Adds that there had never been a 'Hurricane of any consequence since 1780 until the present'.

7 March 1848. James Kirk, Tobago to Sir William Jardine, Jardinehall. Concerns his financial status following the failure of the 'West India Bank

Kirk to Jardine

Letter Summaries pg 8

Reference GD472/126

Title Letters from James Kirk, Tobago to Sir William Jardine, Jardinehall concerning the wildlife, particularly the ornithology of Tobago, and related matters

Dates Feb 1847-Jun 1849 NAS Catalogue - browse - details of record (nrscotland.gov.uk) NAS Catalogue - browse - details of record (nrscotland.gov.uk)

Access status Open

Description Comprising

18 February 1847. James Kirk, Tobago to Sir William Jardine, [Jardinehall]. Concerns his taming of a 'Cockrico', the need for clogs for the negroes and other matters.

19 March 1847. James Kirk, Roxburgh, Tobago to Sir William Jardine, Jardinehall. Concerns the dispatch of three live 'Cockricos' to Jardinehall 'one of the males is very tame indeed he is rather troublesome by the liberties he takes in entering the House leaping upon the Tables, Sideboard & C he roosts upon the trees at large in the flower garden'. Discusses diet and habits of the birds; adds 'he is very bold and pugnacious and has on several occasions attacked a little negro child!'.

3 April 1847. James Kirk, Tobago to Sir William Jardine, Jardinehall. Discusses the 'Cockricos' prospective diet in Britain and his forthcoming visit to Trinidad, Guina and Barbados. Regrets Sir Robert Schornbugh's departure without visiting 'some others of our Islands when he was in Barbados'.

ARTICLE ON HURRICANE DAMAGE NEXT PAGE

7 December 1847. James Kirk, Tobago to Sir William Jardine, Jardinehall. Informs him of the 'violent hurricane with which it pleased God to afflict us on the 17th Octr last - it carried Roxburgh House right before it and everything in it'. Details description of damage but adds 'strange to say 7 human beings escaped without a broken bone'. Bemoans the loss of many of his natural history books 'upwards of 240 volumes, all gone!'.

20 February 1848. James Kirk, Tobago to Sir William Jardine, Jardinehall. Relates to the rebuilding and repair operations to the estate 'what with the losses by the hurricane the failure of our only Bank, the unrenumerating price of W[est] I[ndian] Produce in the British Market and the want of specie to pay our labourers have all but brought things to a stand still'. Adds that there had never been a 'Hurricane of any consequence since 1780 until the present'.

7 March 1848. James Kirk, Tobago to Sir William Jardine, Jardinehall. Concerns his financial status following the failure of the 'West India Bank

243

HURRICANE AT TOBAGO.

The last West India Mail brings an account of an awful hurricane which visited the Island of Tobago, on the night of the 11th of October. The day had been very sultry, and towards evening the indications of an approaching hurricane became frequent. At ten o'clock it burst forth with great fury, the wind blowing from west to north and accompanied by rain and lightning. It continued to rage for three hours, and when the morning broke, a dreadful scene of devastation presented itself. The face of the country had been swept by the winds, and the fruits of the husbandmen, as well as many of their dwellings, were scattered to the winds.

The dwelling-houses on estates generally, have suffered terribly. Some were entirely swept away, and their inhabitants were obliged to resort for shelter, to any field which offered a present protection against the elements.

Trees, the growth of many years, which withstood the violence of all preceding hurricanes, were bent and twisted like willow wands, and presented themselves denuded of foliage, stripped of their branches, and in many an instance torn up by the roots and cast to a distance. The canes which had looked healthy and luxuriant, have been in every case prostrated, as if a destroying torrent of water had passed over them, and torn their leaves into shreds. Those most advanced suffered most severely. The less advanced plants presented a more encouraging appearance, but afforded no hopes that they will fully recover from their effects. Throughout the island, 30 great houses (or managers' houses) were completely destroyed; 31 ditto severely injured; 26 works completely destroyed, 33 ditto severely injured; 456 settlers' houses destroyed, 176 ditto greatly injured. In Scarborough, Rocky Vale, Monkey Town, Lower Town of Scarborough, & otherwise in the vicinity of Scarborough alone—122 houses of all descriptions (including outbuildings) were totally destroyed; 84 ditto greatly injured. The loss of life was estimated at nineteen only. The whole of the barracks were unroofed, and some of the side walls blown down; the officers' quarters were entirely stripped of their verandas, roofs, and shingles, windows and doors blown in and broken, part of the roof of the hospital blown down, canteen, ordnance stores and out-building in ruins; one soldier of the 19th regiment killed, and another seriously injured; several soldiers of the 1st West India regiment also seriously injured by the falling of the ruins. The loss of stores and arms was immense. The damage to the barracks rendered it advisable to send all the white troops to Trinidad.

Kirk to Jardine - Letter Summaries pg 9

which has suspended payments'. Adds, 'as I am a unfortunate Shareholder ... my time has been so much engaged with attendance at frequent meetings trying to come to arrangements with the creditors'.

8 May 1848. James Kirk, Buecoo, [Tobago] to Sir William Jardine, Jardinehall. Thanks him for his offer to 'replace works blown away'. Discusses the work of 'the Revd Mr Smith' and other matters. (Endorsed: 'Ans'd 16 June 1848.')

5 June 1848. James Kirk, Buecoo, [Tobago] to Sir William Jardine, Jardinehall. Concerning various Island and wildlife matters, the aftermath of the hurricane and his desire for a Leister 'such as I saw you killing the Salmon and Sea Trout with in 1844' to go fishing with in order to collect marine specimens. Encloses (not present) a drawing of Tobago by a Captain Campbell I think in 1793 the evening previous to the taking of the Island by the English'.

21 July 1848. James Kirk, Buecoo Estate, Tobago to Sir William Jardine c/o H E Strickland, Tewkesbury. Discusses his queries concerning various species of birds and mammals. Adds that he has now finished some landscapes of Tobago and that he is to meet Dr John Davey 'Brother of Sir Humphrey he is here inspecting Hospitals, he is a great geologist ... I am carrying Specimens to him and expect valuable information'.

20 August 1848. James Kirk, Buecoo, Tobago to Sir William Jardine, Jardinehall. Concerns the acquisition of a parrot for Jardine, the dispatch of specimens and other matters.

6 October 1848. James Kirk, Tobago to Sir William Jardine, Jardinehall. Relates to specimens dispatched aboard the Helen for London, the arrival of a parcel via James Ewing & Co. and other matters.

20 November 1848. James Kirk, Buecoo, Tobago to Sir William Jardine, Jardinehall. Discusses in detail various species or specimens such as the 'Adult White-Necked Humming Birds'.

19 June 1849. James Kirk, Woodlands Estate, Tobago to Sir William Jardine, Jardinehall. Concerns the transportation of specimens to Britain and a miscarried parcel for him from Sir William Jardine. Encloses a note of specimens of eggs and seeds which accompanied letter.

Level	File
Extent	13 items

Kirk to Jardine Letters

Full size illustration (partly coloured) of Jasmine leaf 'food of caterpillar of No 56/58' showing eggs attached, n.d.

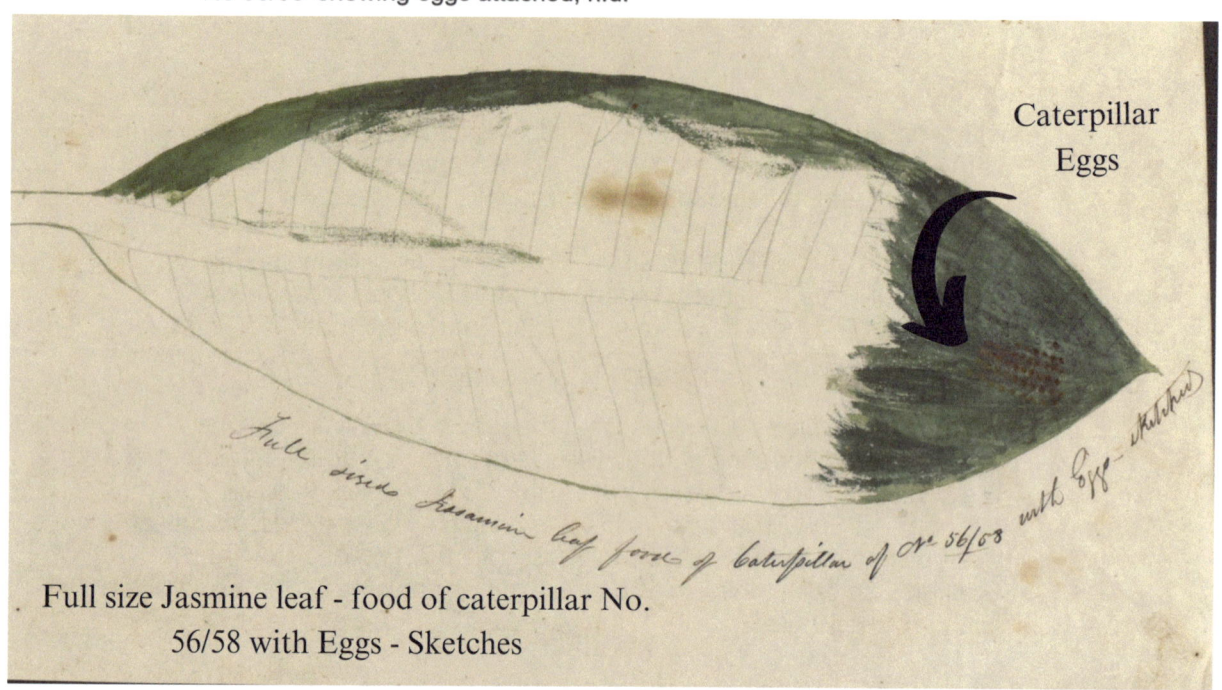

Caterpillar Eggs

Full size Jasmine leaf - food of caterpillar No. 56/58 with Eggs - Sketches

The Jasmine leaf real vs depiction.

Rendering from preliminary drawing above.

The Jasmine flower real vs depiction.

KIRK
AND
BIRDS

Birds from Tobago

Jardine and Kirk developed a deeply engaging relationship, forged through their shared passion for Ornithology. In Kirk's first letter to Jardine, he described the awe he felt upon visiting Jardine's private natural history museum and library, reputed to be the finest in Britain. This must have been a remarkable experience for the young James Kirk. Upon arriving in Tobago and encountering its diverse and vibrant bird population, Kirk conceived a method for documenting the birds of Tobago. He reintroduced himself to Jardine and proposed a business relationship centered on preserving birds for Jardine's renowned Natural History Museum.

A simple browser search using the terms "James," "Kirk," and "Birds of Tobago" reveals a Wikipedia page that includes information about the process Kirk undertook to name one of these birds.

Short-tailed swift

Article   Talk

From Wikipedia, the free encyclopedia

The **short-tailed swift** (*Chaetura brachyura*) is a bird in the Apodidae, or swift family.

Taxonomy [edit]

The species was first formally described as *Acanthylis brachyura* in 1846 by the Scottish naturalist Sir William Jardine, based on the observations of Mr. Kirk, a resident of Tobago.[2]

Bird named after James Kirk

The red-rumped woodpecker (Veniliornis kirkii) is a species of bird in the subfamily Picinae of the woodpecker family Picidae. It is found from Costa Rica south to Peru and east to Brazil, Guyana, and Trinidad and Tobago.

The Kirkii is said to be named after James Kirk as he was the one to first observe and log this bird's description and habits.

Other Kirkii's exist in different locations around the globe. Such as, Dryobates kirkii found off the east coast of Africa.

Migration area of Kirk's Kirkii. As far east of Tobago and south west as Ecuador

Birds that Kirk Prepared for Jardine

These birds represent some of the taxidermy work done by James Kirk and sent to Sir William Jardine. They are in the possession of an descendant of Jardine. She shared this photo with me, and I am very much appreciative to have this picture of his birds.

The pictures are housed on the on the Clan Jardine's Facebook page, h*ttps://www.facebook.com/groups/730007090504064*

KIRK
SUGAR AND THE ENSLAVED

Kirk as Estate Manager for Captain Houston Stewart, RN (Royal Navy)

GCB is the Most Honourable Order of the Bath

Admiral of the Fleet Sir Houston Stewart, GCB (3 August 1791 – 10 December 1875) was a Royal Navy officer and briefly a Liberal Party Member of Parliament. After serving as a junior officer in the Napoleonic Wars, Stewart became commanding officer of the third-rate HMS Benbow in the Mediterranean Fleet and took part in the bombardment of Acre during the Egyptian–Ottoman War. He went on to be Captain-Superintendent of Woolwich Dockyard and then Controller-General of the Coastguard.

Most Honourable Order of the Bath breast star of a Knight / Dame Grand Cross (Civil Division)

August 1833s. Kirk states in a letter to Sir William Jardine that he has now left his 'old residence for promotion' and is now the sole agent for Captain Houston Stewart RN.

The estate was Roxbro; Roxbrough; or Roxborough.

This was the estate that James Kirk, SR resided until his death.

Labor and Money Issues Experienced by James Kirk Plantation Manager and Owner as revealed in his personal letters to Sir Jardine

This is the first mention by Kirk of the conditions since Slavery ended.

4 October 1838 ... Kirk's increasing workload 'consequent upon the late change which has taken place in the conditions of our labouring population' which has prevented him from pursuing 'matters connected with Nat. History'.

More frustrations of Kirk toward government and "labouring population"

22 March 1839. Adds that 'the influence of Government of late with our labouring population has altogether unsettled their minds so that no steady labor can be depended upon - our local laws have been disallowed the Governor and legislature at variance and the Negros opinion of Independence is that it cannot be exhibited without impudence'.

Kirk's workload each month.

3 April 1845. James Kirk, Woodland's Estate, Tobago to Sir William Jardine, Jardinehall. Apologises for not dealing with Jardine's scientific queries, due partly to his increasing duties 'my charge of Estates embracing all corners of the Island that what with regulating shipments, keeping cash accounts, collecting returns and paying 900 salaries monthly ... you can readily imagine I have not much time to spare on the arrival of a packet'

Asking for the clog for his workers, Could this be one of the reasons that James Kirk Sr, was so respected. The large contingency of Labourers attending his funeral was mentioned in his obituary

15 September 1846. Asks him for 'something new in the West Indies, namely four dozen pairs of Lockerby Clogs' of various sizes.

Again expresses the need for clogs for the labouring class.

18 February 1847. James Kirk, Tobago to Sir William Jardine, [Jardinehall]. Concerns his taming of a 'Cockrico', the need for clogs for the negroes and other matters.

Specie is money in terms of coins instead of paper money

20 February 1848. Relates to the rebuilding and repair operations to the estate 'what with the losses by the hurricane the failure of our only Bank, the unrenumerating price of W[est] I[ndian] Produce in the British Market and the want of specie to pay our labourers have all but brought things to a stand still'.

March 1848. Concerns his financial status following the failure of the 'West India Bank which has suspended payments'. Adds, 'as I am a unfortunate Shareholder ... my time has been so much engaged with attendance at frequent meetings trying to come to arrangements with the creditors'.

The Plantation System of Slavery

The plantation system of the British West Indies
https://runaways.gla.ac.uk/minecraft/index.php/the-plantation-system-of-the-british-west-indies/

With the Incorporating Union of 1707, Scotland gained access to the already established English Empire in the Americas. Although relative latecomers to the New World, England had established control over a diverse land mass that was known as the British Empire by 1708. In North America, colonies were established in Virginia, Newfoundland and New England. Further south, the British West Indies were created in successive eras of colonial expansion.

In the first phase from the 1600s, the islands of Barbados and Jamaica were settled as well as St Kitts, Nevis and Antigua. After the Seven Years War (1756-63), Great Britain gained control of Grenada, Dominica, St Vincent and Tobago, whilst Trinidad, St Lucia and Demerara were added after victories in the Napoleonic and Revolutionary Wars (1793-1815). The third phase colonies of Berbice and Essequibo merged with Demerara to become British Guiana (now Guyana) in 1831.

The integrated plantation was the economic foundation of the first British Empire. The system was established and refined on Barbados, which became the richest colony in the West Indies after colonisation in 1625. At first, the exportation of indentured servants – primarily vagrants, criminals and political and religious exiles from Scotland, England and Ireland – provided the tobacco and cotton plantations with a labour force.

However, the planters eventually developed a sugar monoculture based on the expropriation of labour from enslaved peoples imported from Africa. Although slavery had been practiced since c.1636, chattel slavery, an English concept, was given its first legal code in Barbados in 1661. Black slaves were classified as the property of the white master and were listed in plantation inventories next to cattle. In the longer term, the Barbados Act of 1661 introduced a new dimension of exploitation across the world; Jamaica and Antigua, South Carolina, Virginia and Maryland all adopted similar slave codes. Thus, a forced system of labour based on class and eventually race maintained the flow of commodities from the New World to the metropolis.

The plantation system in the British West Indies depended on the existence of a black majority population who were exploited and managed by a smaller, white ruling class. For example, Jamaica was essentially a rural society with most of the population resident along the coast. At the beginning of the nineteenth century, the white population was around 20,000-25,000, whilst the enslaved population was 354,000. Both enslaved and free workers mainly worked on sugar and coffee plantations known as estates or adjoining cattle pens that provided livestock for the plantation economy. The white population of the British West Indies consisted of proprietors, a supervisory class, professionals and skilled tradesmen.

In the early stages of the English West Indies, it was common for proprietors to be resident on their estates. But many others returned to live in luxury as wealthy absentees, based on the proceeds of slavery. In Jamaica in 1775, for example, one-third of the landholders were absentees. In smaller islands, it could be higher. Of the 100 estates in Tobago in 1808, around half were owned by absentee proprietors. Absenteeism was sometimes viewed as a curse and meant the British West Indies did not develop into settler colonies as in North America.

Terms for the supervisory class varied island to island although in general, Solicitors, bookkeepers and overseers managed plantations and estates. Newcomers to Jamaica usually started employment as bookkeepers, although they had little to do with accounts instead supervising the enslaved who worked in the sugar cane fields from dawn until midnight or in the factories boiling sugar. Bookkeepers superintended gangs of enslaved people with the use of black drivers, trusted slaves who sometimes administered punishment. The bookkeepers themselves were subordinate to overseers (known as 'managers' in the Windward and Leeward Islands), and had responsibility for superintending several gangs of enslaved people. Solicitors were above overseers in the hierarchy, with responsibility for managing several estates at once and directly answerable to the proprietor whether they were resident or absentees. The Solicitor was a position of some importance in colonial society.

CANE-HOLEING.

There were also a professional class of white people on the island – doctors, lawyers, administrators, clerks – who offered specific services in the plantation economy. Similarly, a skilled class of tradesmen – masons, bricklayers, blacksmiths and carpenters – serviced the plantation infrastructure, usually depending on skilled enslaved labour in gangs to build houses, windmills or sugar boiling houses.

The prospect of work attracted many fortune seeking Scots to the British West Indies in search of fortune. Known as sojourners, young men – sometimes brothers, cousins and nephews of merchants – travelled in the hope of accumulating rapid fortunes and the aim of returning home to buy landed property. For example, there was large scale Scottish migration to the West Indies during the period 1750-1800, especially from Glasgow and her outlying ports. Around 17,000 young Scotsmen are estimated to have travelled in this period to the region particularly to Grenada, Jamaica, St Vincent and Trinidad although Jamaica was the principal destination. Some took up professional positions in the plantation economy, whilst others became planters, if they had the appropriate finance. Others worked their way up the plantation economy and upward social mobility was based on capital derived from working on plantations and, if they became successful, slave-ownership. Bookkeepers, overseers and tradesmen strived to accumulate capital t o purchase enslaved people, who could be hired out as 'jobbing slaves' to work on other estates. Successful overseers sometimes became attorneys which attracted higher rates of pay.

The dream for many was to purchase a plantation and then return home as an absentee. There are several examples of Scots who accumulated large fortunes. In Antigua, major sugar plantations were owned by the Dunbar, Harvey, Grant, Young, Douglas and Maxwell families. There was also a Scottish contingent in Nevis and St Kitts and adventurers such as Colonel William McDowall and Major James Milliken became owners of large sugar plantations and resident slaves. With wealth and status secured, they returned to live in sprawling landed estates in the west of Scotland. Sometimes fortune were reported in the national press. Dr James Black spent a career in Jamaica, no doubt tending to enslaved people and passing them fit for work on sugar estates, and was worth over £18,000 when he died in Glasgow in 1835. Thus, a career in the plantation economy could lead to riches for the white population, based on the expropriation of labour and wealth from enslaved people.

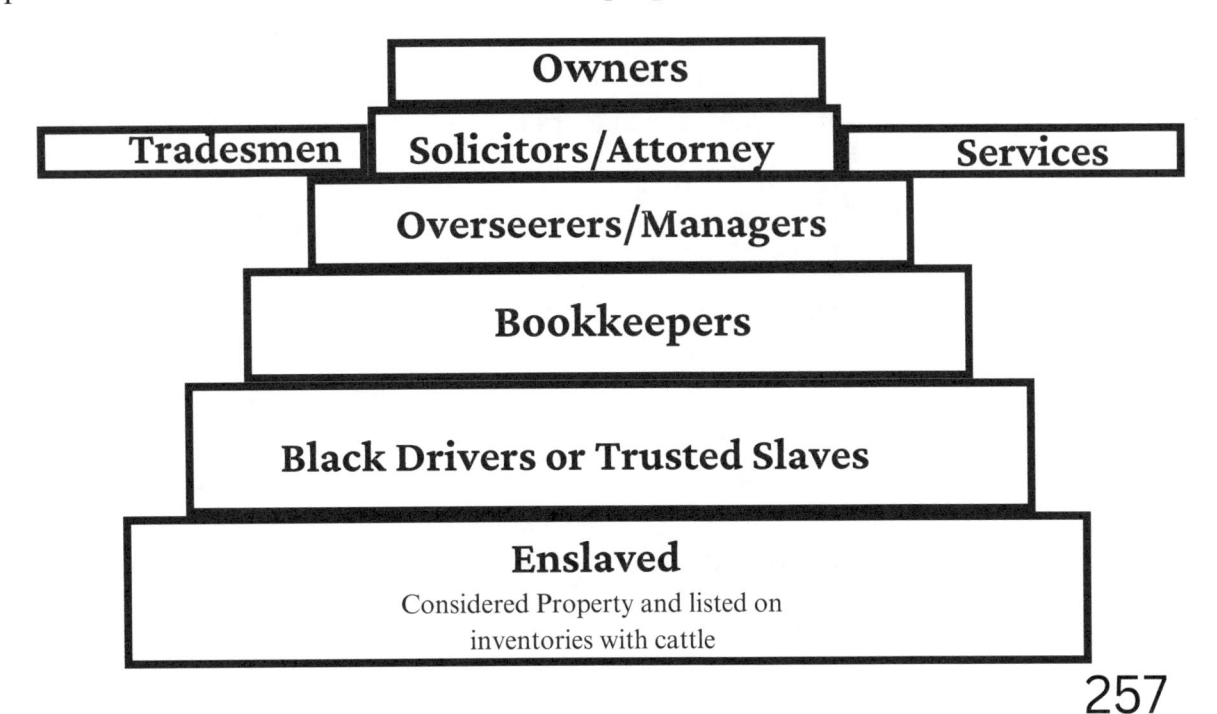

Owners

Tradesmen | **Solicitors/Attorney** | **Services**

Overseerers/Managers

Bookkeepers

Black Drivers or Trusted Slaves

Enslaved
Considered Property and listed on inventories with cattle

The Metayers of Tobago

Emancipation in 1834 did not hit Tobago nearly as hard as Trinidad since Tobago had no free crown lands for ex-slaves to squat upon and thus those who did not emigrate were compelled to continue working for the planters. In order to keep sugar estates going, the metayage system, which was a form of sharecropping, developed. Under the system, the metayer (sharecropper) occupied a piece of land on which he/she planted cane.

At harvest time, the estate owner supplied carts which drew cut canes to the mill where they were processed into rum and sugar of which the metayer received a percentage. In addition, the metayer was often allowed permission to build a cottage on the estate and provision grounds.

Over a decade later (1847) falling sugar prices and the failure of estates in the West Indies for want of labour saw the bankruptcy of the West India Bank which provided credit to many of Tobago planters. The lack of financing for machinery upgrades and labourer wages meant that the planters were more dependent on the metayers than ever. Even so, the production of sugar plummeted.

By 1862 the following could be written: "The metayer system was first introduced in this island in 1843 by Mr Cruickshank, the then proprietor of the Prospect estate; and it was generally resorted to in 1845. Such was the depression at that time, that had not the labourer been induced to work for a share of the produce, the estates, for want of means to pay in money for labour, must have gone out of cultivation.

"Under such a system of cultivation there can be no farming; the labourer cultivates his field so long as it remains in heart; it is not his interest to manure it; for as soon as it ceases to produce what will remunerate him for his labour he moves off to a fresh field; there is an entire absence of implemental husbandry; and, owing in a great measure to the bad faith in which, on both sides, the contract is too often carried out, what it done is imperfectly done, mind from many causes yields little return. I have known canes so planted to remain on the land two years without being cropped."

The collapse of the West India Bank meant that estates had to be sold in Tobago at low prices. It saw the emergence of a black planter class wherein men who were formerly slaves and who had amassed considerable savings became estate owners. Some estates were forced to sell small plots to peasant cultivators which saw the establishment of an agrarian peasant class which survives with a strong and independent spirit in the current generations of Tobagonians.

by Angelo Bissessarsingh

Article prepared by:
<u>National Archives of Trinidad and Tobago</u> and is posted to the same.

After slavery was abolished in the British Empire, British taxpayers paid an estimated 20 million pounds in reparations to slave owners in Britain and its colonies?

According to author Nicholas Draper (2010), approximately 16 million pounds were paid to owners of enslaved peoples in the West Indies specifically—a total that equals billions of pounds in today's values. In Trinidad, the estimated total paid to slave owners was 1,021,858 pounds, while 233,367 pounds were issued to those who owned enslaved peoples in Tobago. An article from 2018 in the UK Guardian Newspaper revealed that it was only in 2015 that British taxpayers finished paying the debt incurred by the British government in order to compensate British slave owners during this time.

When the Slavery Abolition Act was passed in 1833, formerly enslaved Black people who worked in the fields were still required to become apprentices for a period of six years. The law, called "An Act for the Abolition of Slavery throughout the British colonies, for promoting the industry of the manumitted slaves, and for compensating the persons hitherto entitled to the services of such slaves" obligated them to work for their former owners without wages for three-quarters of the work week, with the exception of children under six years old.

The law also accommodated the concerns of slave owners in the British colonies who believed that the abolition of slavery infringed on their property rights. According to Selwyn Cudjoe (2018), some slave owners like William H. Burnley—one of the richest planters in Trinidad—had even lobbied for compensation leading up to the passing of the Act.

Through the Slavery Abolition Act, which came into effect on August 1st 1834, the British Parliament appointed a Compensation Commission to determine which slave owners in the colonies should receive compensation for losing ownership of the enslaved. This Commission required slave owners to submit claims (see Photo 1), along with supporting documents proving ownership.

Rules for the classification of slaves and their corresponding values were also established by members of the Commission. Photo 2 shows some of these values, which were published in the Port of Spain Gazette on July 15th 1834.

This process of compensation was documented and preserved in claims that included the name of the estate, the claim number, the name of the claimant, the number of slaves being filed for compensation, the name of the slave owner and the date the claim was filed.

If the claims were validated, the slave owner received compensation. The claim pictured in Photo 1 was filed by Manuel P. Farfan of Monte Alegre estate in Guanapo for 11 slaves on September 5th 1834.

At the National Archives of Trinidad and Tobago, we have slave compensation claims made between 1834 and 1835 in Trinidad.

PHOTOS ON NEXT PAGE
Photo 1 shows a compensation claim filed by Manuel P. Farfan in 1834.
Photo 2 shows an article in the Port of Spain Gazette that included values assigned to enslaved people occupying different roles.
Photo 3 shows the first Page of an amendment made in 1836 to the Slavery Abolition Act, regarding compensation to slave owners.
These records are all part of the National Archives of Trinidad and Tobago's collections.

References:
Draper, Nicholas. The Price of Emancipation: Slave-Ownership, Compensation and British Society at the End of Slavery. Cambridge University Press, 2010.
Manjapra, Kris. "When Will Britain Face up to Its Crimes against Humanity?" The Guardian, Guardian News and Media, 29 Mar. 2018,

Cudjoe, Selwyn R. Slave Master of Trinidad: William Hardin Burnley and the Nineteenth Century Atlantic World. University of Massachusetts Press, 2018.
Beckles, Hilary. Britain's Black Debt: Reparations for Caribbean Slavery and Native Genocide. University of the West Indies Press, 2013.
Context | Legacies of British Slavery, https://www.ucl.ac.uk/lbs/project/context/.

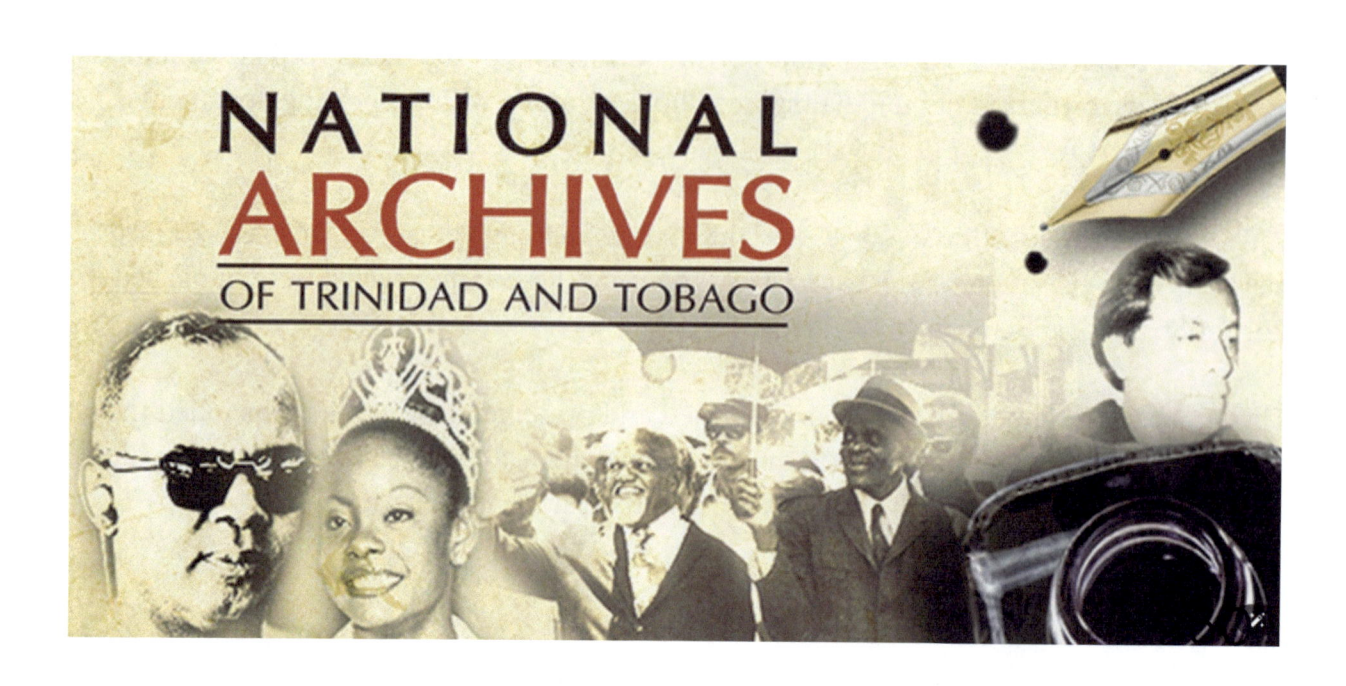

Photos from preceding article

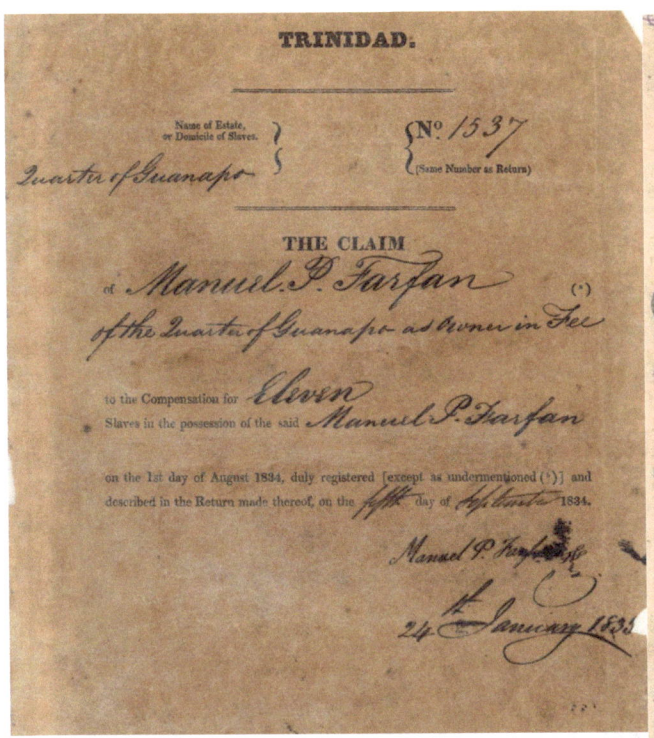

Photo 1

Photo 3

Photo 2

These are the registers that kept track of the enslaved on a plantation. **Glamorgan 1828**

32. Glamorgan Estate

Tobago 1st Jany 1828.

Schedule — Annual Return of Plantation Slaves.

This Return of James Kirk for the Plantation called Glamorgan in the parish of St. Mary for the total number of all Slaves belonging or attached thereto, or usually worked or employed thereon; with a true and distinct Account of all Births and Deaths therein; and of all other Additions to, or Deductions from the Stock of Slaves from whatever cause, between the first day of Jany 1827 and the first day of Jany 1828.

Total No. of Slaves as per Return made up to the 1st of Jany 1827:

Males	Females
79	125

Increase by Births

Names of Males	Females	Colour	Date of Birth	Mothers Name
	Celia	Black	1827 31st May	Venus
	Afia	Black	15th Novr	Peggy

Total Increase by Births — 2

Decrease by Deaths

Males	Females	Colour	Date	Cause of Death
Tobago		Black	1827 4th Jany	Old Age & Debility
Quashy		Yellow	15th August	Leprosy and Invalid
Joe		Black	21st July	Old Age & bad Sores
Jupiter		Black	15th Novr	Old Age & Debility

Total decrease by deaths — 4

Total Slaves Seventy Seven Males & One Hundred and Twenty Seven Females, in all Two Hundred & Four Slaves.

(Signed) **James Kirk**, Manager.

Sworn to before me this 19 day of January 1828 to be a true and distinct Account, according to the Registry Bill of this Island.

Signed **John Shadband**, Deputy Registrar.

Henry Yeaty, Registrar.

Glamorgan Estate
Tobago — 1st January 1829
Schedule — Annual Return of Plantation Slaves

The Return of James Kirk for the Plantation called Glamorgan in the Parish of Saint Mary for the total number of all Slaves belonging or attached thereto, or usually working or employed thereon; with a true and distinct account of all Births and Deaths thereon, and of all other additions to or Deductions from the Stock of Slaves from whatever cause between the first day of January 1828 and the first day of January 1829.

Total no. of Slaves as per Return made up to 1st January 1828:

Males	Females
77	127

Increase by Births

Names of Males	Females	Colour	Date of Birth	Mothers Name
Ebenezer Duncan		Mestize	20th January 1828	Lucy
William		Mulatto	1st November	Louisa

Total Increase by Births: 2

Decrease by Deaths

Males	Females	Colour	Date	Cause of Death
	Beauty	Black	6th May 1828	Old Age and Dropsy
	Eola	Black	2nd July	Worms and Teething
	Hannah	Black	5th July	Premature labor & fever
John		Black	16th July	Influenza
Ebenezer Duncan		Mestize	23rd August	Worms and Teething
Phillip		Black	13th August	Sores and Debility
	Phyllis	Black	7th October	Extreme old age
John		Black	7th October	Consumption
	Angelique	Yellow	11th October	Dropsy
Jacky		Black	16th November	Mal d'Estomach

Total Decrease by Deaths: 5   5

Total Slaves — Seventy Four Males & One Hundred and Twenty Two Females
In all — One Hundred and Ninety Six Slaves

(Signed) James Kirk
Manager

Sworn to before me this 13th day of January 1829 to be a true and distinct account according to the Registry Bill of this Island.

(Signed) Henry Yeates
Registrar

Henry Yeates
Registrar

Glamorgan Estate

Tobago 1st January 1830

Annual Return of Plantation Slaves

Schedule — The Return of James Kirk for the Plantation called Glamorgan in the Parish of Saint Mary for the total number of all Slaves belonging or attached thereto, or usually worked or employed thereon, with a true and distinct account of all Births & Deaths thereon, and of all other Additions to or Deductions from the Stock of Slaves, from whatever cause between the first day of January 1829 and the first day of January 1830.

Total number of Slaves as per Return made up to 1 January 1829	Males	Females
	74	122

Increase by Births

Names of Males	Females	Colour	Date	Mother's Name
Jim	—	Black	21 June	Polly
Allan	—	do	8 Novr.	Queen
—	Beauty	do	9 Decr.	Peggy
Total Increase by Births 2	1			

Total Slaves — Seventy six Males & One Hundred & Twenty three Females.

In all — One Hundred & Ninety nine.

(Signed) James Kirk
Manager

Sworn to before me this 9 day of January 1830 to be a true and distinct account according to the Registry Bill of this Island.

(Signed) H. Yeates
Registrar

Henry Yeates
Registrar

Glamorgan Estate

Tobago, 1st January 1831

Annual Return of Plantation Slaves

Schedule. The Return of James Kirk for the Plantation called Glamorgan in the Parish of St Mary for the total number of all Slaves belonging to attached theretill or usually worked or employed thereon, with a true and distinct account of all Births & Deaths thereon and of all other additions to or deductions from the stock of Slaves from whatever cause, between the first day of January 1830 and the first day of January 1831.

Total number of Slaves as per Return made up to 1st January	Males	Females
	76	123

Increase by Births

Names of Males	Females	Colour	Date	Mother's Name
William		Black	15th March	Nelly
	Leba	do	9 July	Mary
	Letitia	Mestee	13 October	Lucy
	Polly	Black	13 do	Charlotte
	Queen	do	8 November	Peggy
Total Increase by Births 1	4			

Decrease by Death

		Colour	Date	Cause of Death
	Phoebe	Black	5th January	Influenza
Rodger		do	2nd March	Maladictima
	Hagar	do	17 April	Old age & debility
William		do	18 July	Debilitus & dysentery & liver
	Rose	do	31 July	Visitation of Providence
	Phyllis	do	7 October	Old age & debility
Total decrease by Death 2	4			

Total Slaves, Seventy five Males & One hundred & twenty three Females

(Signed) James Kirk
Manager

Sworn to before me this 31st day of January 1831 to be a true and distinct account according to the Registry Bill of this Island

(Signed) Henry Yeates
Registrar

Henry Yeates
Registrar

Glamorgan Estate

Tobago 1st January 1832
Schedule — Annual Return of Plantation Slaves

The Return of Jas. Kirk for the Plantation called Glamorgan in the Parish of Saint Mary for the total Number of all Slaves belonging or attached thereto, or usually settled or employed thereon, with a true and distinct account of all Births and Deaths thereon and of all other additions to or deductions from the Stock of Slaves from whatever Cause between the first day of January 1831 and the first day of January 1832.

Total Number of Slaves as per Return made up to 1st January 1831	Males	Females
	75	123

Increase by Births

Names of Males	Females	Color	Date	Mothers Name
	Nanny	Black	4th June	Venus
	Lucy	do.	6th Octr.	Phoebe

Total Increase by Births — " — 2

Decrease by Deaths

Males	Females	Color	Date	
Wain		Black	11th March	Water in the Chest
	Fanny	do.	1st May	Old age and debility
Boatswain		do.	26th do.	Mal d'Estomac
	Eve	do.	2nd Septr.	Old age & Leprosy
Prince		Yellow	6th do.	Mal d'Estomac
Max		do.	9th Octr.	Venereal Affection
Davie		Black	13th do.	Old age & Palsy
	Jane	do.	26th Novr.	Sores & general debility

Total Decrease by Deaths — 5 — 3

Total Slaves. Seventy Males and One Hundred and Twenty Two Females.
In all One hundred and Ninety Two.

Signed, James Kirk
Manager

Sworn to before me this 31st day of January 1832 to be a true and distinct Account according to the Registry Bill of this Island.
Signed, Henry Yeates
Registrar

Henry Yeates
Registrar

Betseys Hope Estate

Tobago 1st January 1832

Annual Return of Plantation Slaves

Schedule. The Return of James Kirk for the Plantation called Betseys Hope in the Parish of Saint Paul for the total Number of all Slaves belonging or attached thereto or usually worked or employed thereon, with a true and distinct Account of all Births and Deaths thereon, and of all other Additions to or deductions from the said Stock of Slaves from whatever Cause between the first day of January 1831 and the first day of January 1832.

Total Number of Slaves as per Return made up to 1st January 1831	Males	Females
	100	115

Increase by Births

Names of Males	Females	Colour	Date	Mother's Name
	Judy Ann	Mustee	27 March	Jean
William		Black	17 May	Felicity
Nero		do	1 August	Mamba
	Elizabeth	Mustee	24 do	Kitty
Tom		Mulatto	2 Septm.	Judy
Fraser		Black	19 October	Ophelia
	Rose	Black	11 Decm.	Amba
Total Increase by Births	4	3		

Decrease by Deaths

Males	Females	Colour	Date	Cause
	Jeanny	Black	1st January	old age & debility
Hamlet		do	9 do	Epilepsy
Good Luck		Yellow	16 Feby	age & debility
Othello		Black	21 do	Bilious Fever
George		do	7 March	Hooping Cough
Archy		do	21 do	old age & debility
John		do	15 April	old age & debility
	Dutchess	do	10 June	debility & sometimes insane
	Clara	do	21 do	debility arising from incontinent ulcers
	Judy	albino	9 Septm.	child bed
Cupid		Black	12 Novm.	old age & bowel complaint
Islay		do	23 do	old age & bowel complaint
Total Decrease by Deaths	8	4		

Total Slaves. Ninety Six Males and one hundred and Fourteen Females.

In all. Two Hundred and Ten.

Signed, James Kirk
Manager

Sworn to before me this 31st day of January 1832 to be a true and distinct Account according to the Registry Bill of this Island

Signed, Henry Yeates
Registrar

Henry Yeates
Registrar

Betseys Hope 1833

Betseys Hope Estate

Tobago 1st January 1833
Schedule — Annual Return of Plantation Slaves

The Return of James Kirk for the Plantation called Betseys Hope, in the Parish of Saint Paul, for the Total number of all Slaves belonging or attached thereto or usually worked or employed thereon, with a true and distinct account of all Births and Deaths thereon and of all other additions to or deductions from the Stock of Slaves from whatever cause between the first day of January 1832 and the first day of January 1833.

Total Number of Slaves as pr Return made up to 1st January 1832	Males	Females
	96	114

Increase by Births

Names of Males	Females	Colour	Date of Birth 1832	Mothers Name
	Nanny	Black	20 March	Katie
	Adelaide	Mulatto	29 April	Nancy
Henry		Cob	20 June	Isabella
	Kate	Black	29 Novem	Betty
Bob		Black	24 Decem	Amba

Total Increase by Births: 2 | 3

Decrease by Deaths

Males	Females	Colour	1832	Cause
Neil Stewart		Cob	2 January	Worms
	Cherry	Black	15 Do	Old age & debility
	Rose	Do	16 Do	debility being sickly from birth
Patterson		Do	10 March	Dysentery
Monday		Yellow skin	20 Do	Consumption
	Polina	Black	31 May	Old age & debility
	Adelaide	Do	25 June	Do
Sancho		Do	25 Do	Consumption
	Jeanny Cove	Do	12 July	Ditto

Total Decrease by Deaths: 4 | 5

Increase by Exchange

Males	Females	Colour	Date 1832	with whom
Wolf		Black	11 May	Lookey Kelsey for herself

Total Increase by Exchange: 1 | —

Decrease by Exchange

Males	Females	Colour	Date 1832	For whom
	Lookey	Mulatto	11 May	Wolf

Total Decrease by Exchange: — | 1

Decrease by Manumission

Males	Females	Colour	Date	
	Jean	Mulatto	15 October	Manumitted
	Judy Ann	Musta	Ditto	

Total Decrease by Manumission: — | 2

Total Slaves.
Continued next Page

Henry Yates
Registrar

Betseys Hope Estate

Tobago 1st January 1834. Plantation

Schedule. Annual Return of Unattached Slaves. The Return of James Kirk for the Plantation called Betseys Hope, in the Parish of Saint Paul, for the Total Number of all Slaves belonging or attached thereto, or usually worked or employed thereon; with a true and distinct Account of all Births and Deaths thereon; And of all other Additions to, or deductions from the Stock of Slaves from whatever Cause between the first day of January 1833, And the first day of January 1834.

Total Number of Slaves as per last Return made up to 1st January 1833	Males	Females
	95	100

Increase by Births

Names of Males	Females	Colour	Date of Births	Mothers' Names
"	Jeanny	Black	January 10th	Phindey
"	Sally	do	do 16	Jean
"	Liddy	do	July 8	Clarissa
Rolly	"	do	do 24	Dido
"	Catherina Ann	Quadroon	September 9	Kitty
Oswald	"	Blk	do 26	Knowledge
"	Belinda	do	November 29	Ophelia

Total Increase by Births: 2 5

Decrease by Deaths

			Date 1833	Cause
"	Sarah	Black	February 2nd	Consumption
Buonoparte	"	do	do 5	Coroners Inquest held Verdict Visitation of God
Smart	"	do	do 18	Consumption
"	Grace	do	do 20	ditto
"	Felicity	do	do 22	Influenza
"	Dandy	do	May 3	diseased heart & Kidney
William	"	Col	June 2nd	Influenza
"	Molly	Blk	August 22	Scrofula
Archer	"	do	September 16	Coroners Inquest held Verdict Visitation of God
Nero	"	do	October 13	Yaws & General debility
"	Molly	do	do 27	Extreme old age & Gen'l debility
Paul	"	Yellow	November 11	Dysentery, Old Age & Gen'l do

Total Decrease by Deaths: 6 6

Decrease by Transfer

			date of	To whom
"	Abba	Black		
"	Agnes	do		To the Heirs of
"	Agnes	do	1st October	John Robley
"	Ann	do	1833	Deceased
"	Betty	do		
"	Bridget	do		

Carried up: " 6

Notes on Mulattoes and Negroes

Source: Journal of the Anthropological Society of London, Vol. 6 (1868), pp. lvii-lx
Royal Anthropological Institute of Great Britain and Ireland Stable URL: http://www.jstor.org/stable/3025277\

Knowing that the Hon. James Kirk, of Tobago, had resided there forty-two years, and is a careful and practical naturalist, he asked him some questions about these people, and received the following answers. He said that mulattoes and mulatresses less frequently cohabited, from motives of pride or convenience, than with either of the paternal races, and that the number of children proceeding therefrom was smaller; but that they were perfectly fertile among themselves, and laughed at the idea of their becoming extinct from lack of fecundity. He thought the moral character of mulattoes inferior to that of either black or white races; for he had a very bad opinion of the morals of all West Indian coloured people. Thus, a man might be convicted of a notorious crime, and be imprisoned for years, and on his release be received into society with acclamation. He thought that some negroes were capable of acquiring a great amount of knowledge; but even the most intelligent were prone to use their learning for unworthy purposes, such as imitating the handwriting of a kind master for the purpose of fraud. Mr. Keans, the Master in Chancery for the Island of Tobago, gave him the same information. A low state of morality was apt to prevail especially amongst the Dissenters, even when very zealous in the promulgation of their creed, and liberal in the support of their ministers, or in contributing to the building of chapels; for instance, several black brothers preferred their neighbours' wives to their own. The black and coloured people of Tobago have been mostly peaceably disposed; the few insurrections known having been induced from Barbadoes or other neighbouring islands. A plot was discovered in due time, some years ago, which had for its object the massacre of the adult male white population, and the appropriation, by lottery, of the white females among the blacks. Mr. Kirk considered the negro but a savage,—a friend when excited, and little to be depended on even in his best moments. He thought men of the Governor Eyre stamp could alone successfully deal with negroes in revolt. He mentioned, however, in extenuation of the negro character, that his own overseer, in whom he has had great confidence a family of pure negro blood which contained two albinos (males), one of whom, marrying a negress, had a family of children, but no albinos.

The DIRECTOR remarked, that statements concerning the intellectuality of the negro were made very coolly now-a-days. The principal uses to which half-castes applied their superior knowledge was forgery. Such a statement respecting the negro was received, some years ago, with loud hisses. The paper itself took a very great range, and would become very useful for reference. The information obtained from Dr. Kirk was exceedingly important; and by a careful collection of such facts, we should gradually get to know something definite, not only of pure races, but of half-castes.

These are James Kirk's unabridged feelings about the different races he encountered as a planter in Tobago.

This was based on real world experiences. His son James JR left Tobago in shame for forging his father's signature on a legal document and obtained payments that did not belong to him.

Later, SR became ill and he needed Jr's help managing the workload that he could no longer complete on his own, so he sent for JR.

James Jr was "forgiven" and welcomed back into full membership of the society and into leadership of the ruling class in Tobago.

KIRK JR AND SR ESTATES

Tobago and the Parishes

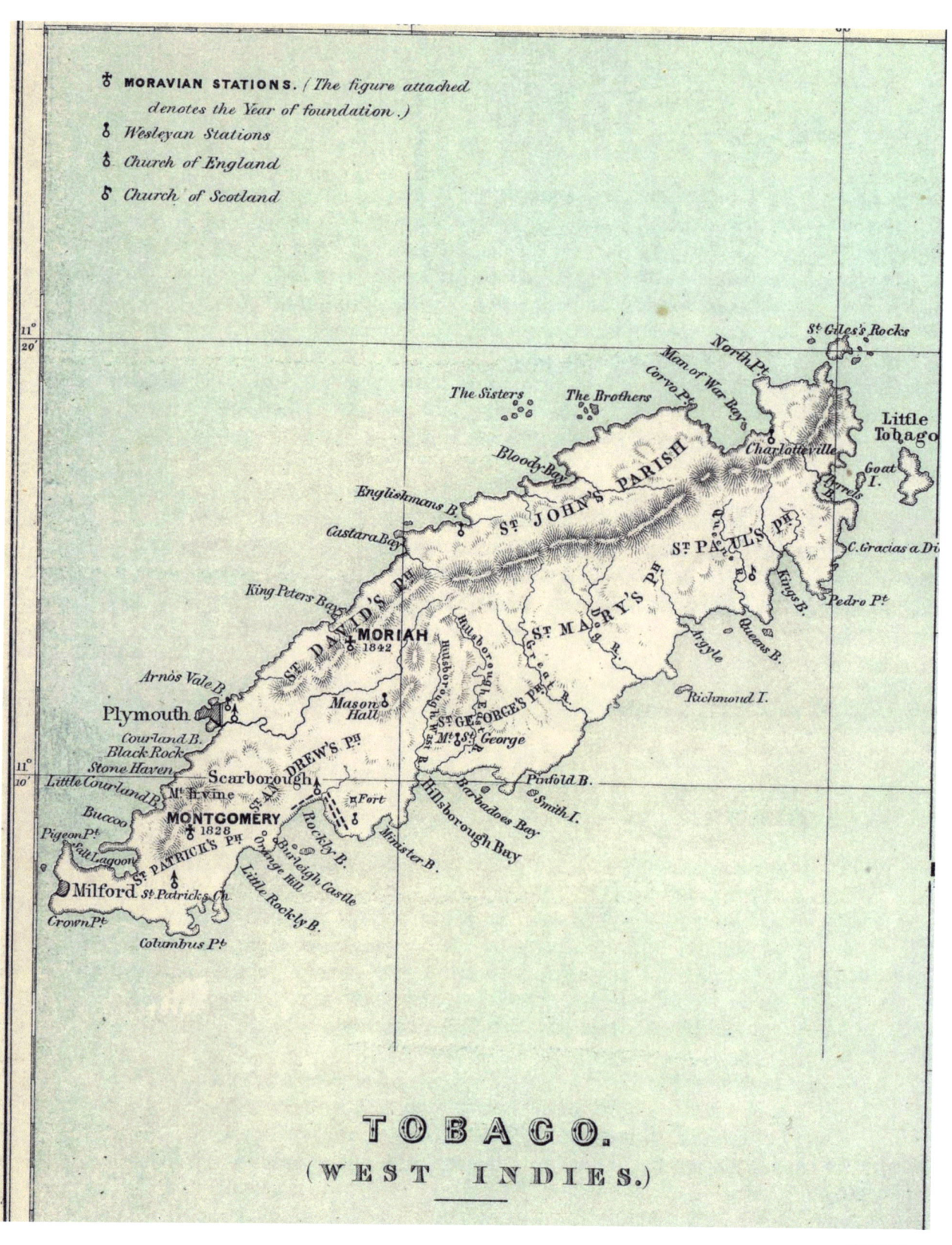

Tobago and the Parishes/Estates

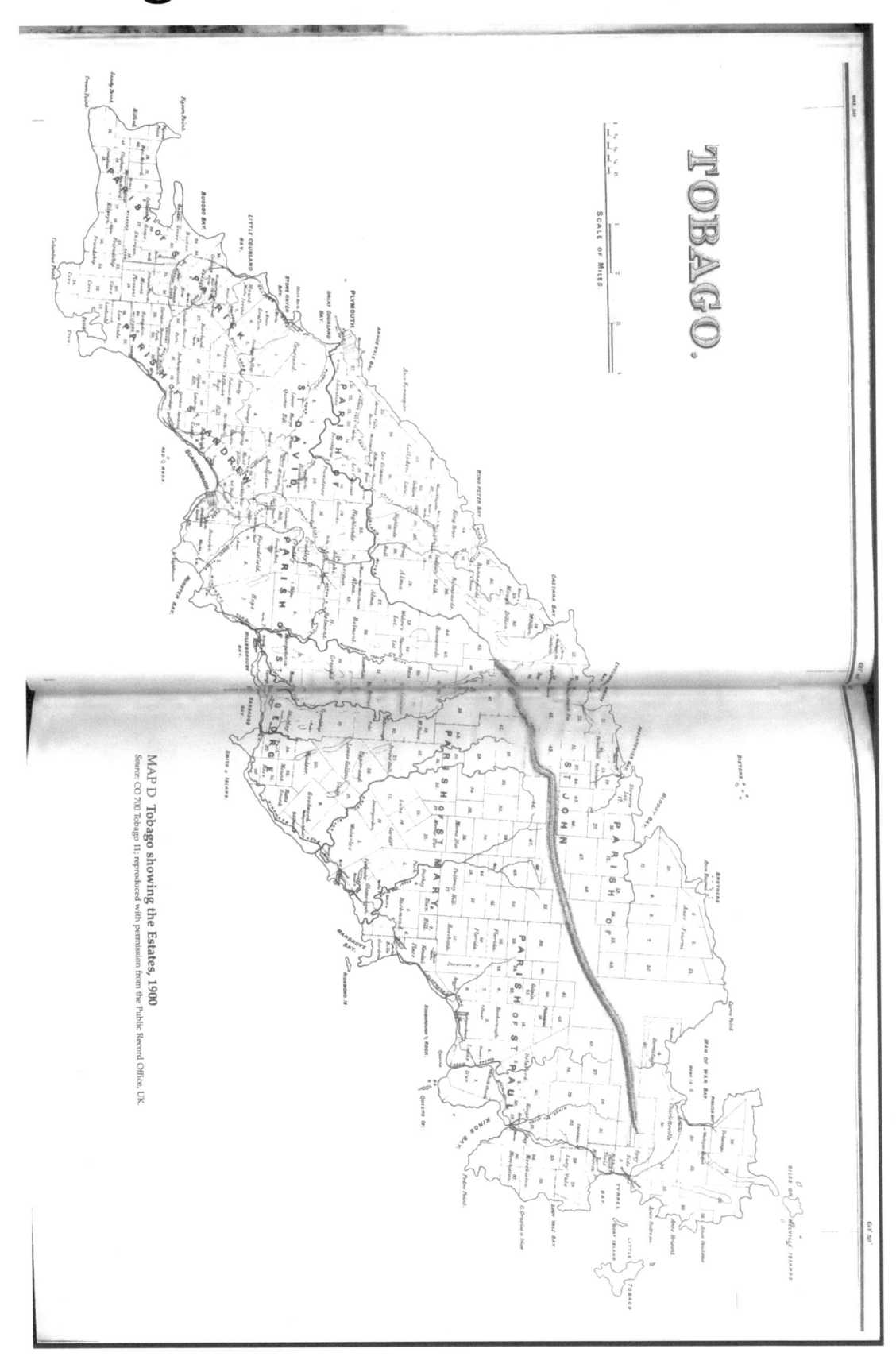

MAP D **Tobago showing the Estates, 1900**
Source: CO 700 Tobago 11; reproduced with permission from the Public Record Office, UK

This chart represents some of the documents available in Tobago Archives.

For the most part, these are mentions of a name in a particular document, such as Jurors or Electors.

The most interesting fact included on this document is the listing that shows James Kirk Jr as part Proprietor of Estates by Marriage

Research for Arleen Froemming
Tobago Archives – records found for the surname Kirk

Tobago Census 1839 to 1841

Name	Parish	Age	Addition	Place of Abode	Calling	Digital Page
James Kirk	St. Andrew	10 years	N/A	Scarborough	N/A	132/559

Most likely the son of James Kirk (Senior)/ Date of census 1839/ DOB circa 1829

Tobago Poll list of an Election (Names of Voters)

Date of Elections	Parish	Name of Voter	Qualification of Voter	Image #
Friday 5th August, 1842	St. David	James Kirk	Attorney for Woodlands Estate	#IMG 8756
7th April, 1843	St. Andrew	James Kirk	Trustee as a (words unreadable)	#IMG 8758
Tuesday 5th September, 1843	St. Paul	James Kirk	Attorney of Roxborough Estate	#IMG 8762

Tobago List of Electors for 1862 to 1870

Parish/Town	Name of Voter	Place of Abode	Qualification of Voter	Image #
St. Paul	James Kirk	Roxborough	Proprietor of Roxborough Plantation	#IMG8770
St Patrick	James Kirk	Roxborough	As Executor & Trustee for the Shirvan & Bon Accord Estates & part of Mount Pleasant.	#IMG8774
St. Patrick	James Kirk (Junior)	Roxborough	Joint Proprietor by right of Wife of Shirvan & Bon Accord Estates & part of Mount Pleasant.	#IMG8774
St. George Scarborough	James Kirk (Junior)	Roxborough	Tenant of the Heirs of Balfour	#IMG8782
St. Mary	James Kirk (Junior)	Roxborough	part Proprietor of houses & lands in Upper Town	#IMG8784
Not listed	James Kirk (Junior)	Roxborough	Tenant of lands called Hatts Grant/ Samuel Wood – Proprietor	#IMG8789
St. David	James Kirk	Roxborough	Proprietor of Studley Park Plantation	#IMG8796
St. George	James Kirk (Junior)	Roxborough	Proprietor of Woodlands Plantation & part Proprietor of Highlands Plantation	#IMG8811
			Proprietor of Studley Park Plantation	#IMG8824

Tobago List of Jurors

Date Empanelled	Name of Juror	Image #
2nd April, 1833	James Kirk	#IMG8840
7th August, 1838	James Kirk	#IMG8871
7th May, 1839	James Kirk	#IMG8873

274

Research for Arleen Froemming
Tobago Census 1839 to 1841

Name	Parish	Age	Addition	Place of Abode	Calling	Digital Page #
George Anderson (*Year circa 1839*)	St. Andrew	25 years	Groom	Scarborough	Not listed	105/559
Romeo Anderson (*Year circa 1839*)	St Andrew	62 years	Mechanic	Riseland	Blacksmith	106/559
Timothy Anderson (*Year circa 1839*)	St. Andrew	80 years	Tradesman	Saint Andrew	Sadler	106/559
Bacchus Anderson (*Year circa 1839*)	St. David	26 Years	Mechanic	Golden Lane	Carpenter	216/559
James Anderson (*Year circa 1841*)	St. David	17 years	Mechanic	Golden Lane	Carpenter	216/559
Robert Cunningham (*Year circa 1839*)	St. Mary	5 months	N/A	Glamorgan	N/A	54/559
Eve Cunningham (*Year circa 1839*)	St. Mary	58 years	An Invalid	Glamorgan	Not listed	55/559
William Cunningham (*Year circa 1839*)	St. Andrew	31 years	Mechanic	Saint Andrew	Not listed	116/559
James Kirk	**St. Andrew**	**10 years**	**N/A**	**Scarborough**	**N/A**	**132/559**
Most likely the son of James Kirk (Senior)/ Date of census 1839/ DOB circa 1829						
John Patterson (*Year circa 1839*)	St. Andrew	66 years	Fisherman	Scarborough	Not listed	144/559
John Patterson (*Year circa 1839*)	St. Andrew	11 years	N/A	Scarborough	N/A	144/559
Robert Patterson (*Year circa 1839*)	St. Andrew	6 years	N/A	Scarborough	N/A	144/559
James Patterson (*Year circa 1839*)	St. Andrew	1 year	N/A	Scarborough	N/A	144/559
Archie Patterson (*Year circa 1839*)	St. Andrew	8 years	Apprentice	Scarborough	Not listed	144/559
James Patterson	St. George	28 years	Mechanic	Nutmeg Grove	Carpenter	91/559
Matthew Witz (*Year circa 1839*)	**St. John**	**29 years**	**Planter**	**Englishman's Bay**	**Attorney**	**22/559**
Matthew Witz (*Year 1841*)	**St. John**	**31 years**	**Planter**	**Englishman's Bay**	**Manager**	**277/559**
Caroline Witz (*Year 1841*)	St. John	8 years	N/A	Englishman's Bay	Dependant on her parents	278/559
Fanny Witz (*Year 1841*)	St John	4 years	N/A	Englishman's Bay	Dependant on her parents	278/559
Catherine Witz (*Year 1841*)	St. John	30 years	Agriculturist	Englishman's Bay	Labourer	278/559
Eve Witz (*Year 1841*)	St. John	5 years	N/A	Englishman's Bay	Dependant on her parents	282/559
Mary Ann Witz (*Year 1841*)	St. John	3 ½ Years	N/A	Englishman's Bay	Dependant on her parents	282/559
Celil Witz (*Year circa 1839*)	St. John	8 years	N/A	Englishman's Bay	N/A	25/559
Wyatt Witz (*Year circa 1839*)	St. John	6 years	N/A	Englishman's Bay	N/A	25/559

Page **1** of **2**

Research for Arleen Froemming
Tobago Census 1839 to 1841

Name	Parish	Age	Addition	Place of Abode	Calling	Digital Page #
Louisa Witz (*Year circa 1839*)	St. George	6 months	N/A	Cradley	N/A	104/559
Lewis (Louis) Witz (*Year circa 1839*)	**St. George**	**25 Years**	**Planter**	**Cradley**	**Not listed**	**101/559**

Tobago Poll list of an Election (Names of Voters)

Date of Elections	Parish	Name of Voter	Qualification of Voter	Image #
Friday 5th August, 1842	St. David	James Kirk	Attorney for Woodlands Estate	#IMG 8756
7th April, 1843	St. Andrew	James Kirk	Trustee as a (words unreadable)	#IMG 8758
Tuesday 5th September, 1843	St. Paul	James Kirk	Attorney of Roxborough Estate	#IMG 8762

Tobago List of Electors for 1862 to 1870

Parish/Town	Name of Voter	Place of Abode	Qualification of Voter	Image #
St. Paul	James Kirk	Roxborough	Proprietor of Roxborough Plantation	#IMG8770
St Patrick	James Kirk	Roxborough	As Executor & Trustee for the Shirvan & Bon Accord Estates & part of Mount Pleasant.	#IMG8774
St. Patrick	James Kirk (Junior)	Roxborough	Joint Proprietor by right of Wife of Shirvan & Bon Accord Estates & part of Mount Pleasant.	#IMG8774
St. Andrew	Barclay Cunningham	Belvedere	Tenant of the House & Land called Belvedere belong to John Coker	#IMG8779
St. George	James Cunningham	Bristol	Proprietor of Cradley Plantation	#IMG8782
St. George	James Kirk	Roxborough	Tenant of the Heirs of Balfour	#IMG8782
Scarborough	James Kirk (Junior)	Roxborough	Part Proprietor of houses & lands in Upper Town	#IMG8784
St. Paul	James Thomas H.B.	Invera	Manager of Invera Plantations	#IMG8789
St. Mary	James Kirk	Roxborough	Tenant of lands called Hatts Grant/ Samuel Wood – Proprietor	#IMG8789
Not listed	James Kirk (Junior)	Roxborough	Proprietor of Studley Park Plantation	#IMG8796
St. David	James Kirk	Roxborough	Proprietor of Woodlands Plantation & part Proprietor of Highlands Plantation	#IMG8811
St. John	Barclay Cunningham	Studley Park	Owner of Ance Fourmie lands	#IMG8814

Page **2** of **2**

Research for Arleen Froemming
Tobago List of Electors for 1862 to 1870

Parish/Town	Name of Voter	Place of Abode	Qualification of Voter	Image #
St. Paul	Frederick M. Witz	Kings Bay Estate	Manager of King's Bay Estate	#IMG8818
St. Mary	James Thomas H.B.	Invera	Proprietor of house & land at Zion Hill	#IMG8818
St. George	James Kirk (Junior)	Roxborough	Proprietor of Studley Park Plantation	#IMG8824
St. George	Barclay Cunningham	Studley Park	Tenant of James Kirk	#IMG8824
St. Andrew	Charles Cunningham (dead)	#5 Calder Hall	Not listed	#IMG8833
St. Andrew	Barclay Cunningham (dead)	Not listed	Not listed	#IMG8833

Tobago List of Jurors

Date Empanelled	Name of Juror	Image #
2nd April, 1833	James Kirk	#IMG8840
11th June, 1833	Matthew Witz	#IMG8844
6th May, 1834	Peter Witz	#IMG8847
5th April, 1834	Henry Cunningham	#IMG8857
7th October, 1837	Louis Witz	#IMG8864
7th August, 1838	James Kirk	#IMG8871
7th May, 1839	James Kirk	#IMG8873
11th June, 1839	Matthew Witz	#IMG8877
1st October, 1839	Louis Witz	#IMG8879

Tobago Marriages

Date of Marriage	Place of Marriage	Name of Groom/Occupation/Abode	Name of Bride/Occupation/Abode	Image#
29th June, 1844	The Church of the United Brethren Moriah/ Parish of St. David	John Cunningham/ Carpenter Woodlands	Juliet Tom/ Agriculturist Indian Walk	#IMG8882
10th May, 1845	Montgomery/ Parish of St. Patrick	John Patterson	Fanny Cato	100/265

TABLE 5.10 Middle District: Owners, Number and Value of Estates, 1881/1882

Owner(s)	No. of estates	AAV or mean AAV (£)	Remarks (including the name(s) of the estate(s))
Thomas Blakely jun.	1	100	Coloured merchant; also owned Parrot Hall Estate, which was listed as 'land' in 1882; Alma Estate.
Craig Castella and Elizabeth Boggett	1	130	Castella was a black man, a former merchant's clerk; owned Mt. St. George Estate; also owned Providence Estate in the Leeward District.
Robert Crooks	1	35	Coloured; owned Breeze Hall Estate; also owned Milford (leeward estate).
A. M. Gillespie and Co.	2	75	British merchant house; biggest creditor to Tobago planters; Sherwood Park and Carnbee estates. See Table 5.13.
William Gordon	1	100	Resident; Calder Hall Estate.
James Hackett	1	100	Hackett was a black man, formerly enslaved; carpenter and shopkeeper who became a planter; owned Belmont; also owned Les Coteaux (leeward estate).
Robert Hutchinson	1	80	UK resident; Cradley Estate.
Walter Irvine II	1	200	UK resident; Bacolet Estate.[24]
Heirs of Frederick Keens	1	70	Deceased white resident; Concordia Estate.
James Kirk sen.	4 (3)[b]	119	Resident Scotsman; died 1874; owned twelve tracts of land of which six were estates. In this district, his estates were Studley Park with Mt. Rose (Montrose) attached, Mesopotamia and Smithfield.
Estate of Mary Kitson	1	70	Friendsfield Estate.
John McCall and others	3	283	Leading planters and merchants; partners with A. M. Gillespie and Co. See the list of the McCall/Gillespie estates in Table 5.13.
Heirs of Piggott	1	60	Lowlands Estate; owned in 1809 by Elphinstone Piggott, Chief Justice; heirs resided in the UK.
Thomas Reid and Co.	1	100	British merchant house owning three estates in 1882; Hope Estate.
Heirs of Robinson Scobie	1	10	Black merchant; Deal Fair Estate, later the Botanic Station.
Estate of William Ward	1	150	Coloured family; Mt. Pelier Estate.
Total	22 (21)	121.8	Total (£) is mean AAV of the units.

Sources: Calculated from Tobago Assessment Roll, 1881/1882; sundry records for the remarks.

Notes:
[a] Numbers in brackets indicate the consolidation of holdings into fewer units. Where the owner had more than one estate, their mean assessed value is given.
[b] Mt. Rose Estate, classified as 'land' on the Assessment Roll, is counted here as an estate since it was worked jointly with Studley Park Estate.

TABLE 5.11 Leeward District: Owners, Number and Value of Estates, 1881/1882

Owner(s)	No. of estates	AAV or mean AAV (£)	Remarks (including the name(s) of the estate(s))
George Agard	1	250	Coloured merchant; migrant from Barbados; Buccoo Estate.
Benjamin Alleyne sen.	1	40	White resident; owned Culloden Estate; managed Charlotteville Estate.
Craig Castella	1	150	Black planter; Providence Estate.
Robert Crooks	1	75	Coloured resident; Milford Estate.
Davidson and others	4	84	Aberdeen lawyers; owned Pigeon Point, Old Grange, New Grange and Grafton estates.
Mary Ann Des Vignes	1	60	Resident white; Craig Hall Estate; owned large property at Mt. Dillon.
A. M. Gillespie and Co. and A. M. Gillespie and others	9 (7)	177	Also owned Cromstain Estate, listed as 'land' on the Assessment Roll. Value of Roselle Estate was not given; therefore the average is based on values for 6 working units. Estates are listed in Table 5.13.
James Hackett	1	200	Black; formerly enslaved; Les Coteaux Estate.
Frances Keens	5	76	Coloured; widow of James Henry Keens, British merchant and former President of the Legislative Council, who died in 1878; Golden Grove, Kilgwyn, Cove, Friendship and Clapham estates.
James Kirk sen.	2	115	Scots planter; died 1874; Highlands and Woodlands estates.
John James Kitson	1	100	Resident family; Arnos Vale Estate.
Heirs of Gordon Turnbull Macdougall	1	180	Coloured family; Runnemede Estate. They also owned Adelphi, not listed as a working estate in 1882.
Duncan Macgillivray	1	50	Scots attorney for A. M. Gillespie and Co.; Franklyns Estate.
Thomas Reid and Co.	2	110	British merchants; Courland and Dunveygan estates.
Thomas Lewis Rowe	1	280	Resident white from Barbados; Mt. Irvine Estate.
John Spicer	2	120	Englishman; master mariner; Shirvan and Bon Accord estates.
Tom and others	1	40	Black owners; Golden Lane Estate.
Total	**35 (33)**	**121.6**	Total (£) is mean AAV of the units.

Sources: Calculated from Tobago Assessment Roll, 1881/1882; sundry records for the remarks.

Note:
[a] Numbers in brackets indicate the consolidation of holdings into fewer units. Where the owner had more than one estate, their mean assessed value is given.

TABLE 5.9 **Windward District: Owners, Number and Value of Estates, 1881/1882**

Owner(s)	No. of estates	AAV or mean AAV (£)	Remarks (including the name(s) of the estate(s))
Dr. James G. and Dr. Richard B. Anderson	1	120	English physicians, druggists and merchants; residents; Castara Estate.
John McCall	4 (3)	125	Scottish resident planter, merchant and estate attorney; died in 1879. See the McCall/Gillespie estates in Table 5.13.
John and James McCall	7 (5)	308	James McCall: Scottish resident planter and merchant. See Table 5.13.
Brutus Murray	1	150	Coloured; former metayer, then estate manager; Pembroke Estate.
Robert H. Pile	2	275	White; resident in Barbados; owned Invera and Roxborough estates; the latter was the scene of the Belmanna uprising, 1876.
James H. B. Thomas	2	95	Resident; born in Grenada; master carpenter, shop owner; estate attorney for Thomas Reid and Co., British merchants; owned Kendal Place and Belle Garden estates.
Total	**17 (14)**	**200.7**	Total (£) is mean AAV of the units.

Sources: Calculated from Tobago Assessment Roll, 1881/1882; sundry records for the remarks.

Note:
[a] Numbers in brackets indicate the consolidation of holdings into fewer units. Where the owner had more than one estate, their mean assessed value is given.

James Kirk, Sr. - Sale of Estates he owned, or managed

The structure of estate ownership in Tobago made it challenging for emancipated individuals to afford purchasing estates or property. However, there are notable examples of Black landowners acquiring significant tracts of land. In 1868, Kent Hector, a carpenter from Mt. St. George, purchased 160 acres, known as Lot No. 20, located in the wooded hills north of Studley Park and Montrose estates. This land was bought from James Kirk Sr., a planter, for £55.

James Kirk's career on the island involved managing estates for absentee owners who resided in Scotland and England. His tenure in Tobago began as an indentured worker under Lord William Robert Keith Douglas, serving on his estate for three years.

This arrangement was typical of the era. British colonial landowners frequently recruited young Scots to manage their estates. For these young men, such opportunities provided a means to elevate their social and economic standing, with the ultimate goal of returning to Scotland to build or purchase grand estates upon achieving financial success.

In 1866, there was an all out effort to sell estates owned/managed by James Kirk Sr. This could have been due to the illness he suffered at this time.

Letters written from James Kirk to Sir William Jardine. Locations - Estates mentioned in letter headings as the return address:

Old Granger - September 10, 1826
Old Granger - September 15, 1826
Betsy's Hope - 2 April 1827,
Betsy's Hope - 27 May 1827
Glamorgan - 21 November 1827
Tobago - 10 May 1828
Glamorgan - 31 July 1828
Glamorgan - 4 March 1829
Betsy's Hope - 13 April 1832
Betsy's Hope - 19 August 1832
Betsy's Hope - September 1832
Betsy's Hope - 1 March 1833
Roxburgh - 12 June 1834
Roxburgh - 6 June 1836
Roxburgh - 17 April 1837
Roxburgh - 2 December 1837
Roxburgh - 25 April 1838
Roxburgh - 4 October 1838
Roxburgh - 17 Mar 1845
Woodlands - 3 April 1845
Tobago - 11 April 1845
Tobago - 12 August 1845
Roxburgh - 18 August 1845
Roxburgh - 5 September 1845
Roxburgh - 19 November 1845

Trinidad Chronicle July 31, 1866

For Sale.

THAT VALUABLE and Seasonable Sugar Estate called

BON ACCORD,

Situate in the Parish of Saint Patrick, comprising 525 Acres or thereabouts, of level land, butted and bounded on the South by the Sea shore, and on the North by a Lagoon abounding with Fish and Turtle, and where there is a

TURTLE CRAWL.

The BUILDINGS are substantial, and there are 89 head of STOCK on the Property, and an excellent WIND MILL, with Stone Tower.

Every thing in good order, and the Estate is capable of making large Crops.

Further particulars may be obtained on application to the Subscriber at Roxburgh.

JAMES KIRK.

THE BARBADOS AGRICULTURAL REPORTER, TUESDAY, JUNE 18, 1872

FOR SALE:

The Undermentioned SUGAR and GRAZING ESTATES, IN THE ISLAND OF TOBAGO.

1. "WOODLANDS."

IN the parish of Saint David, with 500 acres of Land, a set of Sugar Works of solid Masonry, with a new horizantal 8 horse Steam Engine, horizantal Mill and Cornish Boiler, 5 Sugar Boilers, a Copper Clarifier, a 300 gallon Still, Megass House, Mule pen, and Bay Store, all covered with red tiles and in good order. A fine dwelling House, situated in a very healthy position, a Cocoa-nut-walk near the beach; with 10 Mules, 11 Asses, 26 Oxen, 9 Cows, 7 Steers, and Heifers and Calves.

2. "MESSOPOTAMIA,"

In the parish of Saint George, with 500 acres of Land, a set of Sugar Works completed (new from the foundation), covered with red tiles and corrugated iron, with Sugar Boilers, Iron Chimney, and Iron Water Wheel and horizantal Mill, megass House small Dwelling House, abundant supply of Water. These Works are situated within yards of the shipping bay. A fine young Cocoa-nut-walk coming on well.

"STUDLEY PARK"

In the parish of Saint George, (adjoining Messopotamia), with 800 acres of land new 12 horse horizantal Steam Engine, horizantal Rollers, cornish Boilers, Iron Chim and an iron Water Wheel (the gearing of the Mill is so arranged as to be driven by w steam), contain in a mill house covered with galvanized iron — a saw Mill, a fine out sugar-works of solid masonry, 400 yards from the beach, with two sets of Sugar-boilers 00 gallon copper Clarifier, and 300 gallon Still, with two Megass Houses, Mule Pen, sev laborers-houses. A set of Sugar-works just completed near the Dwelling House, cov ith red tiles, and corrugated iron, with 5 Sugar-boilers, two 300 gallon Clarifiers, an orse Beam engine, horizantal Mill, cornish Boiler, and Donkey Engine for feeding Bo d an iron Chimney, a Megas house, a fine Cocoa-nut-walk, a large Dwelling Hous lid masonry, with a Water Tank supplied by a spring, a new wooden Dwelling Ho of and sides covered with shingles, 2 very large reservoirs.

James Kirk, Jr. - Tobago Estates he owned, managed, or mentioned

James Kirk - Tobago Estates he owned or managed

"Green Hill and Friendships"

Also in the parish of Saint George, with 1200 acres of land, adjoining Mesopota[mia] [an]d Studley Park.

"MONTROSE,"

Adjoining Studley Park with 300 acres of land, and

"HATTS GRANT"

In the parish of Saint Mary, adjoining Montrose, with 240 acres of land (the gre[ater p]ortion of these 1740 acres is available for pasture, and would yield a good return if [w]ell stocked.) With 14 Mules, 50 Oxen, 30 Cows, 20 Steers and Heifers, 20 Cal[ves] [t]otal 134

'CALEDONIA,'

4. THE "OBSERVATORY,"

In the parish of Saint John, with about 200 acres of Land, part rented to laborers for provisions grounds, the whole suitable for growing Cocoa.

For Particulars Apply to the Proprietor

JAMES KIRK, JNR,
Studley Park, Tobago.

Or to WILLIAM LAURIE, ESQR.,
Bridgetown, Barbados.

Or to THOMAS REID, ESQR.,
3, Tanchurch Buildings, London.

And if the Properties be not sold before Friday, the 23rd day of August next, they will on that day at 12 o'clock (noon), be put up for public Competition, in the Court House of Scarborough, Tobago.

June 18th, 1872.

Inverara, (with part of *Argyle,*)

With 1000 acres of Land, in the parish of Saint Paul, with a 12 horse Vertical Steam Engine, horizantal mill, (with gearing to be worked by steam or water), Cornish Boiler, a Wooden Water Wheel, 2 steam Clarifiers, 5 sugar boilers and double Tayches, a new 300 gallon Still, megass house, a fine set of Sugar Works of solid masonry lately recovered and situated within half a mile of the beach. A fine Cocoa-nut-walk and some Cocoa. A fine residence with water near. With 6 Mules, 20 Oxen, 15 Cows, 10 Steers and Heifers, 9 Calves, Total 60.

Roxbro, (with part of *Argyle.*)

With 1000 acres of Land, and adjoining *Inverara*, with a fine set of Sugar Works of solid masonry, with a new 12-horse horizantal steam Engine and mill, cornish boiler, 2 Clarifiers, 5 sugar boilers and double Tayches, and an Iron Water Wheel, a new 500 gallon Still, the set of sugar works, within half a mile of the beach. A fine Cocoa-nut-walk, a fine new and large Dwelling House and several laborers' houses, with 16 Mules, 6 Asses, 28 Oxen, 15 Cows, 10 Steers and Heifers, 8 Calves, Total 83.

MC LELLAN'S GRANT,

Adjoining *Roxbro*, with 300 acres of Land.

THESE PROPERTIES

ARE WELL WATERED AND ABOUND IN HARDWOOD,

James Kirk, SR. - Death Announced to Government

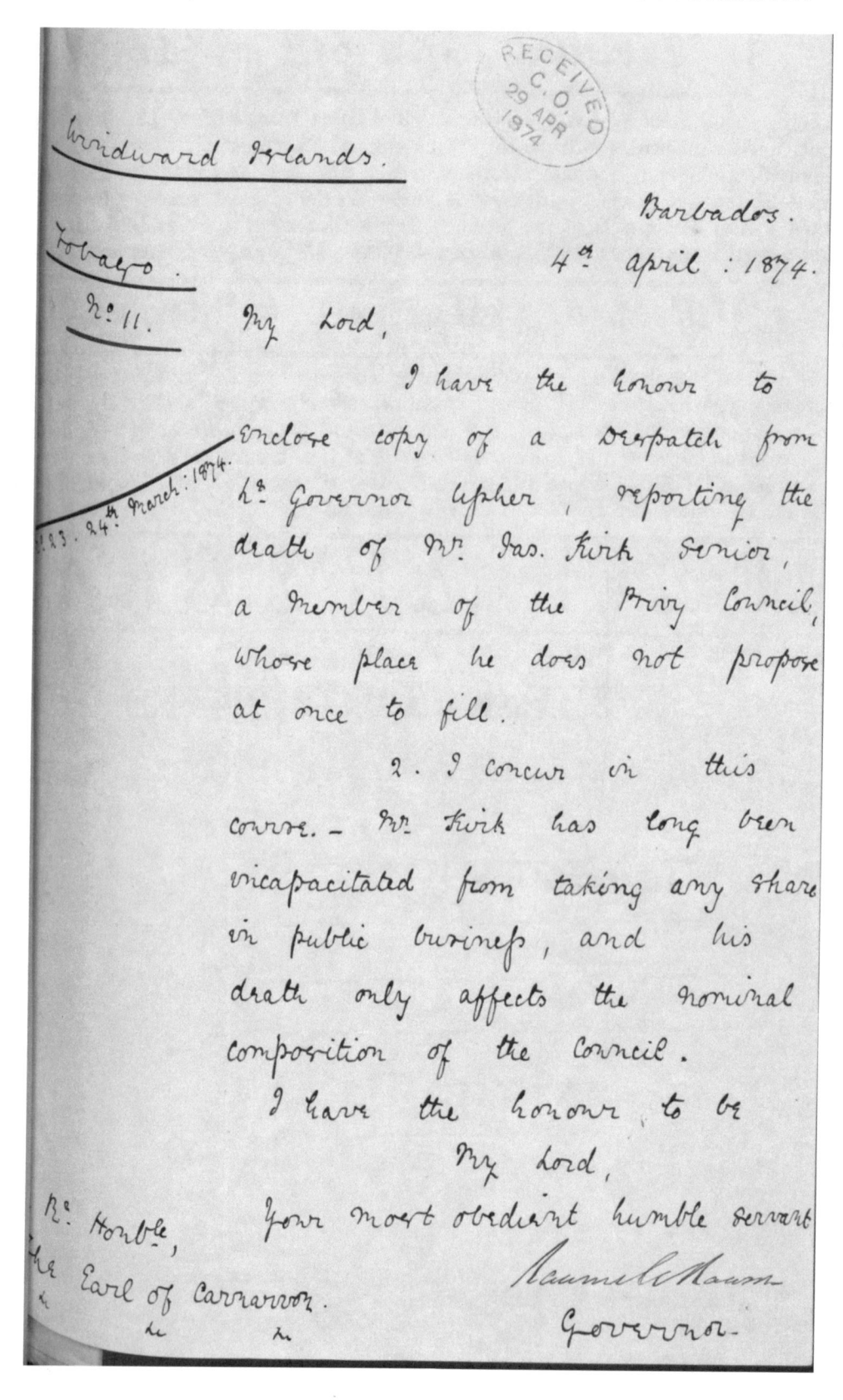

Windward Islands.

Tobago.

No. 11.

Barbados.
4th April: 1874.

My Lord,

I have the honour to enclose copy of a Despatch from Lt. Governor Upsher, reporting the death of Mr. Jas. Kirk Senior, a member of the Privy Council, whose place he does not propose at once to fill.

2. I concur in this course. — Mr. Kirk has long been incapacitated from taking any share in public business, and his death only affects the nominal composition of the Council.

I have the honour to be
My Lord,
Your most obedient humble servant

Rawson W. Rawson
Governor.

The Honble,
The Earl of Carnarvon.

Notification to Barbados of the passing of James Kirk, SR. since he was a member of the Privy Council. It references his condition in the last years of his life.

Enclosure.

Lt. Governor Ussher to Governor Rawson.

Copy 1

Government House
Tobago. 24th March. 1874.

No. 23.   Sir,

I have the regret to announce that Mr. James Kirk, Senior, a member of the Privy Council, and a Justice of the Peace for this island died on the 21st instant.

2. Mr. Kirk's name has been long known in connection with Tobago — He has temporarily administered the Government of this island, and was at one time an extensive proprietor.

3. I am not at

His Excellency,
Governor Rawson. C.B.

KIRK JR

the rest of the story.

James Kirk, Jr. The Criminal

James Kirk JR, fell from a privileged life in politics and social standing to a 2 years Prison sentence (not Hard Labor). The story is outlined in a letter written by J. Goodridge Anderson. He was the brother of Richard Benjamin Anderson who was married to Minnie Paterson (nee Kirk).

James Kirk Jr. left Tobago for a time after forging his father's signature on important documents involving a significant sum of money.

He returned to the colony at his father's request when James Kirk Sr. began to experience declining health. For four years leading up to his death in 1874, Kirk Sr. was bedridden due to paralysis. It is believed that the convalescence period he took in the 1840s was an early indication of the illness that would later incapacitate him. His condition progressively worsened, leaving him unable to fulfill the demanding responsibilities of managing his estates and those he oversaw for absentee landowners.

Recognizing his limitations and the urgency of securing a successor, Kirk Sr. pleaded with his son to return to Tobago. Without James Jr., there was no heir to continue his work or manage the properties under his care. In response, James Jr. returned to Tobago around 1860, though the exact length of his absence is unclear.

By 1879, James Kirk Jr., now a white planter and member of the Executive Council and police force, played a pivotal role in arresting Henry Francis, the First Revenue Officer, on charges of embezzlement. Following this event, James Jr. was appointed to the position himself, marking a significant step in his professional life.

A folk song, recalled by Mrs. Eileen Guillaume (1916-2004), remarked on his descent to equality with the blacks:

Granderry wall, high wall
Granderry wall, Granderry wall
Granderry nuh buil' for me one [alone]
White darg a' guh—Jim Kirk!
Black darg a' guh
White darg a' guh—backra Jimmy!
Alla' we a' one, Oh!*"

PRISON WALLS IN FORT GEORGE, TOBAGO.

JAMES KIRK JR.

MEANING THAT JAMES KIRK WAS NOW ON THE SAME LEVEL AS THE LABOURERS ON THE ISLAND AS DESCRIBED IN SUSAN CRAIG-JAMES BOOK "THE EVOLUTION OF SOCIETY IN TOBAGO: 1838 TO 1900".

Were this the only tale of the Kirks, it would have been a remarkable story of achievement and legacy. However, a letter written to the editor of several Caribbean publications reveals a story of tragedy and scandal in the years following James Kirk Sr.'s passing.

The letter details the troubled aftermath involving his only son, James Kirk Jr. At some point, James Jr. had become estranged from his father. Yet, at his father's insistence, he returned to Tobago, where he was initially welcomed with respect and admiration.

Upon his return, James Jr. was made a justice of the peace, appointed Inland Revenue Officer, elected to the Board of Health, and served on both the Legislative and Privy Councils. He was also tasked with managing his father's estate as its executor, along with other responsibilities like collecting license fees for dogs.

However, the letter, penned by Dr. James Goodrich Anderson—the brother of Dr. Richard Benjamin Anderson, Minnie Kirk's second husband—paints a much darker picture. In it, Dr. Anderson accuses James Jr. of forgery and theft of state funds totaling $500. He claims James Jr. fled from justice and was later apprehended in Toco.

The letter also accuses James Jr. of gambling, drinking, and squandering the inheritance meant for his four sisters. Of these, only Catherine was able to reclaim her share of the estate, thanks to her husband's efforts. He secured a fifth of the estate, which was excluded from the forced auction of the family's plantation. The other three sisters, along with other beneficiaries, received nothing due to James Jr.'s mismanagement.

Dr. Anderson further expressed outrage over what he perceived as preferential treatment in James Jr.'s sentencing. He received a two-year prison term without hard labor, which Anderson attributed to the privileges of his social standing. Eventually, James Jr. was transferred to a prison in Grenada, presumably to minimize the disgrace and hardship inflicted upon the family. The misfortunes of the family did not end there. James Jr.'s son—or perhaps nephew—Henry George Thomas Kirk declared bankruptcy in 1896 and passed away in 1912 at the age of 59. Despite the family's difficulties, Henry was well-regarded in his obituary as one of the great plantation managers and landowners of his time.

Yet, even Henry's life was not without incident. A local news report recounts a chaotic event where his horse, startled while tied at an inn, broke loose. The runaway horse and carriage caused widespread damage, rampaging through streets, destroying storefronts, and injuring several bystanders before being stopped. The article made no mention of the horse's condition, but the carriage was reportedly destroyed.

J Goodridge Anderson's newspaper

Government by the Crown.

(From Tobago *Daylight*.)

LETTERS
To the Right Honourable Her Majesty's Principal Secretary of State for the Colonies.

No. 1.

My Lord,—In addressing myself to the Right Honourable Her Majesty's principal Secretary of State for the Colonies, I do not address the individual who may at this or any other particular time be the recipient of the five thousand a year paid to the Right Honourable Lords for her's representation of the state of the official body here. I will now give another more particular and more recent.

In November last, the Honourable James Kirk, Member of the Executive Council, Inspector of Police and of Inland Revenue officers, a Justice of the Peace, etc., was prosecuted by the Government for forgery of public documents and embezzlement of public monies. He was duly committed on three charges of each of these offences, and at the trial before the Supreme Court, after some progress had been made with the case for the Crown, Kirk suddenly withdrew his plea of not guilty and formally pleaded guilty. He was sentenced to two years imprisonment, and the Crown Prosecutor, for reasons with which Your Lordship ought to be familar, with which everyone in this island is thoroughly familar, said he should not go on with the other cases. During the time that Kirk had the opportunity of doing so, he relieved the Colonial Treasury of about five hundred and thirty-seven pounds, of this you, My Lord, are directly responsible. For, on the first of May, 1883, now two years ago, I wrote to Mr. Harris, Secretary to the Royal Commissioners, who had then just visited this island.

Written by the Brother of Richard Benjamin Anderson

"Mr. James Kirk is Inspector of Police, he is also, being on the Council, styled The Honourable. His history is instructive. Many years ago Mr. James Kirk forged his father's name, and for a long time Tobago knew him not. The father finding himself growing old, made overtures of peace, and Mr. James Kirk returned to Tobago. The old man in due course died, Mr. James Kirk inherited his property subject to the payment of portions to his four sisters. One of these being blessed with a strong minded husband, has received hers, the others, are still minus, and, Mr. James Kirk having got through the property, they are likely to remain so. I hold a power of attorney from a Miss Richardson to recover for her possession of an estate which she was induced by fraud on Kirk's part to mortgage to him. . . . It is a sad thing for a colony like this when a man like Kirk, notorious as a forger, a drunkard, a liar, a fraudulent trustee, and a debtor to every one that will trust him, holds so high a place in it, and his example cannot but tell, as it does with the worst effects, on the force under his control."

I do not know, My Lord, if Mr. Harris brought that letter under Your Lordship's notice. If he did not he sadly neglected his very plain duty in the matter; if he did, you My Lord, have still more grossly neglected yours. For, unless it is to be looked upon as a natural and proper state of things that an Inspector of Police and of Inland Revenue Officers who is also a member of the Executive Council, shall be "notorious as a forger, a drunkard, a liar, a fraudulent trustee, and a debtor to every one that will trust him" it was your manifest and bounden duty to have taken steps for ascertaining the truth or otherwise of my assertions with regard to Kirk and if they were found to be untrue, to have taken the necessary steps to have me punished for so foul and malicious a libel, while if you found them to be true, as you would have done had you chosen to look for the truth, it was still more your duty to remove him from a place for which he was so outrageously unfit. You did not take these steps, you shamefully neglected your duty towards us and towards Kirk, and you are, My Lord, directly responsible for the frauds and defalcations committed by Kirk since I gave you this information as to his character and antecedents, and no amount of sophistry can clear you of that responsibility.

Leaving you, My Lord, for a time, to consider the position you occupy in connection with this matter.

I have honour to subscribe myself,
Your Lordship's most obedient servant,
J. GOODRIDGE-ANDERSON

Investigation into James Kirk, JR and Theft as a Inland Revenue Officer

Defalcations - someone who has legally required financial duties and misuses or misappropriates funds.

COURT HOUSE, SCARBOROUGH,
31st December, 1884.

Sir,—We have the honor to submit this the 1st part of our report on the matters referred to in the Commission dated 25th Novr., 1884.

1. Our first sitting was held on Friday the 28th Novr. 1884, when the Hon'ble L. G. Hay was elected Chairman. It was decided at this sitting that, as in the opinion of the Commissioners it was of the first importance to ascertain with as little delay as possible the extent of the defalcations believed to have been committed by Mr. J. Kirk, our inquiry should primarily be directed solely to this end; and that having reported thereon we should, at greater leisure, undertake the 2nd part of our task, viz. that of enquiring into and reporting upon the working, in all its branches, of the Excise Ordinance 1881, &c.

2. This part of our Report, therefore, deals only with the defalcations; and we would here briefly state the manner in which we set about to unravel—what proved to be a most tangled skein of transactions.

3. In the first place it should be stated that our enquiry extended to the period commencing 1st January, 1882 and ending 20th November 1884. We procured for the purposes of that enquiry, through the Acting Inspector of Inland Revenue Officers, all the Distillers' Stock Books; and from the same source we obtained a great number of documents consisting of Distillers' Quarterly Returns, Licensed Traders Monthly Returns, the Weekly Reports of Inland Revenue Officers, Counterfoils of Permit Books, &c. It may not be out of place to record here our acknowledgment of the ready and valuable help afforded to us by the above-mentioned officer (Mr. L. Witz.)

4. We further obtained from the Treasury a complete list of all Rum duties paid into that Department for the period mentioned in para. 3, and also lists of the Rum duties paid during the same period by the principal Licensed traders.

5. We commenced our labours by carefully comparing the Distillers' Stock Books with their Quarterly Returns, noting discrepancies and omissions. We would shortly explain the importance of such a comparison.

6. The Distiller's Stock Book should contain a true account of all Rum made and all Rum delivered from the Distillery. His Quarterly Return—to the truth of which he has to declare before a Magistrate—should be a brief recapitulation of his transactions. These Returns are sent to the Inspector of Inland Revenue Officers. It is, therefore, obvious that whether the entries in the Stock Book be true or not the Return will be made to correspond with them, otherwise the Distiller will render himself liable to prosecution for making a false Return.

7. In many of the Returns we discovered omissions of several Stock Book transactions this pointed to one of two things, either that the Distiller had knowingly or carelessly omitted to mention these transactions—which would be highly improbable—or that the Inspector of Inland Revenue Officers, through whose hands only the Returns passed before being audited, had by some means falsified them.

8. In order to ascertain who was at fault we requested the attendance of the Distillers concerned and examined them as to these Returns, they emphatically declared them to be forgeries, and such we may add they appeared to be, to us, on the face of them.

9. On examination of the Counterfoils of the Permits issued by Mr. Kirk mention of these omitted transactions were likewise wanting. This we were, of course, prepared for; as under the present system of Audit the issue of regular permits, under the circumstances, would have led to detection. That system appears to be, briefly, as follows:—The Auditor calls upon the Inspector to produce the Distillers' Quarterly Returns together with the Permit Books, these are compared and reference is made to the Payments at the Treasury to see if they also correspond. The Distillers' Stock Books and the Licensed traders Monthly Returns, it seems, were never called for; therefore to commit fraud without being detected it became necessary to manufacture the Returns and to make the Permit Counterfoils agree with them; a difficult and hazardous process, but one that has been very extensively adopted and apparently by only one person viz: Mr. Kirk.

10. Had further proof been wanting to convince us of Mr. Kirk's guilt in the matter of the forged Returns it was amply supplied by the production of certain loose Quarterly Returns which came to us with the other papers procured by Mr. L. Witz. These Returns had evidently not been audited, but on examination they proved to be the originals of some of the forged ones, and contained the items which the latter omitted; they were further identified by the Distillers whose signatures they bore.

11. In almost every instance where a transaction had been omitted (in a forged Return) no payment had been made into the Treasury in respect thereof, although there was abundant proof that the purchaser of the rum had paid the duty—and without doubt to Mr. Kirk.

12. In addition to the omissions referred to we found in these forged Returns certain entries of deliveries of Rum from the Distilleries—which transactions, on examination, we found had never taken place. This appeared to us the more un-accountable, involving as those entries did the payment into the Treasury of Rum duties to correspond. The only explanation we can offer on this point is that probably from time to time Mr. Kirk felt that the falling off of the receipts under the Excise Ordinance might appear suspicious and to allay that suspicion he entered these fictitious transactions and paid the duty which they represented.

13. We attach hereto a table which gives the following particulars:—

All the deliveries that have been made from the Distilleries from the 1st January 1882 to 20th November 1884; the amounts of Rum duty paid by the purchasers of rum during that period; and the amounts that have paid into the Treasury in respect of rum duties for that time. Where an amount has been paid by the purchaser and not been paid by Mr. Kirk into the Treasury, we have debited the latter with the amount. Where sums have been paid into the Treasury on account of transactions which never took place, as mentioned in para. 12, we have credited those sums to Mr. Kirk, and where Mr. Kirk has short paid or paid in excess into the Treasury we have debited or credited him with the amounts accordingly. It will be seen by this table that Mr. Kirk has over paid the sum of £74. 17. 2 and short-paid the sum of £612. 14. 10. We thus find that the defalcations amount to £537. 17. 8.

14. In the course of our enquiry we have found nothing that would justify us in forming the opinion that there was anything like collusion either by the Distillers or on the part of Mr. Kirk's subordinates.

We would, however, remark that the Stock Books, with perhaps one or two exceptions, were in a most discreditable state, and were strong proofs of the want of supervision on the part of the Excise Officers; this was especially the case in the books of the Leeward District and notably of those of LesCoteaux and Shirvan Distilleries, in the book of the latter the quantity of rum delivered from the Distillery is shewn to be in excess of what was distilled!

The evidence of Mr. Cunningham to which we would draw Your Honor's attention—in connection with other matters that came before us, is to say the least of it highly unsatisfactory.

15. We forward herewith a mass of evidence which, we venture to think, are clearly points to the conclusions at which we have arrived.

We have, &c.,

L. G. HAY, *Chairman.*
HERBT. H. SEALY,
JOHN McKILLOP.

His Honour
J. W. CARRINGTON, Esqre., D.C.L.,
Administrator.

Tobago.

AN OFFICIAL IMPRISONED!

The events of the sittings of the Supreme Court in its Criminal Jurisdiction, which came to a close on Thursday, have been something out of the usual run of our ordinary humdrum proceedings on such occasions. The centre of attraction was as may be supposed, the case of The Honourable James Kirk, Inspector of Police and of Inland Revenue Officers, who stood committed on three separate charges each of forgery and embezzlement. The particulars of these charges were so fully reported, and so freely commented upon, by us at the time of the prelimininary investigation before the Police Magistrate, that it is unnecessary for us to go into any details to-day, while the mismanagement of the case by the Government, which we brought into notice at the same time, is of sufficient importance to require separate attention, which we shall bestow upon it later. The case, which was twice postponed owing to causes which have been duly reported in the columns of this paper, was the last one to be taken, and came to an abrupt and somewhat dramatic termination by the Counsel for the defence announcing, on the re-assembling of the Court after luncheon, that his client had resolved to discontinue the defence, and to throw himself on the mercy of the Court. The condition in which Mr. Abbott appeared in Court, a condition disgraceful at any time, but utterly inexcusable on such an occasion as this, and his only too apparent inability to deal effectually with his client's defence, was doubtless the cause of the course taken by the prisoner. On the wisdom, or otherwise, of that course it is not for us to pronounce an opinion, but we may express a regret that a man who could frame such an appeal as that of the prisoner to the Court for a lenient sentence, should have been in such a position as to render such an appeal necessary. The sentence, two years imprisonment without hard labour, seems to meet the requirements of the case as before the Court, and we fully concur with what fell from the lips of His Honor the Acting Chief Justice as to the relative severity of punishments when inflicted on different classes of offenders, or possibly we should rather say on offenders who have been brought up in different social positions. Penalties that would barely be productive of discomfort when awarded to the lowest classes, would entail the severest torture when inflicted on persons tenderly nurtured, and we cannot but think that the Acting Chief Justice exercised a sound judgement, as well as evinced a thorough appreciation of all that his sentence meant to a man like Kirk, in giving him a punishment that at first sight looks extremely lenient. * * *—*News.*

...Kirk Inspector of Police and of Inland Revenue Officers in Tobago, was brought before the police magistrate of Port of Spain and remanded on a charge of defrauding the Government of Tobago. It appears that the accused had escaped to Toco, in Trinidad, where he was arrested. Being unwell, he was placed under medical treatment. He has since been sent back to Tobago for examination.

LETTER TO CA PURSER FROM HER BROTHER-IN-LAW JAMES WITZ, DATED 12 FEBRUARY 1881.

Thann, Alsace 12.2.81

My very dear sister Kate,

    I was very happy to learn by your letter of 5th ult. That your dear husband was getting better after having been ailing of late & I sincerely hope that Dr. Purser has since then been continuing in his convalescence & that the rest of your family are quite well. I think it a good change for Mr. James Kirk to have given up the life of a planter, he now has his fixed income without any risk or uncertainty whereas had he continued in his former calling any failure might have been ascribed to his want of attention or foresight.

Generation Two Maternal

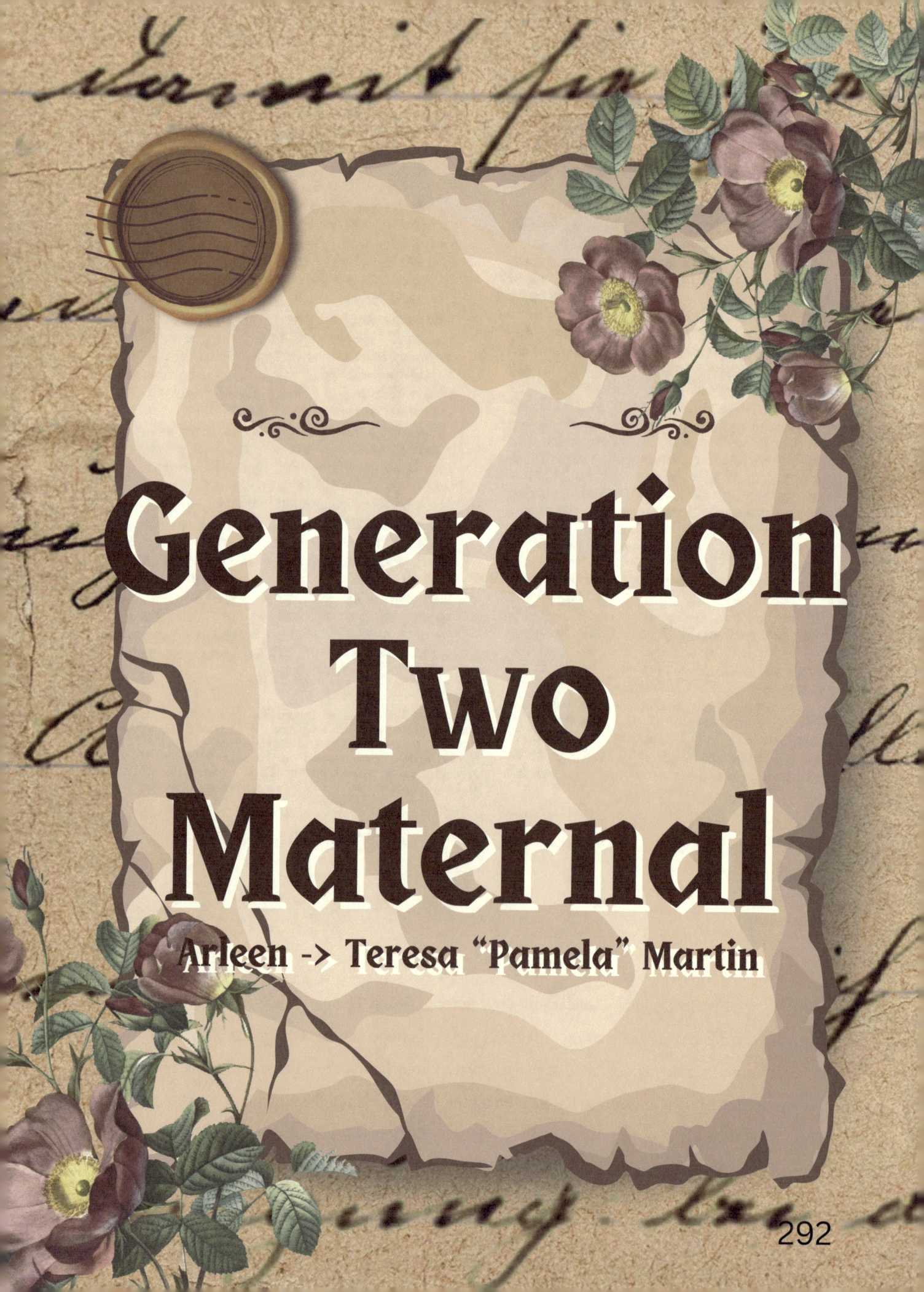

Arleen -> Teresa "Pamela" Martin

HISTORY OF TERESA "PAMELA" AUDRA MARTIN

QUICK FACTS:

BORN
PORT OF SPAIN, TRINIDAD

PARENTS
JOSEPH GABRIAL MARTIN
THERESA BERTHA STOUTE

CHILDREN
CAROL-LYNN THERESA
ARLEEN LORRAINE OLIVE
BRENT ALLAN DAVID

CELEBRATION OF LIFE FOR PAMELA SHEPPARD
by Carol Sheppard

Hello and Welcome to the Celebration of Life for Pamela Sheppard. I would like to start by thanking everyone who came in-person and on Zoom. In a few minutes, I will mute everyone so that we do not have a cacophony of unrecognizable noise. This service will most likely be short because I am leading it, and because I didn't ask anyone for help or how to do this kind of thing. Stubbornness runs in this family, nah?

Psalm 23

The Lord is my Shepherd, I shall not want

He maketh me to lie down in green pastures,

He leadeth me beside the still waters

He restoreth my soul

He leadeth me in paths of righteousness for His namesake

Yea, though I walk through the valley of the shadow of Death,

I will fear no evil,

Thy rod and thy staff, they comfort me

Thou preparest a table in the presence of mine enemies,

Thou anointest my head with oil

My cup runneth over

Surely goodness and mercy shall follow me all the days of my life

And I will dwell in the house of the Lord forever.

Amen

My Mother

My mother, Pamela Martin Sheppard was born on December 10, 1934, in Trinidad, West Indies. She was the oldest of eight children. Her four surviving siblings are Anthony Martin, Eleonore Martin, and Gregory Martin.

Pam married my father, David Sheppard, on April 16, 1955. They were married for 66 years at the time of her passing, which is quite an accomplishment for the times that we now live in. Pam and David had three children, me, Carol Sheppard, Arleen Froemming, and Brent Sheppard, who passed away on May 3, 2020. I almost brought his ashes with me today.

After marrying my dad, David Sheppard, they moved to Montreal Canada. 10 years after moving to Canada, they moved to California. Two years later, they moved back to Trinidad. Then two years later, in the early 1970s, they moved from Trinidad to Florida, in the United States, where she remained for the rest of her life. When I tell people how many times we moved, they asked me if my dad was in the military. Nope, just a young man with dreams that crossed country lines.

Mom was very artistic. She loved to draw and paint. From a young age, I remember her drawing. She painted and hung her art in her house, some of which I have now, but unfortunately, most was lost. Some of the things I found in her room when I cleaned it, were drawing pencils, canvas, and drawing paper. She also knitted doilies, blankets, toilet paper covers, and sweaters. I have a blanket. And Arleen does too. Not a fan of the doilies Mom, sorry!

Mom also used to play the piano and sing. In her golden years, she loved to listen to music and often would break out into song or hummed. She always wanted to have music on. I bought her two iPads. I also bought her a Bluetooth speaker so that she could hear her music through the iPad. Although I tried, she did not know how to use any of it.

She and Dad survived many things during their life together, including Hurricane Michael, when they lived in Panama City Beach, but it destroyed their place of residence and all their belongings. They began to learn to live on very little as they shuffled from Panama City Beach to North Carolina back to Florida.

Mom was a grandmother and great grandmother to many and a great-great grandmother to one. Had she lived to the end of October, she would have been a great-great grandmother to two.

I had made my mind up to come on a Saturday to take her shopping for shoes, because she always commented on my shoes. She told me to look for shoes for her, and I did, but I could never be sure she would like them. I finally found a pair that I thought she would like. I was excited to surprise her with them. I called Dad the Friday night before to let him know that I was coming the next day and that I would take Mom shopping. That is when I found out Mom was in the hospital. She would never come home. She would never see the shoes I bought for her.

When Arleen, Dad, Brian, and I went to see Mom for the last times, she kept asking us what was new with us. I told her that this, this situation, was what was new. Later, she asked me where I was sleeping that night. I told her that I had to go home. I wish that I had stayed.

Watching my mother refuse all life-sustaining treatment made me realize that she is the strongest woman I have ever known in my life. I think sometimes, she just did not know where to apply that strength. I think we can all agree that we would hope to shuffle off this mortal coil that quickly and with that much dignity, grace, and peace.

I would like to end this here little speech by saying goodbye Mom. I love you. I miss you so much already. I know you hear me talking to you every day.

by Carol Sheppard

I would like to close with my mother's own words, called

Thoughts on Life

Be Thankful for every day. Do that best with what life hands you but know you are not in total control. Accept with serenity the things you cannot change. Be cheerful so you can life others while lifting yourself and you will become stronger, and your burden will lighten. The angels will sure smile on and with you. Self-pity brings stagnation, sorry and the inability to further develop. It will be a magnet for negativity.

Be thankful for every little thing; the sun, air, water, health, family, food and on and on. You will develop deep gratitude and attract better things to you. Be grateful for any strength you develop, for you will develop it. You will be an example to others but do it for yourself for you know full well that the admiration of others is fleeting and tenuous, as is life.

Pam

Teresa Pamela Audra Martin
Birth Certificate

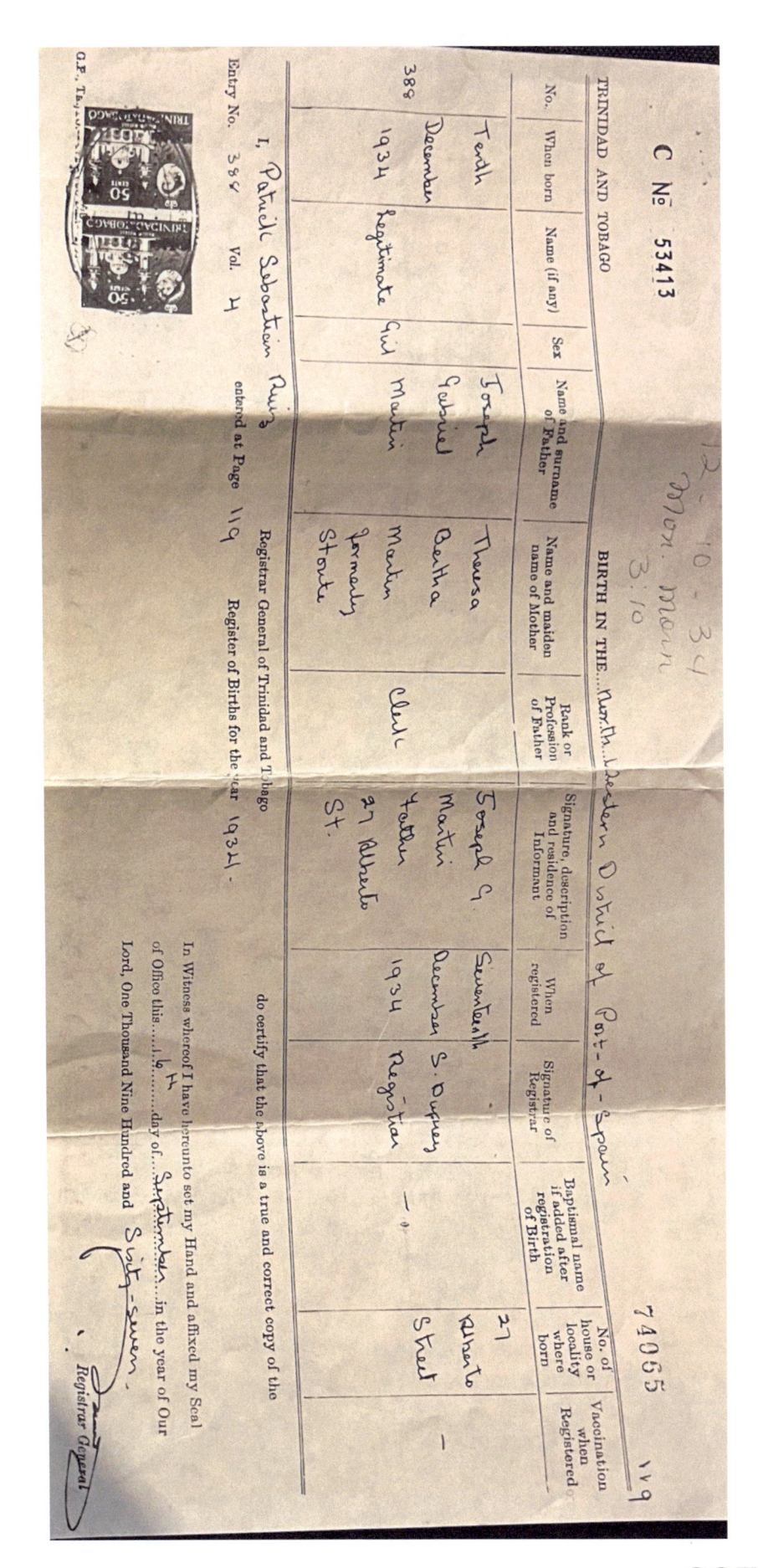

C No. 53413

TRINIDAD AND TOBAGO

BIRTH IN THE North Western District of Port-of-Spain

No.	When born	Name (if any)	Sex	Name and surname of Father	Name and maiden name of Mother	Rank or Profession of Father	Signature, description and residence of Informant	When registered	Signature of Registrar	Baptismal name if added after registration of Birth	No. of house or locality where born	Vaccination when Registered
389	Teath December 1934	Legitimate Girl		Joseph Gabriel Martin	Theresa Bertha Martin formerly Stark	Clerk	Joseph G. Martin Father 27 Alberto St.	Seventeenth December 1934	Leonard S. Dupres Registrar	—	27 Alberto Street	—

12-10-34
Mon. Moon
3.10

I, Patrick Sebastian Quiro, Registrar General of Trinidad and Tobago do certify that the above is a true and correct copy of the
Entry No. 389 Vol. 4 entered at Page 119 Register of Births for the year 1934.

In Witness whereof I have hereunto set my Hand and affixed my Seal of Office this......6......day of.....September.....in the year of Our Lord, One Thousand Nine Hundred and Sixty-seven.

Registrar General

74055
119

Teresa Pamela
Audra Martin
Birth Registration

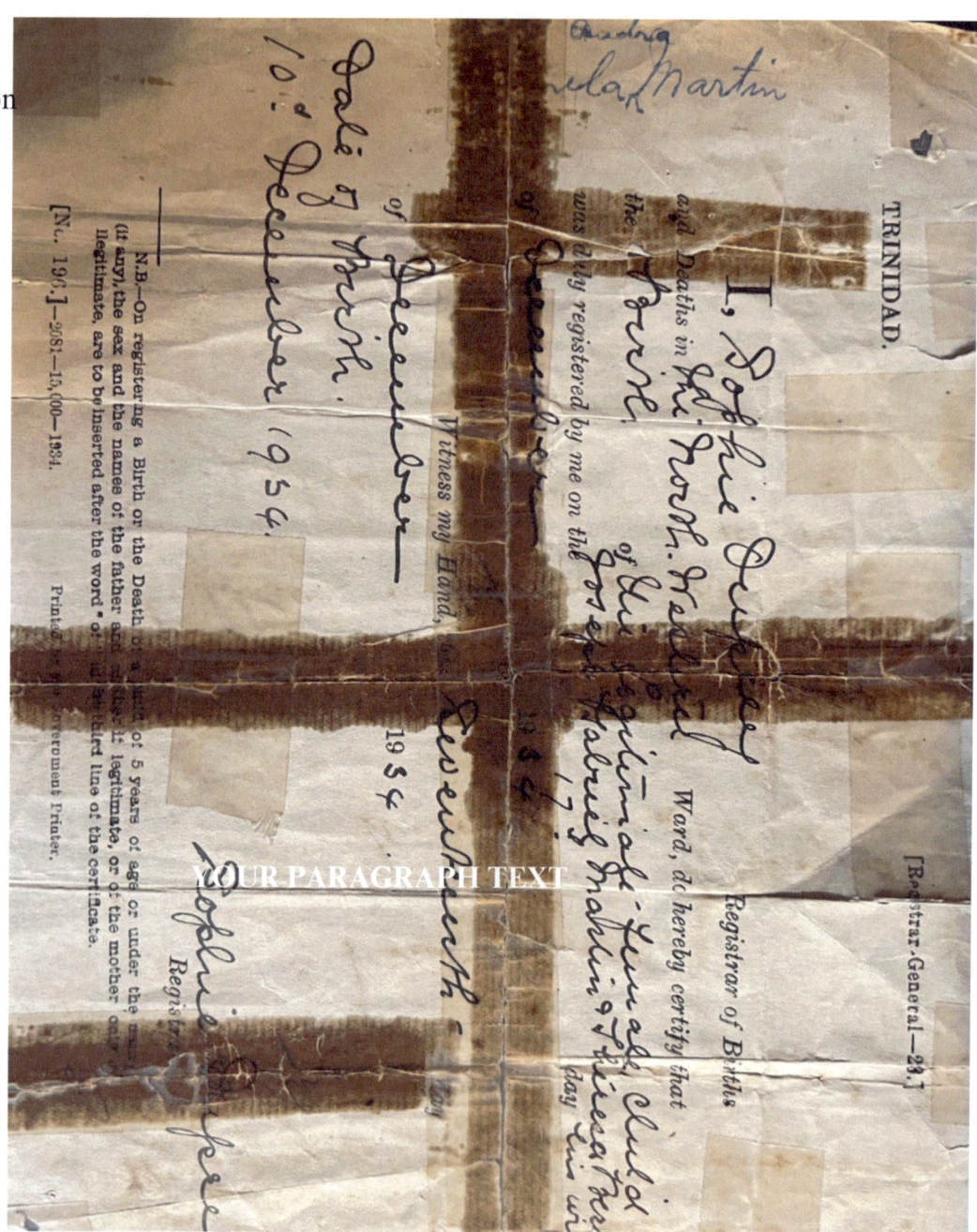

I, *Sophie Duprey*, **Registrar of Birth**
And Deaths in *the North (illegible)* **Ward, do hereby certify that**
The *Birth* **of** *(illegible) Legitimate female child of*
Joseph Gabriel Martin and Theresa Bertha his wife
was duly registered by me on the 17th day
of December **1934**
Witness my hand the *Seventeenth of*
December 1934
Date of Birth
10 December 1934
Sophie Duprey
Register

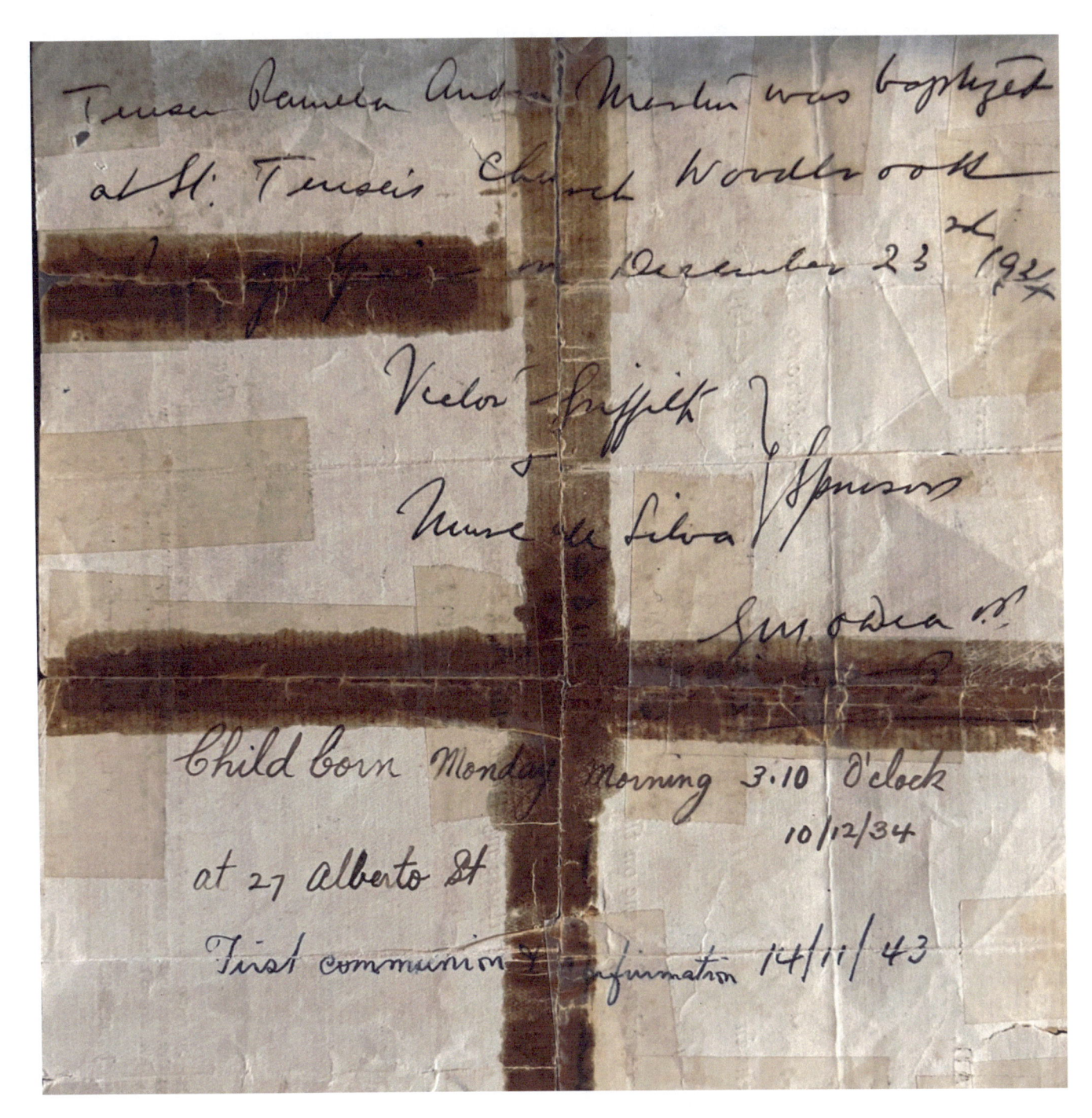

Additional Ordinances for
Teresa Pamela Audra Martin was baptized
at St Teresa's church Woodbrook
Port of Spain in December 23rd 1934

Victor Griffith   Sponsers (?)
Nuise (?) de Silva

Child born Monday Morning 3:10 O'Clock
10/12/1934   (December 10, 1934)
at 27 Alberto Street
First Communion & Confirmation 14/11/43 (November 14, 1943)

PASSPORT

TRINIDAD AND TOBAGO

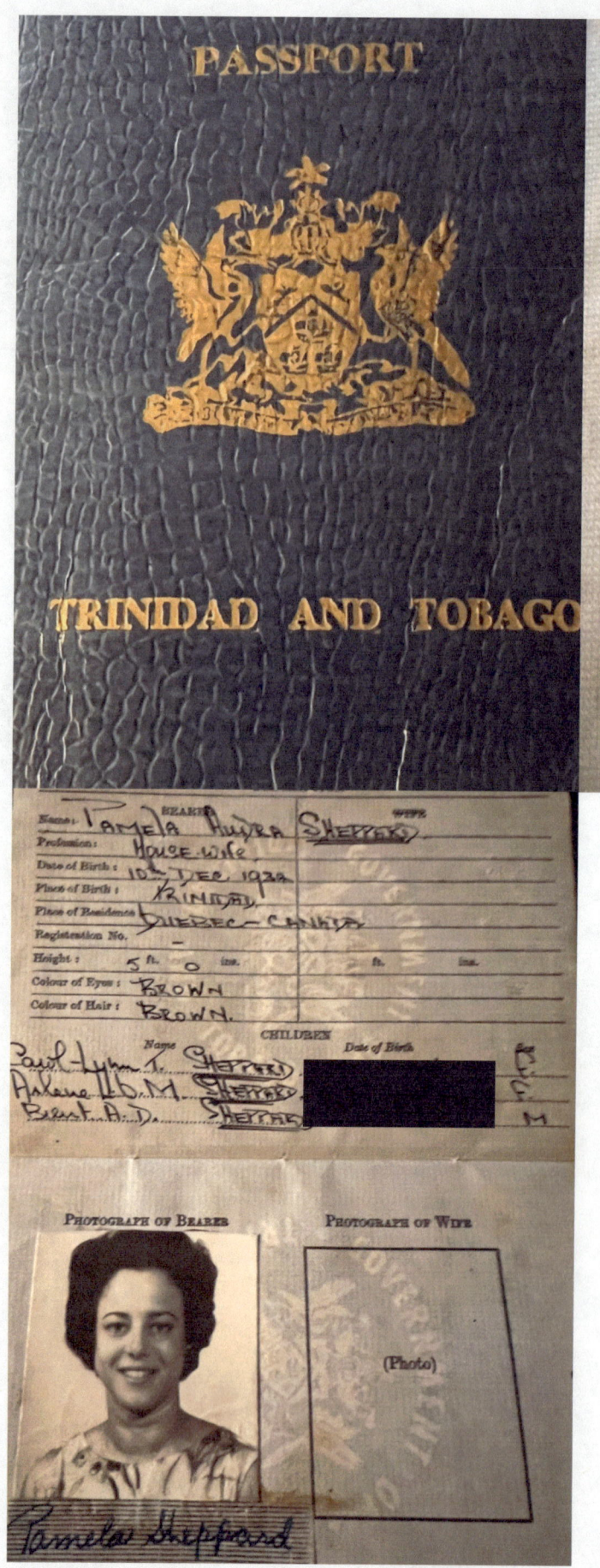

This Passport contains 20 pages

PASSPORT
TRINIDAD AND TOBAGO

No. of Passport: 46125
Name of Bearer: Mrs. PAMELA AUDRA SHEPPARD
Accompanied by ~~his Wife~~ (or Maiden name): MARTIN
and by THREE (3) children

NATIONAL STATUS: Citizen of Trinidad and Tobago

A Citizen of Trinidad and Tobago is a citizen of the British Commonwealth.

BEARER Name: Pamela Audra Sheppard **WIFE**
Profession: Housewife
Date of Birth: 10th Dec 1932
Place of Birth: Trinidad
Place of Residence: Quebec - Canada
Registration No.:
Height: 5 ft. 0 ins.
Colour of Eyes: Brown
Colour of Hair: Brown

CHILDREN
Name	Date of Birth	
Paul Lynn T. Sheppard		
Arlene D.M. Sheppard		M
Brent A.D. Sheppard		M

PHOTOGRAPH OF BEARER — PHOTOGRAPH OF WIFE

Pamela Sheppard

300

Teresa Pamela Audra Martin Death Certificate

STATE OF FLORIDA
BUREAU of VITAL STATISTICS
CERTIFICATION OF DEATH

STATE FILE NUMBER: 2021199734
DATE ISSUED: MARCH 7, 2022
DATE FILED: OCTOBER 5, 2021

DECEDENT INFORMATION
NAME: PAMELA AUDRA SHEPPARD
SEX: FEMALE   SSN: 262-27-9477   AGE: 086 YEARS
DATE OF DEATH: SEPTEMBER 30, 2021
DATE OF BIRTH: DECEMBER 10, 1934
BIRTHPLACE: TRINIDAD, WISCONSIN, UNITED STATES
PLACE OF DEATH: HOSPICE
FACILITY NAME OR STREET ADDRESS: VITAS HEALTHCARE
LOCATION OF DEATH: LECANTO, CITRUS COUNTY, 34461
COUNTY: CITRUS
RESIDENCE: 1900 W ALPHA COURT, LECANTO, FLORIDA 34461, UNITED STATES
OCCUPATION, INDUSTRY: SECRETARY, UNKNOWN
EDUCATION: HIGH SCHOOL GRADUATE OR GED COMPLETED
EVER IN U.S. ARMED FORCES? NO
HISPANIC OR HAITIAN ORIGIN? NO, NOT OF HISPANIC/HAITIAN ORIGIN
RACE: WHITE

SURVIVING SPOUSE / PARENT NAME INFORMATION
(NAME PRIOR TO FIRST MARRIAGE, IF APPLICABLE)
MARITAL STATUS: MARRIED
SURVIVING SPOUSE NAME: DAVID SHEPPARD
FATHER'S/PARENT'S NAME: JOSEPH MARTIN
MOTHER'S/PARENT'S NAME: THERESA STOUT

INFORMANT, FUNERAL FACILITY AND PLACE OF DISPOSITION INFORMATION
INFORMANT'S NAME: CAROL SHEPPARD
RELATIONSHIP TO DECEDENT: DAUGHTER
INFORMANT'S ADDRESS: 2560 62ND AVE APT NO. 255, ST PETERSBURG, FLORIDA 33702, UNITED STATES
FUNERAL DIRECTOR/LICENSE NUMBER: SEAN MCGAN, F020006
FUNERAL FACILITY: MCGAN CREMATION SERVICE LLC F187922
65 N FLORIDA AVENUE, INVERNESS, FLORIDA 34453
METHOD OF DISPOSITION: DONATION
PLACE OF DISPOSITION: MEDCURE
ORLANDO, FLORIDA

CERTIFIER INFORMATION
TYPE OF CERTIFIER: CERTIFYING PHYSICIAN
MEDICAL EXAMINER CASE NUMBER: NOT APPLICABLE
TIME OF DEATH (24 HOUR): 0230
DATE CERTIFIED: OCTOBER 1, 2021
CERTIFIER'S NAME: JOHN D GELIN
CERTIFIER'S LICENSE NUMBER: ME24036
NAME OF ATTENDING PRACTITIONER (IF OTHER THAN CERTIFIER): NOT APPLICABLE

CAUSE OF DEATH AND INJURY INFORMATION
MANNER OF DEATH: NATURAL
CAUSE OF DEATH - PART I - AND APPROXIMATE INTERVAL: ONSET TO DEATH
a. AORTIC ANEURYSM — DAYS
b. VASCULAR DISEASE — MONTHS
c.
d.

PART II - OTHER SIGNIFICANT CONDITIONS CONTRIBUTING TO DEATH BUT NOT RESULTING IN THE UNDERLYING CAUSE GIVEN IN PART I:

AUTOPSY PERFORMED? NO
AUTOPSY FINDINGS AVAILABLE TO COMPLETE CAUSE OF DEATH?
DATE OF SURGERY:
DID TOBACCO USE CONTRIBUTE TO DEATH? UNKNOWN
REASON FOR SURGERY:
PREGNANCY INFORMATION: NOT PREGNANT WITHIN PAST YEAR
DATE OF INJURY: NOT APPLICABLE   TIME OF INJURY (24 HOUR):   INJURY AT WORK?
LOCATION OF INJURY:
DESCRIBE HOW INJURY OCCURRED:

PLACE OF INJURY:
IF TRANSPORTATION INJURY, STATUS OF DECEDENT: TYPE OF VEHICLE:

, STATE REGISTRAR

REQ: 2023729269

WARNING: THE ABOVE SIGNATURE CERTIFIES THAT THIS IS A TRUE AND CORRECT COPY OF THE OFFICIAL RECORD ON FILE IN THIS OFFICE. THIS DOCUMENT IS PRINTED OR PHOTOCOPIED ON SECURITY PAPER WITH WATERMARKS OF THE GREAT SEAL OF THE STATE OF FLORIDA. DO NOT ACCEPT WITHOUT VERIFYING THE PRESENCE OF THE WATERMARKS. THE DOCUMENT FACE CONTAINS A MULTICOLORED BACKGROUND, GOLD EMBOSSED SEAL, AND THERMOCHROMIC FL. THE BACK CONTAINS SPECIAL LINES WITH TEXT. THIS DOCUMENT WILL NOT PRODUCE A COLOR COPY.

DH FORM 1947 (03-13)
CERTIFICATION OF VITAL RECORD

Favorite Picture of mom

Beautiful young or old

Teenage Pam - Love the messy room

Unknown, Arleen, Elenore, Carol, Pam

Pam, Arleen, Elenore, Carol

Barbara Ann, Gail, Pamela, Dorothy

Pam, Arleen, Carol, Brent

Joseph, Pam, Theresa

Generation Two
Siblings Of
Teresa Pamela Audra Martin

Family Tree

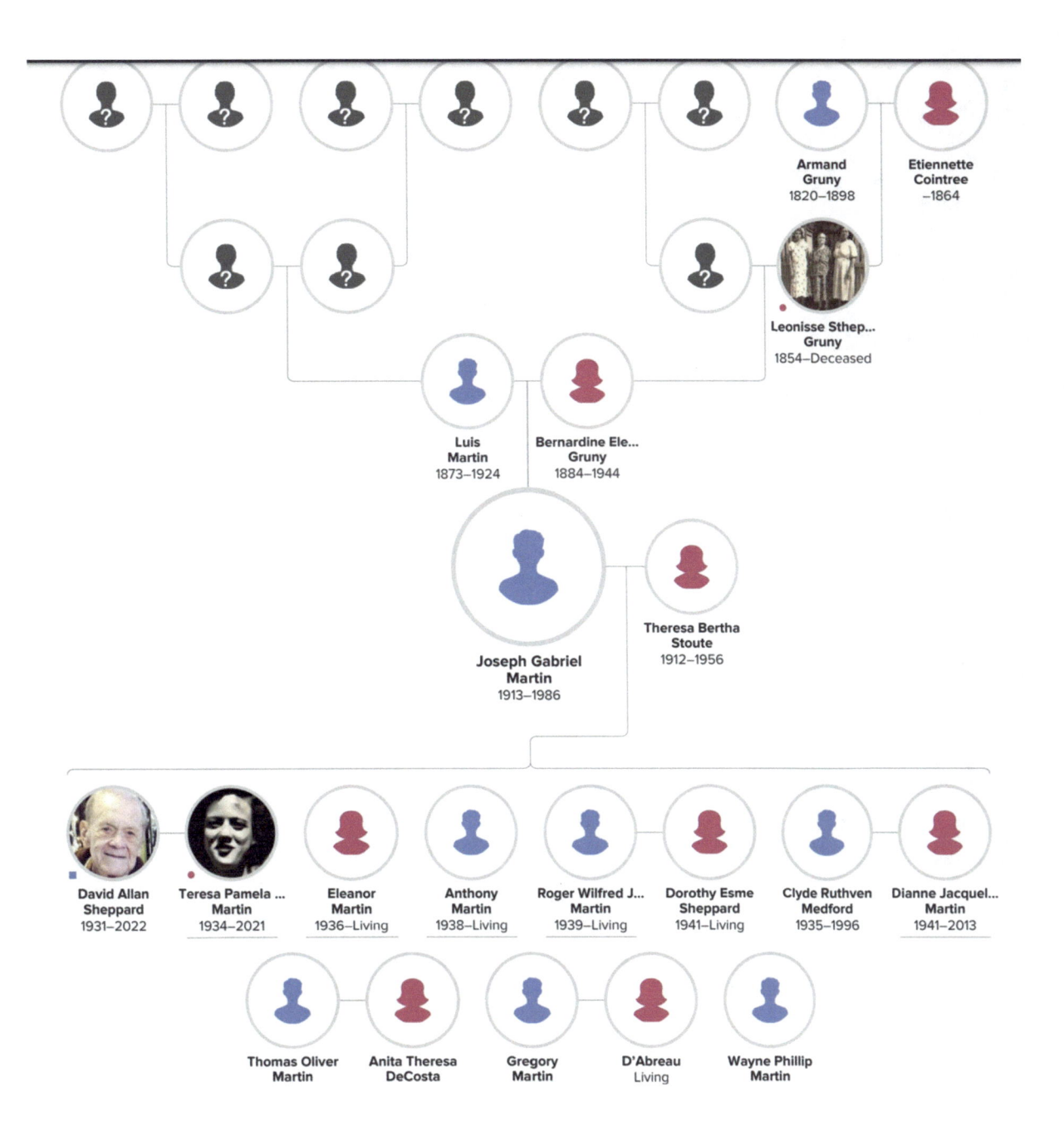

Generation 1 (Great-great-grandparents):
- Armand Gruny (1820–1898) — Etiennette Cointree (–1864)

Generation 2:
- Leonisse Sthep... Gruny (1854–Deceased)

Generation 3 (Grandparents):
- Luis Martin (1873–1924) — Bernardine Ele... Gruny (1884–1944)

Generation 4 (Parents):
- Joseph Gabriel Martin (1913–1986) — Theresa Bertha Stoute (1912–1956)

Generation 5 (Children and spouses):
- David Allan Sheppard (1931–2022) — Teresa Pamela ... Martin (1934–2021)
- Eleanor Martin (1936–Living)
- Anthony Martin (1938–Living)
- Roger Wilfred J... Martin (1939–Living) — Dorothy Esme Sheppard (1941–Living)
- Clyde Ruthven Medford (1935–1996) — Dianne Jacquel... Martin (1941–2013)

Generation 6 (Grandchildren):
- Thomas Oliver Martin — Anita Theresa DeCosta
- Gregory Martin — D'Abreau (Living)
- Wayne Phillip Martin

305

ELEONORE

Eleonore was the second child of Joseph and Theresa. Ellie was born on April 1, 1936. She was always different. She considered herself the black sheep of the family. The fact that she thought this made it so.

In her teens she was beautiful. Pam and Eleonore were the reason we had many family social events at our home in Mt. Lambert, Trinidad. Our dad loved to dance the waltz. At these gatherings he would dance with his daughters and any woman who would dance with him.

Eleonore was flighty. At one time she was in a contest for Ms. Trinidad and Tobago. Here we were in a club and Eleonore was strutting her stuff on stage with the other women striving to be Ms. Trinidad and Tobago. Everything was going fine until it was Eleonore's turn. She started walking across the stage with her head facing the floor. She was not smiling. Had no energy. Looked defeated. I felt like hiding under my table. It came as no surprise when she ended up around last place. This was as a result of my dad's overbearing rearing of his children.

Eleonore had a wonderful boyfriend by the name of Lance de Montbrun. He worshiped the ground she walked on. She dumped him for a guy who was quite the opposite, Fido. Nothing good came of this union.

Ellie always spoke of voices that spoke to her. She believed she knew things without knowing how she knew it. Out of the blue she would give a verbatim account of a conversation that took place twenty or thirty years ago. Strange stuff.

Updated March 28, 2022
Ellie migrated to Australia and married a guy whose last name is Inman. He was a caregiver but dressed like Davy Crockett, pointed steel toe boots and a hat. As soon as I saw him, I knew she couldn't have loved him. They adopted two boys, Bradley and Marcus. Ellie pushed Inman to invest in real estate. When the children were around five and six years old, she took the children with her and moved to Canada.

She settled in the small town of Thorold, Ontario. She got married to Eddy Stennit. Eddy was the caretaker of a ship that travelled throughout the Welland Canal. In the winter he was the only one on board looking after the ship. There she invested in about three properties. Thorold is situated some 90 minutes by car west of Toronto.

Today Ellie is living in a home for the elderly at Millennium Trail Manor in Niagara, Ontario. She walks with the help of a walking stick and a walker. Mentally she is in and out. Extremely forgetful. One son, Mark, lives in Niagara, and the eldest, Bradley, lives in Kamloops, B.C.

Family Group Sheet

Name: Eleanor Lorraine Martin *
Birth: 1 APR 1936 in Trinidad and Tobago, West Indies.
Spouses: Arthur Reid
Inman
Father: Joseph Gabriel Martin
Mother: Theresa Bertha Stoute

Spouse: Arthur Reid

Spouse: Inman
Birth: Australia.
Death: Deceased.

Children of Eleanor Lorraine Martin and Inman: 2

Name: Bradley Inman

Name: Marcus Inman

* The correct spelling of her name is Eleonore

Anthony by Anthony Martin

Anthony Martin, the third child, but first male of Joseph and Theresa Martin, was born with an irregular heartbeat on June 12, 1938. I always thought that Pam and Ellie were smarter than I was. I was quieter when compared to my siblings close to me in age. At one time, our father offered to buy us a brand new bike if we came first in class. I tried for a while, but when I saw it was not possible, I gave up. Growing up I knew my father's dad died when he was only 12 years old. I also knew he had had to drop out of school to support his mother and his four siblings. He was bombastic, boastful, and not the greatest of fathers. I assigned his lack of parental skills to his lack of a normal childhood. For this reason, I forgave him for the terrible way he raised his children. At one time when I was working for him, he fired me. My sister Pamela was living in Montreal, Quebec, Canada. I asked her to sponsor me to come to Canada.

Within the first week of my arrival, I got a job with The Bank of Nova Scotia. This job was very beneficial in furthering my education. I remember shortly after my arrival I found myself staring up at the tall buildings in wonderment. I needed to absorb this new environment. I started taking long walks while meditating where I came from and where I'm going. The first thing I had to do was to learn to walk like a homosapien should. I could not stand straight with my shoulders high and pulled back without concentrating on doing so. I felt there was a monkey on my back. I had to get it off. The monkey was my father. I resolved that one day I would be worth more money than my father ever had.

I left The Bank of Nova Scotia in order to move to Toronto, Ontario, Canada. There, I had three different jobs before buying a hardware store. While running the hardware store with Wanda, I started to invest in real estate. At one time we owned 35 rental properties and some investment land. Some of these were in partnership with another businessman. At this time, I figured I had realized my dream to be wealthier than my dad.

Then it all hit the fan and I headed south financially. My greatest supporter, Wanda, was stricken with colon cancer. She died on May 20, 1988. I then entered into two unfortunate relationships with disastrous results, both financially and emotionally. During this period, I reverted to my saving grace, meditation. My health deteriorated. I then developed high blood pressure. At this point I figured if I don't get rid of the real estate Ibelieve your mind, or what you are thinking, leads you to where you are going. This is a very powerful tool.

I knew that Nelson Mandela of South Africa spent 40 years in jail because he was accused of "Conspiring to use terroristic tactics" Apartheid is 'segregation on grounds of race.' The South African government was based on segregation of race. would physically and bodily head south too. I strongly believe Mandela was anti-segregation, he spent 40 years in jail for committing no crime. Although he was locked in jail for 40 years, his body was locked in, but his mind was elsewhere. On his release he was promptly elected The President of South Africa. He forgave all the people who put him in jail. You can't heal yourself without forgiving all those who did you wrong.

While I was in dreadful relationships, I recognized they were of my own fault. I live my life, the good and the bad with no regrets. Eventually I emerged on the other side. I moved from Whitby, Ontario to Peterborough, Ontario and promptly obtained memberships in three senior social clubs and one other club. I started playing bid euchre, train, shuffleboard and other sports. It was while playing shuffleboard that I met my future wife, Nancy Olan.

The parallels between Nancy and myself are uncanny. She too lost her spouse to cancer. She too used to own a hardware store. We had one friend in common whom she knew since childhood and lost track of after this friend had gotten married and moved away. When Wanda and I moved from Montreal to Ontario this person became our neighbour. Nancy knew Carol before she got married and Wanda and I knew Carol after she had gotten married. Nancy adopted two children, a baby girl she named Susan and a baby boy she named David.

Before Nancy changed her daughter's name to Susan, her name was Trina. Trina is my daughter's name. Uncanny. A few months after meeting me, Nancy threw an 80-year birthday party for me. We invited about 100 of our friends and family to this birthday party. I was speechless. Things went so well that a few months later we got married and invited some 100 people to the wedding. A lucky man, twice.

We enjoy a wonderful friendship and marriage. With Wanda, I was spectacularly lucky, and with Nancy, I am spectacularly lucky too. I got married when I was 80 years old, on Sept 15, 2018. At our wedding, I made my debut as a singer when I sang to her Gene Autry's version of "Have I Told You Lately That I Love You." Nancy's two children and all her family get along well with my two children and grandchildren. Nancy also has one great granddaughter, Langly, who is a darling.

Name:	Anthony Carrlyle Martin	
Birth:	n Trinidad and Tobago, West Indies.	
Spouses:	Nancy Lunn	
	Wanda McDermott	
Father:	Joseph Gabriel Martin	
Mother:	Theresa Bertha Stoute	

Spouse:	Nancy Lunn
Birth:	

Spouse:	Wanda McDermott
Birth:	Montreal Canada.

Children of Anthony Carrlyle Martin and Wanda McDermott: 2

Name:	Jay Martin

Name:	Trina Martin

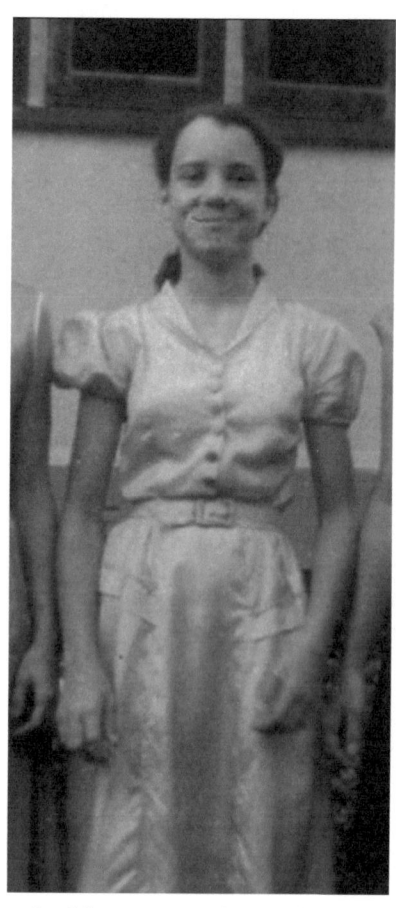

JACKIE by Donna Carla

To sum up my parents Jackie (nee Martin, daughter of Joseph & Theresa Martin) & Clyde Medford (son of Thornhill Medford & Evelyn (nee Edwards) is a really difficult task. Clyde's motto could be "Where I am now is the most important place and time" and Jackie lived her life to the fullest, making every moment of every day count because she knew that life is precious and tomorrow isn't guaranteed.

My mum's, mum Theresa (Stoute) died when mum was 15yrs old. Leaving a husband and 8 children. Her father Joseph then married Gwendolyn and they had 6 more children. My dad was from a small family, he only had one brother. My dad's, dad Thornhill died when he was 13yrs old. My parents were complex people, loyal, determined, strong-willed with a finely tuned sense of humour, though mum was more of a practical joker.

They had a strong work ethic and played just as hard but their love of family & commitment to each other never faltered. They both had tempers but they never held grudges. When they butted heads we all hid especially when playing cards. Dads competitiveness knew no bound and he was never shy in displaying it. Mum always held her ground - certainly interesting dynamics. Dad never passed judgement and mum was mischievous and a real people-person, within seconds of meeting someone she would become a friend. Sending Christmas & birthday cards and letters forever. Mum was an avid artist doodling on every bit of paper she touched - newspapers, magazines envelopes etc. She also loved crossword puzzles and sleeping. Mum could sleep anywhere and easily, before an airplane even taxied up the runway she would be asleep. They balanced each other out. They were almost two extremes but one sweated the small stuff and the other, well he let her. Their marriage lasted till dad passed away.

My earliest memories are of a home filled with friends. There was always music parties, card games, and great holidays with family and friends. Staying at Blanchisseuse or down The Islands. Memories of being woken up by dad (Clyde) in the wee hours to replace his partner in a game of 500. Heaven forbid the game ended or for that matter if anything ended. No one should ever leave a party because according to Clyde "once the first person leaves then everyone leaves" Mum was formidable and focused she was the ambitious one.

Truly the family owe a lot to mum for instilling a sense of purpose and to dad for his generosity of spirit. Clyde played competitive cricket, something he had to give up after a severe car accident but he continued to play social sports. Clyde also built an extremely large avery to house his collection of international birds.

For a man who couldn't make a cup of coffee he would boil eggs, mash vitamins and hand feed his birds. He would sit in the garden with his rum & coke and his cigarettes and watch the birds for hours. He also loved to fish and along with good friends would go deep sea fishing and bring back a boot full of fish to share with the neighbours. This courageous family emigrated from Trinidad & Tobago arriving in Australia on the 9th March 1971.

Jackie drove this decision having experienced fear for herself and her children, she recognised that their island home was no longer safe. Clyde was reluctant, his mother Evelyn had recently become a widow again and lived next door. His only brother was in care and Clyde loved T&T, the lifestyle, the music, the food and his people but he would trust his wife's reasoning. From idea to implementation things moved fast - a total whirlwind of activity. They sold their home, gave away possessions and gifted Clyde's mum their car and appliances, they partied long and hard with friends, not knowing what lay ahead; only knowing that this chapter of their lives was closing.

They flew to Barbados staying with friends and saying goodbye to more family & friends & everything they loved. They then flew to Martinique to board the ship bound for Australia. Jackie's youngest brother Wayne (from her dad & mum) would travel with them to Australia where he would live with his older sister Eleanor and her husband Fred. They lived in Alexandria in close proximity to the city of Sydney. (A far cry from his family & friends & the relaxed tropical T&T) He was lonely and sad but he finished his schooling and then returned to T&T. (I have fond memories of a gentle loving soul).

Australia was also home to Clyde's cousins and a few of Jackie's siblings. It was so far away that there would be little chance of toing and froing - this was going to be a permanent move. Many of their friends and family were choosing Canada and the Australian government took such a long time to approve their application that Canadian residency was also sought & secured. Clyde's cousin Ron Waller and his wife Bev were living in Harbord on the northern beaches of Australia and they offered to accommodate them until they found a home. Jackie & Clyde had lived in Cascade on acreage and now they were all staying in a one bedroom flat. Cramped was an understatement ~ 4 adults, 2 children and lots of suitcases, but the laughter and love abound.

Clyde and Donna didn't settle in as easily as Darrell and Jackie. Their appearance stood out as Australia was coming out of the "white australia policy" Both Jackie and Clyde secured good, permanent employment. Clyde was hired the very next day whilst Jackie enrolled the children in school immediately, 48 hours after arriving in Australia Jackie had found a unit (a tiny 2 bedroom apartment in Harbord near the school and transport. That first weekend they purchased a new car & on the Monday Jackie also started working in the city of Sydney like Clyde.

They had to catch a ferry from Manly to Sydney. A short beautiful, invigorated 40 minute ride across Sydney Harbour. Jackie lasted 2 days. The long hours of travel on top of a full working day, food to cook, children to school took its toll and the reality of having to secure local employment was a necessity. Jackie secured another local job the very next day. (You could literally start your job in the morning quit by lunch & commence new employment the next day.)

In a short time Jackie & Clyde built their new home in Cromer, as this was closer to Jackie's work. Every weekend Clyde would pick up gardening tools and Jackie sewed the curtains to complete their new home. They worked hard both mentally and physically to build a new life. The children joined sporting clubs something they would excel at over time. They all made lots of friends and their almost weekly parties were eagerly anticipated by all. Clyde's obsession with music continued and the local neighbourhood were educated on calypso, soca, R&B, reggae to name a few.

Jackie and Clyde's house was the hub. Clyde built a game room very masculine in appearance. Filled it with his snooker table and friends, all the days of the week. Rugby became the spectator sport with Wednesday and Sunday screening with the boys at their home. Cards were a central part of family life and the games were loud, competitive and quite possibly aggressive. People remember these two unique individuals. Mum for her dedication and support and Clyde for his friendship with everyone regardless of colour, creed, religion or status. In later years Clyde played tennis and then golf became the weekend obsession.

Mum continued to study and was very successful in her career. They worked hard and valued friendships - Holidaying annually with friends & family. Dad passed away from cancer very quickly whilst mum battled it for a long time. They made a new life and developed solid friendships. Dads funeral was so large that everyone couldn't fit in the church and we had two large services in two different states for mum. They left behind a daughter Donna and a son Darrell as well as grandchildren and a grandchild. They instilled a strong sense of self in their children as well as a legacy of love and support.

Family Group Sheet

Name:	Dianne Jacqueline Martin	
Birth:	30 MAR 1941 in Trinidad and Tobago, West Indies.	
Spouses:	Clyde Ruthven Medford	
	David Paterson	
Death:	18 FEB 2013 in Australia; age: 71.	
Burial:	2013.	
Father:	Joseph Gabriel Martin	
Mother:	Theresa Bertha Stoute	

Spouse:	Clyde Ruthven Medford
Birth:	15 AUG 1936 in Trinidad and Tobago.
Marriage:	1963 in Trinidad and Tobago.
Death:	17 JUN 1996 in Cromer, New South Wales, Australia; age: 59.
Burial:	Davidson, Northern Beaches Council, New South Wales, Australia.
Father:	Theodore Sinclair Medford
Mother:	Evelyn Edwards

Spouse:	David Paterson

Children of Dianne Jacqueline Martin and Clyde Ruthven Medford: 2

Name:	Donna Carla Medford
Birth:	in Port of Spain, Trinidad and Tobago.
Spouses:	Graham Brent Rimmer
	Brent Joseph Arneaud
	Guy Antoine Laube

Name:	Darrell Anthony Russell Medford
Birth:	in Port of Spain, Trinidad and Tobago.
Spouses:	Cathy Marriage: Australia.
	Michelle Kaminski Marriage: Australia.

Clyde and Jackie

Donna

David, Darrell, Jackie, Clyde, Pam, Arleen

314

TOMMY

Tommy, the sixth child, was a very gentle soul who wouldn't hurt a fly. Born on April 12, 1946, Tommy was lean and small. There was perhaps something wrong with the alignment of one or both of his eyes. He met his future wife Anita in Trinidad. They eventually migrated to Queensland, Australia. Queensland is located in the northeast part of Australia about 1,775 km. from Sydney.

This is an 18.5 hour drive to Sydney. Queensland has a population of some 5.2 million people. Tommy might have moved there because his Uncle Frankie and their family had migrated there earlier. His sister Eleonore also used to live there. Tommy was very close to his Uncle Frankie's children, especially Paddy. Tommy worked at a sort of Trust Company as a conscientious employee for many years. Eventually Tommy got promoted to a managerial position. He claimed his underlings didn't respect him enough for him to do a good job, so he requested he be demoted back down to his previous job. He didn't like managing or having to worry about his other co-workers. He got his wish and continued in this position until retirement.

In our living room in Trinidad, we had a lovely Bentley piano. At least Pam, Ellie, and Tony started taking piano lessons. Of these the only one who played it decently was Pamela. If you were to meet Tommy, he would be apt to say, "Hi I'm drunkard Tommy. Everybody calls me that." It came as quite a surprise to discover that Tommy played both the guitar and the piano. In fact, Paddy had a band that played in nightclubs. Would you believe Tommy was a member of that band?

While I was on holiday in Australia, Tommy flew down to meet me and Jackie. We had a jam session in Jackie's living room singing some old favourite calypsos. Tommy was a fun-loving guy. Loved a good time, but he was also a very good husband and parent. One of his sons turned out to be a kickboxer. Amazing.

Tommy eventually died from cancer. It startled me to discover my only two siblings that lived in Australia, Jackie and Tommy, both died of cancer. My brother-in-law, and Jackie's husband Clyde, also died of cancer. Was it something in the atmosphere?

Family Group Sheet

	Name:	Thomas Oliver Martin
	Birth:	12 Apr 1946 in Trinidad and Tobago, West Indies.
	Spouse:	Anita Theresa DaCosta
	Death:	30 JUN 2016 in Australia; age: 70.
	Father:	Joseph Gabriel Martin
	Mother:	Theresa Bertha Stoute

	Spouse:	Anita Theresa DaCosta
	Birth:	in Port of Spain, Trinidad and Tobago, British West Indies.
	Marriage:	
	Father:	Fred DaCosta
	Mother:	Mary Olive Elizabeth Nola Anderson

Children of Thomas Oliver Martin and Anita Theresa DaCosta: 5

	Name:	Brent Thomas Martin
	Birth:	

	Name:	Debbie Gail Martin
	Birth:	

	Name:	Jason Martin
	Birth:	

	Name:	Terese Anita Martin
	Birth:	

	Name:	Wayne Martin
	Birth:	

GREGORY

Gregory, the seventh child of Joseph and Theresa Martin, was born on March 4, around 1941. His first wife Angela, lived in Mt. Lambert within the block from our house. After they were married, Gregory and Angela migrated to Ontario, Canada. It wasn't long after that they separated. Angela ended up living in England and Gregory moved back to Trinidad. Gregory had something in common with our father, he could talk incessantly about business. It was always business, business, and more business. That was about 95% of our dad's conversation. In this way Gregory was like his father.

After he returned to Trinidad it became a surprise to learn he was of the Baha'i faith. This is a relatively new religion founded in the 19th century, somewhere near Iran and the Middle East. Our mother and father were Roman Catholics, and it was common knowledge we were all Catholic. It was no surprise that Gregory eventually ended up self-employed. The last knowledge of him was that he partnered with a high up member of the Baha'i faith who had access to money. Gregory is alive and lives in Trinidad at the time of this writing (December 12, 2021.)

Family Group Sheet

Name: Gregory Martin
Birth: Trinidad and Tobago, West Indies.
Spouse: Angela DaBreau
Father: Joseph Gabriel Martin
Mother: Theresa Bertha Stoute

Spouse: Angela DaBreau

Children of Gregory Martin and Angela DaBreau: 3

Name: Kevin Martin

Name: Nastassia Martin
Partner: Andres Helmersson

Name: Rhea Martin
Spouse: Jermany Scott

318

WAYNE Phillip

Wayne, the last and eighth child was just a baby when his mother died in March 1956. He was approximately three years old at the time of her death, somewhere around 1953. My last memory of him was of a neglected child who would rock himself incessantly on the living room rocking chair. Back and forth, back and forth he would go. The amazement was that he seldom cried. If he did cry there would be no one to take care of him. His mother's death was probably hardest on him.

Shortly after he got his driver's license, he died in a horrific auto accident. The year he died is also unknown, probably around 1970. Gregory would probably know.

Generated on August 30th, 2024
Sheppard, Kirk, Begg, Gruny, Martin
Wayne Martin

Family Group Sheet

Name: Wayne Martin
Birth: 18 JUL 1954 in Trinidad and Tobago, West Indies.
Death: 1975 in Trinidad and Tobago; age: 20.
Father: Joseph Gabriel Martin
Mother: Theresa Bertha Stoute

Children of Wayne Martin and Unknown: 2

Name: Nigel Martin

Name: Sydney Martin

319

Eleonore, Pamela, Jackie, Theresa holding baby

Pam, Jackie, Elenore

Tony

Tommy, Wayne (standing) Gregory

Generation Two
Half Siblings Of Teresa Pamela Audra Martin

Joseph Gabriel Martin
and
Gwendolyn Stewart

Joseph and Gwendolyn
Back Row: Wayne, Joseph, Gwendolyn, Tommy, Gregory
Front Row: Michelle, Marcus, Louis, Dean, Judy

In a conversation with Judy, I asked her to describe her family and siblings. Her response was heartfelt: they were tight-knit, strong, and of high moral character. She emphasized that they always knew exactly who they were—Martins. Judy acknowledged that it might have been challenging growing up in the shadow of Joseph's children with Theresa, but they were never intimidated. Instead, they remained resilient, self-assured, and deeply aware of how hard they had worked to keep the family together, especially after Gwendolyn passed away at a young age.

When Gwendolyn met and married Joseph, she was 22 years younger than Joseph, and Judy Stewart/Martin, the daughter of Gwendolyn, just 5 months old was sent to live with her grandparents at that time. Gwendolyn watched over Joseph's 3 young sons: Wayne, Tommy, and Gregory.

Judy stayed with her grandparents until she was four years old. Her surname was changed Martin since Joseph had always promised to adopt her. Joseph and Gwendolyn worked tirelessly to build their business. The business was truly a family effort—sometimes deliveries were made directly to their home, and everyone pitched in. The success of the business was a testament to their collective hard work and dedication.

When Gwendolyn passed, Joseph moved to the United States, where he met and married Ethel B. Rosenthal, affectionately nicknamed Candy. Candy had a penchant for older, "foolish" men who were generous with their money, and Joseph seemed happy to oblige. Joseph's children remember his frequent requests for financial support from the family business, which Candy seemed to enjoy.

Despite the challenges, Joseph's move to the U.S. brought new opportunities for the family. He was able to sponsor Judy's immigration to America, and in turn, Judy sponsored her siblings who wished to follow. This led to a period of travel and connection between the U.S., Canada, and Trinidad, creating a unique blend of familial ties across borders.

Children of Joseph and Gwendolyn

Michelle:

Lives in NJ with her life partner. On her time off from work she loves soccer, fishing, camping, white water rafting, loved watching the London 2012 Olympics. She loves her life and all of her family.

Charles, Michelle, Judy and Louis

Charles Dean Martin married MICHELLE DaBreau in 1983. The couple had four children Joshua, Sarah Megan Dominique.

When he returned to Trinidad, he immediately started to work in the family business. Everything went very quickly with his wife. There was a lot of static with his employment duties and his wife.

Generation Three Paternal

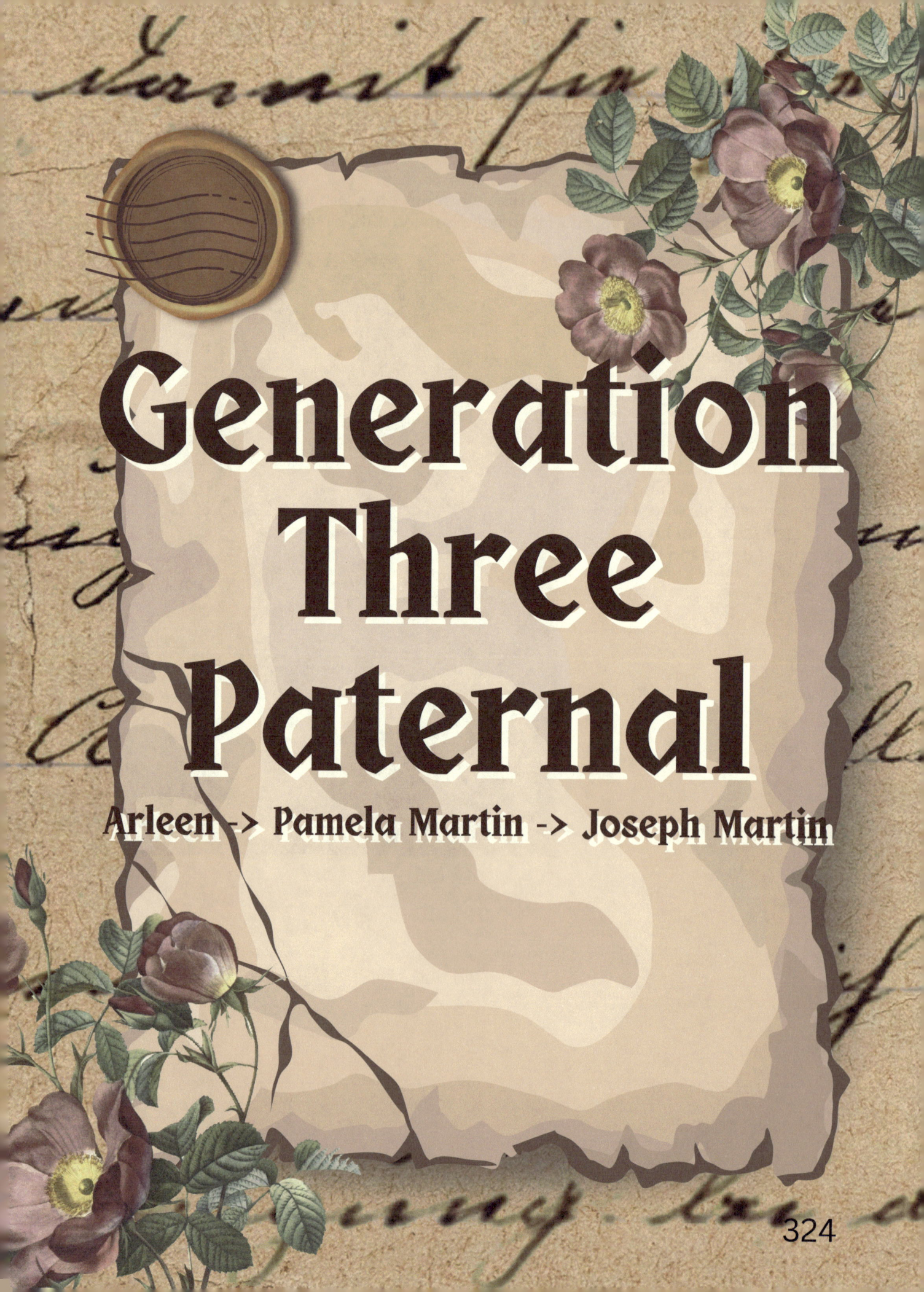

Arleen -> Pamela Martin -> Joseph Martin

HISTORY OF JOSEPH GABRIEL MARTIN

QUICK FACTS:

BORN
TRINIDAD AND TOBAGO

PARENTS
LUIS MARTIN
"ELEONORE GRUNY

CHILDREN
TWO FAMILIES WORTH

Joseph Martin's Life by Anthony Martin

Joseph was born on March 18, 1913. His father, Louis Martin, died suddenly when Joseph was only 12 years old. Being the eldest child, Joe had to quit school in order to provide for his mother and his siblings. In those days social benefits were non-existent. First, he started selling provisions like yams, dasheen taro, bananas, peas, cucumber, tomatoes etc. This he did for many years. While doing this his friend Rita said to him "Joe you are a wonderful guy, but your English is terrible. You should try and continue your education."

Joe started taking correspondence courses from England. Joe was an extremely bright and driven man. He eventually spoke excellent English and read a lot when he had the chance. Eventually he got out of the provision business and started a wine business. This he named Trinidad Wine and Liquor Industry. His products were well-known throughout the island. He also exported products to many other West Indies Islands. Eventually he got out of this business and ventured into wholesaling appliances.

The island had a company that imported parts for fridges and stoves etc. and assembled them in Trinidad. This company had about three wholesalers who provided retail items to retail stores and also to local people. Joseph was one of these wholesalers. In this business, he became a big fish in a small pond. Joseph was a very well-respected man on the island. He made his millions in Trinidad.

One day he was riding his bicycle down the street when he saw two young women walking along the sidewalk. He knew the one nearest to the road but had no idea who the other one was. He asked the one nearest to him "What's your friend's name?" She said her name was Theresa Stout. After speaking to her for a while, he said to his friend "One day she is going to be my wife." After he rode off, Theresa said to her friend "That's a very brash man."

After Joe and Theresa were married, they started having children immediately. First there was Pamela, then Eleonore, Tony, Jackie, Tommy, Gregory and finally, Wayne, for a total of eight children. Theresa was not the disciplinarian. It was always, "Wait till your father comes home." When Father came home, it was not rare for him to unfold his belt, and on the rare occasion, the buckle end would be at the far end. Joseph had a very forceful personality. He could be as charming as the best of them, but he was also extremely bombastic.

His forcefulness impacted all his children in an extremely negative way. Yet he wanted the very best for his children. He was also a very loving and fun parent. We all loved and admired him greatly. We all knew he was bordering on genius. He loved all his children. Growing up I also knew that as smart as he was, there were deep holes in his understanding of things. I knew this was because he had to exit the school system at an extremely young age.

After bearing eight offspring, my mother found herself pregnant again. In those days, we didn't have birth control medication. My sister, Pamela, told me that because our dad told our mother that he didn't want any more children, our mother sought the aid of a midwife. For some reason, things didn't go as planned and she died of tetanus. Blood poisoning. It was such a horrific death that it haunts me to this day. Theresa died in March of 1956.

Joseph was driving his car on the Eastern Main Road, when he felt some discomfort. He pulled over to the side of the road and stopped his car. Shortly after that he was found dead in the car behind the steering wheel. He died of a ruptured stomach. He died in 1986 at age 73.

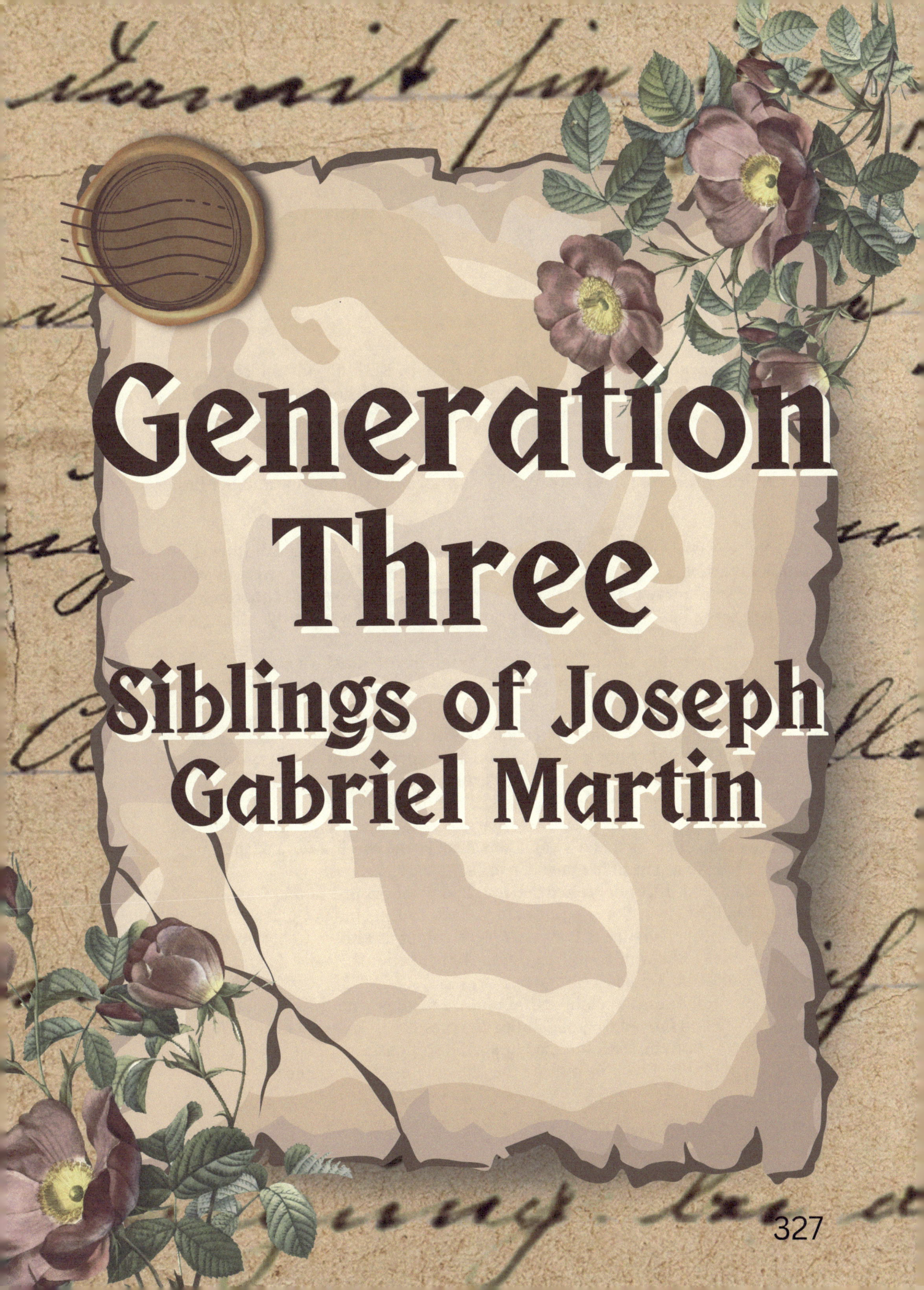

Generation Three
Siblings of Joseph Gabriel Martin

Information From Tony Martin about Joseph Martin's Siblings

- Joseph Martin DOB March 18 1913. Died 1985 from a heart attack at age 73.
- Frank Martin DOB May 11 1915. Died in 1975 from a heart attack at age 60.
- Carmen Martin DOB Feb. 14,1917 Died 2006 from Alzheimer's disease at age 89.
- Matty Martin DOB March 12,1922, Died 2022 from old age at 100.
- Marie Martin DOB Nov.23, 1924. Died Mar 4, 2004 from a heart attack at age 78.h Martin 2022

From Other Sources:

Joseph Martin owned Martin's Marketing on Eastern Main Road - which was the dividing line between between Port of Spain and San Juan. Some of the houses that the Martins lived in were Clifford Street in Belmont and they went to St. Francis Church. They also lived in 17th 1st Street in Mt Lambert.

Eleonore Gruny was Joseph's mother. She was born in Guadeloupe and her father was from France.

Teresa Stoute was his wife, but I don't have any info on her mother or father. I do have that her mother married a man named Cuthbert and lived on O'Conner Street in Woodbrook Trinidad. Teresa had two half sister who were nuns at Holy Name School in Port of Spain. One of the Sister's name was Barbara Cuthbert. I don't know what the other sister was named.

I do not know the name of the church that the family attended when they lived in Woodbrook and I think that Teresa is buried at ?Woodbrook Cemetery on Mucurapo Road in St. James.

Information From Tony Martin **(corrections bolded)**
- Joseph Martin's father name is Louis Martin who **was from St Kitts, West Indies. His family before him came from Madeira, Portugal.**
- Prior to the marriage of Louis Martin & Eleonore Gruny in T'dad., (the parents of Joseph Martin) Louis was previously married and had three daughters from that marriage. **One of his daughter's name was Audry, and this is a form of the name given to Pamelas Martin as one of her middle names.**
- After Louis died, Eleonore remarried and had a son named Sonny Cavalho, Joseph Martin's half brother. Sonny eventually moved to England got married and died there.
- Eleonore's mother's name is Leonise Gruny. She was known to her grandchildren as Mama Nisse. (She wanted to be a doctor but ended up a mid-wife and delivered babies in Guadelope and Trinidad
- Leonisse's mother died in childbirth. Leonisse's father's name is Armand Gruny who was from France and moved to Guadeloupe to command a military installation on the Island.
- Eleonore was born in 1885 and died at age 59 from an aneurism.
- Author's note: I had trouble putting the above in proper sequence.

Descendancy

1. Luis Martin b: ABT 1893 in Saint Kitts and Nevis, Saint-Christophe-et-Niévès. d: 24 NOV 1924 in Port of Spain, St George, Trinidad; age: 31.
+ Bernardine Eleonore Angelique Gruny b: 28 MAY 1884 in Pointe-à-Pitre, Guadeloupe. m: 1930 in Port-of-Spain, Port-of-Spain, Trinité-et-Tobago. d: 1944 in Trinidad, West Indies; age: 59.
   2. Joseph Gabriel Martin b: 18 MAR 1913 in Port of Spain, Trinidad and Tobago, British West Indies. d: 5 SEP 1986 in Port-of-Spain, Trinidad and Tobago; age: 73.
   + Theresa Bertha Stoute b: 4 JUL 1912 in Woodbrook, Port of Spain, Trinidad, W.I.. m: 10 June 1934 in Port of Spain, Trinidad and Tobago, British West Indies. d: 1956 in Trinidad and Tobago, West Indies; age: 43.
      3. Teresa Pamela Audra Martin b: 10 DEC 1934 in Port of Spain, Trinidad. d: 30 SEP 2021 in Lecanto, Citrus, Florida, USA; age: 86.
      + David Allan Sheppard b: 20 NOV 1931 in Port of Spain, Trinidad and Tobago, British West Indies. m: 16 Apr 1955 in Montreal, Canada. d: 02 Aug 2022 in Lecanto, Citrus, Florida, United States; age: 90.
      3. Eleanor Lorraine Martin n Trinidad and Tobago, West Indies.
      + Arthur Reid
      + Inman b: Australia. d: Deceased.
      3. Anthony Carrlyle Martin in Trinidad and Tobago, West Indies.
      + Nancy Lunn
      + Wanda McDermott
      3. Roger Wilfred Joseph Martin in Port Of Spain, Trinidad.
      + Dorothy Esme Sheppard Port Of Spain, Trinidad. m: 01 Oct 1960 in Port-of-Spain, Trinidad and Tobago, British West Indies.
      3. Dianne Jacqueline Martin b: 30 MAR 1941 in Trinidad and Tobago, West Indies. d: 18 FEB 2013 in Australia; age: 71.
      + Clyde Ruthven Medford b: 15 AUG 1936 in Trinidad and Tobago. m: 1963 in Trinidad and Tobago. d: 17 JUN 1996 in Cromer, New South Wales, Australia; age: 59.
      + David Paterson
      3. Thomas Oliver Martin b: 12 Apr 1946 in Trinidad and Tobago, West Indies. d: 30 JUN 2016 in Australia; age: 70.
      + Anita Theresa DaCosta Port of Spain, Trinidad and Tobago, British West Indies. m: 5 NOV 1967.
      3. Wayne Martin b: 18 JUL 1954 in Trinidad and Tobago, West Indies. d: 1975 in Trinidad and Tobago; age: 20.
      3. Gregory Martin
      + Angela DaBreau
   + Gwendolyn Stewart b: Aruba, Aruba. m: 1966 in Port of Spain, Trinidad and Tobago, West Indies. d: 1978 in Trinidad and Tobago, West Indies.
      3. Louis Martin b: Dec 1958. d: Deceased in United States.
      3. Dean Martin b: Trinidad and Tobago, West Indies. d: 27 SEP 2021.
      3. Mark Martin
      3. Michelle Martin
      3. Peggy Martin
   + Ethel B Rosenthal b: MAR 1933 in California, USA. m: 11 Aug 1978 in Clark, Nevada.
   2. Francis John Martin b: 11 MAY 1915 in Port of Spain, Trinidad and Tobago, British West Indies. d: 3 APR 1975 in Australia; age: 59.
   + Rita Barbara D'Abreau b: ABT 1917. d: 18 SEP 1994 in Australia; age: 77.
      3. Michael Godfrey Martin b: 9 MAR 1944 in Trinidad and Tobago. d: 31 DEC 2001 in Brisbane City, Queensland, Australia; age: 57.
      + Karoline Therese MCDONAGH 1 in Sydney New South Wales Australia. m: 16 SEP 1972. d: 26 JUN 2012 in Parkwood Queensland Australia; age: 61.
      3. Dennis Martin b: Port of Spain, Trinidad, W.I.. d: Deceased in Australia.
      3. Mickey Martin b: Port of Spain, Trinidad, W.I.. d: Deceased in Australia.
   2. Carmen Candida Martin b: 14 Feb 1917 in Port of Spain, Trinidad and Tobago. d: 6 JUN 2006 in Boca Raton, Palm Beach, Florida, USA; age: 89.
   + Bennie Edward Zaruba b: 08 Jan 1915 in Omaha, Douglas, Nebraska, United States. m: 27 AUG 1947 in New York City, New York, USA. d: 12 NOV 1960 in San Diego, California, USA; age: 45.
      3. Kyrline M Zaruba b: ABT 1938.
      3. Brenier V Zaruba b: ABT 1949 in California.
      3. Gerard Edward Zaruba b: 11 OCT 1950 in San Diego, California. d: 21 May 1971 in San Diego, California, USA; age: 20.
   + Leland Richard McPhie b: 10 MAR 1914 in Salt Lake City, Salt Lake, Utah, United States. m: 11 Nov 1967 in San Diego, San Diego, California, United States. div: Sep 1969 in San Diego City, California, USA. d: 3 SEP 2015 in San Diego, San Diego, California, United States; age: 101.
   + William S Murphy b: ABT 1924. m: 12 FEB 1972 in San Diego City, California, USA.
   2. Marguerite Martin b: 12 MAR 1922 in Trinidad and Tobabo. d: 15 Jun 2022; age: 100.
   + Juvenal Rodrigues b: Nov 24 1923 in Port-of-Spain, Trinidad and Tobago. d: 5 Jan 1994 in Montreal, Quebec, Canada; age: 70.
      3. Gerald Rodriguez
      3. Jennifer Rodriguez b: Port, of, Spain, Trinidad and Tobago. d: Deceased in Vancouver, British Columbia, Canada.
      3. Maria Rodriguez
      3. Mary Rodriguez
      3. Michael Rodriguez
      3. Nicole Rodriguez
      3. Paula Rodriguez
   2. Marie Louise Martin b: 22 NOV 1924 in Port of Spain, Trinidad and Tobago. d: 31 MAR 2004 in San Diego, California, USA; age: 79.
   + John Francis O'Hagan Jr b: 23 MAY 1928 in AL. m: 24 SEP 1949 in San Diego, California, USA. d: 23 AUG 2014 in San Diego CA; age: 86.
      3. Joseph Michael O'Hagan b: 3 SEP 1953 in California. d: 3 SEP 1953 in San Diego; age: 0.
      3. John Patrick O'Hagan b: 3 SEP 1953 in California. d: 4 SEP 1953 in San Diego; age: 0.
   + Unknown
      3. Gary DeSilva
   2. Audry Martin b: Trinidad. d: Deceased in netherlands.

Marie Martin and Gary De Silva and his posterity

Marie Martin and Gary De Silva and his posterity

Born: 18 Jan 1945 • Trinidad and Tobago
Gary was born to Marie Martin and fathered by an American soldier. Marie, being quite young left Gary to be raised by Olga and Curtis de Silva and he adopted their last name. Marie and Gary maintained their relationship throughout their lives.

Gary was well respected and well connected throughout his life. He was generally a happy soul, so he was also well liked.

He was married three times. What ever was the disposition of those marriages, I do not know. But I do have a tree for Gary and his lines.

Cristel states of her father that he was very well respected as an accountant and businessman and well connected in Trinidad as everyone seemed to know him, and to this day she still runs into people who knew him and loved him.

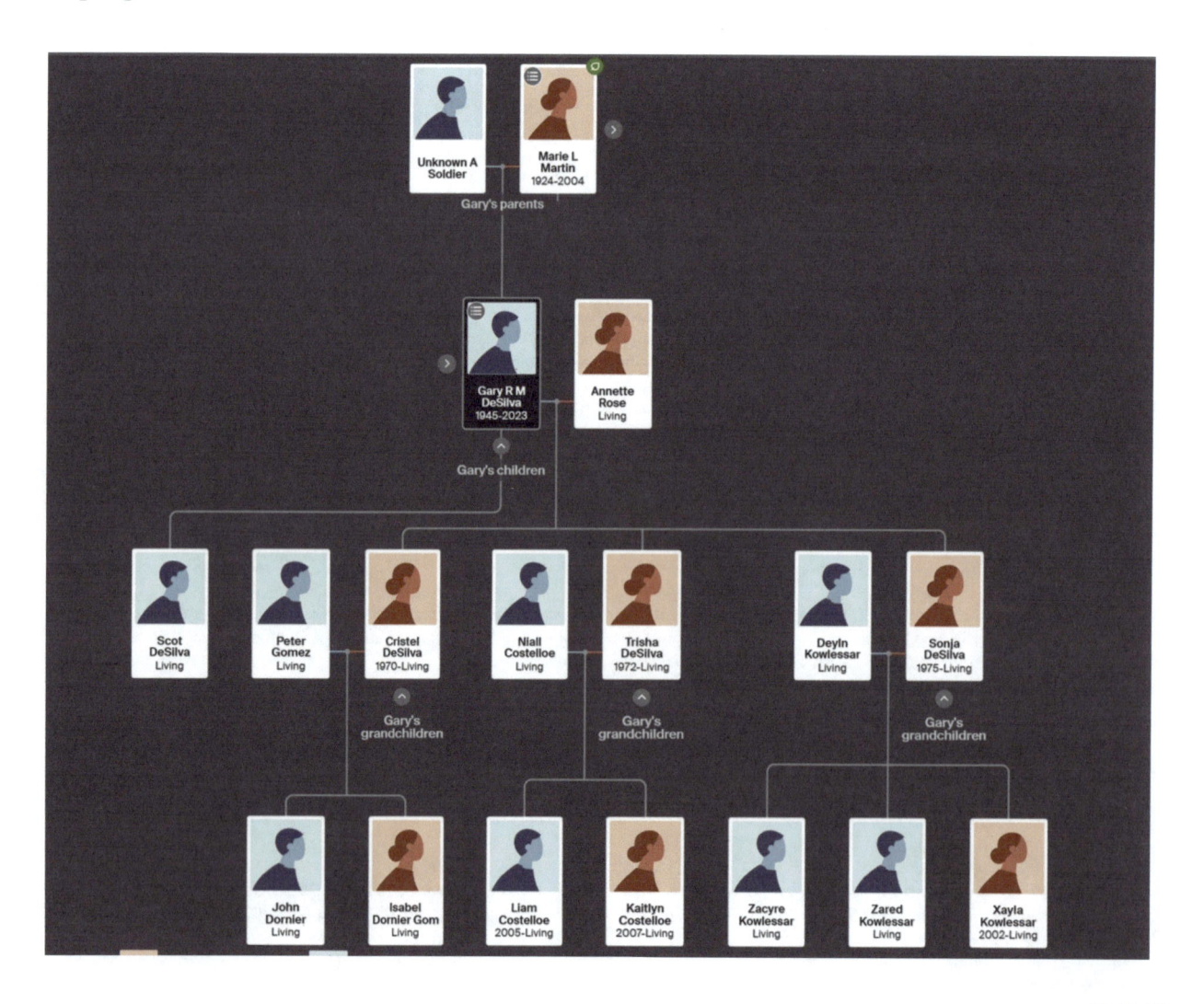

Gary young and as a young man

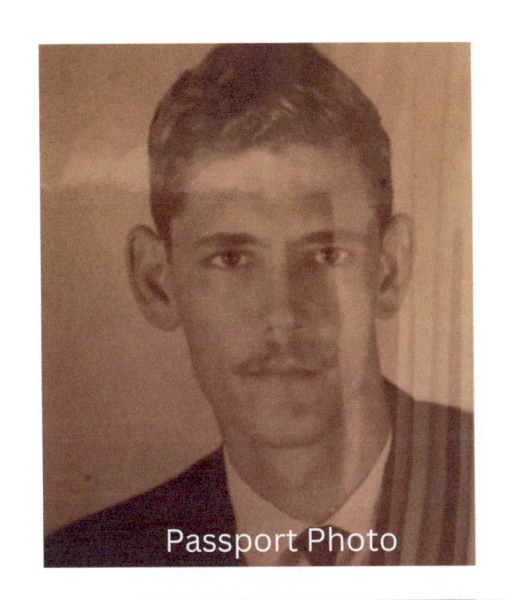

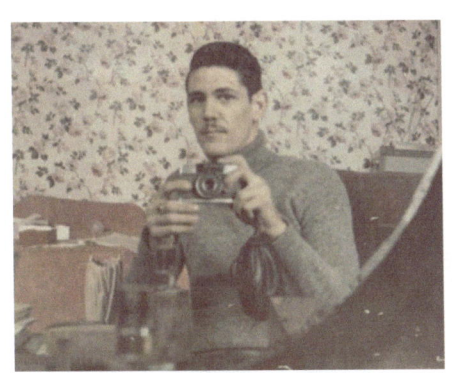

Childhood

Passport Photo

The Photographer

Gary Liming

Gary the father

Gary and his second wife, Annette Rose. Together they had three children: Cristel, Sonja and Trisha

The three girls are pictured below with Gary

Gary the Fun Loving Guy

Gary and his daughter, Cristel

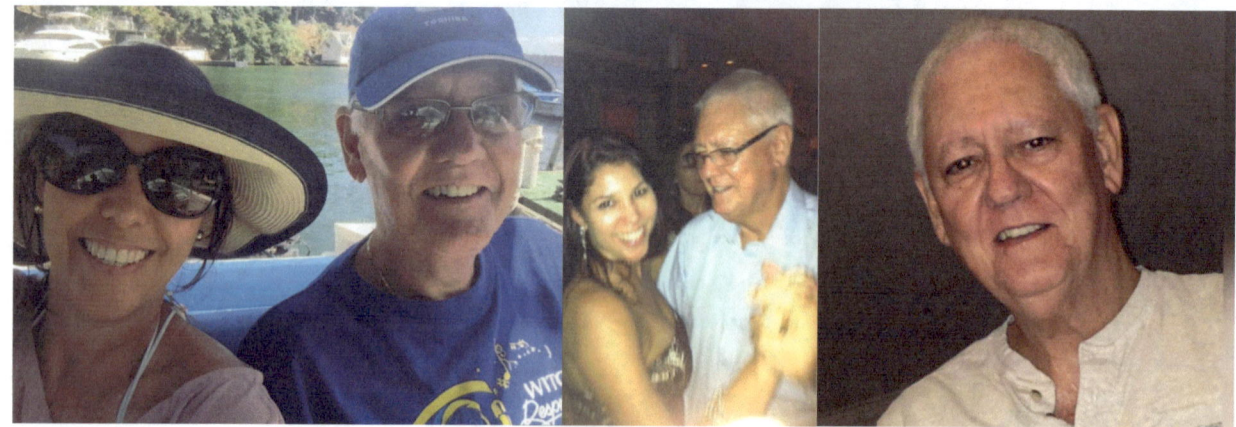

Generation Three Maternal

Arleen -> "Pamela" Martin -> Theresa Bertha Stoute

HISTORY OF THERESA BERTHA STOUTE

QUICK FACTS:

BORN
PORT OF SPAIN
TRINIDAD

PARENTS
FATHER - UNKNOWN
MARIE STOUTE

CHILDREN
LOVING MOTHER OF 12

336

Theresa Stoute by Anthony Martin

My mother's maiden name is Theresa Stout. Theresa was a very sensitive and likable person. She was distinguished by a very dark mole in the middle of the small cup just below the bottom of her nose. She was liked by all who knew her. A very quiet but positive presence. Nothing is known about the Stoute family. In those days family history was not part of the conversation. Theresa's stepdad's last name was Cuthbert. They are not blood-related.

Theresa had a stepsister whose name is Rita Cuthbert. Rita had three sisters: Gloria, Barbara and Manna. I don't remember meeting Rita's sisters. From time to time Rita used to visit us in our home in Mount Lambert. Rita and my mother used to spend their time talking in the kitchen. I never knew what they talked about. Rita was a strikingly attractive woman. As a very young boy I was attracted to her beauty and graciousness.

This is all I know about my mother's family history. After bearing eight offspring, my mother found herself pregnant again. In those days, we didn't have birth control medication. My sister, Pamela, told me that because our dad told our mother that he didn't want any more children, our mother sought the aid of a midwife. For some reason, things didn't go as planned and she died of tetanus; blood poisoning. It was such a horrific death that it haunts me to this day. Theresa died in March of 1956.

Tommy Wayne Gregory

Anthony

Pamela Jackie Eleonore

Joseph Pamela Theresa at Pamela's going away party, She was leaving to marry the love of her life in Montreal.

Theresa and her children

337

Gwendolyn Stewart by Anthony Martin

At Theresa's passing, Pamela was 22. She was the eldest of Joseph's eight children, while Wayne, the youngest, was just three years old. After their mother, Theresa, passed away, Joseph struggled to care for Wayne. This was an especially difficult time for the young boy, who was often left alone, spending hours rocking back and forth in a chair. Recognizing the need for help, Joseph sought a solution and soon found it in Gwendolyn, a woman at least 22 years his junior.

She had a daughter, Judy, about 4 months old. Judy was sent to live with her grandparents and was with them until she was 4 years old. Gwendolyn did this to provide proper care to Wayne. She proved to be a kind and loving woman, as well as a good mother. Together, Gwendolyn and Joseph had about five children.

By this time, Joseph's first five children had left Trinidad, relocating to Canada and Australia. While they were away, Joseph frequently compared the children from his first marriage with those he had with Gwen, often telling the latter that the older siblings were superior. This created resentment, and Gwen's children grew up harboring ill feelings toward their half-siblings.

Ethel B Rosenthal aka Candy

When Gwendolyn passed away, all of Joseph's children were grown. Around this time, he visited his sister Carmen in California. During an outing at a club, Joseph loudly asked, "Would any lady here like to marry a millionaire?" A Jewish woman named Candy accepted the challenge. Candy worked as an agent for movie actors, including Telly Savalas, and was also a real estate agent.
Before their wedding, Joseph visited me in Whitby, Ontario, Canada, and invited me to attend the ceremony in Las Vegas. I declined, as I didn't think it was a good idea and tried to dissuade him from going through with it. He insisted, saying he would pay all expenses to fly everyone from California to Las Vegas and cover my travel costs as well.

After the wedding, Candy persuaded Joseph to fly back and forth to Israel and convinced him to invest heavily in real estate in California. Meanwhile, Joseph's children were managing his business in Trinidad, but Candy's influence led him to withdraw so much capital from the business that it became unsustainable.

The marriage soon began to deteriorate. Candy started to demean Joseph and showed him little respect. Their disputes eventually escalated to the point of legal proceedings. During one court appearance, the judge asked Joseph, "Mr. Martin, you are a very smart businessman. How was it possible for you to get yourself into this situation?" Joseph could only reply, "Your Honour, I don't know."

By the end, the couple's disagreements became petty, with fights over even trivial items.

Generation Four Paternal

Arleen -> Pamela -> Joseph -> Luis Martin

HISTORY OF
Luis Martin aka Luiz or Louis

QUICK FACTS:

BORN
ST. KITTS

PARENTS
UNKNOWN

CHILDREN
JOSEPH, MATTI, MARIE, FRANK, CARMEN

Luis (Louis) Martin

Born about 1873 - St Kitts
Died 24 November 1924, Port of Spain, Trinidad and Tobago, British West Indies.
It was known to Luis's family that he had a connection to Madeira, Portugal. Madeira is the largest island off the coast of Portugal, and many people from the region emigrated to the West Indies as indentured servants.

Luis was born in St. Kitts and later settled in Trinidad. Before marrying Eleonore Gruny, he was married and had three daughters, with one known daughter named Audry. Audry was the namesake for Pamela Martin's middle name, Audra. While in Trinidad, Luis made a living by buying, repairing, and reselling homes. He was also one of the founding members of the Trinidad Portuguese Club. Prior to entering the real estate business, he owned a grocery store. Luis passed away on June 1924 from a heart attack.

At the time of his death, Joseph Martin was 11 years old and was forced to leave school to work and help support his family.

Luis's family was part of the emigration wave from Madeira, Portugal, to the Caribbean in the mid-1800s. A combination of circumstances led to the importation of farm laborers from Madeira to the region.

Before the arrival of the Madeirans, enslaved Africans and indentured servants were used in St. Kitts and Nevis to work the islands' many sugar cane plantations. Slavery was abolished in the British West Indies in 1834, and the enslaved population was granted a four-year transition period called "apprenticeship" before full freedom was given. However, this led to a labor shortage on the islands, as plantation owners and sugar merchants struggled to find workers. Additionally, a cholera epidemic devastated the poorer former slave population, further reducing the workforce.

At the same time, Madeira experienced a series of crises. A civil war raged from 1828 to 1834, followed by a devastating potato famine in 1847, known as the "Ano da Fome" or "Year of Hunger," and finally, a series of vine diseases affected wine production from the 1850s through the 1870s. As a result, many unemployed farm laborers from Madeira emigrated, seeking better opportunities in the West Indies.

Between 1847 and 1870, about 1,180 Madeirans arrived in St. Kitts. Initially, they did not assimilate with either the white plantation owners or the black laboring class. However, after their terms of indenture expired, many chose to remain in the region rather than return to Madeira. They often opened small shops in Kittitian towns, eventually becoming middle-class citizens with increased social status.

Luis Martin and Bernadine Eleonore Angelique Gruny.

Shortly before Luis' death at age 51.

REPUBLIC OF TRINIDAD AND TOBAGO

CERTIFICATE OF DEATH

Name:	LUIS MARTIN
Age:	51 YEAR(S)
Rank/Profession:	CLERK
Informant Name:	A GREGORIO
Informant Address:	74 OXFORD STREET
Informant Description:	UNDERTAKERS
Country of Birth:	ST. KITTS
Place of Death:	19 CHARLES STREET
Cause of Death:	MITRAL STENOSIS
Date of Death:	19TH JUNE, 1924
Sex:	MALE
Medical Examiner:	DR HARTLEY
Registration Date:	20TH JUNE, 1924
Name of Registrar:	E WILSON TELFER
Registration District:	SOUTH WESTERN DISTRICT OF PORT OF SPAIN
Entry No:	106
Notes:	

ISSUED UNDER MY HAND AND SEAL OF OFFICE ON 23RD SEPTEMBER, 2022

REGISTRAR GENERAL

CERTIFIED TRUE AND CORRECT EXTRACT FROM THE REGISTER OF DEATHS, HELD BY REGISTRAR GENERAL'S DEPARTMENT MINISTRY OF THE ATTORNEY GENERAL AND LEGAL AFFAIRS

DA00554222

Generation Four++ Paternal

Arleen -> Pamela -> Joseph -> Bernadine "Eleonoree" Angelique Gruny

HISTORY OF BERNADINE ELEONORE ANGELIQUE GRUNY

QUICK FACTS:

BORN
BASSE-TERRE
GUADELOUPE

PARENTS
FATHER - UNKNOWN STOUTE
LEONISSE STHEPHANIE GRUNY

CHILDREN
LOVING MOTHER OF 6

All of the Guadeloupe Birth Records are written in French. They provide a record detail in the language of your choice. Record located at Filae.com

Bernardine Eléonore Angélique GRUNY

Birth
The 28 may 1884
POINTE-A-PITRE (Pointe-à-Pitre, Guadeloupe)

➕ Import into my tree

Details

Bernardine Eléonore Angélique GRUNY

Parent
- Léonisse Stéphanie GRUNY

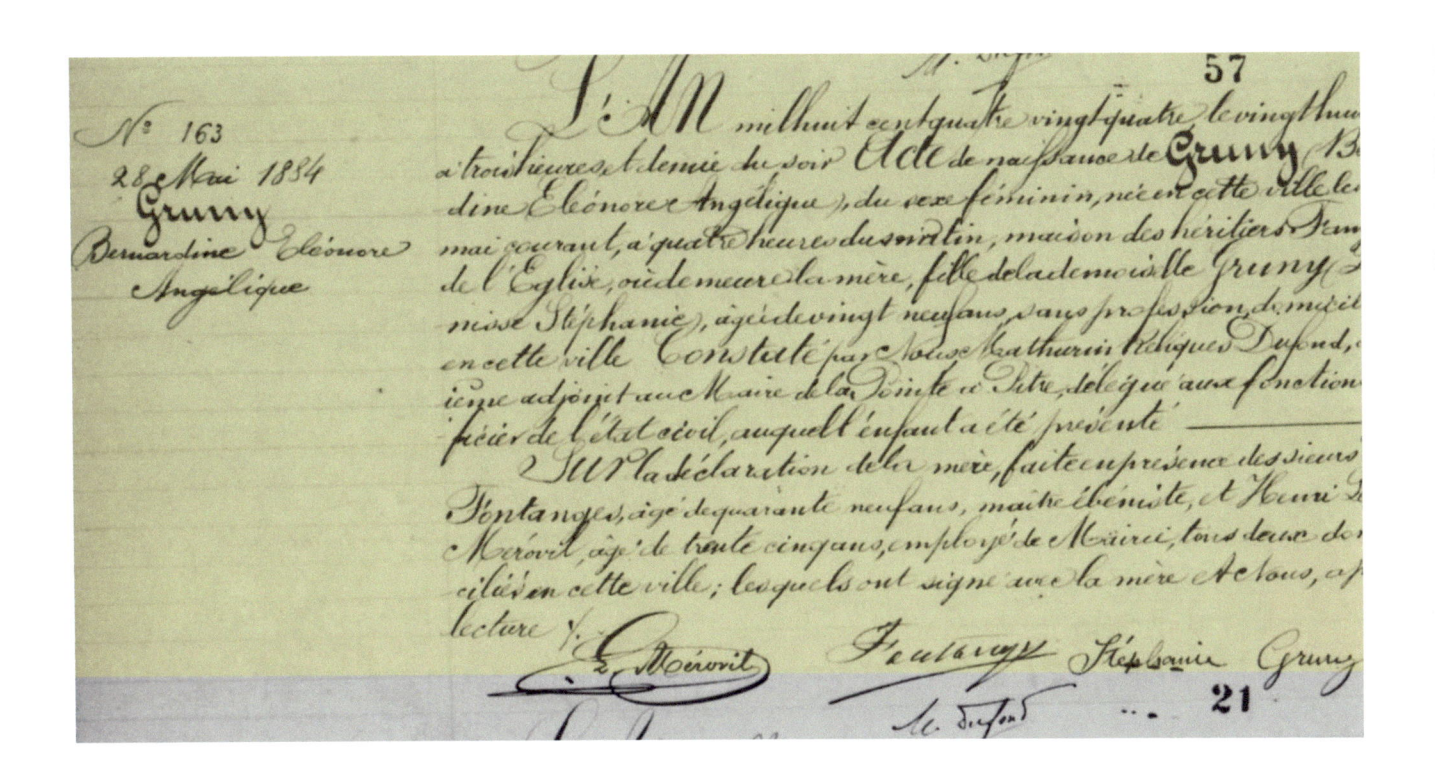

Bernardine Eleonore Angelique Gruny 1884–1944 • LZ4L-LHW

Details | Time Line | Sources (3) | Collaborate (0) | Memories (0) | Ordinances

Louis Martin
1893–1924 • KX4R-Y1B
Marriage: about 1910
Port-of-Spain, Port-of-Spain, Trinidad and Tobago

Bernardine Eleonore Angelique Gruny
1884–1944 • LZ4L-LHW

✓ Preferred

∧ Children (5)

- Joseph Gabriel Martin
  1913–1986 • L529-LWN
- Francis John Martin
  1915–1975 • L56X-1JX
- Carmen Candida Martin
  1917–2006 • LT1F-WN5
- Matty Martin
  1922–Living • G628-2T1
- Marie Louise Martin
  1924–2004 • L568-XK5

➕ Add Child

Henry Carvallo
Deceased • L568-N4L
No Marriage Events

Bernardine Eleonore Angelique Gruny
1884–1944 • LZ4L-LHW

➕ Add Spouse

Leonisse Stephanie Gruny
1854–Deceased • L568-NG6

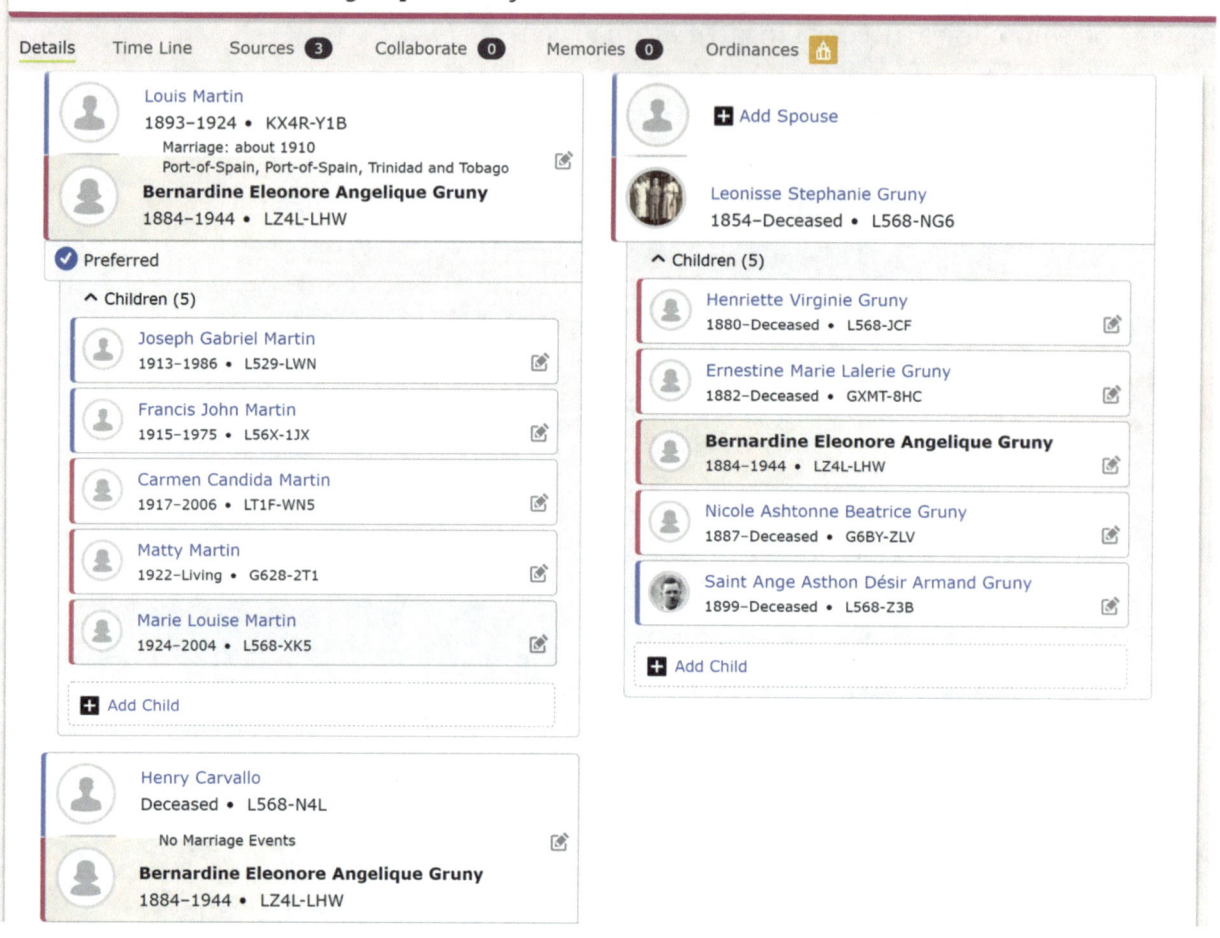

∧ Children (5)

- Henriette Virginie Gruny
  1880–Deceased • L568-JCF
- Ernestine Marie Lalerie Gruny
  1882–Deceased • GXMT-8HC
- **Bernardine Eleonore Angelique Gruny**
  1884–1944 • LZ4L-LHW
- Nicole Ashtonne Beatrice Gruny
  1887–Deceased • G6BY-ZLV
- Saint Ange Asthon Désir Armand Gruny
  1899–Deceased • L568-Z3B

➕ Add Child

ELEANORE

ELEANORE AND LEONISSE

ELEANORE

Eleanor Gruny Martin
Joe's Mother

Here is my grandson, Harrison, with his three-times great-grandmother, Eleonore Gruny Martin. When Harrison was born, I studied his face, trying to figure out who he resembled. At first, I couldn't identify anyone. However, when I later saw a picture of Eleonore Gruny Martin, the resemblance was undeniable. It was like looking at a doppelganger—an exact match. It felt like two pieces of a puzzle finally coming together. After 120 years, I finally discovered who Harrison resembled. It was absolutely incredible.

Child: Harrison Fischer
Mother: Cady Ann Howell
Grandmother: Arleen Sheppard Froemming
Great Grandmother: Pamela Audra Martin Sheppard
Great Great Grandfather: Joseph Gabriel Martin
Great Great Great Grandmother: Bernadine Eleonore Angelique Gruny

Generation Four

Siblings of
Bernardine Eleonore Angelique Gruny

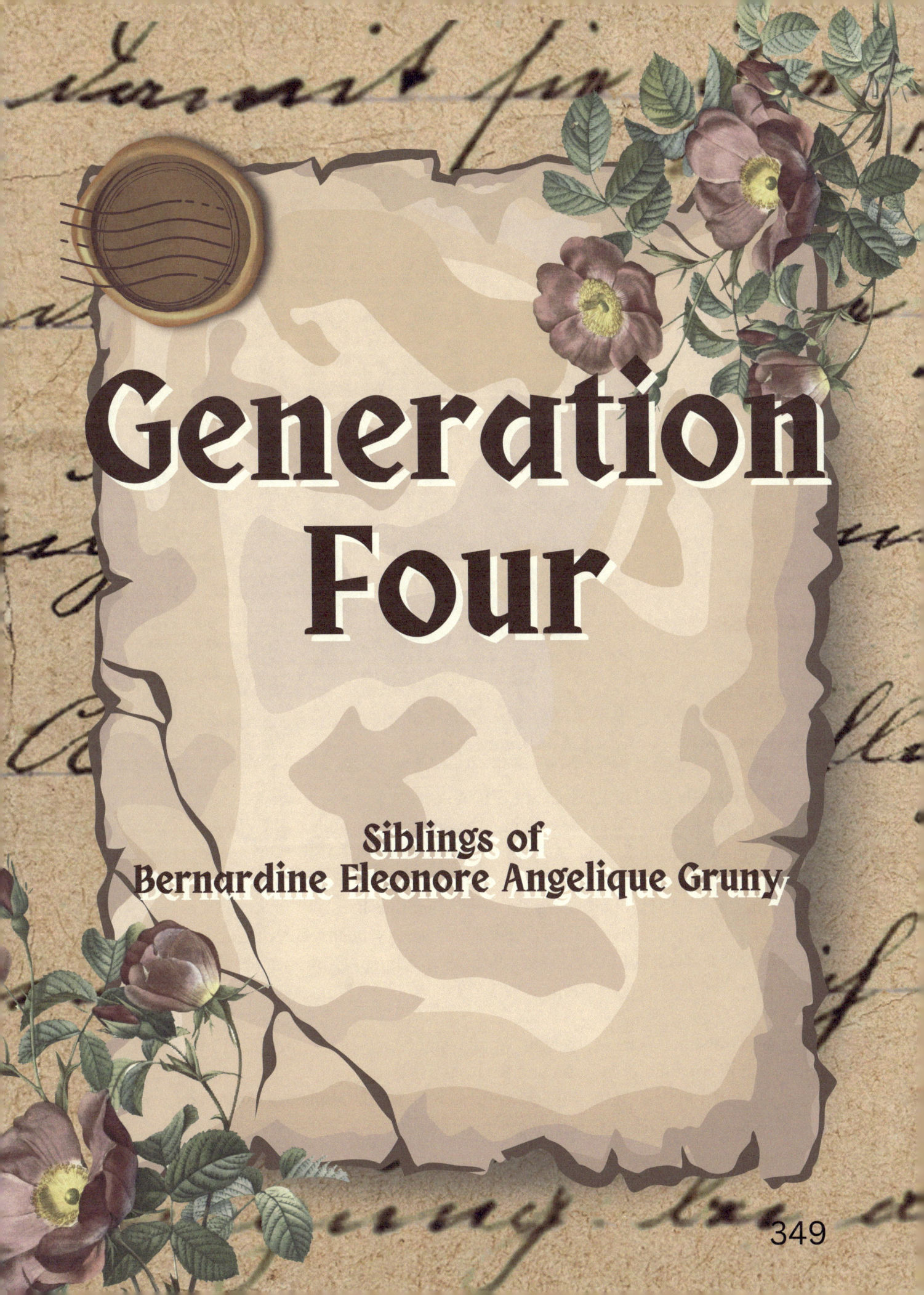

Henri Jules Virassamy

Birth

Henri Jules VIRASSAMY

Birth
The 3rd of April 1878
Pointe-A-Pitre
(Pointe--Pitre, Guadeloupe)

Details

Henri Jules VIRASSAMY

Parents
- Vadivel VIRASSAMY
- Léonisse Stéphanie GRUNY

Source : Death

Henri Jules VIRASSAMY

Death
The 29 april 1882
POINTE-A-PITRE (Pointe-à-Pitre, Guadeloupe)

[Import into my tree]

Details

Henri Jules VIRASSAMY

Parents
- Vadivel VIRASSAMY
- Léonisse Stéphanie GRUNY

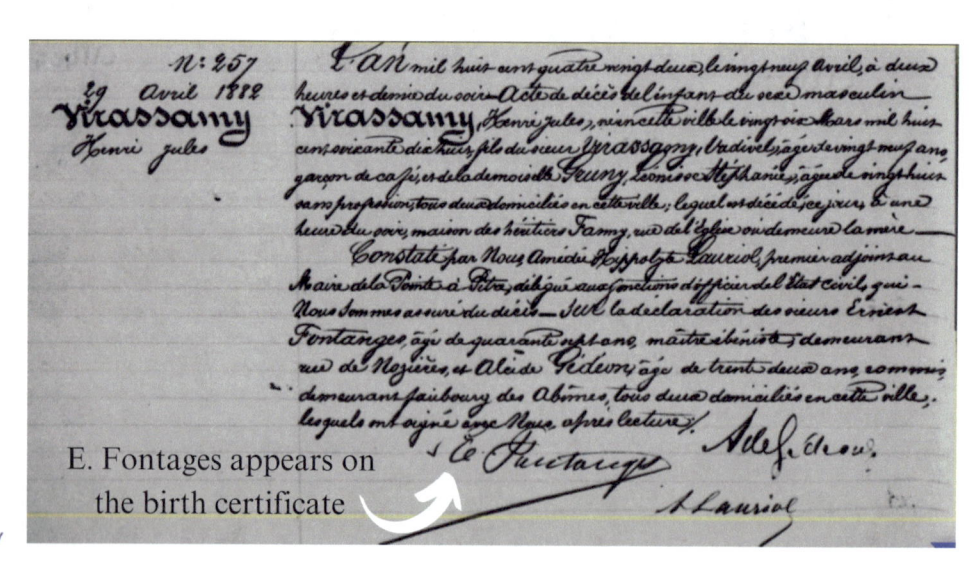

E. Fontages appears on the birth certificate

TRANSCRIPTION OF DEATH CERTIFICATE:

On April 29, 1882 at 2:30 in the evening, the death of the male child VIRASSAMY Henri Jules, born in this city on March 26, 1878 son of Vadivel VIRASSAMY age 29, coffee boy and miss GRUNY Léonise Sthéphanie, age 28, without profession, both reside in this city in the house of the heirs FAMY church street where the mother lives.

On the statements of Ernest FONTANGES 47 years old, carpenter living in Rue de Nozières and Alcide GEDEON 32 years old, clerk, living in Faubourg des Abîmes both resident in this city.

The name "Virassamy" is most likely of Tamil origin and is predominantly found among people from the Tamil community in India and Sri Lanka. After Slavery ended in the Caribbean islands, people from East India were often brought to work in plantations in the Caribbean. More than likely, Vadivel was such an indented person.

On Henri's birth certificate, Vadivel is listed as a coffee worker. Immediately, my mind went to Barista. That proves when we learn something about the past, we often try to frame it in the present. More than likely Vadivel worked at a plantation that had coffee as a product.

WIKIPEDIA The Free Encyclopedia

Coffee production in Guadeloupe

Coffee production in Guadeloupe, an overseas region of France in the Caribbean Sea, has had commercial importance at various times in its history.[1] The island's coffee heritage is being promoted through ecotourism.[2]

History

18th century In 1720, Sir Gabriel de Clieu, based in Martinique, was successful in cultivating coffee,[3] and some beans were planted on nearby Guadeloupe in 1721.[4] Coffee and cotton production increased between 1730 and 1790, decreasing reliance on sugarcane.[5] During this period, coffee cropland increased from 15 hectares to almost 7,000 hectares.[5] By the late 18th century, the cropland had spread from its principal location, at Basse-Terre, to the southwestern area of Grande-Terre.[5]

19th century In the early 19th century, the plantations that remained were mostly in higher elevations of Basse-Terre.[6] In 1842, Guadeloupe faced a coffee crisis.[7] The plantations here and in other West Indian Islands were ravaged by the larvae of *Elachista Coffeella*.[8] Sugarcane production gained dominance with 59% of cultivated land containing the crop in 1856, 45% in 1895, and 66% in 1939.[6] In 1891, with increased import duty on coffee, its growth got a boost.[9] However, residual coffee agriculture continued to supplement the income for some families due to the low local economic activity. The work of Jules Rossignon (died 1883) is mentioned in a Pan American Union publication in 1902. Here, Rossignon states that Guadeloupan coffee was similar to that from Martinique, not easily distinguishable, with similar price points. He described the Guadeloupe bean as "glossy, hard, and long, clean, of an even green color, somewhat grayish", and that it was exported in barrels and hemp bags. Within the "ordinary classes" of coffee, some of the grains were "smaller, rounder, and somewhat curved". Rossignon also mentions that coffee produced in Îles des Saintes was superior.[10] In 1899, Guadeloupe exported 1,587,000 pounds (720,000 kg) of coffee.[10]

20th century Commercially grown coffee varieties recorded in 1913 by Dumont were the *arabica* and *liberica*; the former variety is of better quality and also growing in larger quantities.[11] He described production methods of the early 20th century in detail, mentioning that after the drying stage, coffee is subject to pounding and the removal of the berry's exterior brown cover, this stage being known as *café habitat* and that after the berry's silver coating is removed, the coffee is known as *cafe bonifieur*.[11] In 1918, coffee was being produced on one-ninth of Guadeloupe's land which was under cultivation and about 7% of the exports attributed to coffee.[12] By 1920, coffee cultivation had lessened.[13] Decrease in coffee production in Guadeloupe is party attributed to tropical storms; strong tropical storms of 1921 and 1928 caused severe damage to coffee trees,[14] the 1921 hurricane affecting Basse-Terre.[15] Coffee exportation in 1914 was recorded as more than 1,000 short tons-force (8,900 kN).[16]

Henriette Virginie GRUNY

Birth
The 08 january 1880
POINTE-A-PITRE (Pointe-à-Pitre, Guadeloupe)

Import into my tree

Details

Henriette Virginie GRUNY

Parent
- Léonisse Stéphanie GRUNY

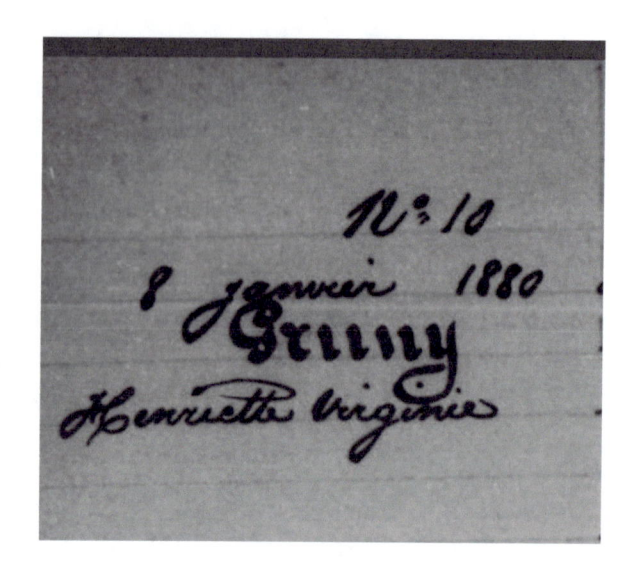

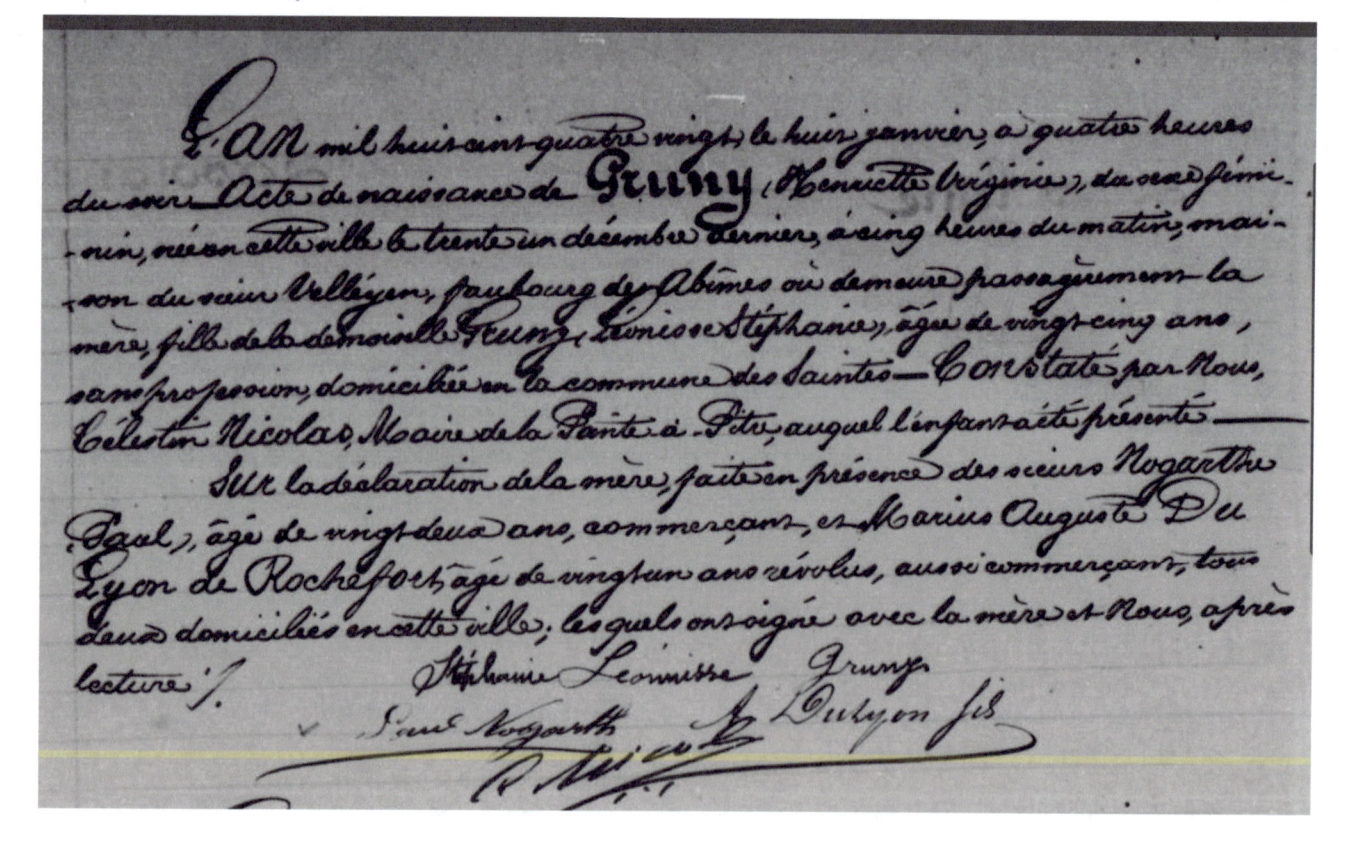

Ernestine Marie Valerie GRUNY

Birth
The 14 september 1882
POINTE-A-PITRE (Pointe-à-Pitre, Guadeloupe)

Import into my tree

Details

Ernestine Marie Valerie GRUNY

Parent
- Léonisse Stéphanie GRUNY

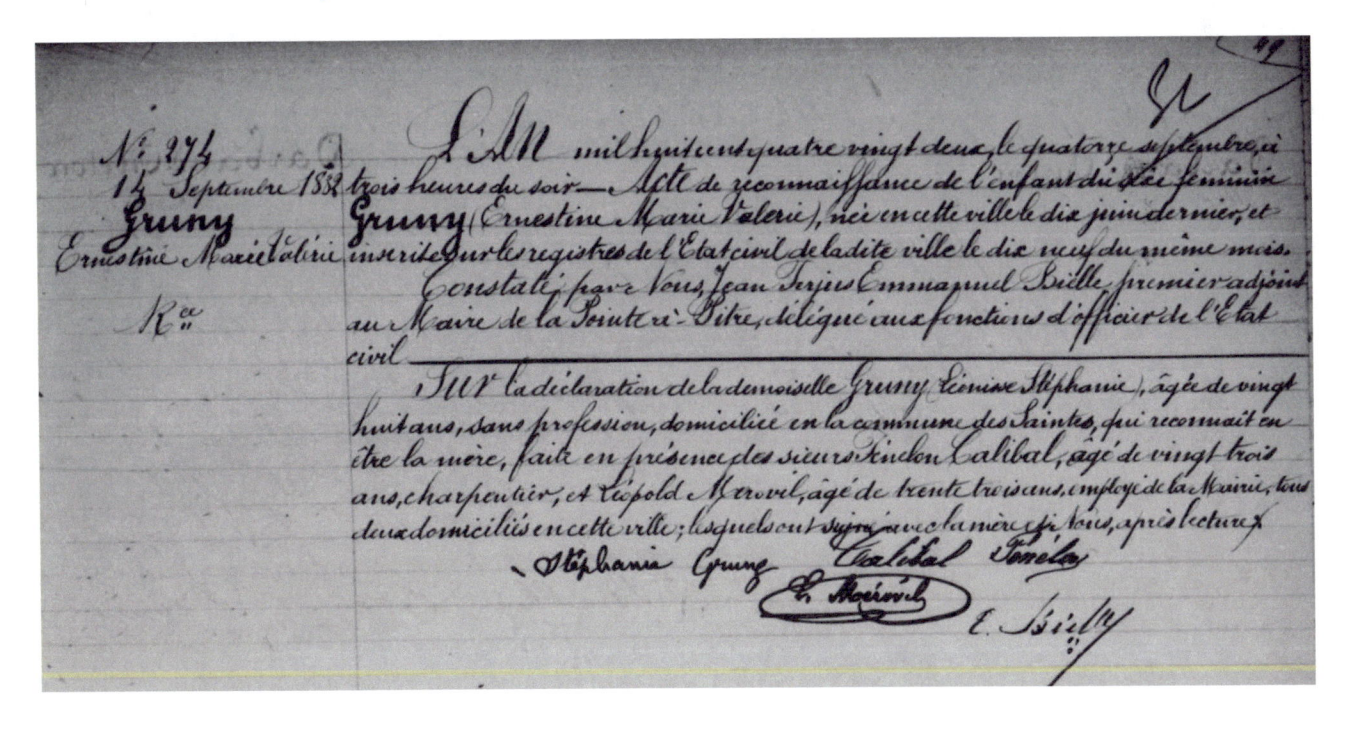

We have a bit more information on Ernestine. She flew to New York so we have her immigration application. On her application she shows "Ernest Gruny" as her father. This never sat well with me as there was no way her father could have the same last name as Leonisse.

There is a possible solution to this, but it can't be verified at the moment, or ever at this point. More about that on the next page.

Ernestine was married twice—first to a man with the surname Alexander and later to someone named Cassino. It seems she also lived in Trinidad for a time, but records indicate she was connected to the French West Indies as well. Additionally, the application references a child named Alfred, though the child's last name is unclear, and it appears he may have been born in France.

From this application, we can glean the name of Ernestine's father: Ernest Gruny. I believe she provided the first name of her and her sibling's father, and what was previously thought to be his first name is actually his last name. Family lore suggests that their father's name is Fontage Gruny. All of these clues point to the possibility that the father of Leonisse's children may have been Ernest Fontage. His name appears on several birth records, but this alone is not sufficient to confirm the connection according to genealogical standards. But logic tells me it is so.

Nicole Asthonne Béatrice GRUNY

Birth
The 16 march 1887
POINTE-A-PITRE (Pointe-à-Pitre, Guadeloupe)

Import into my tree

Details

Nicole Asthonne Béatrice GRUNY

Parent
- Leonisse Stéphanie GRUNY

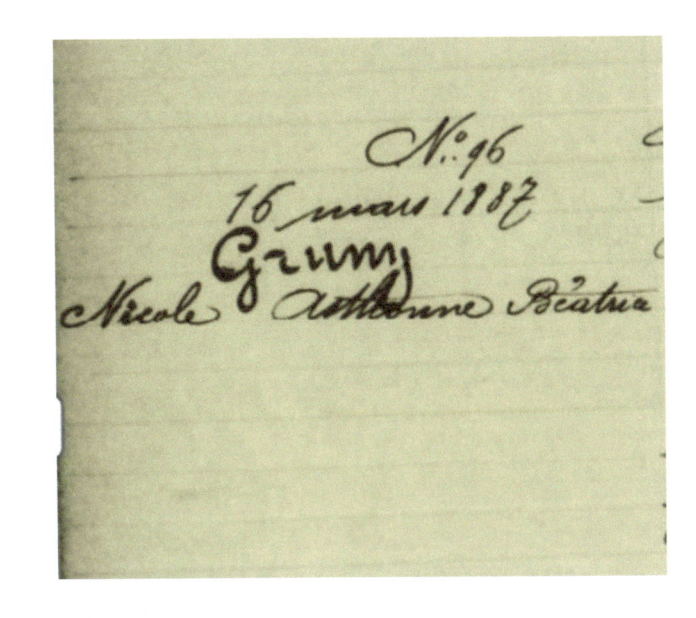

Ernest Fontages appears again.

Saint Ange Asthon Désir GRUNY

Birth
The 08 august 1889
POINTE-A-PITRE (Pointe-à-Pitre, Guadeloupe)

➕ Import into my tree

Details

Saint Ange Asthon Désir GRUNY
Parent
- ? GRUNY

I have a soft spot for Saint Ange. His was the first birth record I found. I was clicking around on MyHeritage.com when I came across his record. I reached out to one of my Facebook groups that helps translate genealogical records, and a gentleman from the group kindly translated the record for me. He also went a step further and did some additional research, which led him to find Leonisse for me. I will forever be grateful for his help. He was incredibly thorough and provided more documented information than I had ever had before. It was through this gentleman that I learned about St. Ange's mother, the infamous "Mama Neisse." From there, I was able to obtain birth records for his siblings, parents, and grandparents, and more recently, for his great-grandparents.

St. Ange

356

St Ange Gruny, HIs wife and two of his 13 Children

Descendancy

1. Saint Ange Asthon Désir Armand Gruny b: 30 JUL 1889 in Pointe-à-Pitre, Guadeloupe. d: 28 FEB 1957 in Port of Spain, Trinidad, W.I.; age: 67.
+ Victoria Eugeina Borrome Lopez b: 26 SEP 1911 in Guiria, Sucre, Venezuela. m: Abt. 1935. d: 1994 in Port of Spain, Trinidad and Tobago; age: 82.

    2. Lydia Josephina Gruny
    + Carl Weekes
        3. Carlene Patricia Weekes
        3. Carlton Weekes
    + Chung Anthony Shampoo
        3. Alberto Shampoo
        3. Jesus Leon Shampoo
    2. Charles Macky Gruny
    + Marites Otero
    2. Anna Gruny
    2. Albertina Gruny
    + Tito Armando Ohep Reyes
    + Unknown
        3. Ana Victoria Ohep
        3. Angel Ohep Gruny
        3. Edwin Armando Ohep Gruny
        3. Juan Casto Ohep Gruny
        3. Tito Alberto Ohep Gruny
    2. Antonio Gruny
    2. Beatriz Gruny
    2. Jose Gruny

        3. Vic Johnaton Gruny
    2. Leonilde Gruny
    + Cleora Theresa Winston
    2. Mignone Ethelbert Gruny
    + John Oswald Martin
Miranda, Venezuela; ag
        3. Carmen Martin
    2. Louis Ernesto Gruny
    2. Yvonne Marie Gruny
    + Kenneth Peter DeAbreu
        3. Cleora Considine
        3. Ursula De Abreu-Este
    2. Linotte Susan Gruny
    + Victor Errol Agostini

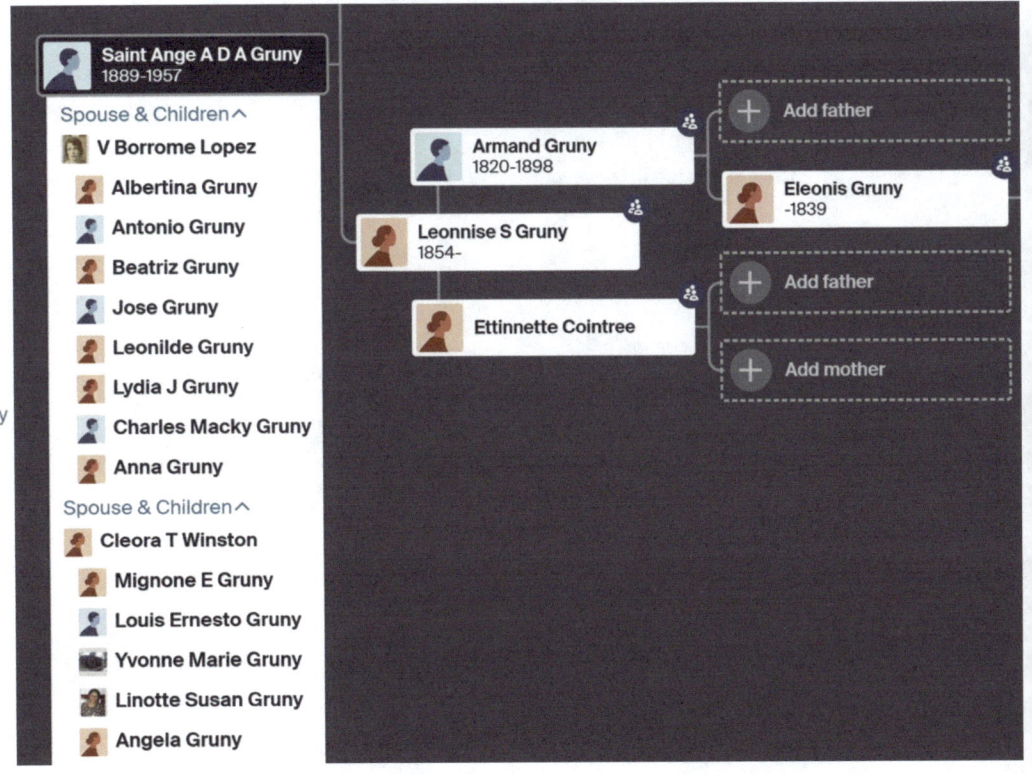

Generation Four++

Arleen -> Pamela -> Joseph -> Bernadine "Eleonoree" Angelique Gruny > Leonisse Gruny

HISTORY OF LEONISSE STHEPHANIE GRUNY

QUICK FACTS:

BORN
GUADELOUPE

PARENTS
ARMAND GRUNY
ETINNETE COINTRE

CHILDREN
LOVING MOTHER OF 6

Birth

The 16 may 1854
TERRE-DE-BAS--LES SAINTES
Anses, Terre-de-Bas)

Details

Léonisse Sthéfanie GRUNY

Parents

- Armand GRUNY
- Etiennette COINTRE

Leonisse was the only surviving child of Armand Gruny and Etiennette Cointre. She is also our direct descendant and mother of "Eleonore" Martin, who is Bernadine Eleonore Angelique Gruny.

Family lore is that Armand was a general who had the favor of Napoleon II, and was awarded governor of Guadeloupe as a reward for his loyalty. It continues that Leonisse involved herself in a relationship with a black soldier and was cast out of the family. She also got herself into a troubled relationship with a man who we think is Ernest Fontages. See Ernestine Gruny for details.

We don't know what happened to her, but she and her children did emigrate to Trinidad. It is said that she delivered many of her grandchildren.

LEONISSE IN THE CENTER, FLANKED BY A GRANDDAUGHTER ON THE LEFT AND A DAUGHTER ON THE RIGHT.

"ELEONORE" AND LEONISSE

Generation Four

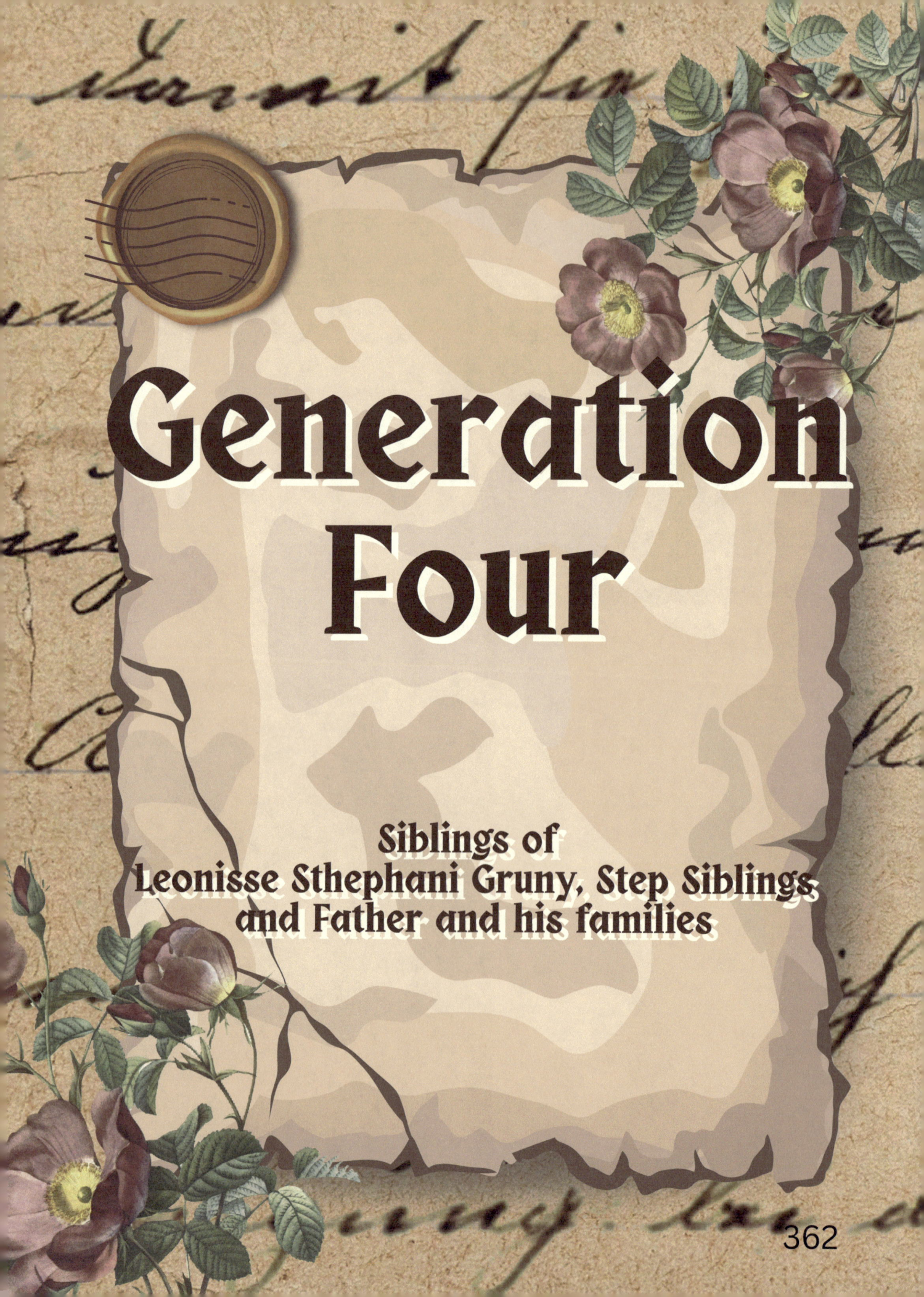

Siblings of
Leonisse Sthephani Gruny, Step Siblings
and Father and his families

Marie Léonie GRUNY

Death
The 02 september 1853
TERRE-DE-HAUT--LES SAINTES (Terre-de-Haut, Guadeloupe)

Details

Marie Léonie GRUNY

Parents

- Armand GRUNY
- Etiennette COINTRE

Marie was the first child of the couple and the first one to pass away on September 2, 1853. A month later, her sister followed her in death on October 8, 1853. Her mother passed a few years afterward.

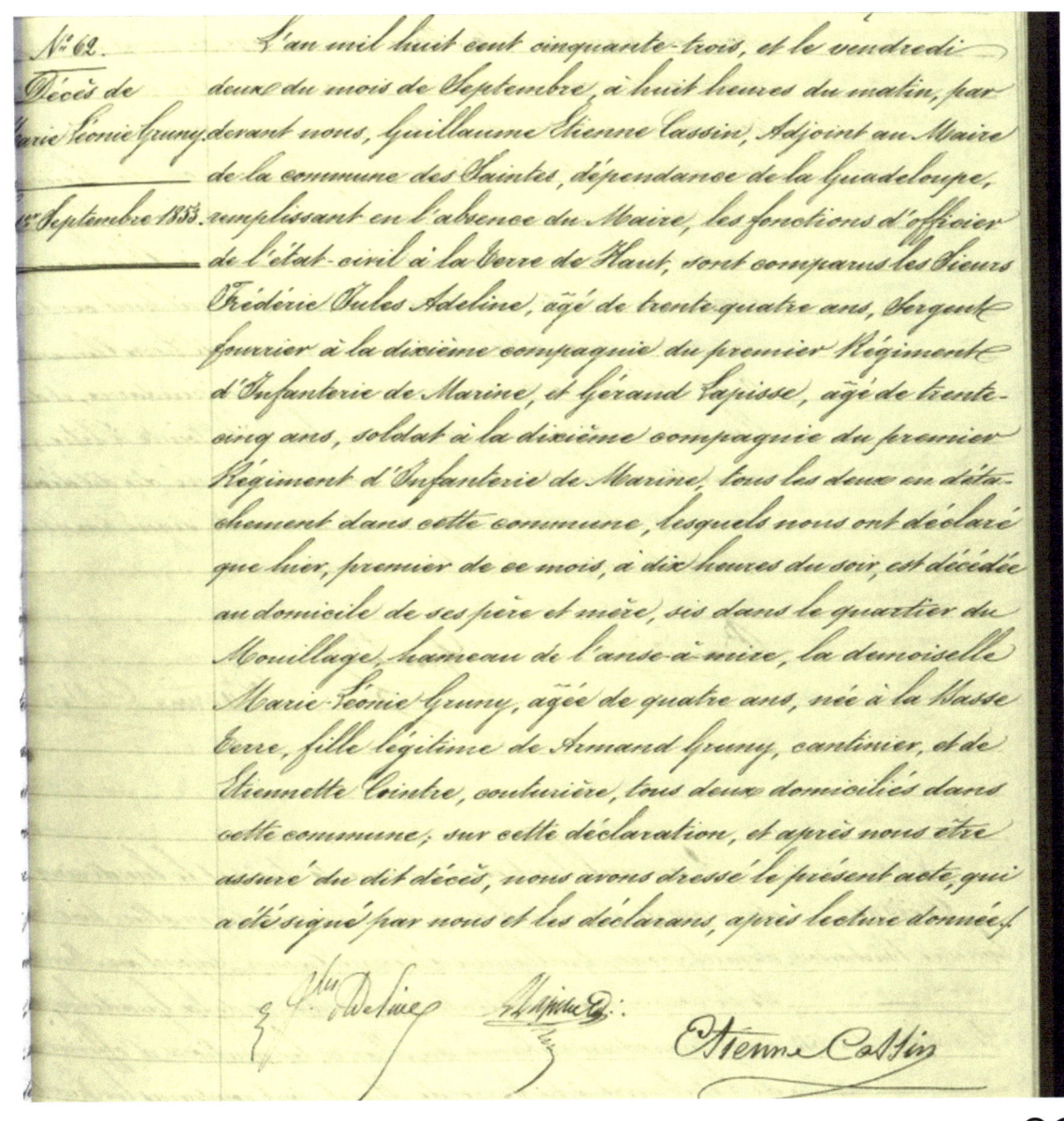

Marie Armantine GRUNY

Death
The 08 october 1853
TERRE-DE-BAS--LES SAINTES (Petites Anses, Terre-de-Bas)

Details

Marie Armantine GRUNY

Parents
- Armand GRUNY
- Etiennette COINTRE

1852 — Birth
The 2nd of August 1852, (Petites Anses) Terre-de-Bas, Guadeloupe, Guadeloupe, Guadeloupe
Daughter of Armand GRUNY and Etiennette COINTRE

1853 — Death (1 year)
The 7th of October 1853, (Petites Anses) Terre-de-Bas, Guadeloupe, Guadeloupe, Guadeloupe

Barbe Marie GRUNY

Birth

The 11 december 1868
TERRE-DE-HAUT--LES SAINTES (Terre-de-Haut, Guadeloupe)

Details

Barbe Marie GRUNY

Parents

- Armand GRUNY
- Anne BABUT

Barbe Marie GRUNY

Death

The 28 april 1877
TERRE-DE-HAUT--LES SAINTES (Terre-de-Haut, Guadeloupe)

Details

Barbe Marie GRUNY

Parents

- Armand GRUNY

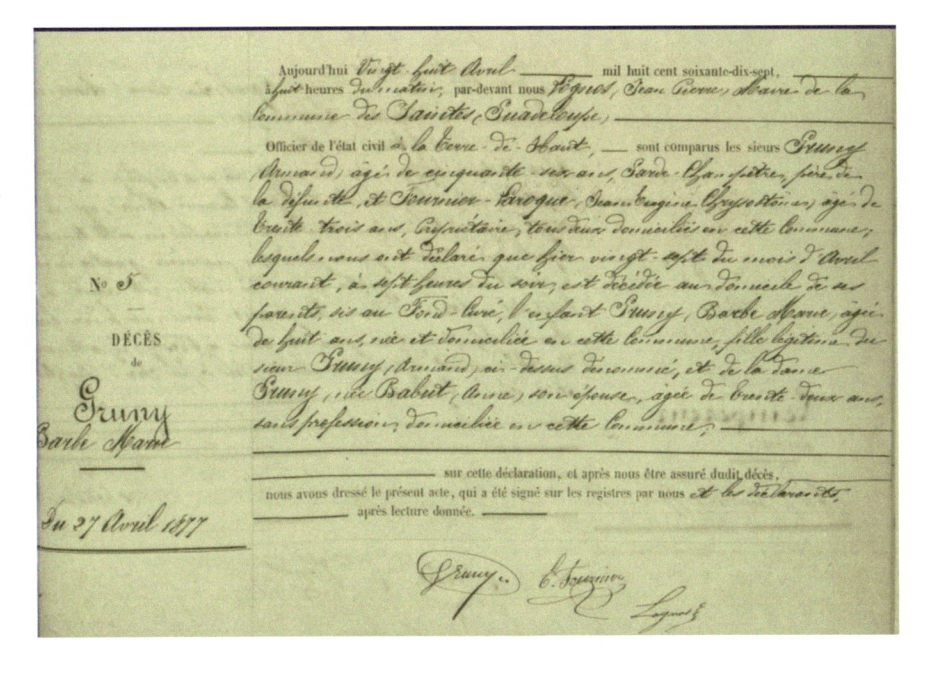

François Désiré GRUNY

Birth
The 02 february 1870
TERRE-DE-HAUT--LES SAINTES (Terre-de-Haut, Guadeloupe)
Details

François Désiré GRUNY

Parents
- Armand GRUNY
- Anne BABUT

François Desiré GRUNY

Death
The 25 august 1905
TERRE-DE-HAUT--LES SAINTES (Terre-de-Haut, Guadeloupe)

Details

François Desiré GRUNY

Parents
- Armand GRUNY
- Marie Anna BABUT

Désir Léon GRUNY

Birth

The 04 august 1871
TERRE-DE-HAUT--LES SAINTES (Terre de-Haut, Guadeloupe)

Details

Désir Léon GRUNY

Parents

- Armand GRUNY
- Anne BABUT

Isidore Armand GRUNY

Birth

The 19 may 1873
BASSE-TERRE (Basse-Terre, Guadeloupe)

Details

Isidore Armand GRUNY

Parents

- Armand GRUNY
- Anne BABUT

Marcel Bienvenu GRUNY

Birth
The 17 april 1875
BASSE-TERRE (Basse-Terre, Guadeloupe)

Details

Marcel Bienvenu GRUNY

Parents

- Armand GRUNY
- Anne BABUT

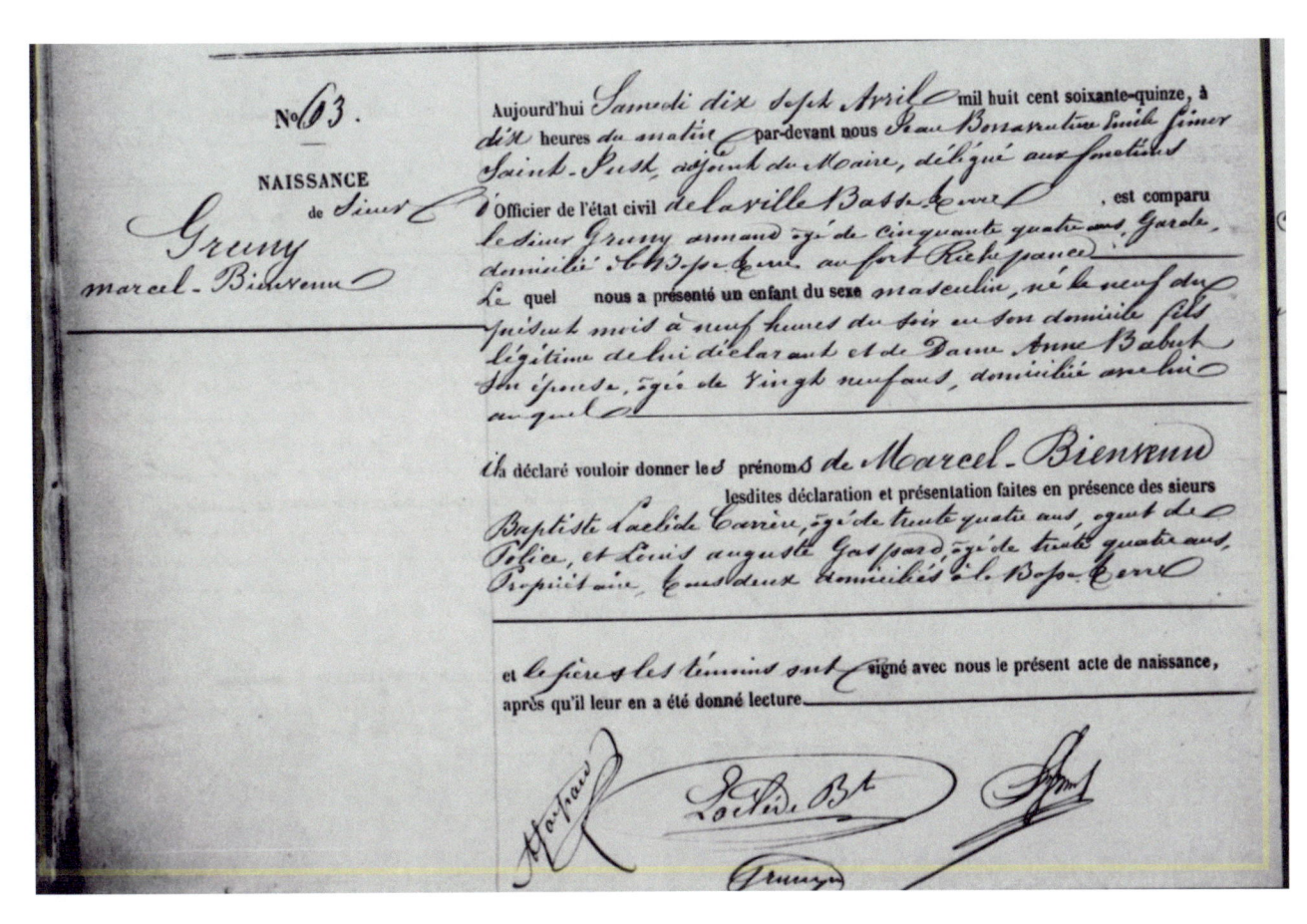

Romain Eugène GRUNY

Birth
The 17 august 1877
TERRE-DE-HAUT--LES SAINTES (Terre-de-Haut, Guadeloupe)
Details

Romain Eugène GRUNY

Parents

- Armand GRUNY
- Anne BABUT

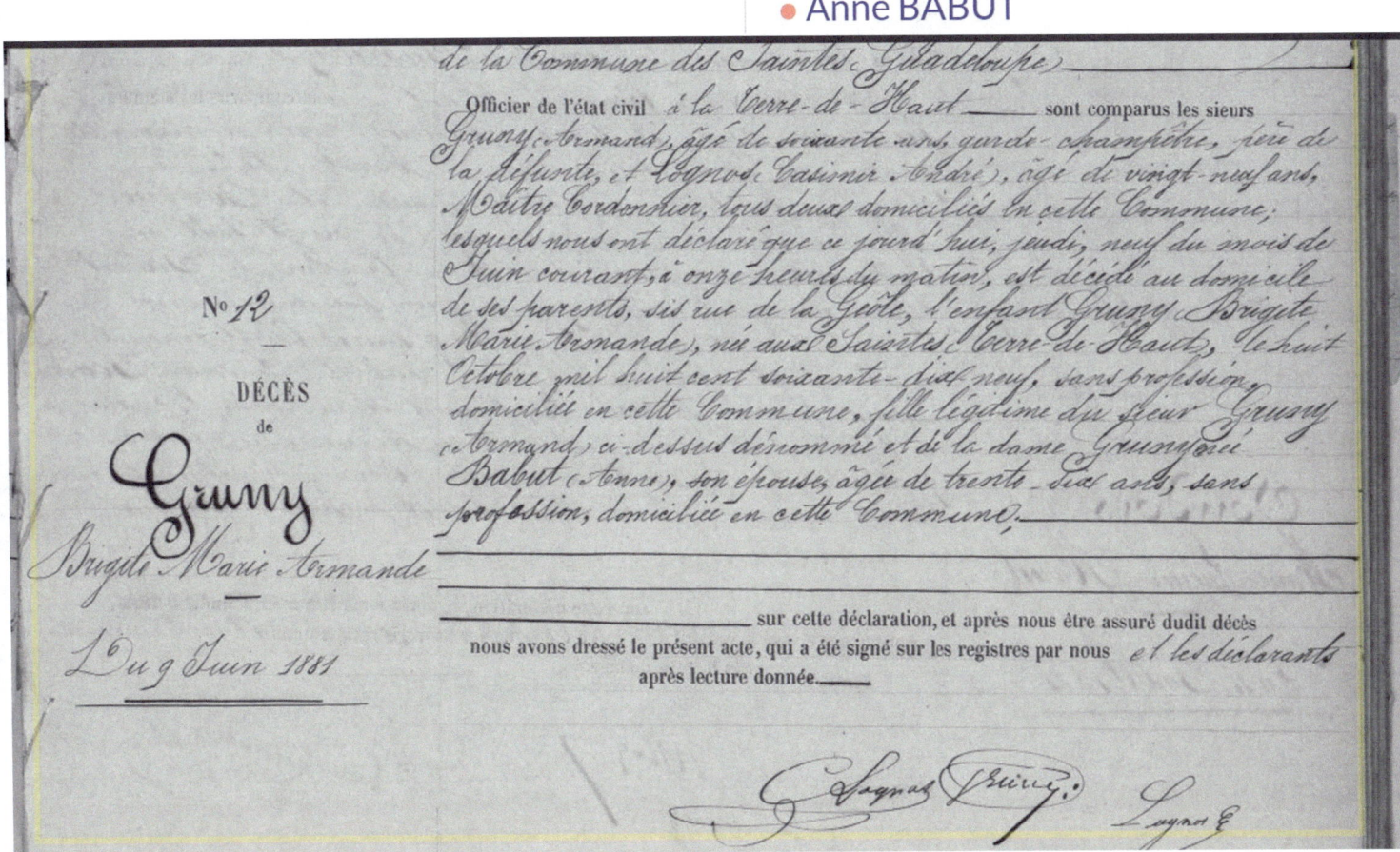

Birth

Brigite Marie Armande GRUNY

Birth

The 16th of October 1879
Terre-De-Haut--Les Saintes
(Terre-De-Haut, Guadeloupe)

Details

Brigite Marie Armande GRUNY

Parents
- Armand GRUNY
- Anne BABUT

Source : Death

Brigite Marie Armande GRUNY

Death

The 09 june 1881
TERRE-DE-HAUT--LES SAINTES (Terre-de-Haut, Guadeloupe)

Details

Brigite Marie Armande GRUNY

Parents
- Armand GRUNY
- Anne BABUT

Tiburce Madeleine Anna GRUNY

Birth
The 18 august 1885
TERRE-DE-HAUT--LES SAINTES (Terre-de-Haut, Guadeloupe)

Details

Tiburce Madeleine Anna GRUNY

Parents

- Armand GRUNY
- Marie Anne BABUT

Pierre Cyriaque GRUNY

Death

The 18 september 1888
TERRE-DE-HAUT--LES SAINTES (Terre-de-Haut, Guadeloupe)

Details

Pierre Cyriaque GRUNY

Parents

- Armand GRUNY
- Marie Anne BABERT

GRUNY

Death
The 09 august 1888
TERRE-DE-HAUT--LES SAINTES (Terre-de-Haut, Guadeloupe)
Details

GRUNY

Parents

- Armand GRUNY
- Marie Anne BABUT

Generation Four

Arleen -> Pamela -> Joseph -> Bernadine "Eleonoree" Angelique Gruny > Leonisse -> Armand Gruny

Armand GRUNY

Birth
The 8th of June 1820
Paris
(📍 Paris, Paris)

Details

The record below is a pension record. I have been trying to get it translated, but have not been able to as of publication of this book.

What I do know is that it shows the pension for Armand Gruny after his death and payable to his youngest child Triburce Madeleine as it lists her as an orphan as she was 13 when her father passed away.

Armand GRUNY

Parent
- Léone GRUNY

  Birth
  Revrours (Seine Et Marne)
  (📍 Seine-Et-Marne, France)

N° d'ordre	NOMS ET PRÉNOMS des officiers, marins ou assimilés et des pères et mères.	GRADES.	DATES de la cessation de l'activité.	du mariage.	du décès.	CONDITIONS dans lesquelles se trouvait l'officier, marin ou autre, décédé, ou circonstances de son décès	NOMS ET PRÉNOMS des veuves et des orphelins.	NAISSANCE. Dates.	Lieux.	QUOTITÉ de la pension.	ÉPOQUE de l'entrée en jouissance de la pension.	DOMICILE.
1	Bruneau (Maurice-Paul)	Pilote de 3e classe à Vahiti.	30 mars 1884.	10 juin 1869.	7 déc. 1899.	Titulaire d'une pension de retraite	ISI (Antoinette)	1845.	Ua-Pu (Îles Marquises).	555f	8 déc. 1899.	Taiohae-Nuka-Hiva (Îles Marquises).
						SECOURS ANNU ORPHELINS.						
2	DELLIARD (Francisque-Louis-Napoléon), marié à BOYER DE LA GIRODAY (Roseline-Louise-Élise-Marie-Joséphine).	Comptable principal au secrétariat du gouvernement de la Cochinchine.	18 juin 1894.	30 sept. 1886.	18 juin 1894. 6 avril 1901.	En possession de droits à une pension de retraite. Titulaire d'une pension de veuve.	IARD (Marie-Gaston-Franque).	9 août 1893.	Saïgon (Cochinchine).	1,100	Du 7 avril 1901 au 8 août 1914.	Tuteur : M. BOYER DE LA GIRODAY, à Saint-Denis (Réunion).
3	GRUNY (Armand)	Gardien-concierge des bâtiments militaires aux colonies.	21 janvier 1873.	28 nov. 1866.	30 avril 1898.	Titulaire d'une pension de retraite.	NY (Tiburce-Madeleine-na).	11 août 1885.	Terre-de-Haut-Saintes (Guadeloupe).	555	Du 21 avril 1898 au 10 août 1906 (1).	Tuteur : M. GRUNY (François), à Saintes (Guadeloupe).
						rescription interrompue.			TOTAL.	2,210		

In Armand's marriage record to Etonnette Cointre, it is stated that Eleonis {no surname] was the mother of her adult and natural son.

Armand (Leonisse's father) had at least two children in the 1880s, and Leonisse also had children during that time.

Armand's second wife, Anne Babut, and the baby she just delivered both died during childbirth on August 9, 1888. Armand lived for approximately 14 more years.

Leonisse is shown to be the mother of a child, Henry Jules Virassamy, with the father indicated. This typically suggests that there was a marriage. However, no marriage record has been found for Leonisse and Vadivel Virassamy, leading to the conclusion that they were not married. Henry Jules Virassamy was four years old when he died in April of 1882. Two of Armand's daughters died in 1883, one in September and one in October.

In Basse-Terre and Pointe-à-Pitre, where they lived, there were outbreaks of yellow fever, cholera, smallpox, and epizootics. All inbound subjects from Trinidad were required to quarantine for seven days upon arrival due to the transmission of these diseases, which were rampant throughout the Caribbean and other regions such as Latin America, Canada, France, and the United States. This could have been the fate of the aforementioned Grunys and possibly even Vadivel Virassamy. However, there is no cause of death listed for Armand's or Leonisse's children who died during this time, nor is there a death record for Vadivel Virassamy.

Armand GRUNY

Birth
The 08 june 1820
Paris 9e (Ancien) (Paris, Paris)

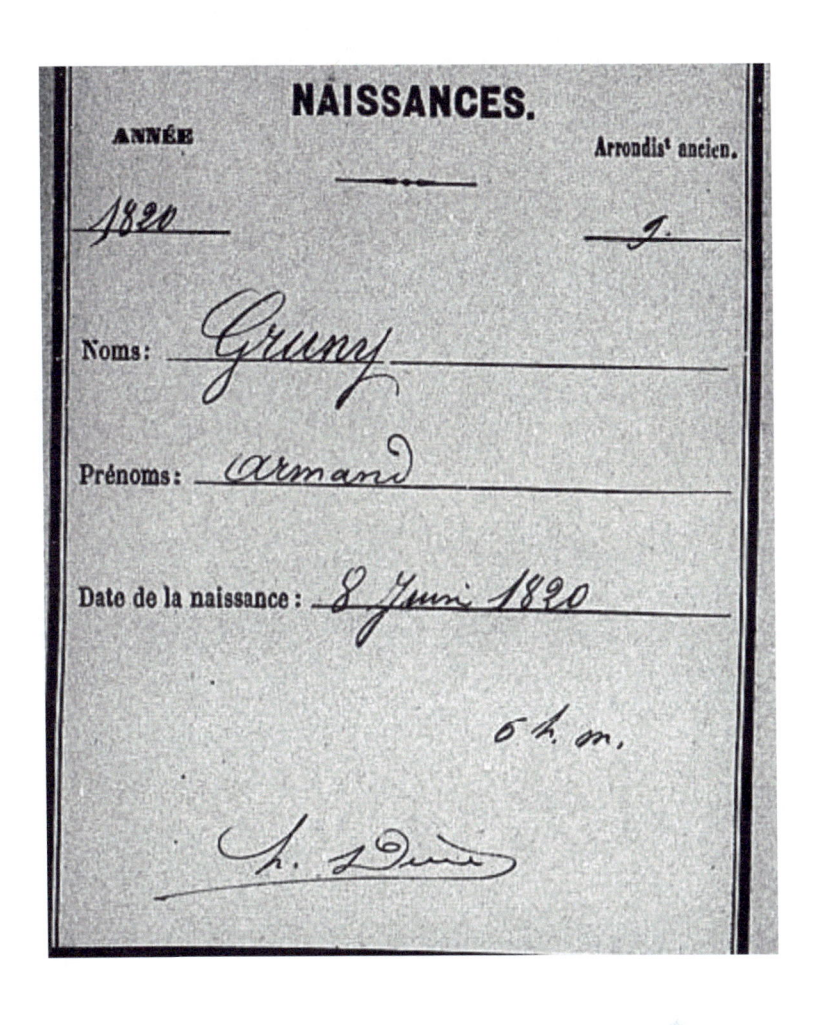

Birth
The 3rd of August 1827, Terre-de-Haut, Guadeloupe, Guadeloupe, Guadeloupe
Daughter of Charles Nicolas COINTRE and Céleste BEDE

Occupation
couturi?re

Marriage with Armand GRUNY
The 24th of April 1851, Terre-de-Bas, 97130, Guadeloupe, Guadeloupe, FRANCE,

Death
The 27th of March 1856, Terre de Haut Fond du Curé, , , , ,

Parents
- CC Charles Nicolas COINTRE 1798 - ?
- CB Céleste BEDE 1809 - ?

> Brothers and sisters

Unions and children
- AG Armand GRUNY 1821 - 1898
- LG Leonie GRUNY 1849 - ?

Etinnette Cointre died in 1856. Leonisse was born in 1854. Armand didn't marry Marie Babut until 1866. We don't know how Leonisse was taken care of over that period of 10 years.

Second Family of Armand Gruny

Armand Gruny
1820–1898 • G6BR-32C

Marie Dite Anne Babut
1847–1888 • GXMY-42X

Marriage
28 Nov 1866
Terre-de-Haut, Guadeloupe

Children (10)

Barbe Marie Gruny
1868–1877 • GXMB-MSX

Francois Desire Gruny
1870–Deceased • GXMB-W3G

Desir Leon Gruny
1871–Deceased • GXMB-RG4

Isidore Armand Gruny
1873–Deceased • GXMY-R33

Marcel Beinvenu Gruny
1875–Deceased • GX9N-D5P

Romain Eugene Gruny
1877–Deceased • GXMB-C1C

Brigite Marie Armande Gruny
1881–1881 • GXMY-R5L

Tiburce Madeleine Anna Gruny
1885–Deceased • GXMY-RKT

Baby Gruny
1888–Deceased • GXMY-TBL

Pierre Cyriaque Gruny
–1888 • GXMB-GZ7

Leonisse would have been twelve years of age when her father, Armand married again. She would have been 14 by the time of her next sibling.

Also, Leonisse's last child was born in 1889, and Armand's was born in 1888.

I believe that these two entries are the same person or twins because of the death date of Marie Babut. She died as a complication of her pregnacy

378

Etiennette COINTRE

Birth
The 3rd of August 1827
Terre-De-Haut--Les Saintes
(Terre-De-Haut, Guadeloupe)

Details

Etiennette COINTRE

- Parents
  - Nicolas COINTRE
  - Léleste BÉDÉ

Marriage

Armand GRUNY
&
Etiennette COINTRE

Marriage
The 24th of April 1851
Terre-De-Haut--Les Saintes
(Terre-De-Haut, Guadeloupe)

Details

Armand GRUNY
Age : 30
- Parent
  - Eleonis GRUNY

Etiennette COINTRE
- Parents
  - Nicolas COINTRE
  - Céleste BÉDÉ

The birth information for Marie Leonie is on the marriage record of Armand and Etiennette. It states her birth details as: born in Basse Terre on 24 August 1849, ... whom they recognize and legitimize by the present {act}.

This record identifies Armand's mother as Eleonis Gruny.

Etiennette COINTRE

1827 (Terre-de-Haut, Guadeloupe) - 1856 (Terre de Haut Fond du Curé,)

● 1 union

Events (3)

1827 — **Birth**
The 2nd of August 1827, Terre-de-Haut, Guadeloupe, Guadeloupe, Guadeloupe
Daughter of Charles Nicolas COINTRE and Catherine Céleste BEDE

1851 (23 years) — **Marriage with Armand GRUNY**
The 24th of April 1851, Terre-de-Haut, Guadeloupe, Guadeloupe, Guadeloupe

Death
The 27th of March 1856, Terre de Haut Fond du Curé, , , ,

Family Circle

∨ Parents

- **CC** Charles Nicolas COINTRE — 1798 - ?
- **CB** Catherine Céleste BEDE — 1806 - 1863

∨ Brothers and sisters

- **LC** Louise Phalnie COINTRE — 1831 - 1896
- **CC** Charlotte Clara COINTRE — 1832 - ?
- **JC** Jean Baptiste COINTRE — 1838 - 1839
- **MC** Marie Catherine COINTRE — 1840 - 1862

∨ Unions and children

- **AG** Armand GRUNY — ? - ?
  - **MG** Marie Léonie GRUNY — 1849 - 1853
  - **MG** Marie Armantine GRUNY — 1852 - 1853
  - **LG** Léonisse Stéfanie GRUNY — 1854 - ?

Source : Military pension

Armand GRUNY

Military Distinction
In 1873

Details

Armand GRUNY

Birth
The 08 june 1820
Paris

Other information

Numéro de décret: Bulletin N° 629
Décret N° 4020

Military Award
Armand GRUNY
Details
Armand GRUNY
Birth
The 8th of June 1820, Paris (Ile-De-France) (location on Paris, Paris)

Type of pension: VARIOUS MILITARY PENSIONS
Date of birth: June 8, 1820
Place of birth: Paris (Ile-de-France)
Home: Guadeloupe
Rank or job: Caretaker of military buildings
Length of service: 47 year(s), 4 month(s), 2 day(s)
Quotation: 565
Reason for pension: Caretaker, with more than 9 years of service to the colonies

That's it folks...

That's it, that is everything I know, and all the supporting evidence I have. I noticed that family didn't like going to familysearch.org or ancestry.com to pull the information and it didn't always provide a cohesive narrative. This is a project that I thought I could finish in a few months that has taken me two years to complete. It is my hope that your life will be edified and enriched by the content of these page.

It is my hope that more members of our family join our Facebook group, **Caribbean Genealogy Struggles**. It is a private group for members of our family. I hope that our family will go there to share feelings, insights and opinions, lots of opinions, about the content of this book that has been my passion for so long.

The information I provided was to the best of my ability. If there are corrections, I can apply them to a future edition. I am willing to do more in the future if necessary. Hopefully, it won't be too necessary. I can't expect that this will be error free. I can only hope.

It has always been my opinion that knowledge of where they came from would benefit our children. Learning about their rich genealogy full of generals, pirates, boat builders, midwives and business men provides our children with a strong sense of identity and belonging, which is essential for their emotional stability as they grow up. For the most part our family was the only ones living in Florida. It was very lonely and I was so jealous of the family that went to Canada because there were so many family members there. I feel like that gives me a first hand perspective on why this work is so important.

Understanding family history can help our children recognize that they are part of a long lineage of individuals who have overcome challenges, made sacrifices, and contributed to their community. This connection to the past can provide them with a sense of security and continuity, fostering self-confidence and resilience. Knowing their ancestors' stories can also offer children valuable life lessons, teaching them how to navigate difficult situations and develop a deeper appreciation for family values and traditions. With this solid foundation, children are more likely to feel grounded, supported, and better equipped to face life's challenges.

With All My Love,
Arleen Froemming

What's Next

I hope to compile traditional family recipes into a Sheppard and Martin family cookbook.

At some point, I will update all of this information into familysearch.org and ancestry.com (excluding information about living relatives).

After the first of the year, I would like to hold some training classes on how to use familysearch.org (free) for any member of the family inspired by genealogy that would like to join.

Made in the USA
Columbia, SC
28 February 2025